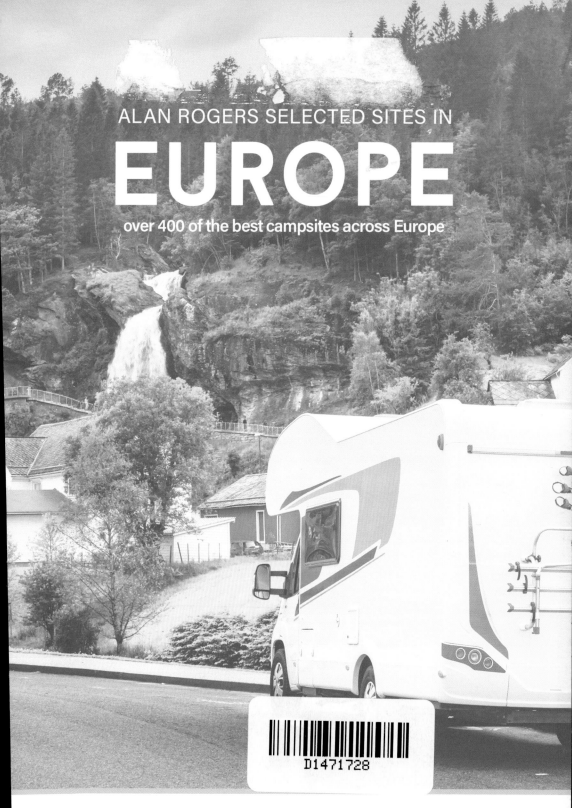

ALAN ROGERS SELECTED SITES IN

EUROPE

over 400 of the best campsites across Europe

alan
rogers

full-colour images
easy-to-use maps
comprehensive writeups

Compiled by: Alan Rogers Travel Ltd

Editorial & Production
Editor: Robin Fearn – enquiries@alanrogers.com
Production & Cartography: Robert Baker
Visual Design: Ben Tully

Advertising
UK Sales: Jo Smethurst – jo@alanrogers.com
Europe Sales: Minou Gurmeet – minou@alanrogers.com

European Advertising Agencies
France: ICCS International Tourism Promotions – info@iccsfrance.com
Spain: Servicios Turisticos Heinze Latzke S.A. – info@servitur-heinze.com
Portugal: Roteiro Lda – info@roteiro-campista.pt
Belgium & Netherlands: CampingMedia – jos@campingmedia.info

Alan Rogers Travel
Chief Operating Officer: Chris Newey
Finance Manager: Alison Harris
IT Manager: Roland Greenstreet

© Alan Rogers Travel Ltd 2019

Published by: Alan Rogers Travel Ltd,
Spelmonden Old Oast, Goudhurst, Kent TN17 1HE
www.alanrogers.com

51st edition - February 2019
ISBN 978-1-909057-91-3

Printed in Great Britain by Stephens & George Print Group

Stay in touch alanrogers.com/signup   **Contact us** alanrogers.com/contact

 facebook.com/alanrogerstravel    twitter.com/alanrogers    instagram.com/alanrogerstravel

Contents and Overview Map

Norway (360)

Sweden (448)

Great Britain (224)

Denmark (64)

Ireland (258)

Netherlands (324)

Germany (192)

Belgium (26)

Czech Republic (54)

Luxembourg (314)

Austria (12)

Switzerland (458)

Slovenia (386)

France (74)

Croatia (42)

Spain (394)

Italy (270)

Portugal (370)

Greece (248)

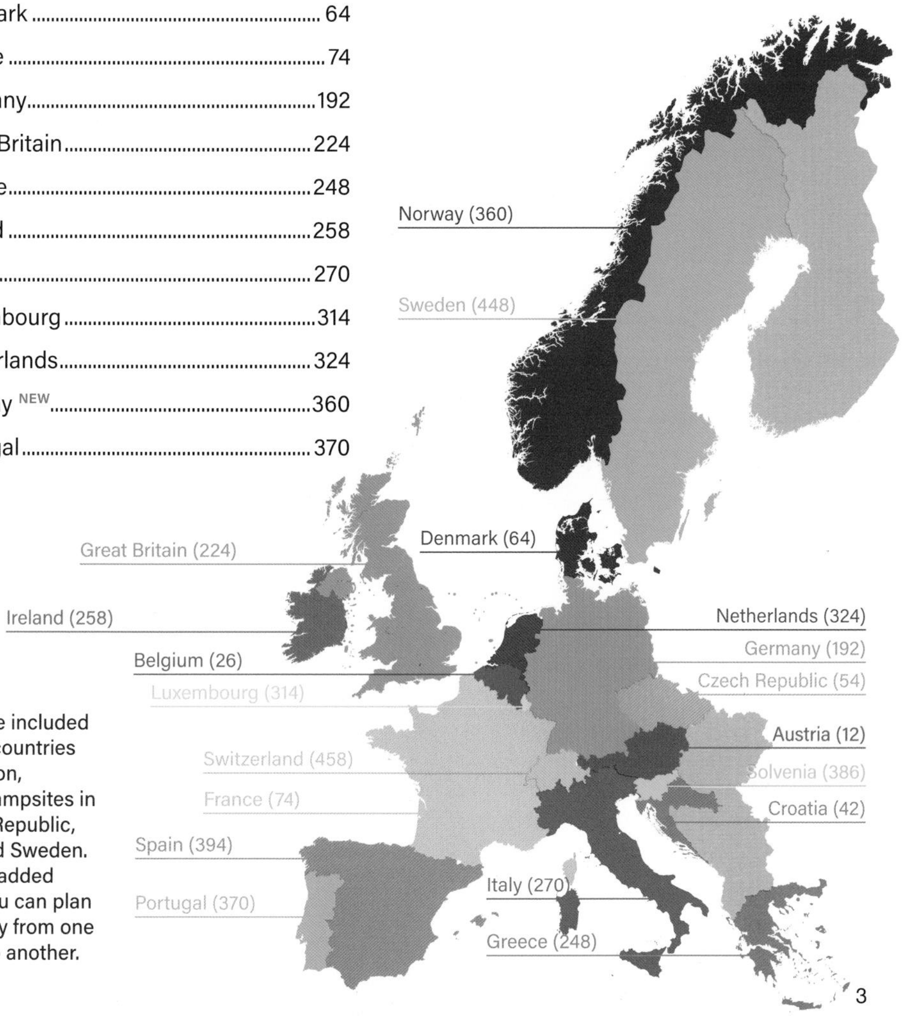

NEW We've included three new countries in this edition, featuring campsites in the Czech Republic, Norway and Sweden. We've also added maps so you can plan your journey from one campsite to another.

3

Alan Rogers launches his first guide 'selected sites for caravanning and camping in Europe'. It contained over 50 "really good sites" personally recommended by Alan Rogers himself and cost 4 shillings, equivalent to 20p in today's money.

1968

'Good Camps Guide for Britain' first published. **1976**

'Good Camps Guide for France' first published. **1985**

After 18 years of steady development and achievement, Alan Rogers seeks retirement. The company was purchased by Clive & Lois Edwards.

1986

First logo introduced to coincide with the 25th anniversary guide. **1993**

'Rented Accommodation in France' first published. **1998**

Aged 81, Alan Rogers passed away after suffering from a long term illness.

2000

Mark Hammerton purchases the Alan Rogers Group. **2001**

Dutch titles launched. **2002**

Italy and Spain guides first published. **2004**

Alan Rogers guides 'go digital'. Selected guides are made available in digital format, some become digital-only guides.

2010

Alan Rogers undergoes a radical rebrand, current logo introduced. **2011**

'An Introduction to Glamping' guide first published. **2012**

The Caravan and Motorhome Club acquires the Alan Rogers Travel Group.

2013

After many years of expansion, the guide range is reduced to it's core titles including 'Britain & Ireland', 'Spain & Portugal', 'Italy, Croatia & Slovenia', 'France' and 'The Big Selection'. **2016**

In 2018 we celebrated our 50th anniversary with a special edition guide with an all-new layout and design.

2018

Since our founding we've published 432 guides, 71 of those have been dedicated to camping in Europe. Welcome to the 51st edition.

2019

Welcome

to the 51st edition

Alan Rogers Guides were first published 50 years ago. Since Alan Rogers published the first campsite guide that bore his name, the nature of European campsites has changed immeasurably.

Back in 1968 many campsites, though well established, were still works in progress having been converted from farms and orchards in the post-war years. Of course, there were fewer to choose from than today and the quality levels varied hugely.

Over the 50 years since the first edition of the Alan Rogers guide, the quality of most campsites has evolved in leaps and bounds. In terms of today's facilities, infrastructure, technology and accommodation types there is very little comparison with what was on offer half a century ago.

Since 1968 we at Alan Rogers have developed longstanding relationships with many campsites. We have worked with different generations of campsite owners and shared with many of them the trials and tribulations along the way. Typically, campsite owners are a hardy breed, passionate about their campsite and ever keen to show it and their region off to every visitor.

The Alan Rogers guides have always aimed to celebrate the variety, recognise the quality and salute the unique (check out our annual awards on pages 10-11). So read on and find the perfect campsite for your next holiday, whatever type of campsite that may be.

Whether you're an old hand in terms of camping and caravanning or are contemplating your first trip, a regular Alan Rogers reader or a new convert, we wish you well in your travels and some pleasurable 'armchair touring' in the meantime!

The Alan Rogers Team

*"Alan Rogers considers that the greatest degree of comfort is obtained by using organised camping sites and, more especially, by using **only the best** of these sites. Alan Rogers' Selected Sites for Caravanning and Camping in Europe 1968 enables you to do just this."*

Alan Rogers
1919 - 2000

Alan Rogers

in search of the 'only the best'

There are many thousands of campsites across Europe of varying quality: this guide contains impartially written reports on over 400, including many of the very finest, in 16 countries. Are there more? Yes, of course, and in countries not included in this book. Online at alanrogers.com you'll find details of many more - over 8,000 campsites.

Put simply, a guide like this can never be exhaustive. We have had to make difficult editorial decisions with the aim of providing you with a selection of the best, rather than information on all – in short, a more selective approach.

We are mindful that people want different things from their choice of campsite so we try to include a range of campsite 'styles' to cater for a wide variety of preferences: from those seeking a small peaceful campsite in the heart of the countryside, to visitors looking for an 'all singing, all dancing' site in a popular seaside resort.

Those with more specific interests, such as sporting facilities, cultural events or historical attractions, are also catered for. The size of the site, whether it's part of a chain or privately owned, should make no difference in terms of quality. The key is that it should be 'fit for purpose' in order to shine and stand out.

If a campsite can identify and understand what kind of campsite it sets out to be, and who it wants to attract, then it can enhance its kerb appeal by developing with that in mind.

By way of example, a lakeside campsite with credentials as a serious windsurfing centre should probably offer equipment for hire, secure storage for customers' own kit, courses and tuition, meteorological feeds and so on.

A campsite in the heart of the Loire Valley might offer guided excursions to local châteaux, weekly tastings of regional wine and cheese, suggested walking or cycling itineraries to local châteaux with entry discounts and so on.

Whatever style of campsite you're seeking, we hope you'll find some inspiration here.

Country

Alan Rogers reference code and on-site information including accommodation count, pitch count, GPS coordinates, Postcode and campsite address.

Campsite Name

A description of the site in which we try to give an idea of its general features – its size, its situation, its strengths and its weaknesses. This section should provide a picture of the site itself with reference to the facilities that are provided and if they impact on its appearance or character. We include details on approximate pitch numbers, electricity (with amperage), hardstandings etc. in this section as pitch design, planning and terracing affects the site's overall appearance. Similarly we include reference to pitches used for caravan holiday homes, chalets, and the like.

Lists more specific information on the site's facilities and amenities and, where available, the dates when these facilities are open (if not for the whole season).

Campsite contact information

Opening dates

Below we list 'Key Feautres'. These are features we think are important and make the site individual.

 Beach nearby

 Dogs allowed

 Open all year

 Fishing

 Watersports

 Golf

This is a QR code. You can scan it with your smartphone and it will take you directly to the campsite listing on our website. Download a QR code app for your phone and try it!

How to use

this guide

The layout of this 2019 guide is the same as our special 2018 anniversary edition but slightly different from previous editions. We still aim to provide comprehensive information, written in plain English in an easy to use format, but a few words of explanation regarding the content may be helpful.

Toilet blocks Typically, toilet blocks will be equipped with WCs, washbasins with hot and cold water and hot shower cubicles. They will have all necessary shelves, hooks, plugs and mirrors. There will be a chemical toilet disposal point and the campsite will provide water and waste water drainage points and bin areas.

Shop Basic or fully supplied, and opening dates.

Bars, restaurants, takeaway facilities and entertainment: We try hard to supply opening and closing dates (if other than the campsite opening dates) and to identify if there are discos or other entertainment.

Swimming pools These might vary from a simple, conventional swimming pool to an elaborate complex with multiple pools and waterslides. Opening dates, charges and levels of supervision are provided where we have been notified. There is a regulation whereby Bermuda shorts may not be worn in swimming pools (for health and hygiene reasons). It is worth ensuring that you do take 'proper' swimming trunks with you.

Leisure facilities For example, playing fields, bicycle hire, organised activities and entertainment.

Dogs If dogs are not accepted or restrictions apply, we state it here. If planning to take a dog, or other pet, we recommend you check in advance.

Opening dates Campsites can, and sometimes do, alter these dates before the start of the season, often for good reasons. If you intend to visit shortly after a published opening date, or shortly before the closing date, it is wise to check that it will actually be open at the time required. Similarly some sites operate a restricted service during the low season, only opening some of their facilities (e.g. swimming pools) during the main season. Again if you are at all doubtful it is wise to check.

Sometimes, campsite amenities may be dependent on there being enough customers on site to justify their opening. Some campsites may not be fully ready by their stated opening dates – grass may not all be cut or perhaps only limited sanitary facilities open. At the end of the season they also tend to close down some facilities and generally wind things down.

We usually give an overview of the pitches, including an approximate quantity. This figure may vary year on year so is rarely absolute.

Awards 2018
by Alan Rogers and the Caravan and Motorhome Club

In 2016 we joined forces with the Caravan and Motorhome Club to present the joint Alan Rogers / Caravan and Motorhome Club Awards for the very first time.

Our awards have a broad scope and before committing to our winners, we carefully consider more than 2,000 campsites featured in the Alan Rogers guides and the Caravan and Motorhome Club 'Venture Abroad' program, taking into account comments from our site assessors, our head office team and, of course, our members & readers.

For the 2018 awards there were nine categories, each with a winner and a highly commended runner-up.

Overall Winners 2018

Alan Rogers	FR17140	Camping Séquoia Parc	France	p124
CAMC	FR07120	Nature Parc l'Ardéchois	France	p144

Progress Award 2018

This award reflects the hard work and commitment undertaken by particular site owners to improve and upgrade their site.

Winner	AU0180	Sportcamp Woferlgut	Austria	p18
Runner-up	NL5630	Vakantiepark Koningshof	Netherlands	p328

Welcome Award 2018

This award takes account of sites offering a particularly friendly welcome and maintaining a friendly ambience throughout readers' holidays.

Winner	FR12080	Camping Club les Genêts	France	p167
Runner-up	CH9430	Camping Lazy Rancho	Switzerland	p461

Innovation Award 2018

Our Innovation Award acknowledges campsites with creative and original concepts, possibly with features which are unique.

Winner	ES86150	KIKO PARK Oliva	Spain	p421
Runner-up	CR6915	Plitvice Holiday Resort	Croatia	p51

Seaside Award 2018

This award is made for sites which we feel are particularly suitable for a really excellent seaside holiday.

Winner	ES80400	Camping Las Dunas	Spain	p398
Runner-up	IT60440	Camping Ca'Savio	Italy	p294

Country Award 2018

This award contrasts with our seaside award and acknowledges sites which are attractively located in delightful, rural locations.

Winner	NL6470	Camping De Papillon	Netherlands	p351
Runner-up	PO8370	Parque Cerdeira	Portugal	p372

All Year Award 2018

This award acknowledges sites which are open all year round.

Winner	FR75020	Camping De Paris	France	p97
Runner-up	ES88020	Camping Cabopino	Spain	p433

Family Site Award 2018

Many sites claim to be family friendly but this award acknowledges the sites we feel to be the very best in this respect.

Winner	FR35020	Castel Camping Domaine des Ormes	France	p79
Runner-up	LU7620	Europacamping Nommerlayen	Luxembourg	p320

Small Campsite Award 2018

This award acknowledges excellent small campsites (fewer than 150 pitches) which offer a friendly welcome and top quality amenities throughout the season to their guests.

Winner	ES90840	Camping la Campiña	Spain	p431
Runner-up	FR66050	Le Haras	France	p177

Video Award 2018

This award reflects sites which have invested significantly in innovative video content and production.

Winner	FR86050	Airotel la Roche Posay Vacances	France	p130
Runner-up	FR41040	Camping Château des Marais	France	p109

Capital Vienna
Currency Euro (€)
Language German
Telephone country code 00 43
Time Zone Central European Time
(GMT/UTC+1)
Tourist Office austria.info/uk

Climate Temperate, with moderately
hot summers, cold winters and snow in
the mountains.

Austria

Austria is primarily known for two contrasting attractions: the capital Vienna with its cathedral, wine bars and musical events, and the skiing and hiking resorts of the Alps. It is an ideal place to visit all year round, for the Easter markets, winter sports and the many cultural and historical attractions, as well as the breathtaking scenery.

The charming Tirol region in the west of Austria is easily accessible, and popular with tourists who flock to its ski resorts in winter. In the summer months it is transformed into a verdant landscape of picturesque valleys dotted with wildflowers, a paradise for walkers.

Situated in the centre are the Lake District, and Salzburg, city of Mozart, with its wealth of gardens, churches and palaces. Vienna's iconic ferris wheel is a must for taking in the beautiful parks and architecture from 200 ft.

The neighbouring provinces of Lower Austria, Burgenland and Styria, land of vineyards, mountains and farmland are off the tourist routes, but provide good walking territory. Further south, the Carinthia region enjoys a mild, sunny climate and is dominated by crystal clear lakes and soaring mountains, yet has plenty of opportunities for winter sports. There are numerous monasteries and churches, and the cities of Villach and Klagenfurt, known for its old square and attractive Renaissance buildings.

Shops 9am to 6.30pm Monday to Friday (often open until 9pm Thursday or Friday in larger cities) and from 9am to 5pm Saturday.

Banks 8am or 9am to 3pm Monday to Friday (open later until 5.30pm on Thursdays). Smaller branches' hours may differ.

Travelling with Children Programs are usually organised for children over the summer period. Many lakes have supervised beach areas. Many museums in Vienna are free for under 18s. Restaurants will have children's menus or prepare smaller portions.

Public Holidays New Year's Day, Epiphany, Easter Monday, Labour Day, Ascension, Whit Monday, Corpus Christi, Assumption 15 Aug, National Day 26 Oct, All Saints' 1 Nov, Conception 8 Dec, Christmas Day, St Stephen's Day (Boxing Day).

Motoring Visitors using Austrian motorways and 'A' roads must display a Motorway Vignette on their vehicle as they enter Austria. Failure to have one will mean a heavy, on-the-spot fine. Vignettes are obtained at all major border crossings into Austria and at larger petrol stations. All vehicles above 3.5 tonnes maximum permitted laden weight are required to use a small device called the 'GO Box'.

See campsite map page 472.

Alan Rogers Code: AU0155
115 pitches
GPS: 47.08012, 10.65940
Post Code: A-6522

Prutz, Tirol

www.alanrogers.com/au0155
info@aktiv-camping.at
Tel: 054 722 648
www.aktiv-camping.at

Open (Touring Pitches):
All year.

Aktiv Camping Prutz

Aktiv-Camping is a long site which lies beside, but is fenced off from, the River Inn. The 115 touring pitches, mainly gravelled for motorcaravans, are on level ground and average 80 sq.m. They all have 6A electrical connections, adequate water points, and in the larger area fit together somewhat informally. As a result, the site can sometimes have the appearance of being quite crowded. This is an attractive area with many activities in both summer and winter for all age groups. You may well consider using this site not just as an overnight stop, but also for a longer stay.

The sanitary facilities are of a very high standard, with private cabins and good facilities for disabled visitors. Baby room. Washing machine. Dog shower. Small shop (all year). Bar, restaurant and takeaway (15/5-30/9; Christmas to Easter). Play room. Ski room. Play area. Children's entertainment. Guided walks. Free shuttle bus to ski slopes. Bicycle hire. Slipway for canoes/kayaks. WiFi over site.

Key Features

 Open All Year

 Pets Accepted

 Disabled Facilities

 Play Area

 Bar/Restaurant

 Skiing

 Bike Hire

 Fishing

Scan me for more information.

Alan Rogers Code: AU0035
5 accommodations
144 pitches
GPS: 47.33735, 11.17860
Post Code: A-6100

Seefeld in Tirol, Tirol

www.alanrogers.com/au0035
info@camp-alpin.at
Tel: 052 124 848
www.camp-alpin.at

Open (Touring Pitches):
All year.

Camp Alpin Seefeld

Camp Alpin Seefeld is a beautifully laid out, modern campsite with first class facilities in an attractive setting almost 4,000 feet above sea level. With excellent views of the surrounding mountains and forests there are 144 large, individual pitches mainly on slightly sloping grass. All have 16A electricity & gas, with ten well placed water points. Some pitches at the back and edge of the site are terraced. This is a quality site for both summer and winter activity, whether you wish to take a gentle stroll or participate in something more demanding, including skiing directly opposite the site.

Excellent heated sanitary facilities include nine private bathrooms for hire, some private cabins. Suite for disabled visitors. Washing machines and dryer. Motorcaravan services. Sauna and solarium. Sunbed cabin. Shop. Bar. Cosy restaurant with a reasonably priced menu. Guest room with games. Play area. Bicycle hire. Apartments to rent. WiFi (free).

Key Features

  Open All Year

 Pets Accepted

 Disabled Facilities

 Play Area

 Bar/Restaurant

 Skiing

Bike Hire

Scan me for more information.

Alan Rogers Code: AU0130
150 pitches
GPS: 47.46699, 12.13979
Post Code: A-6305

Itter, Tirol

Camping Itter Tirol

www.alanrogers.com/au0130
info@camping-itter.at
Tel: 053 352 181
www.camping-itter.at

Open (Touring Pitches):
All year excl. 16-30 November.

This well kept site with 150 touring pitches and good facilities is suitable both as a base for longer stays and also for overnight stops, as it lies right by a main road west of Kitzbühel. It is on sloping ground, but most of the pitches are on level terraces. Some pitches are individual and divided by hedges and most have 8/10A electricity, cable TV connections, water and drainage. Space is usually available. There is a toboggan run from the site in winter. Good walks and a wealth of excursions by car are available nearby. There is some daytime road noise.

The main sanitary facilities are heated and of very high standard. The newest section has a large room with private cubicles. Some of these have vanity style washbasins, others have baths or showers. Two slightly larger units for families, with baby baths. Facilities for disabled visitors. Washing machines and dryers. Motorcaravan services. Cooking facilities. Fridge. Small shop, bar/restaurant (both closed Nov). Heated swimming pool (16 x 8 m) and paddling pool (1/5-30/9). Sauna and solarium. Excellent playground and indoor playroom for wet weather. Youth room. Animation programme (Jul-Aug). WiFi over site (charged). Dog shower. Ski and drying rooms. Good English spoken.

Key Features

 Pets Accepted

 Disabled Facilities

 Swimming Pool

 Play Area

 Bar/Restaurant

 Skiing

Scan me for
more information.

Alan Rogers Code: AU0265
10 accommodations
200 pitches
GPS: 47.57427, 12.70602
Post Code: A-5092

St Martin bei Lofer, Salzburg

www.alanrogers.com/au0265
home@grubhof.com
Tel: 065 888 2370
www.grubhof.com

Open (Touring Pitches):
All Year

Park Grubhof

Park Grubhof is a beautifully laid out, level and spacious site set in the former riding and hunting park of the 14th-century Schloss Grubhof. The 200 touring pitches, all with 12-16A electricity, have been carefully divided into separate areas for different types of visitor – dog owners, young people, families and groups, and a quiet area. There are 167 very large pitches (at least 120 sq.m), all with electricity, water and drainage, many along the bank of the Saalach river. Although new, the central building has been built in traditional Tirolean style using, in part, materials hundreds of years old reclaimed from old farmhouses. The result is most attractive. On the ground floor you will find reception, a cosy café/bar, a restaurant and a small shop, and on the first floor, a deluxe sauna, beauty and wellness suite, two apartments and a relaxation room.

Three attractive, modern sanitary units constructed of wood and glass provide excellent facilities. Large family bathrooms (free with certain pitches, to rent in winter). Washing machine, dryer and drying gallery. Gym upstairs (€5 membership). Recreation and conference room and a small library. Saunas, steam bath and massage. Ski and canoe storage room. Motorcaravan services. Luxury dog shower. Shop, restaurant and bar. Adventure-style playground. Youth room. Playroom. Watersports. Cabins to rent. Hotel and B&B accommodation. WiFi throughout (charged).

Key Features

 Pets Accepted

 Disabled Facilities

 Play Area

 Bar/Restaurant

 Skiing

 Bike Hire

 Fishing

Scan me for more information.

Alan Rogers Code: AU0180
40 accommodations
300 pitches
GPS: 47.28372, 12.81695
Post Code: A-5671

Bruck an der Glocknerstraße, Salzburg

www.alanrogers.com/au0180
info@sportcamp.at
Tel: 065 457 3030
www.sportcamp.at

Open (Touring Pitches):
All year.

Sportcamp Woferlgut

Sportcamp Woferlgut, a family run site, is one of the best in Austria. It lies in the village of Bruck at the northern end of the Großglocknerstrasse mountain road in the Hohe Tauern National Park, near the Zeller See. The level, grass pitches are marked out by shrubs and each has 16A metered electricity, water, drainage, cable TV socket and a gas point. The site's own lake is popular for swimming and sunbathing, and has an adventure timber ropeway and playground. A free entertainment programme for kids of all ages is provided during the peak periods. The first class toilet and shower facilities, as well as a wellness center and 5 pools, has everything you need for a relaxing stay in the Austrian mountains.

Three modern sanitary blocks have excellent facilities including private cabins and underfloor heating. Washing machines and dryers. Facilities for disabled visitors. Family bathrooms for hire (some with bathtubs). Motorcaravan services. Shop, bar, restaurant and takeaway. Heated outdoor pool and children's pool as well as a swimming lake with rope garden. TV rooms and lounge with library. Gym with bathing house and adventure center with sauna. Three playgrounds, indoor playroom and children's cinema. Fun train. Tennis and horses' meadow for Pony rides. Bicycle hire. Watersports and lake swimming. Crazy golf course. WiFi over site (charged).

Key Features

 Open All Year

 Pets Accepted

 Disabled Facilities

 Swimming Pool

 Play Area

 Bar/Restaurant

 Skiing

 Bike Hire

Scan me for more information.

Alan Rogers Code: AU0210
100 pitches
GPS: 47.49370, 13.34700
Post Code: A-5023

Salzburg, Salzburg

www.alanrogers.com/au0210
office@camping-nord-sam.com
Tel: 0662 66 04 94
www.camping-nord-sam.com

Open (Touring Pitches):
18 April - 6 October

Camping Nord-Sam

The centrally-located campsite on the outskirts of the city of Salzburg has been managed by the Lex family for the past 60 years. Only 700 metres from the motorway exit "Salzburg Nord", it is not only the perfect place to stay while passing through, but for leisure and recreational holidays as well. With its approximately 100 pitches, this well-maintained campsite, set amongst lush greenery and blooming flowers is the ideal starting point for the 3.5 km distant city. It is also suitably located for day trips to the Salzkammergut (lake district), the Ice Caves, the Salt Mines and many more sights. A bus stop and bike path to the city centre are right on the doorstep. The complex is equipped with a swimming pool, newly-renovated sanitary facilities with free showers, washing machine & dryer, new toddler playground, bike rental, kiosk with basic food, cafeteria and Wi-Fi. A restaurant (150m) and supermarket (300m) are also nearby.

One big sanitary block equipped with toilets, showers, washing- and drying machines. Cafeteria. Mini market. Ticket counter. Outdoor pool. Bicycle hire. Information point. Bus stop on the doorstep. Hicking path. Bicycle path. WiFi (charged).

Key Features

Pets Accepted

Swimming Pool

Play Area

Bar/Restaurant

Bike Hire

Scan me for more information.

19

Alan Rogers Code: AU0440
29 accommodations
272 pitches
GPS: 46.63141, 13.39598
Post Code: A-9620

Hermagor, Carinthia

www.alanrogers.com/au0440
camping@schluga.com
Tel: 004342 822 051
www.schluga.com

Open (Touring Pitches):
All Year

Schluga Camping

Schluga Camping situated in a flat valley with views of the surrounding mountains. The touring pitches are 100-120 sq.m; many with water, drainage, and satellite TV connections. Electricity connections are available throughout (16A). Mainly on grass covered gravel on either side of tarmac surfaced access roads, they are divided by shrubs and hedges. The site is open all year, to include the winter sports season, and has a well kept, tidy appearance, although it may be busy in high season. English is spoken. There is an impressive wellness centre with saunas, spas and relaxation areas.

Four sanitary blocks (a splendid new one, plus one modern and two good older ones) are heated in cold weather. Most washbasins in cabins and good showers. Family washrooms to rent. Baby rooms and suite for disabled visitors. Washing machines and dryers. Drying rooms and ski rooms. Motorcaravan services. Well stocked shop (1/5-30/9). Bar/restaurant with terrace (closed Nov). Heated indoor (all year) and outdoor (May-Oct) swimming pools. Natural swimming pond (500 sq.m). Playground. New kindergarten and youth games room. Bicycle hire. Sauna. Solarium. Steam bath. Fitness center. TV room. Internet point. Kindergarten programme for small children. Playing field. Dog walking area. WiFi throughout (charged).

Key Features

 Open All Year

 Pets Accepted

 Disabled Facilities

 Swimming Pool

 Play Area

 Bar/Restaurant

 Skiing

 Bike Hire

Scan me for more information.

Alan Rogers Code: AU0351
142 pitches
GPS: 47.73058, 13.47779
Post Code: A-5360

St. Wolfgang, Upper Austria

www.alanrogers.com/au0351
office@berau.at
Tel: 061 382 543
www.berau.at

Open (Touring Pitches):
1 March - 31 December.

Seecamping Berau

This level, grassy site with 142 touring pitches lies directly on the Wolfgangsee and is a couple of kilometres away from the town of St. Wolfgang. It has its own beach, from which there are wonderful mountain views, and a landing stage for water-based activities. All pitches have TV connections, water points and free WiFi, are between 70 and 90 sq.m. and are set among trees. The 6A electricity supply can be upgraded to 13A. The site has a restaurant, which is open to the public, and a pizzeria and bar. This is a relaxed and friendly site, with activities and facilities to suit visitors of all ages. Dance evenings, beer festivals and Caribbean-themed nights, are just a few examples of the on-site entertainment on offer.

Modern washing facilities are housed in the main restaurant building. Family bathrooms to rent. Facilities for children and disabled visitors. Washing machines and dryers. Motorcaravan services. Shop. Restaurant, bar and pizzeria. Wellness facilities. Watersports equipment hire. Play area. Children's club. Evening entertainment. WiFi throughout.

Key Features

 Pets Accepted

 Play Area

 Bar/Restaurant

 Skiing

Scan me for more information.

Alan Rogers Code: AU0515
50 pitches
GPS: 47.18080, 14.21570
Post Code: A-8842

Sankt Peter am Kammersberg,
Steiermark

www.alanrogers.com/au0515
info@camping-bellaustria.com
Tel: 035 367 3902
www.camping-bellaustria.com

Open (Touring Pitches):
28 March - 27 October.

Camping Bella Austria

Bella Austria caters predominantly for fixed tents and chalets, with 50 pitches for tourers. It is well located for exploring southwest Styria, the beautiful Mur valley, and the Niedere Tauern alps (highest point Greimberg 2,472 m). To the north, snow-capped Greimberg sits high above the site whilst in other directions you can see pine-clad slopes and Alpine pastures. Not too far away is the small ski resort of Turracher Hohe. Bella Austria is an ideal base for discovering traditional Austria by bicycle, on foot or in a horse-drawn carriage. The site also offers a unique range of workshops. The level, unmarked pitches all have access to 16A electricity, water and drainage. Some road noise is audible.

The modern sanitary blocks provide ample and clean facilities including toilets, hot showers and washbasins. Washing machine. Bar and restaurant. Wellness centre. Heated swimming pool (11/6-23/9). Sauna. Indoor and outdoor play areas. Volleyball. Basketball. 5-a-side football. Entertainment programme (July/ Aug). Electric bicycles for hire. WiFi in library/TV room.

Key Features

 Pets Accepted

 Disabled Facilities

 Swimming Pool

 Play Area

 Bar/Restaurant

 Skiing

 Bike Hire

Scan me for
more information.

Alan Rogers Code: AU0525
5 accommodations
50 pitches
GPS: 47.16319, 14.73828
Post Code: A-8741

Weisskirchen, Steiermark

www.alanrogers.com/au0525
campingpark@fisching.at
Tel: 035 778 2284
www.camping50plus.at

Open (Touring Pitches):
1 April - 30 October.

50plus Campingpark

This small site is unusual in that it only accepts clients over 50 years of age. It is a high quality site with an attractive setting in the Steiermark region, west of Graz. There are 50 large, level pitches (100-130 sq.m), all equipped with 6A electricity, water, drainage and cable TV connections. Most pitches are on hardstanding. A number of chalets and holiday apartments are also available to rent. There is a small swimming lake which is surrounded by an attractive garden and sunbathing area. The site's bar/snack bar is inviting with a selection of homemade dishes on offer.

Two excellent modern toilet blocks were very clean, with free controllable showers. No facilities for children or disabled visitors. Laundry room. Bar, snack bar and shop (all 1/4-30/10). Outdoor swimming pool (1/5-30/9). Swimming lake. Tennis. Bicycle hire. Activity programme. Chalets and apartments to rent. WiFi (charged).

Key Features

 Adults Only

 Pets Accepted

 Swimming Pool

 Bar/Restaurant

 Bike Hire

Scan me for more information.

Alan Rogers Code: AU0406
6 accommodations
130 pitches
GPS: 46.66518, 13.97695
Post Code: A-9570

Ostriach am See, Carinthia

www.alanrogers.com/au0406
camping@parth.at
Tel: 042 432 7440
www.parth.at

Open (Touring Pitches):
1 April - 30 October, 26 December - 6
January.

Parth Seecamping

On the southern shore of Lake Ossiach, in the heart of
Carinthia, close to the borders with Italy and Slovenia, this
site offers spas, saunas and a range of health treatments. It
also serves as a base from which to explore the attractive
countryside of southern Austria on foot, by bicycle or by car.
The level touring pitches all have electricity connections,
additional pitches have mobile homes to rent. The site has
a private beach where you can have a gentle swim or take
advantage of some of the varied activities that are organised.
There is even a distillery providing drinks for the restaurant!

Sanitary block with open-style washbasins, hot showers, family
rooms and facilities for children and disabled visitors. Laundry.
Dogs' room with shower and hair dryer. Fridge and cooking
facilities. Self-service market. Restaurant serving fish buffets
and steak dinners. Bathing and children's pools. Wellness suite
with sauna, steam room, massage, manicure and pedicure, and
yoga. Gym. Beach volleyball, golf, kayaking, climbing, canyoning,
glacier walking, judo, mountain-biking, tennis, riding, scuba
diving, sailing and surfing organised. Dance lessons. Large
adventure playground and indoor playroom with electronic
games, PlayStation and cinema. Children's club (over 4 yrs)
and entertainment for teenagers and adults. WiFi over the site
(charged).

Key Features

 Pets Accepted

 Play Area

 Bar/Restaurant

 Bike Hire

Scan me for
more information.

Alan Rogers Code: AU0190
29 accommodations
90 pitches
GPS: 47.13640, 13.12990
Post Code: A-5640

Bad Gastein, Salzburg

www.alanrogers.com/au0190
office@kurcamping-gastein.at
Tel: 064 343 0205
www.kurcamping-gastein.at

Open (Touring Pitches):
All year.

Kur Camping Erlengrund

Kur-camping has been run by a friendly Dutch family for ten years and is open all year. It lies in Bad Gastein, a valley in southern Salzburgerland between the Grossglockner and the Hohe Tauern mountains. This valley is one of the most beautiful in Austria, famous for its spas and wonderful mountain scenery. There are 100 generous pitches of which 90 are for touring. Fifty are on hardstandings and all have varying amounts of shade. All have 16A electricity (2-pin sockets) and most are fully serviced, including gas and a TV point. The campsite has all the necessary facilities for summer and winter camping.

Modern, well equipped, heated toilet block with all necessary facilities including baby room and toilet for seniors. Winter drying room and ski store. Washing machine/dryer (tokens). Motorcaravan services. Fresh bread to order. Outdoor swimming pool with sunbathing area, (1/6-30/9). Sauna and fitness room. Playground. Trampoline. TV, library and games room. Guided walks and cycle routes from site. WiFi throughout (free).

Key Features

 Open All Year

 Pets Accepted

 Disabled Facilities

 Swimming Pool

 Play Area

 Skiing

Scan me for more information.

Capital Brussels
Currency Euro (€)
Language French is spoken in the south, Flemish in the north, and German in the eastern provinces.
Telephone country code 00 32
Time Zone CET (GMT/UTC+1)
Tourist Office belgiumtheplaceto.be

Climate Temperate climate similar to Britain.

Belgium

A small country divided into three regions, Flanders in the north, Wallonia in the south and Brussels the capital. Belgium is rich in scenic countryside, culture and history, notably the great forest of Ardennes, the historic cities of Bruges and Gent, and the western coastline with its sandy beaches.

Brussels is at the very heart of Europe and is a must-see destination with its heady mix of shops, bars, nightlife, exhibitions and festivals – a multi-cultural and multi-lingual city that is a focal point of art, fashion and culture. In the French-speaking region of Wallonia lies the mountainous Ardennes, home to picturesque villages rich in tradition and folklore. It is a favourite of nature-lovers and walkers who enjoy exploring its many castles and forts. The safe, sandy beaches on the west coast run for forty miles. The cosmopolitan resort of Ostend with its yacht basin and harbour offers year-round attractions including a carnival weekend and a Christmas market, and the myriad seafood restaurants will suit every taste. Bruges is Europe's best preserved medieval city, crisscrossed by willow-lined canals, where tiny cobbled streets open onto pretty squares. After visiting the many museums and art galleries, why not sample some of the delicious chocolate for which the city is famous

Shops Hours vary widely. Generally open 10am to 6.30pm Monday to Saturday, sometimes closed for an hour for lunch.

Banks 8.30am to 3.30pm or later on weekdays and some also on Saturday morning.

Travelling with Children Many cities have museums and other attractions that run activity days and programs for chrildren. Entrance fees for many attractions are reduced for those under 12. In much of Flanders there are special rates for young people under 26.

Public Holidays New Year's Day, Easter Monday, Labour Day, Ascension, Whit Monday, National Day 21 Jul, Assumption, All Saints' 1 Nov, Armistice Day, Christmas Day. Some government services may also be closed on King's Day 15 Nov.

Motoring For cars with a caravan or trailer, motorways are toll free except for the Liefenshoek Tunnel in Antwerp. Maximum permitted overall length of vehicle/trailer or caravan combination is 18 m. Blue Zone parking areas exist in Brussels, Ostend, Bruges, Liège, Antwerp and Ghent. Parking discs can be obtained from police stations, garages, and some shops.

See campsite map page 473.

Alan Rogers Code: BE0550
34 accommodations
469 pitches
GPS: 51.12965, 2.77222
Post Code: B-8620

West Flanders, Flanders

www.alanrogers.com/be0550
nieuwpoort@kompascamping.be
Tel: 058 236 037
www.kompascamping.be

Open (Touring Pitches):
28 March - 12 November.

Kompas Nieuwpoort

Not far from Dunkerque and Calais and convenient for the A18 motorway, this large, well equipped and well run site with 1056 pitches caters particularly for families. There are many amenities including a heated pool complex, a range of sporting activities, play areas and a children's farm. The 469 touring pitches, all with 10A electricity, are in regular rows on flat grass in various parts of the site; 120 also have a water point and waste water drainage. With many seasonal units and caravan holiday homes, the site becomes full during Belgian holidays and in July and August.

Five modern, clean and well maintained toilet blocks include washbasins in cubicles, controllable showers and excellent facilities for families, young children and disabled visitors. Dishwashing and laundry rooms. Washing machines and dryers. Motorcaravan services. Supermarket, bakery, restaurant, takeaway and café/bar (all w/ends low season, otherwise daily). Swimming pools (heated and supervised) with slide, paddling pool and pool games (17/5-14/9). Bicycle hire. Tennis. Extensive adventure playgrounds. Multisports court. Entertainment programme in July/Aug. WiFi throughout (charged).

Key Features

 Pets Accepted

 Disabled Facilities

 Swimming Pool

 Play Area

 Bar/Restaurant

 Bike Hire

Scan me for more information.

Alan Rogers Code: BE0560
26 accommodations
173 pitches
GPS: 51.15644, 2.75329
Post Code: B-8434

West Flanders, Flanders

www.alanrogers.com/be0560
info@delombarde.be
Tel: 058 236 839
www.delombarde.be

Open (Touring Pitches):
All year.

Camping De Lombarde

De Lombarde is a spacious, good value holiday site between Lombardsijde and the coast. It has a pleasant atmosphere and modern buildings. The 380 pitches are set out in level, grassy bays surrounded by shrubs, all with 16A electricity, long leads may be needed. Vehicles are parked in separate car parks. There are many seasonal units and 21 holiday homes, leaving 173 touring pitches. There is a range of activities and an entertainment programme in season. This is a popular holiday area and the site becomes full at peak times. A pleasant stroll of one kilometre takes you into Lombardsijde. There is a tram service from near the site entrance to the town and the beach.

Three heated sanitary units are of an acceptable standard, with some washbasins in cubicles. Facilities for disabled visitors. Large laundry. Motorcaravan services. Shop, restaurant/bar and takeaway (1/4-31/8 and school holidays). Tennis. Boules. Fishing lake. TV lounge. Entertainment programme for children. Outdoor fitness equipment. Playground. WiFi in bar. ATM. Torch useful. Max. 1 dog.

Key Features

 Open All Year

 Pets Accepted

 Disabled Facilities

 Play Area

 Bar/Restaurant

 Fishing

Scan me for more information.

Alan Rogers Code: BE0665
8 accommodations
32 pitches
GPS: 51.21136, 4.90298
Post Code: B-2460

Antwerp, Flanders

www.alanrogers.com/be0665
kempen@florealgroup.be
Tel: 014 556 120
www.florealgroup.be/en/page/
kempen-lichtaart-en.html

Open (Touring Pitches):
All year.

Camping Floreal Kempen

This is an attractive woodland site and a member of the Floreal group. It is located close to the well known Purperen Heide, a superb nature reserve with 15 scenic footpaths leading through it. There are 228 pitches, of which only 32 are reserved for touring units. These are of a good size (100 sq.m. or more), all with 16A electricity and most with their own water supply. Two simple cabins are available for hikers, as well as fully equipped mobile homes. There are some good leisure facilities, including tennis and a multisports pitch, as well as a popular bar and restaurant.

Three modern, heated toilet blocks are well equipped with some washbasins in cabins and have facilities for children and disabled visitors. Hairdryer. Laundry facilities. Motorcaravan services. Washing machine. Shop, bar, restaurant and takeaway (all year). TV room. Tennis. Play area. Multisports terrain. Pétanque. Mobile homes to rent (one adapted for disabled users). Free WiFi over site.

Key Features

 Open All Year

 Pets Accepted

 Disabled Facilities

 Play Area

 Bar/Restaurant

Scan me for
more information.

Resort De Kempen

Resort De Kempen offers something for everyone: a holiday environment for all age groups, with nothing lacking for the discerning holidaymaker. Of the 228 touring pitches, 25 are used by a tour operator. All the pitches have a fresh water tap, waste water disposal and 6A electricity connection. The main attraction is an indoor pool complex with a central swirl-pool, two shallow pools for toddlers, a long water flume, a jacuzzi and sun beds (cheaper for campers). There is provision for wheelchair users. A retro tavern, restaurant and snack bar overlook the lake with its beach.

A single modern sanitary block includes an excellent children's room (bath in the shape of a car, raised showers, child-size toilets, baby station). There is a further block with family bathrooms. Toilet facilities in the pool complex. Laundry facilities. Motorcaravan services. Restaurant. Bar. Tavern. Takeaway (July/Aug). Shop. Play areas including an area for 5-12 year olds. Boules. Lakes for fishing. Lake with beach area and slide. Bicycle hire.

Alan Rogers Code: BE0800
228 pitches
GPS: 51.21004, 5.17187
Post Code: B-2400

Antwerp, Flanders

www.alanrogers.com/be0800
info@europarcs.nl
Tel: 0031 88 70 80 90
en.europarcs.nl

Open (Touring Pitches):
All Year

Key Features

 Open All Year

 Pets Accepted

 Disabled Facilities

 Swimming Pool

 Play Area

 Bar/Restaurant

 Bike Hire

 Fishing

Scan me for more information.

Alan Rogers Code: BE0647
107 accommodations
70 pitches
GPS: 51.22980, 4.97985
Post Code: B-2460

Antwerp, Flanders

Camping Houtum

www.alanrogers.com/be0647
info@campinghoutum.be
Tel: +32 14 859 216
www.campinghoutum.be

Open (Touring Pitches):
All year.

This quietly situated, family owned campsite can be found on the outskirts of Kasterlee, famous for its gastronomic restaurants. There are 177 pitches, 70 for touring, all with 10A electric hook-ups, water and drainage. These pitches will be relocated to a new area of the site with upgraded facilities. On-site amenities include an excellent children's play area and a popular bar and restaurant.

New toilet block (2013) with facilities for families and disabled visitors. Launderette. Motorcaravan services. Bar. Restaurant and takeaway (open daily July/Aug, then Wed. and weekends). TV room. Playground. Boules pitch. Free WiFi over part of site.

Key Features

 Open All Year

 Pets Accepted

 Disabled Facilities

 Play Area

 Bar/Restaurant

Scan me for more information.

Alan Rogers Code: BE0760
24 accommodations
244 pitches
GPS: 51.17343, 5.53902
Post Code: B-3950

Limburg, Flanders

www.alanrogers.com/be0760
info@goolderheide.be
Tel: 0032 89 469 640
www.goolderheide.be

Open (Touring Pitches):
1 April - 30 September

Goolderheide Familiepark

A large family holiday site with 900 individual pitches, Goolderheide has been owned and operated by the same family for many years and has an excellent pool complex and playgrounds. There are many seasonal and rental units, plus around 250 touring pitches with 6/10/16A electricity, all in a forest setting. The pitches are of variable size and access roads are quite narrow. The outdoor pool complex has two large pools (one of Olympic size), a slide and a paddling pool. There is also a fishing lake, and a lake with a small sandy beach. An enormous area is devoted to a comprehensive play area with a vast range of equipment.

Four sanitary buildings provide an ample supply of WCs and washbasins in cabins, but rather fewer preset showers. Family facilities. Two en-suite units for disabled visitors (key access). Laundry facilities. Dishwasher. Shop, bar and takeaway (daily in July/Aug, w/ends and public holidays in low season). Takeaway. Swimming pools. Tennis. Fishing. Boules. Minigolf. Play area and assault course. Extensive programme of activities (July/Aug).

Key Features

 Pets Accepted

 Disabled Facilities

 Swimming Pool

 Play Area

 Bar/Restaurant

 Bike Hire

 Fishing

Scan me for
more information.

Alan Rogers Code: BE0784
5 accommodations
126 pitches
GPS: 50.95387, 5.66198
Post Code: B-3630

Limburg, Flanders

www.alanrogers.com/be0784
info@kikmolen.be
Tel: 089 770 900
www.kikmolen.be

Open (Touring Pitches):
1 April - 31 October.

Recreatieoord Kikmolen

This is a large and very lively site situated around a large, artificial lake which also serves as the site swimming pool. The campsite is targeted at a family clientele. Large pitches are spread throughout the site, with the 126 for touring which are separated from around 500 seasonal and rental units. The pitches are on grass and all have 6A electricity and water. Dogs are officially not accepted but when we visited there were many dogs on the site. Two water slides run into the large artificial lake (not fenced and unsuitable for young children). The site is within the national park, in an Area of Outstanding Natural Beauty. Although large, it is geared towards families and is ideal for those with younger children.

Eight modern blocks are spread throughout the site, and one was rebuilt for 2012. All have good facilities with some washbasins in cabins, and hot water is charged through a prepaid SEP key system. One disabled toilet per block which is unlocked and used by all. Two restaurants and bars. Takeaway. Well stocked shop. Games room. Lake swimming with water slides. Sports field. Lively activity and entertainment programme. Bicycle hire.

Key Features

 Pets Accepted

 Disabled Facilities

 Swimming Pool

 Play Area

 Bar/Restaurant

 Bike Hire

Scan me for more information.

Alan Rogers Code: BE0610
8 accommodations
337 pitches
GPS: 51.04722, 3.68333
Post Code: B-9000

East Flanders, Flanders

Camping Blaarmeersen

www.alanrogers.com/be0610
camping.blaarmeersen@gent.be
Tel: 092 668 160
www.stad.gent/blaarmeersen

Open (Touring Pitches):
1 March - 31 October.

Blaarmeersen is a comfortable, well managed municipal site in the west of the city. It adjoins a sports complex and a fair sized lake which together provide facilities for a variety of watersports, tennis, squash, minigolf, football, athletics track, roller skating and a playground. There are 337 pitches for touring units, these are flat, grassy, individually separated by hedges and mostly arranged in circular groups, all with electricity. There are 43 hardstandings for motorhomes, plus a separate area for tents with barbecue facilities. There is noise from the nearby city ring road. There is a good network of paths and cycle routes around the city.

Five sanitary units of a decent standard vary in size. Showers and toilets for disabled visitors. Laundry. Motorcaravan services. Shop, café/bar (both daily). Takeaway. Sports facilities. Playground. Fishing. Bicycle hire. Lake swimming. Communal barbecue. WiFi.

Key Features

 Pets Accepted

 Disabled Facilities

 Play Area

 Bar/Restaurant

 Bike Hire

 Fishing

Scan me for more information.

Alan Rogers Code: BE0708
12 accommodations
74 pitches
GPS: 50.24167, 6.09306
Post Code: B-4790

Liège, Wallonia

www.alanrogers.com/be0708
info@hohenbusch.be
Tel: +32 (0)80 227 523
www.campinghohenbusch.be

Open (Touring Pitches):
30 March - 3 November

Camping Hohenbusch

Camping Hohenbusch is located in the Our valley on the edge of the Ardennes and 30 km. from the Grand Prix circuit at Spa-Francorchamps. This is a well equipped site with a new swimming pool, restaurant and even a children's petting zoo. There are grassy pitches which are a good size, all with 5A (Europlug) electricity, water and drainage, with a number of smaller pitches available for hikers. Hohenbusch also boasts a number of luxury pitches which are 150 sq.m. and equipped with satellite TV connections. A number of mobile homes are available to rent, as well as rooms in the main building.

Excellent sanitary facilities with family shower rooms. Laundry facilities. Small shop. Bar. Snack bar and takeaway. All open all season. Swimming pool (heated 30/5-31/8). Paddling pool. Play area. Petting zoo. Bicycle hire. Entertainment and activities in peak season. Mobile homes and rooms to rent. WiFi throughout (charged).

Key Features

 Pets Accepted

 Disabled Facilities

 Swimming Pool

 Play Area

 Bar/Restaurant

Scan me for
more information.

Alan Rogers Code: BE0740
15 accommodations
120 pitches
GPS: 50.41203, 5.95317
Post Code: B-4970

Liège, Wallonia

www.alanrogers.com/be0740
fb220447@skynet.be
Tel: 080 863 075
www.eaurouge.eu

Open (Touring Pitches):
All year.

Camping l'Eau Rouge

A popular, lively and attractively situated site, l'Eau Rouge is in a sheltered valley close to Spa and the Grand Prix circuit. There are 140 grassy pitches of 110 sq.m. on sloping ground either side of a central road (speed bumps) – 120 for touring units, 80 with 10A electricity (70 with water and waste water), the remainder for static units. The main building houses the busy reception, shop, bar and the main sanitary facilities. There are plenty of sporting activities in the area including skiing and luge in winter. The site is close to the motor race circuit at Spa-Francorchamps and is within walking distance for the fit. The site's Dutch owners have completed a five year programme upgrading the infrastructure and have other ideas in the pipeline.

A brand new environmentally friendly toilet block has showers (on payment), private cubicles, and facilities for babies and children. Motorcaravan services. Washing machine. Shop. Baker calls daily at 08.30 (in season). Takeaway (in summer). Bar. Boules. Archery (free lessons in high season). Playground. Entertainment in season. WiFi over part of site (charged). Max. 2 dogs.

Key Features

 Open All Year

 Pets Accepted

 Disabled Facilities

 Swimming Pool

 Play Area

 Bar/Restaurant

 Fishing

Scan me for more information.

Alan Rogers Code: BE0700
78 accommodations
200 pitches
GPS: 50.50758, 5.91952
Post Code: B-4845

Liège, Wallonia

www.alanrogers.com/be0700
info@campingspador.be
Tel: 087 474 400
www.campingspador.com

Open (Touring Pitches):
1 April - 7 November.

Camping Spa d'Or

Camping Spa d'Or is set in a beautiful area of woodlands and picturesque villages, 4 km. from the town of Spa (Pearl of the Ardennes). The site is on the banks of a small river and is an ideal starting point for walks and bicycle trips through the forests. With over 300 pitches in total, 200 are for touring and 20 are reserved for tents. The touring pitches have an open aspect, most are slightly sloping and all have 10A electricity connections. The remainder are used for private mobile homes. Indoor accommodation is provided for groups of up to 50 persons. The bar and restaurant, brightly illuminated with coloured lights outside, offer a cosy environment for eating and drinking. This campsite is within easy reach of many tourist attractions.

Key Features

 Pets Accepted

 Disabled Facilities

 Swimming Pool

 Play Area

 Bar/Restaurant

 Bike Hire

One new large, bright and cheerful sanitary block and one new smaller, prefabricated block, both with all the usual facilities. Room for visitors with disabilities. Laundry. Shop. Bar, restaurant (weekends only in low season) and takeaway. Outdoor heated swimming pool (1/5-15/9). Play area with good equipment. TV in bar. Goal posts and two boules pitches. Entertainment during July/Aug. Mountain bike hire. Maps for mountain biking and walking on sale at reception. WiFi over site (charged).

Scan me for more information.

Alan Rogers Code: BE0670
142 accommodations
276 pitches
GPS: 50.09647, 5.28570
Post Code: B-6927

Luxembourg, Wallonia

www.alanrogers.com/be0670
info@parclaclusure.be
Tel: 084 360 050
www.parclaclusure.be/en

Open (Touring Pitches):
All year.

Camping Parc la Clusure

A friendly and very well run site, Parc la Clusure is highly recommended. Set in a river valley in the lovely wooded uplands of the Ardennes, known as the l'Homme Valley touring area, the site has 469 large, marked, grassy pitches (276 for touring). All have access to electricity, cable TV and water taps and are mostly in avenues off a central, tarmac road. There is some noise from the nearby railway. There is a very pleasant riverside walk; the river is shallow in summer and popular with children (caution in winter). The site's heated swimming pool and children's pool have a pool-side bar and terrace.

Three excellent sanitary units, one heated in winter, include some washbasins in cubicles, facilities for babies and children. Facilities for disabled campers. Motorcaravan services. Well stocked shop, bar, restaurant, snack bar and takeaway (25/3-6/11). Swimming pools (30/4-18/9). Bicycle hire. Tennis. New playgrounds. Organised activity programme including canoeing, archery, abseiling, mountain biking and climbing (summer). Caving. Fishing (licence essential). WiFi over site (free). Max. 1 dog in July/Aug.

Key Features

 Open All Year

 Pets Accepted

 Disabled Facilities

 Swimming Pool

 Play Area

 Bar/Restaurant

 Skiing

 Bike Hire

Scan me for
more information.

39

Alan Rogers Code: BE0735
71 accommodations
193 pitches
GPS: 50.23127, 5.62583
Post Code: B-6960

Luxembourg, Wallonia

www.alanrogers.com/be0735
info@petitesuisse.be
Tel: 084 444 030
www.petitesuisse.be

Open (Touring Pitches):
All year.

Petite Suisse

This quiet site is set in the picturesque countryside of the Belgian Ardennes, a region in which rivers flow through valleys bordered by vast forests where horses are still usefully employed. Set on a southerly slope, the site is mostly open and offers wide views of the surrounding countryside. The 193 touring pitches, all with 10A electricity, are either on open sloping ground or in terraced rows with hedges in between, and trees providing some separation. Gravel roads provide access around the site. To the right of the entrance barrier a large wooden building houses reception, a bar and a restaurant.

All the facilities that one would expect of a large site are available. Showers are free, washbasins both open and in cabins. Baby room. Laundry room with washing machines and dryers. Shop, restaurant, bar and takeaway (4/4-2/11). Heated outdoor swimming pool (1/5-1/9), paddling pool and slide. Sports field. Tennis. Bicycle hire. Playground and club for children. Entertainment programme during school holidays. Varied activity programme, including archery, canoeing, climbing, abseiling and walking. WiFi (charged).

Key Features

 Open All Year

 Pets Accepted

 Swimming Pool

 Play Area

 Bar/Restaurant

 Skiing

 Bike Hire

Scan me for more information.

Alan Rogers Code: BE0711
160 accommodations
299 pitches
GPS: 49.83861, 5.25122
Post Code: B-6880

Luxembourg, Wallonia

www.alanrogers.com/be0711
info@campingbertrix.be
Tel: 061 412 281
www.campingbertrix.be

Open (Touring Pitches):
28 March - 12 November.

Ardennen Camping Bertrix

Bertrix is located at the heart of the Belgian Ardennes, between the towns of Bastogne and Bouillon and overlooking the hills of the Semois valley. Part of a Dutch chain, the site has over 400 terraced pitches of which 299 are for touring, all with 10A electricity, and 43 also have water and drainage. A variety of seasonal caravans are sited among them and there is a friendly feel to the area. Some pitches are available with children's play huts on stilts! A wide range of imaginative activities are organised in the holidays, including some exciting excursions on horseback to the nearby working slate mine.

Five well appointed toilet blocks, one with facilities for disabled visitors. The central one has a large laundry. Motorcaravan services. Shop for basics and bread. Excellent restaurant and bar (closed low season on Tues. and Thurs) has satellite TV and Internet access and a terrace overlooking the large, heated swimming and paddling pools (27/4-16/9, supervised high season). Tennis. Bicycle hire. Children's games room. Woodland adventure trail. Ardennes chalets and holiday homes to rent. WiFi in part of the site (charged). Max. 1 dog in July/Aug.

Key Features

 Pets Accepted

 Disabled Facilities

 Swimming Pool

 Play Area

 Bar/Restaurant

 Bike Hire

Scan me for more information.

Capital Zagreb
Currency Kuna (Kn)
Language Croatian
Telephone country code 00 385
Time Zone CET (GMT/UTC+1)
Tourist Office croatia.hr

Climate Predominantly warm and hot in summer with temperatures of up to 40C.

Croatia

Croatia has developed into a lively and friendly tourist destination, while retaining the unspoilt beauty and character of its coastal ports, traditional towns and tiny islands with their secluded coves. Its rich history is reflected in its Baroque architecture, traditional festivals and two UNESCO World Heritage sites.

The most developed tourist regions in Croatia include the peninsula of Istria, where you will find the preserved Roman amphitheatre in Pula, the beautiful town of Rovinj with cobbled streets and wooded hills, and the resort of Umag, with a busy marina, charming old town and an international tennis centre. The coast is dotted with islands, making it a mecca for watersports enthusiasts, and there is an abundance of campsites in the area. Further south, in the province of Dalmatia, Split is Croatia's second largest city and lies on the Adriatic coast. It is home to the impressive Diolectian's Palace and a starting point for ferry trips to the islands of Brac, Hvar, Vis and Korcula, with their lively fishing villages and pristine beaches. The old walled city of Dubrovnik is 150 km. south. A favourite of George Bernard Shaw, who described it as 'the pearl of the Adriatic', it has a lively summer festival, numerous historical sights and a newly restored cable car to the top of Mount Srd.

Shops Hours vary widely. In high-season 8am to 8pm weekdays and until 2pm or 3pm on Saturdays. Some shops take a break from 2pm to 5pm.

Banks 8am or 9am to 8pm weekdays and 7am or 8am to 1pm or 2pm Saturdays.

Travelling with Children Beaches are safe and many cycle trails are suitable for all ages. Many museums and historical attractions run programs and activity trails. Child fees are applicable for under 9s. The dining scene is relaxed, many restaurants including upmarket ones will offer a kids menu or smaller portions.

Public Holidays New Year's Day, Epiphany, Easter Monday, Labour Day, Corpus Christi, Anti-Facist Resistance Day 22 Jun, Statehood Day 25 Jun, Thanksgiving 5 Aug, Assumption, Independence Day 8 Oct, All Saints' 1 Nov, Christmas Day, St. Stephen's Day 26 Dec.

Motoring There are still some roads which leave a lot to be desired but things have improved dramatically in the last few years. Roads along the coast can become heavily congested in summer and queues are possible at border crossings. Tolls: some motorways, bridges and tunnels. Cars towing a caravan or trailer must carry two warning triangles. It is illegal to overtake military convoys.

See campsite map page 474.

Alan Rogers Code: CR6716
600 accommodations
1911 pitches
GPS: 45.29672, 13.59442
Post Code: HR-52465

Porec, Istria

www.alanrogers.com/cr6716
camping@valamar.com
Tel: 052 465 010
www.camping-adriatic.com/lanterna-
camp-porec

Open (Touring Pitches):
3 April - 3 October

Lanterna Premium Camp

This is a well organised site and one of the largest in Croatia with high standards and an amazing selection of activities, and is part of the Camping Adriatic by Valamar group. Set in 80 hectares with over 3 km. of beach, there are 3,000 pitches, of which 1,911 are for touring units. All have 16A electricity and fresh water, and 255 also have waste water drainage. Pitches are 60-120 sq.m. with some superb locations right on the sea, although these tend to be taken first so it is advisable to book ahead. There are wonderful coastal views from the new glamping area with seven luxury tents and private infinity pool. A member of Leading Campings group.

The sixteen sanitary blocks are clean and good quality. Facilities for children and baby care areas, some Turkish style WCs, hot showers, with some blocks providing facilities for disabled visitors. Laundry service. Three supermarkets sell most everyday requirements. Fresh fish shop. Four restaurants, bars, snack bars and fast food outlets. Swimming pool and paddling pools. Sandpit and play areas, with entertainment for all in high season. Tennis. Bicycle hire. Watersports. Boat hire. Minigolf. Riding. Internet café. Jetty and ramp for boats. WiFi (free). Impressive new glamping area. Dogs are accepted in certain areas.

Key Features

 Pets Accepted

 Disabled Facilities

 Beach Access

 Swimming Pool

 Play Area

 Bar/Restaurant

 Skiing

 Bike Hire

Scan me for
more information.

Alan Rogers Code: CR6713
5 accommodations
600 pitches
GPS: 45.34363, 13.54815
Post Code: HR-52466

Novigrad, Istria

www.alanrogers.com/cr6713
camping@laguna-novigrad.hr
Tel: 052 858 680
www.camping.hr/campsites/
aminess-maravea

Open (Touring Pitches):
15 April - 2 October.

Aminess Maravea

Previously known as Camping Mareda; Aminess Maravea is in a quiet coastal location 4 km. North of the small picturesque town of Novigrad. Backed by oak woods and acres of vineyards, the site slopes down to a half bay and has 600 touring pitches, all with 16A electricity, either set on shallow terraces or slightly sloping gravel/grass. Mature trees provide shade, and many pitches have views over the sea; 95 pitches are fully serviced. The site has an attractive, rocky sea frontage with areas for sunbathing, a good size swimming pool, a restaurant bar and a café, all with sea views.

Five modern toilet blocks, one excellent one refurbished in 2013, have British and Turkish style toilets, washbasins in cabins and hot showers. Family shower room. Child size toilets and washbasins. Laundry with sinks and washing machine. Motorcaravan services. Supermarket. Beach restaurant, coffee bar and bar with terrace. Seawater swimming pool. Play area. Tennis. Fishing. Boats, kayaks, canoes and pedaloes for hire. Bicycle hire. Games hall with video games. Organised entertainment. Free WiFi.

Key Features

 Pets Accepted

 Disabled Facilities

 Beach Access

 Swimming Pool

 Play Area

 Bar/Restaurant

 Bike Hire

 Fishing

Scan me for
more information.

Alan Rogers Code: CR6728
20 accommodations
433 pitches
GPS: 45.15548, 13.61032
Post Code: HR-52450

Vrsar, Istria

www.alanrogers.com/cr6728
camping@valamar.com
Tel: 052 465 010
www.camping-adriatic.com/orsera-camp-porec

Open (Touring Pitches):
1 April - 8 October

Orsera Camping Resort

This is a very attractive site with a 900 m. shoreline from which there are stunning views over the sea to the islands and very often there are spectacular sunsets. This 30-hectare site with direct access to the old fishing port of Vrsar has 535 pitches of which 433 are available to touring units. Marked and numbered, the pitches vary in size with 90 sq.m. being the average. There is some terracing but the pitches to the north of the site are on level ground and offer better views. Ample shade is provided by mature pines and oak trees. All pitches have 10/16A electricity.

The modern and well maintained sanitary blocks are distributed over the site and have mainly British style WCs. Free showers, hot and cold water to washbasins. Some have facilities for disabled visitors. Facilities for babies and children. Motorcaravan services. Laundry. Supermarket (1/5-15/9). Bar/restaurant and takeaway (1/5-15/9). Sports centre. Cinema. Bicycle hire. Fishing. Watersports (no jet skis). Only electric barbecues are permitted. Free WiFi throughout.

Key Features

 Pets Accepted

 Disabled Facilities

 Beach Access

 Play Area

 Bar/Restaurant

 Skiing

 Bike Hire

 Fishing

Scan me for more information.

Alan Rogers Code: CR6744
420 pitches
GPS: 44.89812, 13.80833
Post Code: HR-52100

Pula, Istria

www.alanrogers.com/cr6744
camping@valamar.com
Tel: 052 465 010
www.camping-adriatic.com/brioni-camp-pula

Open (Touring Pitches):
All Year

Brioni Sunny Camping

Situated on a small peninsula within sight of the Brijuni National Park (comprising 14 islands) and within easy reach of Pula, Brioni Sunny Camping is a quiet and useful base from which to tour in a scenically attractive and historically interesting region. The site has 420 touring pitches under ample shade, all with 10A electricity and 272 with fresh water taps. On mainly level grass and gravel, the pitches are numbered with some terracing. Part of the site is devoted to a youth hostel which shares the site facilities. A diving club is based on the site, the clear seawater being ideal for snorkelling.

Three sanitary blocks, one with facilities for disabled visitors. Cleaning and maintenance needed some attention when we visited. Baby room. Laundry room. Small supermarket and kiosk selling fruit, vegetables and bread (10/5-15/9). Restaurant. Beachside snack bar. Play area. Boat rental. Internet access.

Key Features

 Open All Year

 Pets Accepted

 Disabled Facilities

 Beach Access

 Play Area

 Bar/Restaurant

 Bike Hire

 Fishing

Scan me for more information.

Alan Rogers Code: CR6605
4 accommodations
50 pitches
GPS: 45.80235, 15.82708
Post Code: 10437

Zagreb, Central

www.alanrogers.com/cr6605
info@campzagreb.com
Tel: 1 3324 567
www.campzagreb.com

Open (Touring Pitches):

Camp Zagreb

The pitches here are laid out in a circular arrangement, linked by wooden pathways. As well as offering 50 camping pitches in 2 sizes (38 x 75m2 and 10 x 100m2) Camp Zagreb also has accommodation in 4 modern wooden bungalows suitable for 2-4 people and a small selection of glamping tents. The wellness suite which overlooks the lake features a water bed, jacuzzi, finish sauna and large sun terrace with lake view. Other activities include a horse riding school and kayak rental (included in the rental price of the glamping accommodation.) The on-site pizza restaurant, with views over the lake, Pizzeria Jezero is highly recommended.

Pizzeria, Cafe Bar, Wellness Centre with Finnish sauna, jacuzzi, relaxation area, sunbathing terrace, water bed, massage and salt room. Beach, BBQ, Pet Shower, Laundry, Dishwashing, Chemical Toilet Disposal Point, Kayak hire, Bike hire, Horse riding school.

Key Features

 Open All Year

 Pets Accepted

 Disabled Facilities

 Play Area

 Bar/Restaurant

 Bike Hire

 Horse Riding

Scan me for more information.

Alan Rogers Code: CR6757
32 accommodations
584 pitches
GPS: 45.01964, 14.57072
Post Code: HR-51500

Krk, Kvarner

www.alanrogers.com/cr6757
camping@valamar.com
Tel: 052 465 010
www.camping-adriatic.com/jezevac-camp-krk

Open (Touring Pitches):
3 April - 30 September

Ježevac Camping Resort

Jezevac Premium Camping Resort is an excellent and well maintained seaside site within walking distance of the pretty town of Krk. It is a large site extending to over 11 hectares and is built on a hillside at the western side of the town. Over 550 pitches, all for touring, are mainly on level terraces, separated by hedges with some shade and a number enjoy views of the bay below. All have 10A electricity, 120 are fully serviced. Some premium beachside pitches are available with water and electricity. The 800 m. long private beach is the focal point and in high season the atmosphere can be very lively.

Six modern, well maintained toilet blocks with free hot showers. Washing machines. Facilities for disabled visitors and children. Motorcaravan services. Shops (1/4-15/10). Restaurants (1/5-1/10) and bars. Takeaway (1/5-30/9). Tennis. Playground. Activity and entertainment programmes and children's club (May-Sept). Fishing. Bicycle hire. Boat launching and sailing. Max. 1 dog. Communal barbecue area. WiFi throughout.

Key Features

 Pets Accepted

 Disabled Facilities

 Beach Access

 Play Area

 Bar/Restaurant

 Bike Hire

 Fishing

 Sailing

Scan me for more information.

Alan Rogers Code: CR6772
100 accommodations
500 pitches
GPS: 44.55555, 14.44166
Post Code: HR-51550

Mali Losinj, Kvarner

www.alanrogers.com/cr6772
info@poljana.hr
Tel: 051 231 726
www.campingpoljana.com

Open (Touring Pitches):
1 April - 21 October.

Camping Poljana

Autocamp Poljana lies on the narrow strip of land in the southern part of Losinj island, just north of the pleasant town of Mali Losinj. With 780 pitches (500 for touring), this site is bigger than it looks. The camping area has been newly laid out with some flat areas and some terraces. The pitches are marked with flowers and shrubs. There are some mature trees for shade and 500 electricity connections. Campers may be able to experience both sunset and sunrise from the same pitch! The toilet facilities are new and well maintained, while a shop and a series of bars and restaurants are available close by.

Toilet blocks, including solar panels for hot water, are entirely up to date and adequate. Family room. Facilities for disabled visitors. Baby rooms. Motorcaravan services. Washing machine. Daily entertainment programmes. Bicycle hire. WiFi throughout (charged). Rock beach with cocktail bar. Marina.

Key Features

 Pets Accepted

 Disabled Facilities

 Beach Access

 Play Area

 Bar/Restaurant

 Bike Hire

 Fishing

Scan me for more information.

Alan Rogers Code: CR6915
53 accommodations
94 pitches
GPS: 44.97357, 15.64799
Post Code: HR-47245

Lika, Rakovica, Dalmatia

www.alanrogers.com/cr6915
info@plitvice.com
Tel: 047 784 192
www.plitvice.com

Open (Touring Pitches):
1 April - 1 October

Plitvice Holiday Resort

Plitvice Holiday Resort is on the Zagreb - Split road, 125 km. South of Zagreb. It is well situated for visiting the beautiful Plitvice National Park. The site is surrounded by meadows, forests, mountains, lakes and waterfalls. There are 94 pitches for touring and six teepees for rent. Some of the average size pitches are on grass or hard ground, with many slightly sloping (levelling blocks useful). Some have part or full shade and all have 16A electricity. There is an excellent restaurant offering local and Croatian dishes along with an international menu. In high season, the site often gets full so early arrival is recommended. The site has recently invested heavily in glamping style accommodation including some impressive treehouses, lake houses and mobile homes.

Two modern toilet blocks with mainly open washbasins, could be stretched at times. Washing machine and dryer. Motorcaravan services. Small shop with fresh bread. Bar/restaurant. Small swimming pool (1/5-1/10). Play areas. Evening entertainment twice a week. Tennis. WiFi (free). The site also has a wide selection of accommodation for rent including tipis, bungalows and apartments.

Key Features

 Pets Accepted

 Disabled Facilities

 Swimming Pool

 Play Area

 Bar/Restaurant

Scan me for more information.

Alan Rogers Code: CR6911
80 accommodations
451 pitches
GPS: 43.51157, 16.19377
Post Code: HR-21218

Trogir, Dalmatia

www.alanrogers.com/cr6911
info@vranjica-belvedere.hr
Tel: 021 798 222
www.vranjica-belvedere.hr

Open (Touring Pitches):
27 March - 20 October.

Vranjica Belvedere

Camping Vranjica Belvedere is 30 km. west of Split, on the beautiful Dalmatian coast. This large terraced site lies on a wooded hillside with magnificent views across the crystal blue sea to the neighbouring islands. There are over 400 average size, marked pitches, the majority with 10/16A electricity (long leads required), some have water and drainage. Rock pegs are advised. A stylish but small swimming pool with sunbeds overlooks the Adriatic Sea. There is a rocky and pebbly beach adjacent to the site offering many watersports. A small area of beach accepts dogs.

Four modern toilet blocks located across the site were still being completed at the time of our visit (facilities for disabled visitors in one block at far end). Laundry. Motorcaravan services. Minimarket. Restaurant, takeaway and beach bar. New children's pool. Tennis. Minigolf. Boules. Multisports court. Watersports. Playground. Bicycle hire. Full family entertainment and sporting activities. Communal barbecues only. WiFi (free).

Key Features

 Pets Accepted

 Disabled Facilities

 Beach Access

 Swimming Pool

 Play Area

 Bar/Restaurant

 Bike Hire

 Fishing

Scan me for more information.

Alan Rogers Code: CR6860
50 accommodations
232 pitches
GPS: 43.44062, 16.68028
Post Code: HR-21310

Omis, Dalmatia

www.alanrogers.com/cr6860
camping@galeb.hr
Tel: 021 864 430
www.kamp.galeb.hr

Open (Touring Pitches):
All year.

Camp Galeb

Galeb is an attractive, grassy, beachside site set beneath mature trees. The River Cetina is just to the north of the site and the pretty port where river meets sea is a powerful attraction complemented by the ancient forts and pirate buildings above. A dramatic, 1,000-metre rock backdrop to the whole site reflects the light differently as the day progresses and the superb sunsets paint it with amazing orange and red hues. The numbered touring pitches are level and most have some shade. However, in high season, units are very close together and there will be little privacy; All are fully serviced (16A Europlug). Some pitches are right at the water's edge, from where there are views of the coast and the island of Brac.

Two sanitary blocks have been renovated to a good standard and both have facilities for disabled campers. Hot water for showers is plentiful and there is a regular cleaning routine. Motorcaravan services. Shop selling basics, bar, restaurant, takeaway (all open all year). Tennis. Play areas. Bicycle hire. Motor scooter hire. Entertainment in high season. TV. Security boxes. Cold boxes. Currency exchange. Beach. Boat launching and boat hire. Windsurfing. Sailing. Gas and electric barbecues only. Communal barbecue. Free WiFi throughout. Organised boat trips.

Key Features

 Open All Year

 Pets Accepted

 Disabled Facilities

 Beach Access

 Play Area

 Bar/Restaurant

 Bike Hire

 Fishing

Scan me for
more information.

Capital Prague
Currency Czech Koruna (CZK)
Language Czech
Telephone country code 00 420
Time Zone CET (GMT/UTC+1)
Tourist Office visitczech.cz

Climate Temperate oceanic climate with warm summers and cold, snowy winters.

Czech Republic

The Czech Republic, once known as Bohemia, is a land of fascinating castles, romantic lakes and valleys, picturesque medieval squares and famous spas. It is divided into two main regions, Bohemia to the west and Moravia in the east.

Although small, the Czech Republic has a wealth of attractive places to explore. The historic city of Prague is the hub of tourist activity and a treasure trove of museums, historical architecture, art galleries and theatres, as well as the annual 17-day beer festival!

The beautiful region of Bohemia, known for its Giant Mountains, is popular for hiking, skiing and other sports. West Bohemia is home to three renowned spas: Karlovy Vary, Mariánské Lázne and Františkovy Lázne, which have developed around the hundreds of mineral springs which rise in this area, and offer a wide variety of restorative treatments.

Brno is the capital of Moravia in the east, lying midway between Prague, Vienna and Budapest. Visitors will admire its beautiful architecture, notably Mies van der Rohe's Villa Tugendhat. North of Brno is the Moravian Karst, where the underground Punkya River has carved out a network of caves, some open to the public and connecting with boat trips along the river.

Shops 9am to 6pm weekdays, some stores open 9am to 1pm on Saturday. Shopping centres have longer opening hours.

Banks 9am to 4pm weekdays, some 9am to 1pm Saturday.

Travelling with Children The country is gradually becoming more children friendly although it lags behind many of its European neighbours when it comes to facilities and accessibility. More often than not restaurants will offer a children's menu. The attractions, mainly historic, aren't geared towards children but still make for an interesting day out.

Public Holidays New Year's Day, Good Friday, Easter Monday, May Day, Liberation Day 8 May, St Cyril & St Methodius Day 5 Jul, Jan Hus Day 6 Jul, Statehood Day 28 Sep, Independence Day 28 Oct, Freedom & Democracy Day 17 Nov, Christmas Eve, Christmas Day, Boxing Day.

Motoring There is a good, well signposted road network throughout the Republic and, although stretches of cobbles still exist, surfaces are generally good. An annual road tax is levied on all vehicles using Czech motorways and express roads, and a disc can be purchased at border crossings, post offices and filling stations. Dipped headlights are compulsory throughout winter. Give way to trams and buses.

See Campsite map 472.

Alan Rogers Code: CZ4695
10 accommodations
180 pitches
GPS: 50.70430, 14.93898
Post Code: CZ-46352

Severocesky, North Bohemia

www.alanrogers.com/cz4695
camping2000@online.nl
Tel: 485 179 621
www.camping2000.com

Open (Touring Pitches):
15 April - 15 September.

Camping 2000

Created from pleasant farm buildings and the fields behind them, Camping 2000 is especially popular with Dutch visitors. It is a good base for exploring Northern Bohemia with Prague (90 km) and the Krkonose mountains (50 km) from a pleasant, rural location. Most of the pitches are of average size (up to 100 sq.m) and numbered, all with 6A electricity. There is little shade and cars parked on the pitches can make the curved rows feel a bit crowded during high season. Further off, there are a few pitches catering for larger units. The social heart of the site is a large barn with a bar and a takeaway serving pizzas and typical Dutch snacks. Outdoors, a terrace overlooks a paddling pool and a larger, circular swimming pool featuring a 48 m. waterslide.

Until an extra new block is built, in high season prefabricated units are used next to the main toilet block. Facilities for disabled visitors. Washing machine and dryer. Shop (July/Aug). Bar and takeaway (May-Sept). Swimming and paddling pools. Bicycle hire. TV room. Five wooden cottages (fully equipped) for hire. WiFi.

Key Features

 Pets Accepted

 Disabled Facilities

 Swimming Pool

 Play Area

 Bar/Restaurant

 Bike Hire

Scan me for more information.

Alan Rogers Code: CZ4680
12 accommodations
100 pitches
GPS: 51.00228, 14.46680
Post Code: 407-77

Šluknov, North Bohemia

www.alanrogers.com/cz4680
info@campingregenboog.com
Tel: 607 513 973
www.campingregenboog.nl

Open (Touring Pitches):
19 May - 30 September.

Camping de Regenboog

Camping de Regenboog enjoys a beautiful location in the north of the Czech Republic and is only 5 km from the border of Germany. The campsite sits on 13 hectares, so the pitches are incredibly spacious. They also have log cabins for rent which sleep up to 6 people. Adjacent to the campsite, there is a recreation lake for swimming and boating, and you can walk or cycle in the nature reserve 'Bohemian Switzerland', as it is perfect for sports enthusiasts and nature lovers. Fresh bread is available from the bakers situated within 50 metres of the site, and the supermarket is only 400 metres away. For dinner, there are a few local restaurants nearby, and the prices are very reasonable. The campsite organises excursions to the nearby Skoda factory & museum.

Key Features

 Play Area

 Skiing

 Bike Hire

Large recreational lake for swimming and boating, Table tennis. Beach volleyball court. Football field. Campfire. Recreation/Youth room. Children's playground. Bowls. Archery (Once or twice a week). Horse riding nearby. Sheep pasture, where every morning the children can help to feed the sheep. Excursions to the Skoda factory/museum. In the main summer holidays (Jul/Aug) there is a recreation programme for all ages, from children's stories to cosy campfire evenings, football tournaments, barbecues and gatherings on Sunday. This all will be done in Dutch, so if you want a translation, this is available. Free WiFi.

Scan me for
more information.

Alan Rogers Code: CZ4555
5 accommodations
36 pitches
GPS: 50.61641, 16.22865
Post Code: CZ-54982

Kralovehradecky, East Bohemia

www.alanrogers.com/cz4555
bert.mien@tiscali.cz
Tel: 491 582 138
www.aktief.cz

Open (Touring Pitches):
1 May - 1 October.

Mini Camping Aktief

Camping Aktief is a small, rural site on the outskirts of the village of Vernerovice. The campsite is close to the Polish border, east of the Krkonose (Giant) Mountains. The spectacular rock formations of Adrspach and Teplice nad Metuji are close at hand. There are just 36 pitches (20 with 6A electricity), located in a tranquil and protected area with many fruit trees. From the campsite, there are good views around the surrounding rolling meadows and hills. The friendly Dutch owners have developed Camping Aktief as an important hiking centre. Plenty of other activities are also organised here, and detailed walking and cycle routes are available (in Dutch). The owners, Bert and Mien van Kampen, are happy to share their knowledge of the local area, including some good restaurants. They also organise special tours, including visits to a local brewery and glassworks. Bikes, mountain bikes and fishing equipment are available for hire on site. In peak season, a weekly barbecue is organised.

Modern toilet block with hot showers and underfloor heating. Sauna. Washing machine. Mobile home to rent. Accommodation in luxuriously converted farm buildings. Bicycle hire. WiFi (free).

Key Features

 Open All Year

 Skiing

 Bike Hire

Scan me for more information.

Alan Rogers Code: CZ4820
15 accommodations
150 pitches
GPS: 50.01152, 14.15022
Post Code: CZ-26712

Stredocesky, Central Bohemia

www.alanrogers.com/cz4820
info@campvalek.cz
Tel: 731 476 741
www.campvalek.cz

Open (Touring Pitches):
1 May - 30 September.

Caravan Camp Valek

Only 2.5 km. from the E50 motorway, this well maintained site creates a peaceful, friendly base enjoyed by families. It has been family owned for 21 years. Surrounded by delightful countryside, it is possible to visit Prague even though it is about 28 km. to the city centre. The site is well grassed and most of the pitches are on level ground to one side of the pool. The other part of the site is on sloping ground and more suitable for tents. Most of the pitches are in the open and not explicitly marked. However this does not appear to cause overcrowding and there is plenty of space. Electricity (10A) is available to all. Some places have pleasant views of the sunbathing area in front of the pool with a pine forested hillock as a backdrop.

The single extremely well maintained toilet block has limited numbers of toilets and showers, but during our visit in high season coped well. Small shop with fresh rolls daily. Waiter service restaurant with terrace has an extensive menu. Communal grill on the terrace. Natural swimming pool (20x60 m; June-Sept) with constantly changing water checked regularly by the authorities to ensure its purity. Extensive games room with arcade machines and Internet. Live musical nights on Saturdays. Tennis.

Key Features

 Pets Accepted

 Disabled Facilities

 Swimming Pool

 Play Area

 Bar/Restaurant

Scan me for more information.

Alan Rogers Code: CZ4720
21 accommodations
170 pitches
GPS: 48.65595, 14.17024
Post Code: CZ-38279

Jihocesky, South Bohemia

www.alanrogers.com/cz4720
info@campingfrymburk.cz
Tel: 380 735 284
www.campingfrymburk.cz

Open (Touring Pitches):
24 April - 20 September.

Camping Frymburk

Camping Frymburk is beautifully located on the Lipno lake in southern Bohemia and is an ideal site. From this site, activities could include walking, cycling, swimming, sailing, canoeing or rowing, and afterwards you could relax in the small, cosy bar/restaurant. It is also possible to enjoy a real Czech meal in one of the restaurants in Frymburk. There are 170 level pitches on terraces (all with 6A electricity, some with hardstanding and four with private sanitary units) and from the lower terraces on the edge of the lake there are lovely views over the water to the woods on the opposite side. A ferry crosses the lake from Frymburk where one can walk or cycle in the woods.

Three immaculate toilet blocks with washbasins, preset showers (charged) and an en-suite bathroom with toilet, basin and shower. Facilities for disabled visitors and families. Launderette. Motorcaravan services. Chemical disposal. Shop, restaurant and bar, takeaway (1/5-15/9). Three playgrounds. Waterpark with water trampolines. Canoe, bicycle, pedalos, rowing boat and surfboard hire. Entertainment (July/Aug). Volleyball competitions. Rafting. Bus trips to Prague. Torches useful. Internet access and WiFi.

Key Features

 Pets Accepted

 Disabled Facilities

 Play Area

 Bar/Restaurant

 Bike Hire

 Fishing

Scan me for more information.

Camping Olsina

Alan Rogers Code: CZ4725
21 accommodations
180 pitches
GPS: 48.74612, 14.11691
Post Code: CZ-38223

Jihocesky, South Bohemia

www.alanrogers.com/cz4725
info@campingolsina.cz
Tel: 608 029 982
www.campingolsina.cz

Open (Touring Pitches):
1 April - 31 October.

Camping Olsina is a part wooded site, with direct access to Lake Lipno and within walking distance of the pretty lakeside village of Cerná v Pošumavi, in southern Bohemia. This is a tranquil site with splendid views across the lake to the hills beyond. There are 180 grassy pitches (150 with electrical connections), and many have lake front positions. There are also 15 chalets (for four people) and six mobile homes (six people). On-site amenities include a shop and restaurant, as well as cycle and boat hire. Cerná v Pošumaví has a yacht club and a windsurfing school with rental facilities.

Two modern sanitary buildings, one serving the camping area, the other serving the rented accommodation. Both are well maintained with open style washbasins and controllable hot showers with sliding doors. Facilities for disabled visitors. Laundry room. Small shop. Restaurant. Bar. Direct lake access. Fishing. Play area. Boat hire. Bicycle hire. Free WiFi over site. Accommodation for rent.

Key Features

 Pets Accepted

 Disabled Facilities

 Play Area

 Bar/Restaurant

 Bike Hire

 Fishing

Scan me for more information.

Alan Rogers Code: CZ4892
2 accommodations
65 pitches
GPS: 49.51050, 16.77440
Post Code: CZ-67953

Jihomoravsky, South Moravia

www.alanrogers.com/cz4892
campingbenesov@hetnet.nl
Tel: 608 280 654
www.camping-benesov.nl

Open (Touring Pitches):
1 May - 1 September.

Camping de Bongerd

This small, well cared for site, owned and run by a Dutch family for 20 years, is in the part of the Czech Republic said to enjoy the most sun. De Bongerd has 65 pitches, all for touring units, with 6A electricity, in two fields with pitching off a gravel access road. One field runs down towards the former farmhouse and pitches here are slightly sloping, although some terraces have been created. Pitches on the second field are arranged on level ground in a circular arrangement. The site is attractively landscaped with young pine trees and colourful flowers. Many activities for children are organised such as film nights, excursions, walks through the site's forest and communal campfires. Trips to the historic cities of Brno and Olomouc are organised, and there is an extensive library.

Key Features

 Pets Accepted

 Swimming Pool

 Play Area

 Bar/Restaurant

 Bike Hire

 Fishing

Two well maintained prefabricated sanitary units supplement facilities in the farmhouse. British style toilets, open washbasins and controllable, hot showers (running free for 7 minutes). Motorcaravan services. New swimming pool with slide. Playground on gravel. Football field. Minigolf. Fishing. Riding. Activities for children. Excursions. Bicycle hire. Free WiFi over part of site. Max. one dog per pitch.

Scan me for more information.

Alan Rogers Code: CZ4895
55 pitches
GPS: 49.27657, 16.45263
Post Code: CZ-66471

Jihomoravsky, South Moravia

www.alanrogers.com/cz4895
camping.hana@seznam.cz
Tel: 607 905 801
www.campinghana.com

Open (Touring Pitches):
20 April - 30 September.

Camping Hana

The caves of the Moravian Karst, the site of the battle of Austerlitz and the castles of Veveri, Pertstejn and Spillberk are all within easy reach of this pleasant, small and quiet campsite. Hana Musilova runs the site to very high standards, speaks excellent English and Dutch and provides lots of local information. There are 55 level, numbered pitches with 10A electricity. Brno, the capital of Moravia and the Czech Republic's second largest city, is a short boat or bus ride away and the village of Veverska Bityska has shops, restaurants, bars and an ATM plus a reasonable, small supermarket. In Brno you can enjoy a good meal in one of the many restaurants or the more ghoulish campers may like to visit the Capuchin monastery crypt where the mummified bodies of monks and local dignitaries dating back from the early 1700s are on display. This is an excellent site on the banks of the river Svratka, where you can savour Czech life in a quiet and leisurely way.

The modernised sanitary block provides ample and clean toilets, hot showers (token, 1st free per person then CZK 10), washbasins and baby changing. Washing machine and dryer. Kitchen and dishwashing facilities. Small shop with essential supplies. Bicycle hire. Free WiFi throughout. Charcoal and gas barbecues allowed.

Key Features

 Pets Accepted

 Disabled Facilities

 Play Area

 Bike Hire

 Fishing

Scan me for
more information.

63

Capital Copenhagen
Currency Danish Krone (DKK)
Language Danish
Telephone country code 00 45
Time Zone CET (GMT/UTC+1)
Tourist Office visitdenmark.com

Climate Generally mild although changeable throughout the year.

Denmark

Denmark offers a diverse landscape all within a relatively short distance. The countryside is green and varied with flat plains, rolling hills, fertile farmland, many lakes and fjords, wild moors and long beaches, interspersed with pretty villages and towns.

It is the easiest of the Scandinavian countries to visit, and distances are short so it is easy to combine the faster pace of the city with the tranquillity of the countryside and the beaches. It comprises the peninsula of Jutland and the larger islands of Zeeland and Funen, in addition to hundreds of smaller islands, many uninhabited.

Zeeland is home to the climate-friendly capital city, Copenhagen, with its relaxing waterside cafés, vibrant nightlife, Michelin star restaurants and the stunning Frederiksborg castle. Funen is Denmark's second largest island, linked to Zeeland by the Great Belt Bridge.

Known as the Garden of Denmark, its gentle landscape is dotted with orchards and pretty thatched, half-timbered houses. It also has plenty of safe, sandy beaches. Jutland's flat terrain makes it ideal for cycling and its long beaches are popular with windsurfers. It's also home to one of the most popular attractions in Denmark, Legoland, and the oldest town in Scandinavia, Ribe.

Shops Hours vary throughout the year. Generally open from 10am to 6pm weekdays and until 4pm on Saturday. Some larger stores may be open Sunday. Supermarkets open from 8am to 9pm.

Banks 10am to 4pm Monday to Friday.

Travelling with Children A country very much tailored to children with a whole host of attractions from theme parks and zoos to family-friendly beaches. Entry to most museums is free. Many campsites have special programs for children during peak season.

Public Holidays New Year's Day, Maundy Thursday, Good Friday, Easter Monday, Prayer Day 17 May, Ascension, Whit Monday, Constitution Day 5 Jun, Christmas Day, Boxing Day, New Year's Eve.

Motoring Driving is much easier than at home as roads are much quieter. Driving is on the right. Do not drink and drive. Dipped headlights are compulsory at all times. Strong measures are taken against unauthorised parking on beaches, with on-the-spot fines.

See campsite map page 475.

Alan Rogers Code: DK2265
100 pitches
GPS: 55.74480, 12.58538
Post Code: DK-2920

Sjælland, Islands

www.alanrogers.com/dk2265
info@campingcopenhagen.dk
Tel: 39 62 36 88
www.campingcopenhagen.dk

Open (Touring Pitches):
7 March - 19 October.

Charlotten-lund Fort

On the northern outskirts of Copenhagen, this unique site is within the walls of an old fort, which still retains its main armament of twelve 29 cm. Howitzers (disabled, of course). There are 65 pitches on grass, all with 10A electricity. The apparent limitation on the space available means that pitches are relatively close together, but many are quite deep. The site is very popular and is usually full every night, so a reservation is necessary. The campsite is only 6 km. from the centre of Copenhagen, with a regular bus service from just outside the site. Alternatively, you could use the excellent cycle network to visit the city. The fort was constructed during 1886-1887 and was an integral link in the Copenhagen fortifications until 1932. A restaurant in the fort (under separate management) has excellent sea views to Sweden and the spectacular Øresund bridge.

Key Features

 Pets Accepted

 Disabled Facilities

 Beach Access

 Bar/Restaurant

 Bike Hire

 Fishing

Sanitary facilities located in the old armoury are newly rebuilt, well maintained and heated. Free showers. Kitchen facilities include gas hobs and a dining area. Laundry. Motorcaravan services. Small café in reception. Restaurant with terrace and views. Bicycle hire. Free WiFi over site. Beach.

Scan me for more information.

Alan Rogers Code: DK2269
23 accommodations
225 pitches
GPS: 55.71800, 11.76064
Post Code: DK-4300

Sjælland, Islands

www.alanrogers.com/dk2269
c-holbaek@fdm.dk
Tel: 59 43 50 64
www.holbaekfjord.dk

Open (Touring Pitches):
All year.

Holbæk Fjord Camping

This site has a peaceful and idyllic setting with views across Isefjorden, the marina and the golf course. It is located close to the seaside village of Holbæk. With a quiet and relaxed atmosphere, the emphasis on is on wellbeing, and it is ideal for those looking for a spot of pampering in the wellness centre. There are 225 grass pitches (100 for touring), all have 16A electricity and are mostly on sloping ground. Many have a view of the fjord. There is a choice of a traditional 'inline' arrangement or one where several pitches are in circles bordered by low hedges. Although promoted as a quiet site, there is a heated pool and other facilities for children. The most important attractions nearby must be at Roskilde, the ancient capital of Denmark (30 km). A thousand years of Danish history is gathered in the cathedral, burial place of 39 Danish kings and queens. The Viking Museum has five original ships on display, costumes and crafts to try. Copenhagen is 60 km. away.

Key Features

 Open All Year

 Pets Accepted

 Disabled Facilities

 Swimming Pool

 Play Area

 Bike Hire

One sanitary block with free hot showers, family room and facilities for disabled visitors (key access). Washing machine and dryer (DKK 30). Campers' kitchen. Bread supplies. Covered, heated swimming pool (1/5-end Oct). Sauna and spa (free). Outdoor fitness. Wellness.. TV room. Play area. Shuffleboard. No entertainment (to preserve the quiet atmosphere). Bicycle and go-kart hire. Caravans and hiker cabins to rent. WiFi (free).

Scan me for more information.

Alan Rogers Code: DK2255
25 accommodations
413 pitches
GPS: 55.17497, 12.10203
Post Code: DK-4640

Sjælland, Islands

www.alanrogers.com/dk2255
info@feddetcamping.dk
Tel: 56 72 52 06
www.feddetcamping

Open (Touring Pitches):
All year.

Feddet Strand Camping

This interesting, spacious site with ecological principles is located on the Baltic coast. It has a fine, white, sandy beach (Blue Flag) which runs the full length of one side, with the Præstø fjord on the opposite side of the peninsula. There are 413 pitches for touring units, generally on sandy grass, with mature pine trees giving adequate shade. All have 10A electricity and 20 are fully serviced (water, electricity, drainage and sewerage). The sanitary buildings have been specially designed, clad with larch panels from sustainable local trees and insulated with flax mats.

Both sanitary buildings are equipped to high standards. Family bathrooms (with twin showers), complete suites for children and babies. Facilities for disabled visitors. Laundry. Kitchens, dining room and TV lounge. Excellent motorcaravan service point. Well stocked licensed shop. Licensed bistro and takeaway (1/5-20/10; weekends only outside peak season). Large, indoor swimming pool and paddling pool (charged). Minigolf. Games room. Indoor playroom and several playgrounds. Event camp for children. Pet zoo. Massage. Watersports. Fishing. WiFi.

Key Features

 Open All Year

 Pets Accepted

 Disabled Facilities

 Beach Access

 Swimming Pool

 Play Area

 Bar/Restaurant

 Bike Hire

Scan me for
more information.

Alan Rogers Code: DK2040
61 accommodations
150 pitches
GPS: 55.83116, 9.30076
Post Code: DK-7323

Vejle, Jutland

www.alanrogers.com/dk2040
info@riisferiepark.dk
Tel: 75 73 14 33
www.riisferiepark.dk

Open (Touring Pitches):
24 March - 23 September

Riis Feriepark

Riis Feriepark is a good quality touring site ideal for visiting Legoland and Lalandia Billund (18 km), and Givskov Zoo (3 km). It is a friendly, family run site with 150 large level, grass touring pitches which are sheltered and surrounded by trees and shrubs. Electricity (13A) is available to all pitches, and 15 comfort pitches also have water and drainage. The outdoor heated pool and water slide complex, and the bar that serves beer, ice cream, soft drinks and snacks, are open all season. There is a small, well stocked shop. The excellent indoor kitchen facilities and an attractive, covered barbecue area are very useful. This is a high-class site suitable for long or short stays in this very attractive part of Denmark.

Two very good sanitary units include washbasins with divider/curtain and controllable showers (on payment). Suites for babies and disabled visitors, family bathrooms (one with whirlpool bath, on payment) and solarium. Laundry. Motorcaravan services. Campers' kitchen. Large sitting room with TV, plus barbecue grill house. Shop. Café. Pool complex (2/6-4/9). Minigolf. Three playgrounds. Trampolines. Outdoor chess. Zip wire. Go-kart track. Train ride for children. Animal farm. Bicycle hire. Cabins to rent. WiFi (charged).

Key Features

 Pets Accepted

 Disabled Facilities

 Swimming Pool

 Play Area

 Bar/Restaurant

 Bike Hire

Scan me for more information.

Denmark

Alan Rogers Code: DK2100
4 accommodations
270 pitches
GPS: 56.16773, 10.73067
Post Code: DK-8400

Århus, Jutland

www.alanrogers.com/dk2100
Info@blushoj.com
Tel: 86 34 12 38
www.blushoj-camping.dk

Open (Touring Pitches):
1 April - 15 September

Blushoj Camping

This is a traditional type of site where the owners are making a conscious effort to keep mainly to touring units – there are only six seasonal units and four rental cabins. The site has 270 pitches on levelled grassy terraces surrounded by mature hedging and shrubs. Some have glorious views of the Kattegat, and others overlook peaceful rural countryside. Most pitches have electricity (10A), but long leads may be required. There is a heated and fenced swimming pool (14x7 m) with a slide and a terrace. The beach below the site provides opportunities for swimming, windsurfing and sea fishing. The owners also arrange traditional entertainment – folk dancing, local choirs, and accordion music some weekends in high season. This is an excellent location for a relaxed family holiday, with numerous excursion possibilities including the beautiful old town of Ebeltoft (4 km), with its shops and restaurants, and the world's largest wooden sailing ship, the Frigate Jylland, now fully restored and open to the public.

Key Features

 Pets Accepted

 Disabled Facilities

 Beach Access

 Swimming Pool

 Play Area

 Bike Hire

 Fishing

One toilet unit includes washbasins with dividers and showers with divider and seat (charged; cleaning can be variable). The other unit has a new kitchen with electric hobs, sinks, dining/TV room, laundry and baby facilities. A heated extension provides six very smart family bathrooms, and additional WCs (including one for disabled visitors) and washbasins. Motorcaravan services. Well stocked shop. Swimming pool (20/5-20/8). Minigolf. Play area. Games room. Beach. Fishing. Internet access. Free WiFi over site.

Scan me for
more information.

Alan Rogers Code: DK2155
17 accommodations
300 pitches
GPS: 57.35502, 10.51185
Post Code: DK-9300

Nordjylland, Jutland

www.alanrogers.com/dk2155
info@hedebocamping.dk
Tel: 98 46 14 49
www.hedebocamping.dk

Open (Touring Pitches):
27 March - 13 September.

Hedebo Strand Camping

Hedebo Strand camping is a family run site with a very warm and welcoming feeling. It has an enviable position on the Kattegat shore. Although it is a large site with 600 pitches, the 300 touring pitches are in a separate section, so it feels more compact. They vary in size (50-190 sq.m) and most have 13A electricity. The ground is slightly sloping with some shade from the hedges that back each row and from the pitches nearest the sea there are beautiful views over the Kattegat. Some hardstanding places are available. The pitches by the sea are much sought after and worth reserving. A footpath will take you to the charming town of Saeby. The owners have a private collection of 150 classic and vintage motorcycles, which guests can view free of charge.

Four large toilet blocks provide good facilities including 17 large family rooms with toilet, child size toilet, controllable showers (DKR 5) and washbasin. Facilities for disabled visitors. Motorcaravan services. Laundry. Campers' kitchen. Supermarket, bar, restaurant and takeaway (all season). Heated outdoor pool with slides (15/6-1/9, 12x8 m). Playground. Multisports pitch. Tennis. Minigolf. Bowling. Fishing. Games room. Some entertainment for children in high season. Beach. WiFi (charged).

Key Features

 Pets Accepted

 Disabled Facilities

 Beach Access

 Swimming Pool

 Play Area

 Bar/Restaurant

 Fishing

Scan me for more information.

Denmark

Alan Rogers Code: DK2142
14 accommodations
198 pitches
GPS: 56.59795, 9.03756
Post Code: DK-7800

Viborg, Jutland

www.alanrogers.com/dk2142
info@skivefjordcamping.dk
Tel: 97 51 44 55
www.skivefjordcamping.dk

Open (Touring Pitches):
18 March - 18 December.

Camping Skive Fjord

This modern site on the northern edge of Skive was built on terraced ground overlooking the fjord in 1994. The grassy, open terraces are arranged on either side of the main tarmac road providing level pitches, most with beautiful views. With grass and gravel access lanes, the terraces and some pitches are separated by bushes and shrubs. Well-lit concrete steps connect the terraces. There is a special, level pitch close to the toilet block for disabled visitors. The site has over 150 pitches for touring units with 10-16A electricity. Although it is possible to swim in the fjord, the site also has its own open-air pool (heated). Other amenities include an attractive games room with table tennis, TV, internet and a small library. Close to the toilet block is a covered communal grill area. This site is an excellent starting point for touring this beautiful area and a good base for those who enjoy fishing (sea trout), surfing, sailing or water skiing.

Modern toilet facilities include washbasins (open style and in cabins) and controllable hot showers. Family shower rooms with baby bath. Baby room. Washing machines, dryers and ironing board. Kitchen. Motorcaravan services. Basics from reception (bread to order). Outdoor pool with small slide and paddling pool. Playground. Cable track. Minigolf. Fishing. Riding. Pétanque. Watersports. WiFi over site (charged). Boat launching. Bicycle hire.

Key Features

 Pets Accepted

 Disabled Facilities

 Beach Access

 Swimming Pool

 Play Area

 Bike Hire

 Fishing

Scan me for more information.

Alan Rogers Code: DK2010
142 accommodations
690 pitches
GPS: 55.54600, 8.13507
Post Code: DK-6857

Ribe, Jutland

www.alanrogers.com/dk2010
info@hvidbjerg.dk
Tel: 75 27 90 40
www.hvidbjergstrand.com

Open (Touring Pitches):
20 March - 18 October.

Hvidbjerg Strand Camping

A family-owned TopCamp holiday site, Hvidbjerg Strand is on the west coast near Blåvands Huk, 43 km. from Esbjerg. It is a high quality, seaside site with a wide range of amenities including a large wellness facility. Most of the 570 pitches have electricity (6/10A) and the 130 'comfort' pitches also have water, drainage and satellite TV. To the rear of the site, 70 new, fully serviced pitches have been developed, some up to 250 sq.m. and 44 with private sanitary facilities. Most pitches are individual and divided by hedges, in rows on flat sandy grass, with areas also divided by small trees and hedges. A member of Leading Campings group.

Five superb toilet units include washbasins, roomy showers, spa baths, suites for disabled visitors, family bathrooms, kitchens and laundry facilities. Bathroom for children decorated with dinosaurs and Disney characters, and racing car baby baths. Motorcaravan services. Supermarket. Café/restaurant. TV rooms. Pool complex, solarium and sauna. Wellness facility. Western-themed indoor play hall. Play areas. Supervised play rooms (09.00-16.00 daily). Barbecue areas. Minigolf. Riding (Western style). Fishing. Dog showers. ATM machine. Free WiFi.

Key Features

 Pets Accepted

 Disabled Facilities

 Beach Access

 Swimming Pool

 Play Area

 Bar/Restaurant

 Bike Hire

 Fishing

Scan me for more information.

Capital Paris
Currency Euro (€)
Language French
Telephone country code 00 33
Time Zone CET (GMT/UTC+1)
Tourist Office franceguide.com

Climate Temperate climate. Warmer in the south and east, wetter in the north and west and snowy in the mountains.

France

From the hot sunny climate of the Mediterranean to the more northerly and cooler regions of Normandy and Brittany, with the Châteaux of the Loire and the lush valleys of the Dordogne, and the mountain ranges of the Alps, France offers holidaymakers a huge choice of destinations to suit all tastes.

France boasts every type of landscape imaginable, ranging from the wooded valleys of the Dordogne to the volcanic uplands of the Massif Central, the rocky coast of Brittany to the lavender-covered hills of Provence and snow-capped peaks of the Alps. The diversity of these regions is reflected in the local customs, cuisine, architecture and dialect. Many rural villages hold festivals to celebrate the local saints and you can also find museums devoted to the rural arts and crafts of the regions. France has a rich cultural heritage with a wealth of festivals, churches, châteaux, museums and historical monuments to visit. The varied landscape and climate ensure many opportunities for outdoor pursuits from hiking and cycling, wind- and sand-surfing on the coast and rock climbing and skiing in the mountains. And no trip to France is complete without sampling the local food and wine.

Shops Opening hours vary throughout the year. In high-season 10am to noon and 2pm to 7pm Monday to Saturday. Shops located in ZTIs (International Tourist Zones) are open longer and including Sunday.

Banks 9am to noon and 2pm to 5pm Monday to Friday or Tuesday to Saturday.

Travelling with Children Perhaps one of the most child-friendly countries in Europe, France has a good mix of cultural sights, historical monuments and other attractions. Each region has something different to offer. Most museums are free for under 18s.

Public Holidays New Year's Day, Easter Monday, Labour Day, VE Day 8 May, Ascension, Whit Monday, Bastille Day 14 Jul, Assumption, All Saints' 1 Nov, Armistice Day, Christmas Day. Good Friday and Boxing Day are only public holidays in Alsace.

Motoring France has a comprehensive road system from motorways (Autoroutes), Routes Nationales (N roads), Routes Départmentales (D roads) down to purely local C class roads. Tolls are payable on the autoroute network which is extensive but expensive, and also on certain bridges.

See campsite map pages 476, 477, 478.

Alan Rogers Code: FR29590
40 accommodations
232 pitches
GPS: 48.14485, -4.26882
Post Code: F-29550

Finistère, Brittany

La Plage de Tréguer

www.alanrogers.com/fr29590
camping-treguer-plage@wanadoo.fr
Tel: 02 98 92 53 52
www.camping-treguer-plage.com

Open (Touring Pitches):
6 April - 29 September.

Set right on the dunes adjacent to a large, sandy beach on the vast sweep of Douarnenez Bay, this is one of only seven campsites in Brittany with direct access to a beach, with no paths or roads to cross. It is an impressive location, not manicured but on the 'wild' side, being a protected area. Tall hedges provide wind shelter, tamarisk grows in profusion, and there are uninterrupted views out to sea. Some pitches nestle in the shelter of the dunes (sandier ground), others are in groups of four or eight, bordered by hedging. There are mobiles homes available to rent. This is a wonderful site for those seeking a natural, maritime setting – it is officially a 'plage sauvage' with the sound of the waves coming free of charge. The owners relatively recently arrived, are enthusiastic and have sensitive plans for updating this unique site.

Key Features

 Pets Accepted

 Disabled Facilities

 Beach Access

 Swimming Pool

 Play Area

 Bar/Restaurant

One central toilet block has showers, washbasins in cabins, and facilities for babies and disabled visitors. Bar, takeaway and shop (July/Aug). Heated outdoor swimming pool with jacuzzi, waterfall for children and paddling pool (1/6-30/9). Play area. Bouncy castle. Multisports court. Games room/TV. Organised entertainment (July/Aug). Direct access to beach.

Scan me for more information.

Alan Rogers Code: FR29000
406 accommodations
68 pitches
GPS: 48.65807, -3.92833
Post Code: F-29660

Finistère, Brittany

www.alanrogers.com/fr29000
contact@les-mouettes.com
Tel: 02 98 67 02 46
www.yellohvillage.co.uk/camping/
les_mouettes

Open (Touring Pitches):
5 April - 8 September.

Camping Les Mouettes

Yelloh! Village Camping Les Mouettes is a sheltered site on the edge of an attractive bay, with access to the sea at the front of the site. In a wooded setting with many attractive trees and shrubs, the 474 pitches include 68 for touring units, all with electricity, water and drainage. The remainder are taken by tour operators and by 406 mobile homes and chalets to rent. At the centre of the 'village' are shops, a bar, a restaurant, an entertainment stage, sports facilities and an impressive heated pool complex with swimming, paddling and water slide pools, plus a 'Tropical river', jacuzzi and sauna. There is also an excellent indoor swimming pool.

A clean sanitary block with controllable showers and washbasins in cabins. There are showers with washbasins and delightful rooms for children and babies. Facilities for disabled visitors. Laundry. Shop (limited hours outside the main season). Takeaway. Bar with TV. Restaurant/pizzeria/grill. Heated pool complex indoor (all season) and outdoor. Beauty salon. Games rooms (special one for under 5s). Play area. Multisports ground. Minigolf. Bicycle hire. Entertainment all season. Large units should phone first. Free WiFi throughout .

Key Features

 Pets Accepted

 Disabled Facilities

 Swimming Pool

 Play Area

 Bar/Restaurant

 Bike Hire

Scan me for more information.

Alan Rogers Code: FR29120
160 accommodations
60 pitches
GPS: 47.81234, -4.22105
Post Code: F-29740

Finistère, Brittany

l'Océan Breton

www.alanrogers.com/fr29120
info@yellohvillage-loceanbreton.com
Tel: 02 98 82 23 89
www.camping-bretagne-
oceanbreton.fr

Open (Touring Pitches):
2 May - 4 September.

L'Océan Breton is a comfortable site in the grounds of a manor house on a river estuary near Pont l'Abbé. The campsite itself has neat, modern buildings and is laid out on flat grass providing 220 pitches (60 for touring units). All have electricity connections (6/10A), some also have water and drainage and around ten pitches have hardstanding. One area is rather open with separating hedges planted, the other part being amongst more mature bushes and some trees which provide shade. Site amenities are of excellent quality. The old Manoir is still open to the public and is used during the high season as a crêperie.

New sanitary facilities including washbasins all in cabins and facilities for babies and disabled visitors. Laundry. Small shop. Restaurant. Takeaway. Large modern bar with TV (satellite) and entertainment all season. Large aquapark with slides and children's pool. Covered, heated swimming pool. Sauna, solarium and small gym. Fitness centre. Play area. Tennis. Pétanque. Games room. Bicycle hire.

Key Features

 Pets Accepted

 Disabled Facilities

 Swimming Pool

 Play Area

 Bar/Restaurant

 Bike Hire

Scan me for
more information.

Alan Rogers Code: FR35020
120 accommodations
160 pitches
GPS: 48.49030, -1.72780
Post Code: F-35120

Ille-et-Vilaine, Brittany

Domaine des Ormes

www.alanrogers.com/fr35020
info@lesormes.com
Tel: 02 99 73 53 00
www.lesormes.com

Open (Touring Pitches):
1 April - 24 September (with all services).

This impressive site in the grounds of the Château des Ormes is in the northeast part of Brittany, in an estate of wooded parkland and lakes. It is busy in high season but peaceful at other times, with an impressive range of facilities and a wide range of accommodation. Of the 700 pitches, 140 are for tourers (most with 6A electricity, some with 16A and their own water and waste water). They are of varying sizes (80-150 sq.m) and there is a choice of terrain – flat or gently sloping, wooded, walled or open. The rest are occupied by tour operators (550) and by mobile homes (120 to rent).

The heated sanitary blocks are of a good standard, with family cubicles (shower and washbasin) and facilities for babies, children and disabled visitors. Motorcaravan services. Supermarket, bar, restaurant, pizzeria and takeaway. Games room, bar and disco. Indoor and outdoor pools, an impressive aqua park and wave pool. Adventure play area. Golf (charged). Bicycle hire. Fishing. Equestrian centre (charged). Minigolf. Tennis. Sports ground. Paintball. Archery. Zip wire. Climbing wall. Cricket club. Charcoal and gas barbecues are permitted. WiFi in bar area free, (elsewhere charged).

Key Features

 Pets Accepted

 Disabled Facilities

 Swimming Pool

 Play Area

 Bar/Restaurant

 Bike Hire

 Fishing

 Golf

Scan me for more information.

Alan Rogers Code: FR56150
106 accommodations
96 pitches
GPS: 47.73048, -2.72801
Post Code: F-56250

Morbihan, Brittany

www.alanrogers.com/fr56150
contact@campingvannes.com
Tel: 02 97 44 66 06
www.campingvannes.com/en

Open (Touring Pitches):
6 April - 17 September

Camping du Haras

Close to Vannes and the Golfe du Morbihan in southern Brittany, Camping du Haras is a small, family run site in a rural location. There are 140 pitches, in a variety of settings, both open and wooded, the pitches are well kept and of a good size, all with electricity (4-16A) and most with water and drainage. Whilst M. Danard intends keeping the site quiet and in keeping with its rural setting, he provides plenty of activities for lively youngsters, including some organised games and evening parties. Adults will enjoy the new wellness area with indoor pool, spa, sauna and massage facilities.

The modern toilet blocks (heated) provide a few washbasins in cabins and controllable showers. Facilities for babies and disabled visitors. Laundry facilities. No shop but basics are kept in the bar. Bar with snacks (May-Oct). Restaurant and takeaway (July/Aug). Outdoor pool with waves and slide (1/5-31/10). Indoor pool complex and spa (6/4-17/9). Play area. Animal park. Trampoline. Minigolf. Organised activities (high season). Free WiFi in reception and bar (charged over site). Possibility of private bathrooms on pitch.

Key Features

 Pets Accepted

 Disabled Facilities

 Swimming Pool

 Play Area

 Bar/Restaurant

 Bike Hire

Scan me for more information.

Alan Rogers Code: FR56450
86 accommodations
97 pitches
GPS: 47.50542, -2.68325
Post Code: F-56370

Morbihan, Brittany

www.alanrogers.com/fr56450
info@manoirdekeranpoul.com
Tel: 02 97 67 33 30
www.manoirdekeranpoul.com

Open (Touring Pitches):
25 March - 25 September.

Manoir de Ker An Poul

Le Manoir de Ker An Poul has an attractive location, close to the sea (700 metres) in the southern Morbihan region. The old manor house is charming and the site has been developed in the grounds. This is quite a large site with around 299 pitches, around half of which are occupied by mobile homes and chalets. There is a large indoor and outdoor pool complex. Many activities are on offer in high season, including evening entertainment and a club for children.

Sanitary facilities include hot showers, washbasins in cabins and facilities for disabled visitors. Laundry facilities. Shop. Bar, restaurant and snack bar. Indoor pool. Outdoor swimming pool and paddling pools. Games room. Multisports pitch. Play area. Bicycle hire. Activity and entertainment programme. Mobile homes and chalets to rent. WiFi in some areas (charged).

Key Features

 Pets Accepted

 Disabled Facilities

 Swimming Pool

 Play Area

 Bar/Restaurant

 Bike Hire

Scan me for more information.

Alan Rogers Code: FR35220
20 accommodations
30 pitches
GPS: 47.76362, -2.12552
Post Code: F-35550

Ille-et-Vilaine, Brittany

www.alanrogers.com/fr35220
contact@art-nature-village.com
Tel: 02 99 08 10 59
www.art-nature-village.com

Open (Touring Pitches):
4 May - 2 October.

Camping Art Nature Village

In peaceful, rural Southern Brittany on the edge of the town of La Gacilly and next to the River Aff, the small campsite of Art Nature Village offers a variety of pitches and accommodation. The 25 touring pitches are spacious (all 120 sq.m) and divided by hedges and there are also luxury tents, trailer caravans and cottages to rent. Vehicles are restricted to certain zones. The nature pitches are green and private, next to the river and near sanitary facilities. Larger comfort pitches have 6A electricity. There is provision for cyclists and ramblers. Designated motorcaravan stopover pitches (16.00-10.00) have hardstanding and are near sanitary and service facilities, but have no electricity.

Renovated sanitary blocks (2012) with washbasins in individual cabins, family bathroom, baby bathroom and facilities for visitors with disabilities. Breakfast room. Bar (July/Aug). Washing machine and tumble dryer. Beauty salon. Secure shed for cyclists and ramblers equipment. Motorcaravan services. Play area. Animation in high season. Hammocks and sun loungers. Fishing in river. WiFi area (free).

Key Features

 Pets Accepted

 Disabled Facilities

 Swimming Pool

 Play Area

 Bar/Restaurant

 Fishing

Scan me for more information.

Alan Rogers Code: FR50070
61 accommodations
230 pitches
GPS: 49.66715, -1.48704
Post Code: F-50330

Manche, Normandy

Camping l'Anse du Brick

www.alanrogers.com/fr50070
welcome@anse-du-brick.com
Tel: 02 33 54 33 57
www.anse-du-brick.fr/en

Open (Touring Pitches):
6 April - 14 September

A friendly, family site, Castel Camping Caravaning l'Anse du Brick overlooks a picturesque bay on the northern tip of the Cotentin Peninsula, eight kilometres east of Cherbourg port. This quality site makes a pleasant night halt or an ideal longer stay destination for those not wishing to travel too far. Its pleasing location offers direct access to a small sandy beach and a woodland walk. This is a mature, terraced site with magnificent views from certain pitches. Tarmac roads lead to the 117 touring pitches (all with 10A electricity) which are level, separated and mostly well shaded by many trees, bushes and shrubs.

New sanitary facilities are kept spotlessly clean and are well maintained. Washbasins mainly in cubicles and pushbutton showers. Provision for children, families and disabled visitors. Laundry area. Possibility of private sanitary on the pitch. Motorcaravan services. Shop (all season), restaurant and bar/pizzeria. Heated swimming pools (indoor all season, outdoor from 1/5). Tennis. Play area. New in 2019: Pump Track on site! Organised entertainment in season. Miniclub (5-12 yrs). Bicycle, SUP and kayak hire. Free WiFi throughout and faster connection for extra fee.

Key Features

 Pets Accepted

 Disabled Facilities

 Swimming Pool

 Play Area

 Bar/Restaurant

 Bike Hire

Scan me for more information.

Alan Rogers Code: FR50000
30 accommodations
100 pitches
GPS: 49.30041, -1.54478
Post Code: F-50250

Manche, Normandy

www.alanrogers.com/fr50000
info@campingetangdeshaizes.com
Tel: 02 33 46 01 16
www.campingetangdeshaizes.com

Open (Touring Pitches):
4 April - 30 September.

l'Etang des Haizes

This is an attractive and very friendly site with a swimming pool complex that has a four-lane slide, a jacuzzi and a paddling pool. L'Etang des Haizes has 160 good sized pitches, of which 100 are for touring units, on reasonably level ground and all with electricity (10A Europlug). They are set in a mixture of conifers, orchard and shrubbery, with some very attractive, slightly smaller pitches overlooking the lake and 60 mobile homes inconspicuously sited. The fenced lake has a small beach (swimming is permitted), with ducks and pedaloes, and offers good coarse fishing for huge carp (we are told!). There are good toilet and shower facilities where children and campers with disabilities are well catered for.

Two well kept and modern unisex toilet blocks have British style toilets, washbasins in cabins, units for disabled visitors, and two family cabins. Small laundry. Motorcaravan services. Milk, bread and takeaway snacks (no gas). Snack bar/bar with TV and terrace (28/6-29/8). Swimming pool complex (28/5-4/9). Play areas. Bicycle hire. Pétanque. Organised activities including treasure hunts, archery and water polo (6/7-22/8). Well stocked tourist information cabin. WiFi (charged).

Key Features

 Pets Accepted

 Disabled Facilities

 Swimming Pool

 Play Area

 Bar/Restaurant

 Bike Hire

 Fishing

Scan me for more information.

Alan Rogers Code: FR50110
50 accommodations
50 pitches
GPS: 48.62762, -1.41600
Post Code: F-50220

Manche, Normandy

www.alanrogers.com/fr50110
infos@campingsaintmichel.com
Tel: 02 33 70 96 90
www.campingsaintmichel.com

Open (Touring Pitches):
31 March - 1 November.

Camping Saint-Michel

This delightful, quiet site is located in a peaceful, rural setting, yet is only 8 km. from the busy tourist attraction of Mont Saint-Michel. The site has 100 pitches which include 50 for touring units and 50 for mobile homes to rent. Electricity connections (6/10A) are available to all pitches and many trees and shrubs provide a good amount of shade. A welcoming reception has a terrace overlooking the pool. The site slopes gently down to a small enclosure of farm animals kept to entertain children and adults alike. Here you can meet Nestor and Napoléon, the donkeys, and Linotte the mare, as well as miniature goats, sheep, chickens and ducks. The owners intend to maintain a quiet and peaceful site, hence there are no discos or organised clubs.

Two small, well maintained toilet blocks have washbasins in cubicles and pushbutton showers. Separate laundry. Baby room. En-suite facilities for disabled visitors. Motorcaravan services. Shop and bar. Heated swimming pool (1/5-30/9). Animal farm. Play area. Games room. Bicycle hire. Internet access and WiFi (free) in reception area.

Key Features

 Pets Accepted

 Disabled Facilities

 Swimming Pool

 Play Area

 Bar/Restaurant

 Bike Hire

Scan me for more information.

Alan Rogers Code: FR61090
7 accommodations
17 pitches
GPS: 48.84327, -0.39821
Post Code: F-61430

Orne, Normandy

www.alanrogers.com/fr61090
larouvre@gmail.com
Tel: 02 33 64 82 40
www.larouvre.fr

Open (Touring Pitches):
25 March - 14 October.

Camping de la Rouvre

Camping de la Rouvre is set on the banks of the River Rouvre, 2 km. from its confluence with the River Orne. There are 17 grassy touring pitches (ten adjacent to the river), almost all with 16A electricity (long leads required) and separated by hedges. An open field accommodates a further 30 units. There are two tents and a wooden chalet for hire. The site is convenient for several ferry ports, with the famous tourist sites of Mont Saint-Michel, Caen, Bayeux, the Normandy landing beaches and the most beautiful treasures of Calvados on the doorstep. The Roches d'Oëtre is a walkers' paradise, with eight walking routes starting from the site. Nearby is the 1,000-kilometre GR36 long-distance footpath running from the English Channel to Spain. The local gorges are a haven for wildlife, and the 150-metre high cliffs, steep rocks and deep gorges, has earned the area the nickname 'The Switzerland of Normandy.'

Key Features

 Pets Accepted

 Disabled Facilities

 Bike Hire

 Fishing

One clean sanitary block has adequate provision with hot showers, one private cabin and facilities for disabled visitors (gravel path). Washing machine. Boules. Communal barbecue. Fishing. Bouncy castle. Bicycle hire. WiFi throughout (charged).

Scan me for
more information.

Alan Rogers Code: FR14340
31 accommodations
51 pitches
GPS: 49.32571, -0.86448
Post Code: F-14710

Calvados, Normandy

www.alanrogers.com/fr14340
camping-laroseraie@orange.fr
Tel: 02 31 21 17 71
camping-calvados-normandie.fr

Open (Touring Pitches):
25 March - 2 October.

La Roseraie d'Omaha

Near a quiet little village in the Calvados region of Normandy, Camping La Roseraie d'Omaha is a rural family site just 4 km. from the sea and close to the D-Day landing beaches. The 51 touring pitches all have electricity (10A, Europlug) and 30 also have a water tap and drain; there is some shade in places. There are also 37 mobile homes and bungalows, most available to rent. The site is close to the N13 Cherbourg-Caen dual carriageway, so is convenient for an overnight stop as well as being a good base from which to explore the Normandy countryside and coastline. Some noise should be expected from the nearby dual carriageway.

Brightly-decorated sanitary facilities with preset showers and most washbasins in cubicles. Unit for disabled visitors. Baby room. Laundry. Shop. Bar and snack bar with TV. Takeaway (1/4-30/9). Heated indoor swimming pool with retractable sides, slides and paddling pool (1/6-15/9). Playground. Volleyball. Minigolf (charged). Boules pitch. Tennis court (charged). Family entertainment programme (July/Aug). Evening activities (1/6-15/9). Bicycle and mountain bike hire. Internet. WiFi over site (charged).

Key Features

 Pets Accepted

 Disabled Facilities

 Swimming Pool

 Play Area

 Bar/Restaurant

 Bike Hire

Scan me for more information.

Alan Rogers Code: FR14400
20 accommodations
63 pitches
GPS: 48.91361, -0.47389
Post Code: F-14570

Calvados, Normandy

www.alanrogers.com/fr14400
camping.normandie@gmail.com
Tel: 02 31 69 70 36
www.camping-normandie-clecy.fr

Open (Touring Pitches):
25 March - 1 October.

Les Rochers des Parcs

Les Rochers des Parcs is a tranquil, natural site located in the lush valley of the River Orne, at the heart of the Suisse Normande. The landscape is undulating, sheltered and in a well preserved environment, which is carefully managed by the owners. There are 90 marked pitches (80-150 m2), 63 for touring, 55 with electricity (6-10A). They are set in a wooded location with varying degrees of shade, and 20 are directly by the river. This is an ideal site for fishermen, and for rock climbing enthusiasts, as there are rock faces close by with a wide range of difficulty levels.

The two toilet blocks (one heated but due for renovation) provide preset showers and washbasins in cubicles. Facilities for children and disabled visitors. Laundry. Shop selling basics (bread to order). Snack bar and takeaway (15/4-30/9). Breakfast service. Minigolf. Boules. Archery. Beach volleyball. Badminton. Bouncy castle. Play area. Mountain bike hire. Free WiFi over part of site.

Key Features

 Pets Accepted

 Disabled Facilities

 Play Area

 Bar/Restaurant

 Bike Hire

 Fishing

 Horse Riding

Scan me for more information.

Alan Rogers Code: FR27070
7 accommodations
115 pitches
GPS: 49.23564, 1.40005
Post Code: F-27700

Eure, Normandy

www.alanrogers.com/fr27070
campingtroisrois@aol.com
Tel: 02 32 54 23 79
www.camping-troisrois.com

Open (Touring Pitches):
15 March - 15 November.

l'Ile des Trois Rois

One hour from Paris, on the banks of the Seine and overlooked by the impressive remains of Château Gaillard (Richard Coeur de Lion), this attractive and very spacious ten-hectare site will appeal to couples and young families. There is easy access to the 115 level, grassy touring pitches in a well landscaped setting, all with electricity (6A), although some long leads may be required. Many pitches back onto the River Seine where you can watch the barges, and most have views of the château. Of the 80 mobile homes, there are seven to rent, leaving lots of space to enjoy the surroundings, including the large lake full of perch and bream for those eager fishermen. Others can try their luck in the Seine.

Four small, heated toilet blocks have showers and washbasins in cubicles. One has facilities for disabled visitors, another has a laundry facility. Motorcaravan services. Heated swimming and paddling pools (15/5-15/9). Bar, restaurant and takeaway (1/6-30/8). Fenced play area. Adult open-air exercise area. Evening entertainment (4/7-30/8). Bicycles and barbecues for hire. Satellite TV. Internet access. WiFi throughout (charged).

Key Features

 Pets Accepted

 Disabled Facilities

 Swimming Pool

 Play Area

 Bar/Restaurant

 Bike Hire

 Fishing

Scan me for more information.

Alan Rogers Code: FR76160
21 accommodations
77 pitches
GPS: 49.69878, 0.27560
Post Code: F-76790

Seine-Maritime, Normandy

www.alanrogers.com/fr76160
camping@aiguillecreuse.com
Tel: 02 35 29 52 10
www.campingaiguillecreuse.com

Open (Touring Pitches):
2 April - 17 September.

l'Aiguille Creuse

L'Aiguille Creuse, conveniently close to Le Havre, is named after a rock, alleged to be hollow, near Etretat. The site is set back from the Côte d'Albâtre in the village of Les Loges, between Etretat and the fishing port of Fécamp. There are 135 good sized grassy pitches, slightly sloping in parts and divided by neat hedges. Of these, 78 are for touring, all with 10A electricity and 14 also with water and drainage. The village is within easy walking distance and buses run from here to Fécamp, Etretat and Le Havre. An alternative and more adventurous way of getting to Etretat is by booking a rail buggy and pedalling yourselves down the hill – you are then brought back up to the village by road in a 'petit train'.

Two modern toilet blocks (one heated, the other open in July/Aug) with unisex toilets (no seats), controllable showers, washbasins in cubicles, baby changing and facilities for disabled visitors and children. Laundry. Motorhome services. Smart new bar (with 30 mins. free WiFi daily). Takeaway (9/7-22/8). Heated pool with retractable roof. New playground. WiFi (charged). Card-operated barrier.

Key Features

 Pets Accepted

 Disabled Facilities

 Swimming Pool

 Play Area

 Bar/Restaurant

Scan me for more information.

Alan Rogers Code: FR80090
24 accommodations
164 pitches
GPS: 50.31406, 1.69541
Post Code: F-80120

Somme, Picardy

www.alanrogers.com/fr80090
camping@valdauthie.fr
Tel: 03 22 29 92 47
www.valdauthie.fr

Open (Touring Pitches):
1 April - 29 September

Le Val d'Authie

This well-organised campsite occupies a fine village location in Picardy in the coastal hinterland and is within 12 km of several sandy beaches, but also has an excellent pool complex, small restaurant and bar. The owner has carefully controlled the size of the site, leaving space for a leisure area with an indoor pool complex. There are 164 pitches in total, but with many holiday homes and chalets (some for hire), there are only 50 for touring units. These are on grass, some are divided by small hedges, with 6/10A electric hook-ups, and ten have full services. Amenities on the site include a fitness trail and running track, a mountain bike circuit and plenty of pleasant paths for evening strolls. High-quality meals can be enjoyed in the site's lovely restaurant which has a superb upstairs room overlooking the pool and gardens (book at busy times).

Good sanitary facilities, some unisex, include shower units and washbasins, washbasins in cubicles and limited facilities for disabled and baby campers. Shop. Bar/restaurant (variable hours). Pools and paddling pools (lifeguards in Jul/Aug). Playground. Club room with TV. Weekend entertainment/animation in season. Multisport field, football, petanque and tennis court. Trampoline. Fitness room with sauna (extra charge). Internet access (free). Bike rental. WiFi throughout (charged).

Key Features

 Pets Accepted

 Disabled Facilities

 Swimming Pool

 Play Area

 Bar/Restaurant

 Bike Hire

Scan me for more information.

Alan Rogers Code: FR80120
47 accommodations
66 pitches
GPS: 50.24976, 1.61196
Post Code: F-80550

Somme, Picardy

www.alanrogers.com/fr80120
lesaubépines@
baiedesommepleinair.com
Tel: 03 22 27 01 34
www.camping-lesaubepines.com

Open (Touring Pitches):
1 April - 1 November.

Flower Camping les Aubépines

This peaceful, family run site is on the edge of the Parc Ornithologique du Marquenterre and is just 1 km. from a beach on the Baie de Somme, a river estuary famous for its resident population of seals. There are 194 pitches, although 128 are occupied by privately owned mobile homes with a few available to rent. Consequently, there are just 66 touring pitches scattered throughout the site. All on level ground, they are of a reasonable to a good size, separated by hedges and trees and with water taps and electricity (3-10A) close by. It is an attractively laid out site which has a relaxed and very French feel and should appeal to those seeking a quiet holiday close to nature. In high season the site has a morning club for younger children, afternoon activities for older ones and some evening family events.

Key Features

 Pets Accepted

 Disabled Facilities

 Swimming Pool

 Play Area

 Bike Hire

Two unisex toilet blocks, fairly basic but clean and in good order. Washbasins in cubicles, pushbutton showers and some larger cubicles with shower and basin. Baby bath and toilet. Facilities for disabled visitors are minimal (no grab rails). Laundry room. Small well stocked shop. Heated outdoor pool (1/5-15/9). Indoor games. Small play area. Bicycle hire. Outdoor fitness machines. WiFi over site (charged).

Scan me for more information.

Alan Rogers Code: FR62010
12 accommodations
146 pitches
GPS: 50.86632, 1.85698
Post Code: F-62340

Pas-de-Calais, Nord/Pas-de-Calais

www.alanrogers.com/fr62010
castels@bien-assise.com
Tel: 03 21 35 20 77
www.camping-la-bien-assise.com

Open (Touring Pitches):
20 April - 15 September

Camping la Bien-Assise

Le Castel Camping de La Bien-Assise is a mature and well developed campsite, the history of la Bien-Assise goes back to the 1500s. There are 198 pitches here, including 4 with hardstanding, mainly set among mature trees with others on a newer field. Connected by surfaced and gravel roads and of a good size (up to 300 sq.m), shrubs and bushes divide most of the pitches. Being close to Calais, the Channel Tunnel exit and Boulogne, makes this a good stopping point en-route, but La Bien-Assise is well worth a longer stay. It is a very popular site which is also used by tour operators, but is well managed and there are no adverse effects.

Three well equipped toilet blocks provide many washbasins in cubicles, showers and baby rooms. Laundry facilities. The main block is in four sections, two unisex. Two motorcaravan service points. Shop. Restaurant. Bar/grill and takeaway (all from mid April). TV room. Pool complex (mid April-mid Sept) with toboggan, covered paddling pool and outdoor pool. Play areas. Minigolf. Tennis. Bicycle hire. WiFi (charged, but free with a drink in the bar).

Key Features

 Pets Accepted

 Disabled Facilities

 Swimming Pool

 Play Area

 Bar/Restaurant

 Scan me for more information.

Alan Rogers Code: FR62190
14 accommodations
61 pitches
GPS: 50.77983, 1.94771
Post Code: F-62850

Pas-de-Calais, Nord/Pas-de-Calais

www.alanrogers.com/fr62190
contact@pommiers-3pays.com
Tel: 03 21 35 02 02
www.pommiers-3pays.com

Open (Touring Pitches):
1 April - 31 October.

Les Pommiers des 3 Pays

This delightful site, close to the Channel ports and the A26 and A16 autoroutes, is on the outskirts of Licques (1 km to the village) in the beautiful Boulonnais countryside. Of the 61 level, grassy pitches, 20 are for touring. All have 16A electricity, water tap and drain, some have rubberised hardstanding. Motorcaravans are especially welcome. The pretty brasserie caters for dining and takeaway in pleasant surroundings near the brand new, heated pool. There is a small, fenced play area for children. A longer stay enables visits to the beaches of the Opal Coast, and many sites of both World Wars, including Dunkirk and Ypres for example.

Two sanitary blocks are equipped with showers, private washing cubicles and facilities for babies. Washing machines and dryers. Sale of bread in the morning. Bar. Restaurant and takeaway. Heated pools. Indoor pool with changing rooms. Activity and entertainment programs (during school holidays). Bicycle hire. Fishing. Chalets and mobile homes to rent. Internet access and free WiFi.

Key Features

 Pets Accepted

 Disabled Facilities

 Swimming Pool

 Play Area

 Bar/Restaurant

Scan me for more information.

Alan Rogers Code: FR77050
60 accommodations
100 pitches
GPS: 49.00294, 2.94141
Post Code: F-77910

Seine-et-Marne, Paris/Ile de France

www.alanrogers.com/fr77050
contact@villageparisien.com
Tel: 01 64 34 80 80
villageparisien.camp-atlantique.co.uk

Open (Touring Pitches):
1 April - 1 November.

Le Village Parisien

If you intend to visit Disneyland, this site is ideally situated, just 12 km. away. Tickets can be purchased at the site, and taxi travel can be arranged. However, the site has more to offer than its proximity to the theme park. There are 260 pitches in total with 100 for touring units. They are reasonably well cared for with mature hedges dividing them (access to some could be difficult for larger vehicles). They include 50 smaller touring pitches, more suitable for tents and motorhomes, with electricity on a flat, grassy area with young trees. The site is close to Charles de Gaulle airport, and there are overhead flights. There is an outdoor pool (unheated) and a second pool with a sliding roof and a shallow area for children. The site offers various activities including tennis and minigolf. Across the road from the entrance is the Canal de l'Ourcq for fishing and kayaking. A towpath alongside the canal is ideal for walking and cycling.

Three toilet blocks are old, but adequate (one closed in low season). Facilities for disabled visitors. Motorcaravan services. Laundry facilities. Small shop and takeaway, bar with entertainment and TV (1/5-15/9). Swimming and paddling pools (1/5-15/9, unheated). Tennis. Play area. Minigolf. Bicycle and kayak hire. Pétanque. Football, volleyball and basketball. Tickets and taxis for Disneyland. WiFi on part of site (charged).

Key Features

 Pets Accepted

 Disabled Facilities

 Swimming Pool

 Play Area

 Bar/Restaurant

 Bike Hire

Scan me for more information.

Alan Rogers Code: FR77180
11 accommodations
35 pitches
GPS: 48.25657, 2.43575
Post Code: F-77760

Seine-et-Marne, Paris/Ile de France

www.alanrogers.com/fr77180
campingiledeboulancourt@orange.fr
Tel: 01 64 24 13 38
www.camping-iledeboulancourt.com

Open (Touring Pitches):
All year excl. Christmas week.

Camping Ile de Boulancourt

In pleasant countryside south of Paris and within easy reach of the Palais de Fontainebleau, this is a traditional, no-frills campsite occupying an attractive location on the bank of the River Essonne. There are 110 pitches on level grassland with groups of trees providing some shade; electricity connections (6A) are available. Nature lovers will be in their element, with woodland paths and waterways surrounding the site, and the forest of Fontainebleau with its major climbing sites and the Parc Naturel Régional du Gatinais Français both a short drive (or an energetic ride) away. A few mobile homes and chalets can be hired, and new ones are planned.

Heated sanitary block with facilities for babies and disabled visitors. Motorcaravan services. Pétanque. Playground. Trampoline. New hospitality room (library, games, kitchen and space for campers). Fishing. Botanical walks. Bicycle hire. WiFi throughout (charged). Picnic evenings and floral workshops in high season.

Key Features

 Pets Accepted

 Play Area

 Bike Hire

 Fishing

Scan me for more information.

Alan Rogers Code: FR75020
81 accommodations
378 pitches
GPS: 48.86885, 2.23473
Post Code: F-75016

Paris, Paris/Ile de France

www.alanrogers.com/fr75020
paris@camping-indigo.com
Tel: 01 45 24 30 00
www.campingparis.fr

Open (Touring Pitches):
All year.

Camping de Paris

A busy site and the only one within Paris, set in a wooded area between the Seine and the Bois de Boulogne. The site is quite extensive but nevertheless becomes very full with many international visitors, with noise well into the night, despite the rules. There are 459 pitches of varying size (including mobile homes) of which 280 are marked, with electricity (10A), water, drainage and TV aerial connections. An improvement and development programme including a new toilet block and restaurant was carried out during the winter of 2014/15. Reservations are made for pitches – if not booked, arrive early in season (mornings).

Four toilet blocks, one modern. Newest block has facilities for disabled visitors but there is no ramped access. All these facilities have heavy use in season. Laundry room. Two motorcaravan service points. Shop. Pizza bar, takeaway and food truck. New central lodge for relaxation. New playground. Bicycle hire. Information service. Shuttle bus to Paris. WiFi in reception. Cottage and wooden Romany-style caravans to rent.

Key Features

 Open All Year

 Pets Accepted

 Disabled Facilities

 Play Area

 Bar/Restaurant

 Bike Hire

Scan me for more information.

Alan Rogers Code: FR52020
39 accommodations
145 pitches
GPS: 48.40644, 5.27109
Post Code: F-52230

Haute-Marne, Champagne-Ardenne

www.alanrogers.com/fr52020
info@laforgedesaintemarie.com
Tel: 03 25 94 42 00
www.laforgedesaintemarie.com

Open (Touring Pitches):
18 April - 4 September.

La Forge de Sainte Mar

This attractive campsite in a secluded valley is accessed through a narrow arched gateway. It was created in 1995 by careful conservation of original forge buildings and the surrounding land. The River Rongeant meanders through the site widening into a small fishing lake. A picturesque bridge links the upper part of the site to the reception area. Grass pitches, 145 for touring units, are of varying sizes on terraces, amongst trees or in more open spaces. Electricity (6A, Europlug) and water are available, and 120 pitches are fully serviced. Ten premium pitches have garden furniture, fridge and barbecue. There are also 39 mobile homes and chalets. Larger units should take care when manoeuvring.

Two sanitary blocks provide all facilities including those for children and disabled visitors. Family shower room. Additional facilities at reception and pool complex. Laundry facilities. Shop, restaurant and bar with terrace. Pizzeria in high season. Heated indoor pool and one for children (18/4-4/9). Play areas. Bicycle hire. Fishing (charged). Games room. Archery. Organised games for children (July/Aug). Programme for adults including wine and cheese tasting and guided walks. WiFi (charged).

Key Features

 Pets Accepted

 Disabled Facilities

 Swimming Pool

 Play Area

 Bar/Restaurant

 Bike Hire

 Fishing

Scan me for more information.

Alan Rogers Code: FR51020
10 accommodations
138 pitches
GPS: 48.93590, 4.38320
Post Code: F-51000

Marne, Champagne-Ardenne

www.alanrogers.com/fr51020
camping.chalons@aquadis-loisirs.com
Tel: 03 26 68 38 00
www.aquadis-loisirs.com

Open (Touring Pitches):
4 March - 3 November

Châlons en Champagne

The location of Châlons, south of Reims and near the A4 and A26 autoroutes, about 300 km. from Calais and Boulogne, makes this an ideal stopover. This site on the southern edge of town now belongs to the Aquadis-Loisirs group. The wide entrance with its neatly mown grass and flowerbeds leads to tidy rows of large pitches separated by hedges, many with taps and drains adjacent. Of the 138 pitches, 89 are on gravel, the rest on grass; 96 have electricity (10A). Some overlook a small lake. Trees abound although there is no shade in some parts. The site is ideally situated for exploring this famous region in the plain of the River Marne and its historical connections.

Three fairly basic toilet blocks (one open only in high season, the other can be heated) include washbasins in cabins, baby room and hairdressing station. Unit for disabled visitors. Laundry facilities. Shop. Bread to order. Open-air bar, snack bar and takeaway (1/5-30/9). Games (pool and babyfoot) and TV rooms. Fishing lake. Playground. Minigolf. Tennis. Volleyball. Boules. Mini-football. Motorcaravan services. WiFi throughout (charged). Ten mobile homes to rent.

Key Features

 Pets Accepted

 Disabled Facilities

 Play Area

 Bar/Restaurant

 Bike Hire

 Fishing

Scan me for more information.

Alan Rogers Code: FR52040
30 accommodations
150 pitches
GPS: 47.81280, 5.32056
Post Code: F-52200

Haute-Marne, Champagne-
Ardenne

www.alanrogers.com/fr52040
croix.arles@yahoo.fr
Tel: 03 25 88 24 02
www.campingdelacroixdarles.com

Open (Touring Pitches):
15 March - 31 October.

Camping de la Croix d'Arles

Only 10 km. from autoroute A31 (exit Langres Sud), this site is ideally located for an overnight stop on your holiday journey, but also has the basics for a more extended stay. There are 180 pitches, of which 150 are for touring units with 10A electricity. Most facilities are near the entrance, as is a flat grassy area mostly used by caravans and motorhomes for overnight stops. A wooded area, where nature has been worked with rather than controlled, provides groups of numbered pitches with lots of shade (leads for electricity of up to 40 m. could be needed). Further on is an area for tents with no electricity supply. A tour operator uses the site. In high season trained staff run a club for children and other activities for all ages. The location is ideally situated for exploring the lakes, rivers, canal, paths and cycle tracks of the region and the beautiful town of Langres.

Key Features

 Pets Accepted

 Disabled Facilities

 Swimming Pool

 Play Area

 Bar/Restaurant

Two modern toilet blocks contain British style WCs, some washbasins in cabins and controllable showers. Facilities for disabled visitors. Baby room. Washing machines, dryer, ironing board and washing lines. Small shop for basics. Restaurant, bar, snack bar and takeaway (1/4-31/10). Swimming and paddling pools (fenced), sauna and jacuzzi in timber chalets (15/5-15/9). Playground. Minigolf. Games rooms. Boules. Mobile homes and chalets for hire. WiFi on part of site.

Scan me for
more information.

Alan Rogers Code: FR88120
25 accommodations
64 pitches
GPS: 48.16826, 6.89025
Post Code: F-88430

Vosges, Lorraine

www.alanrogers.com/fr88120
info@camping-closdelachaume.com
Tel: 03 29 50 76 76
www.camping-closdelachaume.co.uk

Open (Touring Pitches):
17 April - 20 September

Au Clos de la Chaume

Sites et Paysages Camping Au Clos de la Chaume is a pleasant site is within walking distance of the town, on level ground with a small stream. The friendly family owners, who are British and French, live on site and do their best to ensure campers have an enjoyable relaxing stay. There are 94 level grassy pitches of varying sizes and with varying amounts of sun and shade. All 64 touring pitches have electricity hook-ups (6/10A) and some are divided by shrubs and trees. The site carries the LPO (League for Bird Protection) label with over 30 species present. There is an attractive, well fenced, new swimming pool and an excellent small adventure-style playground. Wine tasting evenings are held in July and August.

Key Features

 Pets Accepted

 Disabled Facilities

 Swimming Pool

 Play Area

Two modern sanitary blocks provide all the necessary facilities for families and disabled visitors. Childrens sanitary facilities. Laundry with washing machines and dryers. Motorcaravan services. Reception keeps basic supplies (June-Aug). New covered swimming pool (1/5-20/9). Play area. Games room with pool table, table football and library. Boules. Volleyball. Ping-pong tables. WIFI throughout (charged) and also a FREE WiFi limited zone.

Scan me for more information.

Alan Rogers Code: FR88410
17 accommodations
147 pitches
GPS: 48.06242, 6.96475
Post Code: F-88400

Vosges, Lorraine

www.alanrogers.com/fr88410
contact@campingvertevallee.com
Tel: 03 29 63 21 77
www.campingvertevallee.com

Open (Touring Pitches):
All year excl. 1 November - 15
December.

Flower Camping Verte Vallée

In one of France's most picturesque regions, amongst the Vosges mountains and the vineyards of Alsace, Verte Vallée enjoys an enviable location just 300 m. from the shore of the Lac de Longemer, and within easy reach of the popular towns of Kaysersburg and Colmar. Of the 147 pitches, 130 are for touring with 4-10A electricity (long leads advisable). The site is open much of the year and winter sports enthusiasts can leave their vehicles on site and use the shuttle bus to their destinations. There are chalets and tent lodges to rent and a large cottage for parties of up to 22.

Shower blocks (one heated with drying room). Washing machines and dryer. Baby room. Shop (fresh bread daily) and takeaway (July/Aug). Motorcaravan services. A cooked meat vendor and a pizza van call twice weekly (July/Aug). Bar (1/6-30/9). Heated outdoor pool (1/5-30/9). Heated indoor pool (1/5-30/9). Tennis. Table tennis. Pool table. Table football. Trampoline. Playground. Indoor games room and TV room. A varied programme of entertainment for all ages is provided all season, including clubs and activities for younger children. WiFi on part of site. There are tennis courts, table tennis, pool tables and table football . A varied programme of entertainment for all ages is provided all season, including clubs and activities for younger children. This is a wonderful site for families with children.

Key Features

 Pets Accepted

 Disabled Facilities

 Swimming Pool

 Play Area

 Bar/Restaurant

 Skiing

 Bike Hire

Scan me for more information.

Alan Rogers Code: FR88110
19 accommodations
125 pitches
GPS: 48.12088, 6.82914
Post Code: F-88640

Vosges, Lorraine

www.alanrogers.com/fr88110
steniole@wanadoo.fr
Tel: 03 29 51 43 75
www.steniole.com/en

Open (Touring Pitches):
1 April - 30 September

Flower Camping la Sténiole

Set in a lovely peaceful, rural area in the heart of the Vosges forest, this attractive site is run by dedicated and friendly couple, Rudi and Natacha, who are constantly improving the site and its facilities. The 125 pitches (4/10A electricity) which are open from 1 April - 15 October are either separated by hedges or beside the water. There is little shade. They also have accommodation for rental year round. The site has an indoor heated pool which is open from May - September and they'll also have a water slide from July 2018. There is a small river which has been used to form a small lake for fishing and swimming and a series of separate ponds (water quality is checked regularly). An atmosphere of relaxation is encouraged and the whole family can have a good time here. The final approach to the site is on a steep single track road, a 250-metre climb in two kilometres.

Two sanitary blocks and additional facilities in the main building include facilities for children and disabled visitors. Washing machines and dryers. Bar and Restaurant (Jul/Aug). Pizza takeaway (Jul/Aug). Indoor heated pool from May to Sept (wth water slide open Jul/Aug). Fishing. Games room with TV and library. Playground. Football. Volleyball. Petanque. Trampoline. Table tennis. WiFi on some areas (free). Apartments, chalets and mobile homes to rent.

Key Features

 Pets Accepted

 Disabled Facilities

 Swimming Pool

 Play Area

 Bar/Restaurant

 Skiing

 Fishing

 Horse Riding

Scan me for more information.

Alan Rogers Code: FR67070
85 accommodations
74 pitches
GPS: 48.33722, 7.28862
Post Code: F-67220

Bas-Rhin, Alsace

www.alanrogers.com/fr67070
giessen@campeole.com
Tel: +33 (0)3 88 58 98 14
www.campeole.com/le-giessen

Open (Touring Pitches):
30 March - 30 September

Camping Le Giessen

Le Giessen is a member of the Campéole group and can be found at the foot of the Vosges mountains, with easy access to many of the best-loved sights in Alsace. Although there is no pool on site, a large complex comprising indoor and outdoor pools with a water slide can be found adjacent to the site, with free admission for all campers. The 74 touring pitches here are grassy and of a good size, mostly with 6A electrical connections and some shaded by mature trees. A number of mobile homes and fully equipped tents are available to rent. A supplement is payable for twin-axle caravans. Various activities are organised in high season including a children's club and disco evenings.

Two toilet blocks with all facilities including controllable hot showers and facilities for disabled visitors. Laundry. Bar (May-Sept). Snack bar/takeaway (July/Aug). Motorcaravan service point. Play area. Multisports court. Activities and entertainment. Bicycle hire. Fishing. Mobile homes and equipped tents to rent. WiFi (charged).

Key Features

 Pets Accepted

 Disabled Facilities

 Swimming Pool

 Play Area

 Bar/Restaurant

 Fishing

Scan me for more information.

Alan Rogers Code: FR68210
109 pitches
GPS: 48.14902, 7.25394
Post Code: F-68240

Haut-Rhin, Alsace

www.alanrogers.com/fr68210
camping@kaysersberg-vignoble.fr
Tel: 03 89 47 14 47
www.camping-kaysersberg.com

Open (Touring Pitches):
1 April - 30 September

Municipal Kaysersberg

Kaysersberg Municipal campsite is in a leafy location by the river, just outside the centre of town, a perfect location for exploring the Alsace wine region. This campsite is for touring only, no rentals on site. The 110 pitches are 80sq.m or larger with electricity and 15 pitches are specifically for campers with dogs. They are grassy and level with shade available and tarmac access roads. Four well equipped sanitary blocks offer disabled access and baby facilities as well as a laundry and dishwashers. A baker delivers to reception daily during peak season.

Four well equipped sanitary blocks, one heated in colder months. Disabled access. Baby room. Laundry. Dishwashers. Bread available at reception. Tennis court. Table tennis. Bowling alley. Children's playground. Games room. TV room. WiFi. Swimming pool 600m. Golf 5km.

Key Features

 Disabled Facilities

 Play Area

Scan me for more information.

Alan Rogers Code: FR67060
48 accommodations
147 pitches
GPS: 48.57551, 7.71506
Post Code: F-67200

Bas-Rhin, Alsace

www.alanrogers.com/fr67060
info@camping-strasbourg.com
Tel: 03 88 30 19 96
www.camping-strasbourg.com

Open (Touring Pitches):
All year.

Camping de Strasbourg

Reopened in July 2015 after a lengthy refurbishment, Camping Indigo Strasbourg is a beautifully designed and built, brand new city site in south-west Strasbourg. During the low season you pick your pitch but in high season and during the time of the Christmas market (when there may be snow!), reservations are advised as the site becomes full. There are currently 90 pitches with electricity connections (6-9A, Europlug). A new central lodge has been added, the sanitary facilities completely rebuilt and a modern café/restaurant opened on site. There is a bus stop 200 m. from the site and the city tram runs into town. The city centre is only 30 minutes' walk. This site is an ideal base from which to explore the city.

Two brand new, heated sanitary blocks with facilities for families and disabled visitors. Washing machines and dryer. Motorcaravan services. Bar, restaurant and takeaway (all 6/7-31/8). Outdoor heated swimming pool (30/4-18/9). Bicycle hire. Free WiFi on part of site. Wood and canvas tents and Romany-style caravans available to rent.

Key Features

 Open All Year

 Pets Accepted

 Disabled Facilities

 Swimming Pool

 Play Area

 Bar/Restaurant

 Bike Hire

Scan me for more information.

Sunêlia Le Fief

Alan Rogers Code: FR44190
227 accommodations
384 pitches
GPS: 47.23486, -2.16757
Post Code: F-44250

Loire-Atlantique, Pays de la Loire

www.alanrogers.com/fr44190
camping@lefief.com
Tel: 02 40 27 23 86
www.lefief.com

Open (Touring Pitches):
6 April - 22 September

Sunêlia Le Fief welcomes all campers on large pitches of 100 m², partly shaded and bordered by lush, established vegetation, and would particularly suit if you are a family with young children or lively teenagers. Le Fief is a well established site only 900 m. from sandy beaches on the southern Brittany coast. It has a magnificent aquapark with outdoor and covered swimming pools, paddling pools, slides, river rapids, fountains, jets and more. The site has 384 pitches, 96 pitches for touring units, all with 8A electricity and varying slightly in size and accessibility. There are also 227 mobile homes and chalets to rent and 39 privately owned units. An impressive Taos mobile home village includes a new Sunny Club for children.

Key Features

 Pets Accepted

 Disabled Facilities

 Swimming Pool

 Play Area

 Bar/Restaurant

 Bike Hire

Bar, restaurant, takeaway (all season) with terrace overlooking the pool complex. Grocery (all season). Heated outdoor pools (1/5 - 22/9). Indoor swimming pool (all season). Wellness Centre. Playground. Padel. Petanque. Archery. Games room. Animation and organized activities (weekends April / June, every day July / August). Bike rental. WiFi on the site (charged). 900m from the city centre and the long sandy beach.

Scan me for more information.

Alan Rogers Code: FR72060
2 accommodations
73 pitches
GPS: 48.22555, 0.13448
Post Code: F-72170

Sarthe, Pays de la Loire

www.alanrogers.com/fr72060
beaumont.sur.sarthe@wanadoo.fr
Tel: 02 43 97 01 93
www.beaumontsursarthe.com

Open (Touring Pitches):
1 May - 30 September.

Camping Val de Sarthe

This delightful, inexpensive riverside site is conveniently located just a short walk from the town and its shops and services. The 73 individual, level and grassy pitches are large, divided by hedges and all have electricity (5A). Some of the pitches including those along the river's edge may require a longer cable. An excellent activity area provides swings and other play equipment, boules pitches, tennis, netball, and a fitness trail. Those intending to stay longer than one night require a barrier card (refundable deposit). Reception opens 10.00-12.00 and 16.00-20.00 in May, June and September, 09.00-12.00 and 15.00-20.00 in July and August. Barrier opens at 07.00.

The central sanitary unit is accessed by a flight of steps although there is a long and fairly steep ramp for disabled visitors. Facilities include some washbasins in cubicles and spacious showers. Laundry facilities. Motorcaravan services. Bread and croissants to order. Activity area. River fishing. Room for campers' use (July/Aug). Double axle caravans are not accepted.

Key Features

 Pets Accepted

 Disabled Facilities

 Play Area

 Horse Riding

Scan me for more information.

Alan Rogers Code: FR41040
39 accommodations
115 pitches
GPS: 47.66580, 1.52877
Post Code: F-41500

Loir-et-Cher, Val de Loire

Château des Marais

www.alanrogers.com/fr41040
info@camping-marais.com
Tel: 02 54 87 05 42
chateau-des-marais.com/en

Open (Touring Pitches):
2 May - 10 September,
accommodation from 16 April.

The Château des Marais campsite is a good base for visiting the château at Chambord and the other châteaux in the Vallée des Rois. The site, providing 115 large touring pitches in avenues, all with electricity (10A), access to water and drainage and ample shade, is situated in the oak and hornbeam woods of its own attractive, small château. Twenty-five designated motorcaravan pitches are on hardstanding and grass. An excellent swimming complex offers pools with two slides, two flumes and a lazy river. There is an on-site tourism office where bookings can be made. Used by a UK tour operator.

Four sanitary blocks have good facilities including some large showers and washbasins en-suite, suitable for visitors with disabilities. Washing machines and dryers. Motorcaravan services. Shop. Bar/restaurant with large terrace. Takeaway. Breakfast service. Swimming complex with heated and unheated pools, slide and cover for cooler weather. Wellness spa centre with massage. Outdoor fitness area. New minigolf course. Bicycle and go-kart hire. Games room. Music/TV room and library in the Manor House. Club for children (high season). Fishing pond. Excursions to Paris, an entertainment programme and canoe trips organised in high season. WiFi throughout (charged).

Key Features

 Pets Accepted

 Disabled Facilities

 Swimming Pool

 Play Area

 Bar/Restaurant

 Bike Hire

 Fishing

Scan me for more information.

Alan Rogers Code: FR37120
205 accommodations
394 pitches
GPS: 47.14870, 0.65480
Post Code: F-37800

Indre-et-Loire, Val de Loire

www.alanrogers.com/fr37120
contact@fierbois.com
Tel: 02 47 65 43 35
www.fierbois.com

Open (Touring Pitches):
26 April - 1 September

Camping Parc de Fierbois

Castel Camping Parc de Fierbois has a wide variety of accommodation to rent if you're not bringing your own caravan or tent. There's a range of Mobile homes, Chalets, Gîtes and Tree houses. The campsite provides plenty of opportunity for a restful family holiday, but there are many activities for everyone if you prefer to be more active. As well as a covered heated pool, you'll also find a water-park complex with toboggans, a children's club, adventure park, including archery and a skate park, and a good restaurant and bar. The region also has a rich heritage for you to discover including chateaux Villandry, Azay-le-Rideau and Chenonceau, as well as many famous vineyards.

Two sanitary blocks are equipped with showers, private washing cubicles and facilities for babies. Washing machines and dryers. Well stocked shop. Bar. Restaurant and takeaway. Heated indoor pool. Outdoor pool with waterslides. Activity and entertainment programmes (in July and August). Bicycle hire. Fishing. Adventure park in the trees. Internet access and WiFi (charged).

Key Features

 Pets Accepted

 Disabled Facilities

 Swimming Pool

 Play Area

 Bar/Restaurant

 Bike Hire

 Fishing

Scan me for more information.

Alan Rogers Code: FR41070
40 accommodations
111 pitches
GPS: 47.49001, 1.25832
Post Code: F-41120

Loir-et-Cher, Val de Loire

www.alanrogers.com/fr41070
camping@grandetortue.com
Tel: 02 54 44 15 20
www.la-grande-tortue.com

Open (Touring Pitches):
9 April - 17 September

Camping la Grande Tortue

In the region that the Kings of France chose to build their most beautiful residences, this pleasant, shaded site has been developed in the surroundings of an old 800-hectare forest, just 1 km. from the banks of the Loire river. For those seeking a relaxing holiday, it provides 169 pitches, including 111 for touring units, all with 10A electricity (119 Europlugs) and 58 with full services. The friendly family owners continue to develop the site with a multisports court and an attractive swimming pool complex. During July and August, they organise a programme of trips including canoeing and riding excursions, as well as twice weekly concerts and shows.

Three sanitary blocks offer washbasins in cabins and pushbutton showers. Facilities for disabled visitors in one block. Laundry facilities. Motorcaravan services. Shop, terraced bar and restaurant with takeaway service (all season). Heated swimming pool covered in poor weather, shallow outdoor pools for children (from 1/5). Trampolines, ball crawl with slide and climbing wall, two bouncy inflatables. Club for children (July/Aug). Multisports court. Bicycle hire (13/4-15/9). WiFi over site (charged). No electric barbecues

Key Features

 Pets Accepted

 Disabled Facilities

 Swimming Pool

 Play Area

 Bar/Restaurant

 Bike Hire

Scan me for more information.

Alan Rogers Code: FR41030
300 accommodations
115 pitches
GPS: 47.54398, 2.19193
Post Code: F-41300

Loir-et-Cher, Val de Loire

www.alanrogers.com/fr41030
info@lesalicourts.com
Tel: 02 54 88 63 34
www.lesalicourts.com

Open (Touring Pitches):
4 May - 1 September

Camping les Alicourts

A secluded holiday village set in the heart of the forest, with many sporting facilities and a super spa centre, Leading Camping les Alicourts Resort is midway between Orléans and Bourges, to the east of the A71. There are 550 pitches, 115 for touring and the remainder occupied by mobile homes and chalets. All pitches have 6A electricity connections and good provision for water, and most are 150 sq.m. (min. 100 sq.m.). Locations vary from wooded to more open areas, thus giving a choice of amount of shade. All facilities are open all season and the leisure amenities are exceptional. A member of Leading Campings group.

Three modern sanitary blocks include some washbasins in cabins and baby bathrooms. Laundry facilities. Facilities for families and disabled visitors. Motorcaravan services. Shop. Boutique. Restaurant. Takeaway dishes available. Bar with terrace. Pool complex. 7 water slides. Spa centre. Library. 6-hectare lake (fishing, bathing, canoes, pedaloes, cable-ski). 9-hole golf course. Adventure play area. Tennis. Minigolf. Boules. Roller skating/skateboarding (bring own equipment). Bicycle hire. WiFi (charged).

Key Features

 Pets Accepted

 Disabled Facilities

 Swimming Pool

 Play Area

 Bar/Restaurant

 Bike Hire

 Fishing

 Golf

Scan me for more information.

LES ALICOURTS RESORT, Glamping Loire-Valley
Spa, Golf, Pool Complex, Fishing
www.lesalicourts.com
Member of the Leading Campings of Europe

les alicourts
sort by nature *****

Alan Rogers Code: FR45010
80 accommodations
120 pitches
GPS: 47.64152, 2.61528
Post Code: F-45500

Loiret, Val de Loire

www.alanrogers.com/fr45010
contact@bardelet.com
Tel: 02 38 67 47 39
www.bardelet.com

Open (Touring Pitches):
13 April - 15 September

Castel les Bois du Bardelet

This attractive, high quality site, ideal for families with young children, is in a rural setting and well situated for exploring the less well known eastern part of the Loire Valley. Two lakes (one for boating, one for fishing) and a pool complex have been attractively landscaped in 18 hectares of former farmland, blending old and new with natural wooded areas and more open grassland with rural views. There are 245 large, level grass pitches with 120 for touring units. All have at least 10A electricity, 15 have water, waste water and 16A electricity, and some 30 have hardstanding. Eight have individual en-suite sanitary units beside the pitch.

Two heated toilet blocks (effectively unisex, one open in high season only) have some washbasins in cubicles, controllable showers, an en-suite unit for disabled visitors and a baby room. Washing machines and dryers. Minimart, bar, takeaway and restaurant (13/4-8/9). Heated outdoor pool (1/5-1/9). Heated indoor pool and children's pool (all season). Wellness centre with sauna, hot tub, Shiatsu massage and beauty treatments. Fitness and jacuzzi rooms. Beach on lake. Games area. Canoeing and fishing. Tennis. Minigolf. Volleyball. Pétanque. Play area with trampoline. Kids' club, sports tournaments, excursions and activities, aquagym, archery (July/Aug). Bicycle hire. Chalets/mobile homes for hire. WiFi (free in bar).

Key Features

 Pets Accepted

 Disabled Facilities

 Swimming Pool

 Play Area

 Bar/Restaurant

 Bike Hire

 Fishing

Scan me for more information.

Alan Rogers Code: FR85915
33 accommodations
79 pitches
GPS: 46.46486, -1.65484
Post Code: F-85440

Talmont-Saint-Hilaire, Vendée

www.alanrogers.com/fr85915
info@camping-leparadis85.com
Tel: 02 51 22 22 36
www.camping-leparadis85.com

Open (Touring Pitches):
1 May - 30 September.

Camping le Paradis

Camping le Paradis can be found close to the popular seaside resort of Talmont-Saint-Hilaire, between Jard-sur-Mer and the larger resort of Les Sables-d'Olonne. Talmont makes up part of the Côte de Lumière, and its 3.5 km. sandy beach (Le Veillon) has longstanding Blue Flag accreditation. There is a free shuttle bus from the campsite to the beach. Pitches here are of average size with limited shade. A number of mobile homes are available to rent. On-site amenities include a covered, heated pool and an all-weather sports pitch (basketball, volleyball, football). The site becomes more active in peak season with a daily children's club and frequent activities for all the family (including evening entertainment).

The single toilet block provides washbasins and showers in cubicles. Laundry. Shop. Bar/snack bar and takeaway (July/Aug). Covered swimming pool. Play area. All weather sports pitch. Activity and entertainment programme (July/Aug). No charcoal barbecues. WiFi over part of site (charged). Max. 1 dog. Mobile homes and caravans to rent.

Key Features

 Pets Accepted

 Disabled Facilities

 Swimming Pool

 Play Area

 Bar/Restaurant

Scan me for
more information.

Alan Rogers Code: FR85770
38 accommodations
164 pitches
GPS: 46.67703, -1.76885
Post Code: F-85220

Coëx, Vendée

www.alanrogers.com/fr85770
reservation@rcn.eu
Tel: +31 85 0400 700
www.rcn.nl/la-ferme-du-latois

Open (Touring Pitches):
6 April - 24 September

La Ferme du Latois

Originally a simple 'camping à la ferme', this site has been developed by a Dutch organisation into an extensive, very well equipped and well-maintained campsite. Located around two attractive fishing lakes, the 164 pitches, most available for touring, are spacious and attractively laid out with plenty of grass, hedges and trees, some young, some mature. All have electricity (6/10A), and a few are very large. There are 38 mobile homes to rent. An old barn has been converted into a large restaurant offering an extensive French menu, including a 'menu du jour'. Also here are a small bar, a shop selling necessary provisions and the reception area.

Two large, modern sanitary blocks built in traditional style have excellent toilets, showers and washbasins in cubicles. Good facilities for disabled visitors. Attractively tiled areas for babies and children, with special toilets, washbasins and showers. Two smaller blocks provide additional facilities. Laundry room with washing machines and dryers. Motorcaravan services. Small shop. Bar counter with terrace. Restaurant. All facilities available all season. Heated outdoor swimming pool with slides. Play area. Bicycle hire. Fishing lakes. Archery (high season). WiFi over site (free). Max. 1 dog. Mobile homes to rent.

Key Features

 Pets Accepted

 Disabled Facilities

 Swimming Pool

 Play Area

 Bar/Restaurant

 Bike Hire

 Fishing

Scan me for more information.

Alan Rogers Code: FR85145
59 accommodations
59 pitches
GPS: 46.75563, -2.00781
Post Code: F-85160

Saint Jean-de-Monts, Vendée

www.alanrogers.com/fr85145
contact@le-tropicana.com
Tel: 02 51 58 62 98
www.le-tropicana.com

Open (Touring Pitches):
14 May - 18 September.

Camping le Tropicana

Le Tropicana is situated in the heart of a vast pine forest, a few kilometres south of Saint Jean-de-Monts. It is only minutes away from a fine sandy beach (gate from site) and all the amenities in Saint Hilaire-de-Riez. This seven-hectare site has a total of 332 pitches with 59 for tourers. They are generously sized (100-130 sq.m), on sandy grass, and all have 10A electricity (long leads may be required). The whole family will enjoy the water park, with its three heated swimming pools with water slides and a toddlers' pool. The extensive high season entertainment and leisure programme caters for all ages and there is also a kids' club.

Three toilet blocks with showers and washbasins in cubicles and facilities for disabled visitors. Baby room. Laundry. Shop (bread to order), bar/restaurant/takeaway (29/6-1/9). Heated indoor swimming pool and paddling pool. Heated outdoor pool with slide, flume and jacuzzi. Wellness centre. Play area. Beach volleyball. Boules. Games room. Children's activities and family entertainment (July/Aug). TV room. WiFi (charged).

Key Features

 Pets Accepted

 Disabled Facilities

 Swimming Pool

 Play Area

 Bar/Restaurant

 Bike Hire

Scan me for more information.

Alan Rogers Code: FR85740
67 accommodations
46 pitches
GPS: 46.80913, -2.11017
Post Code: F-85160

Saint Jean-de-Monts, Vendée

Aux Coeurs Vendéens

www.alanrogers.com/fr85740
info@coeursvendeens.com
Tel: 02 51 58 84 91
www.coeursvendeens.com

Open (Touring Pitches):
23 April - 17 September.

This is a delightful little site, a real find for those wishing to enjoy the beaches and lifestyle of this stretch of coastline without the razzmatazz of some of the neighbouring sites. It is family run and everywhere there is attention to detail: flower tubs beside the road as you drive in, whitewashed stones for the pitch numbers, engraved designs on the washbasin mirrors, even plugs for the dishwashing sinks! There are 46 touring pitches, all with electricity available (10A), and a further 69 with mobile homes and chalets, all but five available for rent.

Two rather dated sanitary blocks are bright, cheerful and kept very clean. Controllable showers, washbasins in cubicles, two pleasant baby rooms. En-suite facilities for disabled visitors (wheelchair users might have minor difficulties accessing this). Laundry. Small shop with takeaway (2/7-28/8). Bar (9/7-28/8). Heated swimming pools (indoor as site, outdoor 1/6-7/9). Fitness equipment. TV and games room. Playgrounds. Trampoline and bouncy castle. Children's club (5-12 yrs, July/Aug). Bicycle hire. Internet access (free). WiFi throughout (free).

Key Features

 Pets Accepted

 Disabled Facilities

 Swimming Pool

 Play Area

 Bar/Restaurant

 Bike Hire

Scan me for more information.

Alan Rogers Code: FR85710
150 accommodations
46 pitches
GPS: 46.47207, -1.72646
Post Code: F-85180

Les Sables d'Olonne, Vendée

www.alanrogers.com/fr85710
lebelair@cybelevacances.com
Tel: 02 51 22 09 67
www.campingdubelair.com

Open (Touring Pitches):
6 April - 3 November.

Camping le Bel Air

Le Bel Air is a well established site close to the Vendée's largest resort, Les Sables-d'Olonne. It is now very much dedicated to mobile homes and chalets, and for 2019 they have introduced mobile homes with private Jacuzzi's. Of its 286 pitches, just 46 are for touring – 40 on grass mostly with electricity (16A), water and drainage and a further six on concrete for motorcaravans. This is a very well equipped site with the focal point being a new and impressive pool complex including a large covered pool and separate outdoor pool.

Five well equipped small sanitary blocks with facilities for babies and disabled visitors. Laundry with washing machines and dryers. Motorcaravan services. Bar, snack bar, takeaway and shop. Heated outdoor pool with children's pool and waterslides (April-Sept). Heated indoor pool with sauna, spa and gym (all season). TV room. Games room. Multisports court. Playground. Bicycle hire. Skate park for teenagers. Charging stations for electric vehicles (new for 2019). Activities in high season. Mobile homes and chalets for rent. Charcoal barbecues not permitted. WiFi throughout (charged).

Key Features

 Pets Accepted

 Disabled Facilities

 Swimming Pool

 Play Area

 Bar/Restaurant

 Bike Hire

 Scan me for more information.

Alan Rogers Code: FR85500
154 accommodations
81 pitches
GPS: 46.67833, -1.91571
Post Code: F-85800

Saint Gilles-Croix-de-Vie,
Vendée

Le Bahamas Beach

www.alanrogers.com/fr85500
info@chadotel.com
Tel: 02 51 54 69 16
www.chadotel.com

Open (Touring Pitches):
2 April - 24 September.

A member of the Chadotel group, le Bahamas Beach is separated from the sandy beach by 600 m. of sand-dunes and the River Jaunay. It is a modern, well-equipped site, very well placed on one of the most popular stretches of the Vendée coast, and attracts a higher proportion of French holidaymakers than many others in the area. The 81 touring pitches are scattered amongst the total of 235, of which 154 are mobile homes. There is one French tour operator (6 pitches). The pitches are grassy, and level on sandy soil, separated by hedges or low bushes and all have easy access to electricity and water. There are few trees and little shelter from the wind off the sea. Maximum unit length permitted is 8.5 m. There is a good range of daytime and evening entertainment for all ages in July and August.

Key Features

 Pets Accepted

 Disabled Facilities

 Swimming Pool

 Play Area

 Bar/Restaurant

 Bike Hire

Two well maintained toilet blocks include washbasins in cubicles, a unit for disabled visitors and baby rooms with bath, shower and toilet. Washing machines and dryers. Bar, snacks and takeaway (25/5-15/9) with limited opening hours in low season. Shop (25/5-15/9). Heated outdoor pool with cover for cooler weather, slide, flume, children's pool and large sun terrace (5/4-20/9). Play area. Minigolf. Football, basketball and volleyball. Bicycle hire. WiFi over site (charged).

Scan me for
more information.

Alan Rogers Code: FR85930
150 accommodations
86 pitches
GPS: 46.47609, -1.49454
Post Code: F-85440

Avrillé, Vendée

www.alanrogers.com/fr85930
forges@franceloc.fr
Tel: 02 51 22 38 85
www.campingdomainedesforges.com

Open (Touring Pitches):
11 April - 27 September.

Domaine des Forges

Arranged in the beautiful grounds of a 16th-century manor house, the 86 touring pitches here are very generous in size (100-200 sq.m) with 16A electricity, water and drainage. Some of the premium pitches with additional services such as Internet access and cable TV carry an extra charge. The owners aim to develop a prestige campsite with the highest quality of services, and they have made an excellent start. A further 150 pitches are occupied by mobile homes, chalets and tents available for hire. A large lake is available for fishing. An extension to the site opened in 2011 with two new toilet blocks, and it will take a little time for trees and shrubs to mature here. A heated indoor pool also opened in 2011, as was an area of 20 hardstanding pitches for motorhomes and a TV room.

Four heated sanitary blocks include facilities for disabled visitors and babies. Laundry facilities. Motorcaravan services. Shop (Apr-Sept). Bar and takeaway. Heated indoor pool with whirlpool (all season). Two heated outdoor pools plus flumes, slides, wading and fun pools for children. Play area. Minigolf. Fishing lake. Multisports area. Boules. Fitness room. Bicycle hire. Gas barbecues only. Internet access and WiFi throughout (charged). One dog per pitch.

Key Features

 Pets Accepted

 Disabled Facilities

 Swimming Pool

 Play Area

 Bar/Restaurant

 Bike Hire

 Fishing

Scan me for more information.

Alan Rogers Code: FR85850
50 accommodations
101 pitches
GPS: 46.64463, -1.73328
Post Code: F-85150

Saint Julien-des-Landes, Vendée

www.alanrogers.com/fr85850
info@la-bretonniere.com
Tel: 02 51 46 62 44
www.la-bretonniere.com

Open (Touring Pitches):
9 April - 30 September.

Camping la Bretonnière

An attractive, modern site on a family farm surrounded by beautiful, peaceful countryside, this site is sure to please. With 165 pitches in an area of six hectares, there is plenty of space for everyone. There are 101 touring pitches, eight tents, eighteen mobile homes, and 20 alpine-style chalets, spread around several fields, some quite open, others with some shade from perimeter hedges. The grassy pitches are all of a generous size with 12/16A electricity (Europlug, long leads may be required). Two swimming pools, both covered, are surrounded by a pleasant terrace, with the bar and reception close by. Also on site is a lovely large fishing lake (fenced) with a pleasant walk all around. The bar and takeaway operate in July/August, ices and essential tinned food items are available from reception, and there is a motorhome service point. A club for children runs in July and August.

Four modern, clean and well appointed toilet blocks are spread evenly around the site, with baby rooms and facilities for disabled visitors at two blocks (may not be open April/May). Motorcaravan services. Small shop, bar, snack bar and takeaway (July/Aug). Two covered swimming pools (15.5x7 m, 11x5 m) and play pool for children. Wellness centre. Playgrounds. Games/TV room. Tennis. Boules. Basketball. Volleyball. Indoor and outdoor football pitches. Fishing lake. Bicycle hire. WiFi (free by bar and reception). Caravan storage.

Key Features

 Pets Accepted

 Disabled Facilities

 Swimming Pool

 Play Area

 Bar/Restaurant

 Bike Hire

 Fishing

Scan me for more information.

Alan Rogers Code: FR17780
44 accommodations
111 pitches
GPS: 46.20383, -1.52042
Post Code: F-17590

Charente-Maritime, Poitou-Charentes

www.alanrogers.com/fr17780
contact@campdusoleil.com
Tel: 05 46 29 40 62
www.campdusoleil.com

Open (Touring Pitches):
1 April - 1 October

Camp Du Soleil

This peaceful campsite is situated on the island of Ré nestled between the beautiful village of Ars en Ré and the beach. They offer a relaxing, family atmosphere amongst wilderness and nature in a small park of 2 hectares. Although a small site, you have a choice of 111 pitches, separated by trees and hedges, and 44 cottages/mobile homes with 2 or 3 bedrooms. There is also a good size pool with a separate paddling pool for babies and young children and all of the facilities you need for an enjoyable camping holiday. You will discover beautiful landscapes, monuments, heritage, local products, marinas, a bird reserve, bike rides in the salt marshes from local cycle paths and the art of simple living.

3 heated sanitary blocks including an accessible unit for disabled visitors. Showers. Baby bath. Laundry facilities. Restaurant, bar and takeaway. Grocery store. TV room. Outdoor pool. Children's playground. Gaming room. Ping Pong. Petanque. Bicycle rental. You also have all of the shops and restaurants of Ars en ré, just 400 metres away.

Key Features

 Pets Accepted

 Disabled Facilities

 Swimming Pool

 Play Area

 Bar/Restaurant

 Bike Hire

Scan me for more information.

Alan Rogers Code: FR17140
400 accommodations
240 pitches
GPS: 45.81095, -1.06109
Post Code: F-17320

Charente-Maritime, Poitou-Charentes

www.alanrogers.com/fr17140
info@sequoiaparc.com
Tel: 0033 (0)5 46 85 55 55
www.sequoiaparc.com

Open (Touring Pitches):
11 May - 1 September

Camping Séquoia Parc

The overall winner of the Alan Rogers Campsite of the Year Awards in 2018, Séquoia Parc is just 7 km from the beach (Marennes-Plage). This is a high-quality family campsite in the heart of the Charente-Maritime region, set in the grounds of La Josephtrie, a castle with beautifully restored outbuildings and courtyard area with a bar and restaurant. The pitches are between 120 and 140m² with 6/10A electricity connections, separated by shrubs providing plenty of privacy. The site has mobile homes, chalets and fully equipped tents for up to 7 people. This is a popular site and reservations are necessary for high season. This site is a member of Leading Campings group.

Three spotless toilet blocks include units with washbasins and showers. Facilities for disabled visitors & children. Large laundry. Motorcaravan services. Supermarket with fresh bread. Restaurant/bar. Take-away with wood oven pizzas. 2000 m² swimming pool complex with water slides, lazy river and large paddling pool. Wellness & Fitness centre with indoor swimming pool, sauna, hammam and Jacuzzi. Massage rooms, spa treatments & fitness area with cardio & weight training equipment. Playgrounds. Multisports pitch. Tennis. Games & TV rooms. Bicycle & pedal-go-kart hire. Entertainment/excursions in high season. Free children's club for children from 4-12 years. Animal farm. Equestrian centre (seasonal). New playgrounds with zipline. WiFi zones (charged).

Key Features

 Pets Accepted

 Disabled Facilities

 Swimming Pool

 Play Area

 Bar/Restaurant

 Bike Hire

 Horse Riding

Scan me for more information.

Alan Rogers Code: FR17220
78 accommodations
111 pitches
GPS: 45.90415, -1.21525
Post Code: F-17480

Charente-Maritime, Poitou-Charentes

www.alanrogers.com/fr17220
info@camping-labrande.com
Tel: 05 46 47 62 37
www.camping-labrande.com

Open (Touring Pitches):
25 March - 3 November.

Camping la Brande

An environmentally friendly site, run and maintained to a high standard, la Brande offers an ideal holiday environment on the delightful Ile d'Oléron. It is situated on the oyster route and close to a sandy beach. Pitches here are generous and mostly separated by hedges and trees, the greater number for touring outfits. All are on level grassy terrain and have electricity hook-ups, some are fully serviced. Some of the most attractive pitches are in a newer section towards the back of the site. The many activities during the high season, plus the natural surroundings, make this an ideal choice for families.

Three clean sanitary blocks (one heated) have spacious, well equipped showers and washbasins (mainly in cabins). Baby facilities. Excellent facilities for disabled visitors. Private facilities (shower, basin and toilet) to rent. Laundry rooms. Motorcaravan services. Superb restaurant/takeaway and bar (July/Aug). Shop (July/Aug). Heated indoor swimming pool (all season). Jacuzzi. Sauna. Playground. Games room. Football field. Tennis. Minigolf. Fishing. Archery (high season). Bicycle hire. Canoe hire. Free WiFi on part of site. No charcoal barbecues. Kids' club. Lending library.

Key Features

 Pets Accepted

 Disabled Facilities

 Swimming Pool

 Play Area

 Bar/Restaurant

 Bike Hire

Scan me for more information.

Alan Rogers Code: FR17340
41 accommodations
157 pitches
GPS: 46.05480, -1.08340
Post Code: F-17340

Charente-Maritime, Poitou-Charentes

www.alanrogers.com/fr17340
contact@camping-port-punay.com
Tel: 05 17 81 00 00
www.camping-port-punay.com

Open (Touring Pitches):
4 May - 23 September

Camping Au Port-Punay

Campsite Au Port-Punay is a friendly and well run site located in Chatelaillon-Plage in the charming fishermen's village Les Boucholeurs, just 300m from the beach. The site is particularly good for families with small children. There are 157 touring pitches laid out on well trimmed grass, with many mature poplars and low shrubs on sunny or partly shaded pitches, or fully equipped rental accommodation. Campsite Au Port-Punay is about 3 hectares and offers you a quiet environment among plants and trees, but if you want hustle and bustle, take the bus 150m from campsite to the centre of La Rochelle, or visit the islands Ré, Oléron and Aix and of course cruise around the Fort Boyard. In 2018 the campsite celebrated its 54th anniversary.

One well maintained large toilet block with good facilities including washbasins in cubicles and large shower cubicles. Large shower and toilet for disabled people and a baby bathroom. Washing machines and dryer in a laundry room. Motorcaravan services. Shop (all season). Bar, restaurant and takeaway (09/06-09/09). Swimming pool (heated May-Sept). Fitness equipment. Games area. Play area. Bicycle hire. High Speed WiFi over site (free of charge).

Key Features

 Pets Accepted

 Disabled Facilities

 Swimming Pool

 Play Area

 Bar/Restaurant

 Bike Hire

Scan me for more information.

Alan Rogers Code: FR16060
3 accommodations
83 pitches
GPS: 45.79761, 0.06284
Post Code: F-16170

Charente, Poitou-Charentes

www.alanrogers.com/fr16060
info@marcodebignac.com
Tel: 05 45 21 78 41
www.marcodebignac.com

Open (Touring Pitches):
1 February - 30 November

Camping Marco de Bignac

The small village of Bignac is set in peaceful countryside not too far from the N10 road, north of Angoulême. This mature, British owned site is arranged alongside an attractive lake. Mature trees fringe the lake which is home to some impressive fish, including carp (fishing is free for guests). In the camping area, the trees are arranged formally to mark 83 touring pitches and three for mobile homes to rent. The pitches are level and offer a mixture of shade with a minimum size of 100 sq.m. Most have 3/6A electricity (long leads may be required). This site is popular and is a peaceful, relaxing location for couples or young families.

Two traditional style toilet blocks have functional, recently refurbished facilities, including those for disabled visitors. Washing machine. Bar and restaurant (April-Oct). Small shop (1/3-30/10). Swimming pool (July-Aug, unsupervised). Football, badminton, tennis, boules and fishing, all free. Library. Play area. Pets' corner. Entertainment in high season. A torch may be useful. Free WiFi at reception and the bar.

Key Features

 Open All Year

 Pets Accepted

 Disabled Facilities

 Swimming Pool

 Play Area

 Bar/Restaurant

 Bike Hire

 Fishing

Scan me for more information.

Alan Rogers Code: FR17600
195 accommodations
52 pitches
GPS: 45.96807, -1.24456
Post Code: F-17190

Charente-Maritime, Poitou-Charentes

www.alanrogers.com/fr17600
contact@camp-atlantique.com
Tel: 02 51 20 41 94
www.campingsignol.co.uk

Open (Touring Pitches):
2 April - 24 September.

Camping Signol

Occupying an eight-hectare site just 800 metres from the sandy beaches, and a short walk from the little port of Boyardville, this campsite has plenty to offer. Of the 340 pitches, just 52 are for touring, set amongst high pine trees, some occupying hillocks, others tucked away among mobile homes. The pitches vary in size and access to some is tight making them unsuitable for larger units. Levelling blocks may be required. Electricity (6A) is available to all, although long leads are sometimes required. There may be a short walk to the water supply.

Three traditional, fully equipped toilet blocks provide washbasins in cubicles and preset showers. Basic facilities for disabled campers and for children. Laundry. Motorcaravan services. Shop, bar/snack bar, takeaway (all season). Two heated swimming pools (indoor all season with sauna, steam room and fitness room; outdoor from 2/4). Massage and beauty parlour. Enclosed play area with seats for parents. Children's club (3-12 yrs, July/Aug). Boules. Evening entertainment (all season). WiFi over site (charged). Gas barbecues only on pitches. Mobile homes and chalets available to rent. Max. 1 dog.

Key Features

 Pets Accepted

 Disabled Facilities

 Swimming Pool

 Play Area

 Bar/Restaurant

 Bike Hire

Scan me for
more information.

Alan Rogers Code: FR86050
78 accommodations
200 pitches
GPS: 46.79965, 0.80945
Post Code: F-86270

Vienne, Poitou-Charentes

www.alanrogers.com/fr86050
info@larocheposay-vacances.com
Tel: 05 49 86 21 23
www.larocheposay-vacances.com

Open (Touring Pitches):
2 April - 24 September.

La Roche Posay

Camping la Roche Posay is set in eight hectares and has direct access to the Creuse river on which fishing and canoes are popular. There are 200 pitches, of which 78 are used for mobile homes to rent. Access around the site is good for larger units. The pitches are all large and 10A electricity is available. This is a good, well run site in very natural surroundings. There is a sense of spaciousness where you can relax in a convivial atmosphere. Many different types of trees offer a mix of shade and the site is pleasantly landscaped.

Two fully equipped, heated toilet blocks, one in each section. Excellent facilities for disabled visitors and children. Bar and takeaway (all season). Snack bar (July/Aug). Outdoor swimming pool with toboggan (May-Sept). Heated, covered swimming and paddling pools. Play area. Games room. Fishing. Canoes. Boules. Riding. Bicycle hire. Entertainment in high season. Free shuttle bus to town. WiFi (free in bar).

Key Features

 Pets Accepted

 Disabled Facilities

 Swimming Pool

 Play Area

 Bar/Restaurant

 Bike Hire

 Fishing

 Horse Riding

Scan me for
more information.

Alan Rogers Code: FR58040
18 accommodations
63 pitches
GPS: 47.00587, 3.90548
Post Code: F-58120

Nièvre, Burgundy

www.alanrogers.com/fr58040
info@campingfougeraie.fr
Tel: 03 86 85 11 85
www.campingfougeraie.com

Open (Touring Pitches):
28 March - 3 October.

L'Etang de la Fougeraie

This is a tranquil and spacious campsite laid out on a hillside deep in the Parc Naturel Régional du Morvan, with views over their lake, across the valley and surrounding hills. The spring water lake is ideal for fishing and swimming. There is a small bar and restaurant serving good quality regional meals and a well-stocked shop with local produce. There are 81 terraced pitches, with 63 for touring, 58 with electricity (10/16A). Recent renovations have included redesigned, level pitches overlooking the lake, fewer steep paths, a new heated, outdoor pool and heated sanitary block. L'Etang de la Fougeraie is a place where you can sit back and relax after a day exploring the surrounding peaceful countryside lying within the Parc du Morvan.

Heated sanitary block with family/disabled room close to entrance, but a fair distance uphill from the lower pitches. Washing machine and dryer. Shop, bar, restaurant and takeaway, heated outdoor pool (all season). Lake swimming. Fishing. Playgrounds. Paintball. Bicycle hire. Caravan storage. American RVs and twin-axle units not accepted. Chalets for rent with TV and DVD player. WiFi (free).

Key Features

 Pets Accepted

 Disabled Facilities

 Swimming Pool

 Play Area

 Bar/Restaurant

 Bike Hire

 Fishing

Scan me for more information.

Alan Rogers Code: FR71180
4 accommodations
85 pitches
GPS: 46.47973, 3.96755
Post Code: F-71160

Saône-et-Loire, Burgundy

www.alanrogers.com/fr71180
info@lachevrette.com
Tel: 03 85 53 11 49
www.lachevrette.com

Open (Touring Pitches):
1 April - 8 October.

Camping la Chevrette

This pretty town site has been leased from the municipality for some years by an enthusiastic, friendly couple. There are 85 neat and tidy pitches which are separated by hedges and flowers decorate the site. The level pitches include 71 with electricity (10A) for touring units and 50 for tents. There are four chalets to rent. At the far end of the site there is a slipway onto the River Loire and it is this aspect that attracts campers with canoes. The site also has its own canoes for hire and include free transfers. Situated on the route of the Voie Verte cycle path, which runs along the Canal du Centre, this is a popular destination for walkers and cyclists.

Four small toilet blocks, one with cold water only, each provide separate facilities for men and women and some washbasins in cabins. Facilities for disabled visitors. Washing machine and dryer in one block. Small restaurant/snack bar and takeaway (all July/Aug). Bread to order. Heated outdoor pool (1/5-7/9). Club room/library with TV for bad weather. Canoe hire and transfers. Fishing and boat launching. Free WiFi over part of site.

Key Features

 Pets Accepted

 Disabled Facilities

 Swimming Pool

 Play Area

 Bar/Restaurant

 Fishing

Scan me for
more information.

Alan Rogers Code: FR21080
9 accommodations
149 pitches
GPS: 46.90718, 4.68560
Post Code: F-21590

Côte d`Or, Burgundy

www.alanrogers.com/fr21080
camping.santenay@aquadis-loisirs.
com
Tel: 03 80 20 66 55
www.aquadis-loisirs.com/en

Open (Touring Pitches):
8 April - 27 October

Camping des Sources

Santenay lies in the heart of the Côte de Beaune, a region renowned for its wine and châteaux, and within easy reach of Beaune. This is a peaceful place to unwind after a day's sightseeing or wine tasting. It is near a long distance cycle and walking track and next to the village sports and leisure area with free access to the swimming pool and paddling pool (1/6-31/8; token from reception). There are 149 comfortable level grassy touring pitches (from 90 to 150 sq. m.) delineated by a variety of trees offering some shade and all with 6A electricity. Twin-axle caravans are not accepted. This pleasant site provides a good base for those wishing to tour this interesting region. There are no organised activities on site, so it will appeal to those happy to make their own entertainment.

The modern, well equipped and very clean toilet block includes facilities for disabled visitors. Motorcaravan services. Laundry facilities. Gas supplies. Shop (15/5-31/8). Games room. Playground. Playing field. Minigolf. Boules. Volleyball. Six new mobile homes for hire. Internet point and WiFi.

Key Features

 Pets Accepted

 Disabled Facilities

 Swimming Pool

 Play Area

Scan me for
more information.

Alan Rogers Code: FR39020
48 accommodations
131 pitches
GPS: 46.52260, 5.67380
Post Code: F-39270

Jura, Franche-Comté

www.alanrogers.com/fr39020
info@camping-surchauffant.fr
Tel: 03 84 25 41 08
www.camping-surchauffant.fr

Open (Touring Pitches):
27 April - 17 September.

Domaine de Surchauffant

In the heart of the Jura lake district, Domaine de Surchauffant is pleasantly situated above the beaches bordering the Lac de Vouglans, which can be reached quickly on foot directly from the site. With only 203 pitches, this site may appeal to those who prefer a more informal atmosphere, however it can be lively in high season. The 131 touring pitches are of a reasonable size and are informally arranged, some are fully serviced and most have electricity (10A). They are divided by hedges and there is some shade. You can also choose to stay in one of their 24 mobile homes or 24 chalets. The lake offers a variety of watersports activities, boat trips, etc. and is used for fishing and swimming (guarded in high season as it shelves steeply).

The sanitary facilities are older in style and are adequate rather than luxurious, but are reasonably well maintained and were clean when we visited. They include some washbasins in private cabins. Modern laundry. Heated swimming pool (200 sq.m) and paddling pool. Two playgrounds. Table tennis. Entertainment (July/Aug). TV room. Small library. Grocers for basic needs and a snack bar opposite campsite. Two restaurants (1 with view over the lake) are located just 200 metres from the campsite. Bicycle hire. Safety deposit boxes.

Key Features

 Pets Accepted

 Disabled Facilities

 Swimming Pool

 Play Area

 Bar/Restaurant

 Skiing

 Bike Hire

Scan me for more information.

Alan Rogers Code: FR39030
189 accommodations
700 pitches
GPS: 46.66435, 5.81315
Post Code: F-39130

Jura, Franche-Comté

www.alanrogers.com/fr39030
chalain@chalain.com
Tel: 03 84 25 78 78
www.chalain.com

Open (Touring Pitches):
26 April - 16 September

Domaine de Chalain

In the unspoilt surroundings of the Jura, in 75 acres of wooded parkland surrounded by cliffs and forests, the Domaine de Chalain offers the perfect combination of relaxation, fun and discovery. On the shores of lake Chalain, this lovely site has a wide range of accommodation options - camping pitches (455 with electricity), mobile homes, bungalows or chalets. With a comprehensive range of leisure activities for children and adults, it's a great family option. There are swimming opportunities and water sports in the lake or Les Lagons aqua park. Indoors there is a heated paddling pool and swimming pool, together with a wellness area with sauna, jacuzzi (over 18s only) and hammam. Outdoors you'll find another paddling pool and swimming pools with water games, jacuzzi, waterslides, multi-lane slides and waterfalls.

The sanitary blocks are well equipped with showers, private washing cubicles and facilities for babies. Additional facilities include The "Le Cottage" restaurant, takeaway, ice-cream vendor, bar, bakery, grocery store, launderette, sports and camping shop which are all located in the heart of the park. At the reception, you will also find all the practical and tourist information you need for your stay, as well as safe hire, Internet terminals, a WiFi hotspot (also available on the campsite for an extra charge) and a cash machine.

Key Features

 Pets Accepted

 Disabled Facilities

 Swimming Pool

 Play Area

 Bar/Restaurant

 Bike Hire

 Fishing

 Sailing

Scan me for more information.

Alan Rogers Code: FR39010
30 accommodations
171 pitches
GPS: 47.00284, 5.66300
Post Code: F-39380

Jura, Franche-Comté

www.alanrogers.com/fr39010
plageblanche@huttopia.com
Tel: 03 84 37 69 63
europe.huttopia.com/en/site/la-plage-blanche

Open (Touring Pitches):
27 April - 25 September.

La Plage Blanche

Huttopia La Plage Blanche is located in the Jura, by the rippling waters of the River Loue. This spacious eight-hectare site has 218 pitches (171 for touring, 40 of these on the riverbank). All are large, grassy and level with 10A electricity (Europlugs). This is a great site for family holidays with its children's activities and themed evenings in the bar/restaurant (DJ or live music) in high season. Other activities include kayaking, canoeing, fishing, fly fishing and woodland walks in the site's own wood. A number of distinctive safari style tents are available to rent.

Three sanitary blocks include showers, washbasins in cabins and facilities for babies and disabled campers. Launderette. Motorcaravan service area. Shop with basics. Bar/snack bar/pizzeria with terrace. Takeaway. Heated swimming and paddling pools (all season). Adults only spa with small pool, jacuzzi and sauna. Play area. Entertainment and activities for children and families. TV room. Library. Volleyball. Boules. River fishing and fishing lake. Woodland walks. Canoeing. WiFi (free).

Key Features

 Pets Accepted

 Disabled Facilities

 Swimming Pool

 Play Area

 Bar/Restaurant

 Fishing

Scan me for more information.

France

Alan Rogers Code: FR19100
72 accommodations
99 pitches
GPS: 45.07530, 1.91699
Post Code: F-19400

Corrèze, Limousin

www.alanrogers.com/fr19100
info@dordogne-soleil.com
Tel: 05 55 28 84 84
www.campingsoleildoc.com

Open (Touring Pitches):
19 April - 15 November.

Camping Au Soleil d'Oc

You will be assured of a very warm welcome, throughout the long season, at this attractive family run site set amongst a variety of tall trees on the banks of the River Dordogne. The large, level, grass pitches, 99 for touring units, all with electricity (6A, Europlug), are mostly separated by neatly trimmed shrubs and hedges. They are set out on two levels; the lower level nearer the river, with fewer static pitches, being some distance from the toilet facilities and sports area. This site should appeal to lovers of watersports and other activities, particularly in July and August when there is plenty to do for all the family.

Two unisex toilet blocks offer all the facilities one would expect. Baby facilities. Motorcaravan services. Shop (July/Aug). Bar (1/7-30/9). Restaurant and takeaway (1/6-30/9). Outdoor pool (15/6-15/10). Indoor pool (19/4-31/10). Swimming in the Dordogne. Canoe hire and organised trips. Volleyball. Football. Pool table and electronic games. Archery. Minigolf. Fishing. Bicycle hire. Guided walks and bike rides. Entertainment programme (July/Aug). WiFi. Torches useful.

Key Features

 Pets Accepted

 Disabled Facilities

 Swimming Pool

 Play Area

 Bar/Restaurant

 Bike Hire

 Fishing

Scan me for more information.

Alan Rogers Code: FR23010
28 accommodations
116 pitches
GPS: 46.37243, 2.20268
Post Code: F-23600

Creuse, Limousin

www.alanrogers.com/fr23010
info.camping-de.poinsouze@
orange.fr
Tel: 05 55 65 02 21
www.camping-de-poinsouze.com

Open (Touring Pitches):
13 May - 13 September.

Le Château de Poinsouz

Le Château de Poinsouze is a well established site arranged on an open, gently sloping, grassy park with views over a small lake and château. It is an attractive, well maintained, high quality site situated in the unspoilt Limousin region. The 116 very large, grassy touring pitches, some with lake frontage, all have electricity (6-20A Europlug), water and drainage and 68 have sewerage connections. The site has a friendly, family atmosphere with many organised activities in main season including a children's club. There are marked walks around the park and woods. All facilities are open all season.

High quality sanitary unit includes suites for disabled visitors. Washing machines and dryers. Motorcaravan services. Shop for basics. Takeaway. Bar and restaurant. Swimming pool, slide, children's pool and new water play area with fountains. Fenced playground. Pétanque. Bicycle hire. Free fishing in the lake, boats and lifejackets can be hired. Sports facilities. Accommodation to rent. WiFi over site (charged). No dogs in high season (14/7-18/8).

Key Features

 Pets Accepted

 Disabled Facilities

 Swimming Pool

 Play Area

 Bar/Restaurant

 Bike Hire

 Fishing

 Sailing

Scan me for more information.

Alan Rogers Code: FR23060
26 pitches
GPS: 45.94720, 1.81260
Post Code: F-23250

Creuse, Limousin

www.alanrogers.com/fr23060
les4saisons0314@orange.fr
Tel: 05 55 64 23 35
www.les-4-saisons.com

Open (Touring Pitches):
All year.

Les Quatre Saisons

Les Quatre Saisons is a small, quiet and rural British owned campsite in the Creuse. The site is open all year round and has been laid out on a large sloping, grassy field without roads or footpaths making movement around the site rather difficult, especially in wet weather. There are 26 undelineated pitches scattered around the site, all with electricity, some having shade. There is another large grassy area for recreation. Access to the site involves a tight turn up into the site from a narrow road and is not suitable for large outfits.

Fully tiled, small shower block with provision for disabled visitors. Washing machine. Homemade bread, preserves and home-grown vegetables for sale. Breakfast service and evening meals available at the farmhouse. Play area. Recreation field. Rooms in main house to rent. WiFi on most of site. Dogs are accepted by prior arrangement.

Key Features

 Open All Year

 Disabled Facilities

 Play Area

Scan me for more information.

Le Pont d'Allagnon

Alan Rogers Code: FR43240
16 accommodations
60 pitches
GPS: 45.38699, 3.26608
Post Code: F-43410

Haute-Loire, Auvergne

www.alanrogers.com/fr43240
centre.auvergne.camping@orange.fr
Tel: 04 71 76 53 69
www.campingenauvergne.com

Open (Touring Pitches):
28 March - 19 October.

Camping le Pont d'Allagnon is a popular and friendly municipal site which is very well run and managed. There are 60 pitches (52 with 10A electricity for tourers) set mainly in rows with shade from mature trees and separated by hedges. The outdoor swimming pool is heated and is open only to campers, while other leisure facilities such as beach volleyball/football, minigolf and boules are shared with the village. This is a tranquil site with a convivial bar/snack terrace. No entertainment is provided though the pleasant village is only 50 metres away with easy access by a footbridge over the river.

Clean sanitary block with separate room for families and disabled visitors. Heated baby room. Small laundry. Motorcaravan services. Bar/snack bar with terrace. Heated swimming pool with disabled access (13/6-15/9). Beach volleyball/football pitch. Basketball. Boules. Fishing in river. Playground. Free WiFi on part of site. Communal barbecue. Chalets to rent. Max. 1 dog.

Key Features

 Pets Accepted

 Disabled Facilities

 Swimming Pool

 Play Area

 Bar/Restaurant

 Skiing

 Fishing

Scan me for more information.

Alan Rogers Code: FR63030
175 accommodations
60 pitches
GPS: 45.56900, 2.94043
Post Code: F-63790

Puy-de-Dôme, Auvergne

www.alanrogers.com/fr63030
contact@camping-europe-murol.com
Tel: 04 73 88 60 46
www.camping-europe-murol.com

Open (Touring Pitches):
26 April - 01 September

Camping l'Europe

L'Europe is, in high season, a lively site, dominated by its mobile homes, on the edge of the little town of Murol. The site is 800 m. from the Lac de Chambon which has a sandy beach and range of watersports. There are 215 level grassy pitches, 60 for touring, all with 10A electricity, water and drainage; they are of a good size with reasonable shade. It has a busy activities programme including evening entertainment. The bar/restaurant overlooks the pool complex and is the site's focal point and entertainment centre. The surrounding area offers many walking and cycling opportunities, and the site organises a number of popular excursions.

Sanitary facilities include washbasins in cabins, showers and provision for disabled visitors. Laundry facilities. Bar, restaurant and takeaway (7/7-28/8). Swimming pool with toboggan and paddling pool (26/4-01/9). Tennis. Archery. Boules. Football. Aquagym. Water polo. Play area and large sports area. WiFi throughout (charged).

Key Features

 Pets Accepted

 Disabled Facilities

 Swimming Pool

 Play Area

 Bar/Restaurant

 Bike Hire

Scan me for more information.

Alan Rogers Code: FR43060
29 accommodations
79 pitches
GPS: 45.12017, 3.79367
Post Code: F-43350

Haute-Loire, Auvergne

Camping Rochelambert

www.alanrogers.com/fr43060
infos@camping-rochelambert.com
Tel: 04 71 00 54 02
www.camping-rochelambert.com

Open (Touring Pitches):
1 April - 30 September.

Flower Camping de la Rochelambert is an attractive and welcoming site can be found in the heart of Auvergne. Extending over four hectares, it is located at the foot of the Château de la Rochelambert and is bordered by a river and a wooded nature trail. There are 79 large pitches here (120 sq.m), mostly well shaded and equipped with 16A electricity. Twelve riverside pitches (no electricity) are perfect for anglers, and the site has a special hut for storing tackle and bait. A number of good quality timber chalets are for rent. The emphasis here is on peace and tranquillity in an idyllic natural setting, and for this reason, the site is run along very environmentally friendly lines.

Key Features

 Pets Accepted

 Disabled Facilities

 Swimming Pool

 Play Area

 Bar/Restaurant

 Fishing

Two well positioned toilet blocks (one heated) are well maintained and kept clean. Baby room. Excellent room for disabled visitors. Modern motorcaravan services. Small shop for basic needs, pleasant bar and terrace (all season). Snack bar/takeaway serving pizza and regional specialities (1/7-30/8). Swimming and paddling pools (1/6-15/9). Sauna (charged). Fishing with chalet for preparation and freezing. Tennis. Archery. Boules. Play area. Entertainment and activity programme (during school holidays). Wooden chalets and two roulottes to rent. WiFi (free).

Scan me for more information.

Alan Rogers Code: FR07110
336 accommodations
137 pitches
GPS: 44.57250, 4.51115
Post Code: F-07170

Ardèche, Rhône Alpes

www.alanrogers.com/fr07110
lepommier@cielavillage.com
Tel: +33 (0)4 75 94 82 81
www.campinglepommier.com

Open (Touring Pitches):
13 April - 10 September

Domaine le Pommier

Domaine le Pommier is an extremely spacious, first class site of ten hectares in 32 hectares of wooded grounds centred around a spectacular pirate themed water park. The site is steeply terraced and has wonderful views over the Ardèche mountains and beyond. Of the 611 pitches, 137 are for touring units, the rest used for a variety of mobile homes and chalets to rent. They are on flat, sandy grass, of a good size and well spaced. Separated by trees and hedges, some have less shade. All have shade and access to electricity and water and all facilities are of a very high standard. The site is not recommended for very large units.

Four excellent toilet blocks, one with underfloor heating, provide all the necessary facilities. Comprehensive shop. Bar/restaurant. Aquapark with exciting slides, paddling pools, etc. Everything opens all season. Boules. Minigolf. Large multi-sports area. Activities for all the family including zip-lining, water polo and kids clubs. Very extensive programme of events on and off site. Entertainment programme in French, English and Dutch. WiFi (charged).

Key Features

 Pets Accepted

 Disabled Facilities

 Swimming Pool

 Play Area

 Bar/Restaurant

Scan me for
more information.

Alan Rogers Code: FR07120
24 accommodations
220 pitches
GPS: 44.39804, 4.39878
Post Code: F-07150

Ardèche, Rhône Alpes

www.alanrogers.com/fr07120
info@ardechois-camping.com
Tel: 04 75 88 06 63
www.ardechois-camping.com

Open (Touring Pitches):
6 April - 12 October

Nature Parc l'Ardéchois

Camping Nature Parc l'Ardéchois is a very high quality, family run site within walking distance of Vallon-Pont-d'Arc. It borders the River Ardèche and canoe trips are run, professionally, direct from the site. This campsite is ideal for families with younger children seeking an active holiday. The facilities are comprehensive and the central toilet unit is of an extremely high standard. Of the 250 pitches, there are 225 for touring units, separated by trees and individual shrubs. All have electrical connections (6/10A) and with an additional charge, 125 larger pitches have full services (22 include a fridge, patio furniture, hammock and free WiFi). Forming a focal point are the bar and restaurant (excellent menus) with an attractive terrace and a takeaway service. A member of Leading Campings group.

Two very well equipped toilet blocks, one superb with everything working automatically. Facilities are of the highest standard, very clean and include good facilities for babies, children and disabled visitors. Laundry facilities. Four private bathrooms to hire. Well stocked shop. Excellent restaurant, bar and takeaway. Heated swimming pool and paddling pool (no Bermuda shorts). Wellness area with sauna, hammam, jacuzzi and 4 seasons-shower. Different types of massage and treatments. Yoga. Gym. Tennis. Very good play area. Organised activities, canoe trips. Bicycle hire. Only gas barbecues are permitted. Communal barbecue area. WiFi throughout (charged).

Key Features

 Pets Accepted

 Disabled Facilities

 Swimming Pool

 Play Area

 Bar/Restaurant

 Bike Hire

 Fishing

Scan me for more information.

Alan Rogers Code: FR07310
38 accommodations
97 pitches
GPS: 44.40547, 4.37916
Post Code: F-07150

Ardèche, Rhône Alpes

www.alanrogers.com/fr07310
roubine.ardeche@wanadoo.fr
Tel: 04 75 88 04 56
www.camping-roubine.com

Open (Touring Pitches):
14 April - 9 September

Camping la Roubine

This site on the bank of the Ardèche has been in the same family ownership for over 30 years. During this time there has been constant upgrading and it must now be considered one of the best sites in the area. There are 97 touring pitches, all with electricity (10A) and quite spacious. Well tended grass, trimmed hedging and mature trees and smart tarmac roads create a calm and well kept atmosphere. The proprietors, M. Moulin and Mme. Van Eck like to welcome their guests and are available to help during the day – they are rightly proud of their well run campsite.

Several small sanitary blocks include washbasins in cubicles and showers. The main toilet block has showers, washbasins in vanity units, a baby bathroom, 2 childrens' bathrooms and facilities for disabled visitors. Laundry. Swimming pools, paddling pool and separate children's pool. Spa with sauna, Jacuzzi, massages and beauty treatments . Tennis. Boules, Fishing. Barbecues only permitted on communal sites. River beach. WiFi throughout (charged).

Key Features

 Pets Accepted

 Disabled Facilities

 Swimming Pool

 Play Area

 Bar/Restaurant

 Fishing

Scan me for more information.

Alan Rogers Code: FR07630
420 pitches
GPS: 44.44470, 4.36630
Post Code: F-07120

Ardèche, Rhône Alpes

Aluna Vacances

www.alanrogers.com/fr07630
contact@alunavacances.fr
Tel: 04 75 93 93 15
www.alunavacances.fr

Open (Touring Pitches):
5 April - 4 November

Nestled on the doorstep of the Ardèche Gorges, surrounded by nature and outdoor pursuits of all varieties; energetic ones such as rafting, cycling and swimming, and relaxing ones like walking, picnicking and exploring nature, camping at Sunêlia Aluna Vacances has something for all the family. This leafy site prides itself on its large 'closer to nature' pitches set on grass, some with hardstanding, measuring 100 to 120 sq.m. Electricity (10A) is available and there are four sanitary blocks throughout the site. There is rental accommodation on site as well as a new water park, both indoor and outdoor pools with many slides, a large restaurant with a terrace and bar, kid's club, a grocery store and a spa. Many sports are available during high season; football, tennis, volleyball, badminton, basketball, table tennis, jeu-de-boules, aquagym and dance, plus an outdoor fitness area.

Key Features

 Pets Accepted

 Disabled Facilities

 Swimming Pool

 Play Area

 Bar/Restaurant

Four sanitary blocks are equipped with showers, private washing cubicles and facilities for babies and disabled guests. Washing machines and dryers. Well stocked shop. Bar with TV. Restaurant and takeaway. Waterpark with heated outdoor pools, indoor pool and slides. Sports and kid's club (seasonal). Tennis & Volleyball court. Table tennis. Boules. Multisports field. Playground. Entertainment programmes. Some off site activities bookable on site (cycling, horse riding, canoeing). WiFi (extra charge).

Scan me for more information.

Alan Rogers Code: FR07410
30 accommodations
134 pitches
GPS: 44.43119, 4.32959
Post Code: F-07120

Ardèche, Rhône Alpes

www.alanrogers.com/fr07410
camping@chapouliere.com
Tel: 04 75 39 64 98
www.lachapouliere.com

Open (Touring Pitches):
24 March - 4 November

Camping la Chapoulière

Camping la Chapoulière is a medium sized site, alongside the Ardèche river, some two kilometres south of Ruoms. Grassy banks allow easy access to the river with a deeper area for bathing. The site is in two areas: the upper level, above the pool, has chalets and touring pitches; the older, more established area is for touring pitches nearer the river, with some chalets/mobile homes close to the restaurant. Trees provide dappled shade. There are 134 fairly level touring pitches (no hedges) on sand and grass, all with 6/8A electricity. This site is a good choice for those who prefer to make their own entertainment, and many visitors return year after year, creating a lively community and a sociable atmosphere.

Modern and adequate sanitary blocks. Facilities for babies and disabled visitors in main block. Preset hot showers and some washbasins in cabins. Washing machine. Shop (June/Aug), bread to order all season. Bar (April-Sept). Restaurant (July/Aug and w/ends). Pizza takeaway. Heated swimming pool. Spa and fitness centre with Hammam and massage. Play area. Games room with large TV screen. Organised activities (July/Aug). Riding trips. River bathing. Fishing. Canoe trips. WiFi on most of site (free).

Key Features

 Pets Accepted

 Disabled Facilities

 Swimming Pool

 Play Area

 Bar/Restaurant

 Fishing

Scan me for more information.

Alan Rogers Code: FR07050
307 accommodations
50 pitches
GPS: 44.41410, 4.27290
Post Code: F-07120

Ardèche, Rhône Alpes

www.alanrogers.com/fr07050
contact@rancdavaine.fr
Tel: 04 75 39 60 55
www.camping-ranc-davaine.fr

Open (Touring Pitches):
12 April - 23 September

Sunêlia Le Ranc Davaine

Sunêlia Le Ranc Davaine is a large, busy, family oriented site with direct access to the River Chassezac. There are approximately 500 pitches with 50 for touring, all with electricity (10/16A) for which very long leads are required (some may cross roads). Most pitches are scattered between static caravan and tour operator pitches on fairly flat, stony ground under a variety of trees, some of which are quite low giving much needed shade. The site can get very busy for much of the season. A lively entertainment programme is aimed at young children and teenagers with an enclosed disco three nights a week until 03.00.

Three fully equipped sanitary blocks, very clean and modern include facilities for people with reduced mobility. Washing machines and dryers. Large shop. Internet access. Bar/restaurant, pizzeria, takeaway. Indoor swimming pool (heated), pools for relaxation and swimming, water slide and water park (all facilities all season, no shorts allowed). Large playground. Tennis. Fishing nearby. Extensive entertainment programme (Jul/Aug). Discos. Fitness area. Free WiFi on part of the site.

Key Features

 Pets Accepted

 Disabled Facilities

 Swimming Pool

 Play Area

 Bar/Restaurant

Scan me for more information.

Alan Rogers Code: FR07540
73 accommodations
127 pitches
GPS: 44.42900, 4.33208
Post Code: F-07120

Ardèche, Rhône Alpes

www.alanrogers.com/fr07540
grandterre@wanadoo.fr
Tel: 04 75 39 64 94
www.campinglagrandterre.com

Open (Touring Pitches):
6 April - 9 September

Camping la Grand Terre

La Grand'Terre is a large campsite offering a comprehensive range of facilities for its visitors. It has 296 pitches (127 for tourers) which are set out in back-to-back rows with plenty of shade. One camping area is particularly shaded. A large modern building housing reception, and the bar/restaurant area is located at the front of the site with an attractive pool complex immediately to the rear. The large parking area at the entrance makes check-in and departure easy. Large outfits may find access to some of the pitches difficult (some narrow roads and overhanging branches) so arrive early in high season.

Key Features

 Disabled Facilities

 Swimming Pool

 Bar/Restaurant

 Bike Hire

Fishing

Four sanitary blocks offer reasonable facilities, but perhaps a long walk from a few locations. Water points are limited. Laundry. Ironing service. Shop (from 06 Apr). Bar (from 06 Apr). Restaurant and fast food service (from 6 Apr). Two heated outdoor pools, 2 waterslides, Jacuzzi and aqua games (06/04 - 09/09). Playground. Tennis. Petanque. TV and games room. Outdoor cinema. Internet access. Gas. Bike rental. Fishing. Charcoal barbecues are not allowed. Useful torches in some areas.

Scan me for more information.

Alan Rogers Code: FR07660
56 accommodations
GPS: 44.43415, 4.41099
Post Code: F-07150

Ardèche, Rhône Alpes

www.alanrogers.com/fr07660
domainedesevenier@orange.fr
Tel: 04 75 88 29 44
www.sevenier.net

Open (Touring Pitches):
30 March - 4 November.

Domaine de Sévenier

Le Domaine de Sévenier is a modern, high quality chalet complex enjoying a hilltop location with fine panoramic views over the surrounding garrigue, a unique mix of oak trees, juniper, rosemary and thyme. There are no touring pitches at this site. Located 4 km. from Vallon-Pont-d'Arc and 800 m. from the pretty village of Lagorce, the domaine is an old winery which has been sensitively converted and offers accommodation in well appointed wooden chalets serving the needs of families, both large and small. Rest and relaxation is the theme here and the restaurant has a good reputation. On-site amenities include a swimming pool and a separate children's pool. The site has links to Nature Parc Camping de l'Ardèche and guests are welcome to enjoy the camping site's evening entertainment.

The sanitary block includes hot showers and provision has been made for disabled visitors. Washing machine. Shop. Bar. Restaurant. Outdoor heated swimming pool. Paddling pool. Activity programme. Play area. Minigolf. Bicycle hire. Fully equipped chalets to rent.

Key Features

 Pets Accepted

 Disabled Facilities

 Swimming Pool

 Play Area

 Bar/Restaurant

 Bike Hire

Scan me for
more information.

Alan Rogers Code: FR73020
18 accommodations
135 pitches
GPS: 45.62248, 6.78475
Post Code: F-73700

Savoie, Rhône Alpes

www.alanrogers.com/fr73020
bourgsaintmaurice@huttopia.com
Tel: 04 79 07 03 45
europe.huttopia.com/en/site/bourg-st-maurice

Open (Touring Pitches):
19 May - 16 October.

Camping Bourg St-Maurice

Huttopia Bourg-Saint-Maurice is on a small, level plain at an altitude of 830 m. on the River Isère, surrounded by mountains and attracts visitors all year round (except for a short time when they close). The site's 153 unseparated, flat pitches (135 for touring) are marked by numbers on the tarmac roads and all have electrical connections (10A). Most are on grass but some are on tarmac hardstanding making them ideal for use by motorcaravans or in winter. Trees give shade in most parts, although some pitches have almost none. Duckboards are provided for snow and wet weather. Formerly known as Camping le Versoyen, this is a good base for winter skiing, summer walking, climbing, rafting or canoeing, or for car excursions.

Two well maintained toilet blocks can be heated and have British and Turkish style WCs. No facilities for disabled visitors. Laundry. Motorcaravan service facilities. No shop but bread available to order. Heated rest room with TV. Small bar with takeaway in summer. Play area. Free shuttle in high season to funicular railway. Free WiFi in central lodge.

Key Features

 Pets Accepted

 Play Area

 Bar/Restaurant

 Skiing

Scan me for more information.

Alan Rogers Code: FR33370
308 accommodations
449 pitches
GPS: 45.36348, -1.14575
Post Code: F-33930

Gironde, Aquitaine

www.alanrogers.com/fr33370
infos@chm-montalivet.com
Tel: 05 33 092 092
www.chm-montalivet.com

Open (Touring Pitches):
31 March - 27 October

Naturist Montalivet

This is a very large naturist village with everything that you could need during your holiday without leaving the site. It has direct access to the ocean with its own beautiful, golden sandy beaches with coastguard surveillance in high season. Watersports are numerous with lessons if you require. The main emphasis here is to keep the family entertained. There are 3,081 pitches, of which 449 are for touring. Pitches are level, on grass or sand and mature trees provide shade in some areas. Diving, dancing classes and surfing are just some of the activities organised here.

Numerous sanitary blocks with facilities for disabled visitors. Launderette. Motorcaravan services. Shops, restaurants and bars (all 31/03-27/10). Two swimming pool complexes (31/03-05/10) with slides and toboggan (16/06-16/09). Children's clubs. Evening entertainment. Playgrounds. Sports grounds. TV rooms and cinema. Large library. Wellness centre offering numerous treatments and massage as well as saunas and jacuzzi. Bicycle hire. Fishing. WiFi throughout(charged). Max. 1 dog.

Key Features

 Naturist Site

 Pets Accepted

 Disabled Facilities

 Beach Access

 Swimming Pool

 Play Area

 Bar/Restaurant

Bike Hire

Scan me for more information.

153

Alan Rogers Code: FR33110
252 accommodations
618 pitches
GPS: 45.22372, -1.16318
Post Code: F-33990

Gironde, Aquitaine

www.alanrogers.com/fr33110
info@cca33.com
Tel: 05 56 09 10 25
www.cca33.com

Open (Touring Pitches):
11 May - 15 September

La Côte d'Argent

Camping de la Côte d'Argent is a large, well equipped site for leisurely family holidays. It makes an ideal base for walkers and cyclists with over 100 km. of cycle lanes in the area. Hourtin-Plage is a pleasant invigorating resort on the Atlantic coast and a popular location for watersports enthusiasts. The site's top attraction is its pool complex, where wooden bridges connect the pools and islands and there are sunbathing and play areas plus an indoor heated pool. The site has 618 touring pitches (all with 10A electricity), not always clearly defined, arranged under trees with some on sand. High quality entertainment takes place at the impressive bar/restaurant near the entrance.

Very clean sanitary blocks include provision for disabled visitors. Washing machines. Motorcaravan services. Grocery store, restaurant, takeaway, pizzeria and bar. Four outdoor pools with slides and flumes (1/6-14/9). Indoor pool (all season). Fitness room. Massage (Institut de Beauté). Tennis. Multisport area. Beach volleyball. Pétanque. Play areas. Miniclub, fitness and organised entertainment in high season. Bicycle hire. WiFi partial site (charged). Charcoal barbecues are not permitted. Hotel (12 rooms).

Key Features

 Pets Accepted

 Disabled Facilities

 Swimming Pool

 Play Area

 Bar/Restaurant

 Bike Hire

Scan me for more information.

Alan Rogers Code: FR33460
533 accommodations
820 pitches
GPS: 44.73439, -1.19598
Post Code: F-33950

Gironde, Aquitaine

www.alanrogers.com/fr33460
reception@lesviviers.com
Tel: 05 56 60 70 04
www.lesviviers.com

Open (Touring Pitches):
30 March - 15 September

Camping les Viviers

Les Viviers is a large family site on the Lège-Cap-Ferret peninsula. There pitches are dispersed around a 33-hectare wood, 400 of which are occupied by mobile homes and chalets. The site borders the Bassin d'Arcachon and is 5 km. from the nearest Atlantic beach. Pitches are well shaded and of a good size. Most have electrical connections. A large range of amenities are on offer, including a well stocked supermarket, restaurant, pizzeria and a twice weekly street market. A lively activity and entertainment programme is on offer in peak season.

Toilet blocks have free preset showers and facilities for children and disabled visitors. Laundry rooms. Private lake and its private beach. Direct access to the Bassin d'Arcachon by the beach. Supermarket (open all the season). Bar/snack bar, restaurant/ pizzeria and takeaway. Pool complex 620m2 with heated and covered pool. Bike hire. Minigolf, ping-pong and tennis court. Gym. Games room. Play area. Entertainment and activity programme. Mobile homes and chalets to rent. WiFi (charged). Gas and charcoal barbecues are not permitted.

Key Features

 Pets Accepted

 Disabled Facilities

 Beach Access

 Swimming Pool

 Play Area

 Bar/Restaurant

 Bike Hire

 Fishing

Scan me for more information.

Alan Rogers Code: FR24450
12 accommodations
140 pitches
GPS: 44.80367, 1.15533
Post Code: F-24250

Dordogne, Aquitaine

www.alanrogers.com/fr24450
contact@campingmaisonneuve.com
Tel: 05 53 29 51 29
www.campingmaisonneuve.com

Open (Touring Pitches):
All year.

Camping Maisonneuve

This family run site is beautifully situated in the Céou Valley, in the Périgord. There are 140 spacious touring pitches, all with 6/10A electricity. Some are well separated, whilst others are on two open, grassy areas. Most pitches have some shade. The site's facilities are grouped around the old farmhouse. Swimming, fishing and canoeing are all possible in the Céou river which borders the site and can be accessed directly. There are also swimming and paddling pools on site and in high season entertainment is organised several evenings each week. This is an excellent location from which to explore the beautiful region of the Périgord.

Three heated sanitary blocks, one has been totally refurbished, are kept clean and tidy. Facilities for babies and disabled visitors. Family shower room. Laundry. Bar (all season). Shop with bread, snack bar, takeaway (all July/Aug). Swimming and paddling pools (1/5-15/10). Minigolf. Play areas. TV room. Games room. Dance evenings. Karaoke. Sports tournaments. Canoe trips. Climbing. WiFi in reception and courtyard (free).

Key Features

 Pets Accepted

 Disabled Facilities

 Swimming Pool

 Play Area

 Bar/Restaurant

Scan me for more information.

Alan Rogers Code: FR24350
66 accommodations
159 pitches
GPS: 44.76228, 1.01412
Post Code: F-24170

Dordogne, Aquitaine

www.alanrogers.com/fr24350
reservation@rcn.eu
Tel: 05 53 29 01 15
www.rcn.nl/moulin-de-la-pique

Open (Touring Pitches):
23 April - 24 September

La Moulin de la Pique

This high quality campsite, set in the heart of the Dordogne, has fine views looking up to the fortified town of Belvès. It is a splendid rural estate where there is plenty of space and a good mixture of trees and shrubs. Set in the grounds of a former mill, the superb traditional buildings date back to the 18th century. There are 219 level pitches with 159 for touring units, all with 10A electricity, a water point and drainage. The remainder are used for mobile homes to rent. The site is ideally suited for families with young and teenage children as there is so much to do, both on site and in the surrounding area.

Four modern sanitary blocks include facilities for disabled visitors. Launderette. Shop (bread to order), bar, restaurant, snack bar and takeaway (all open all season). Swimming pools (two heated). Recreational lake. Playgrounds. Outdoor fitness area. Library. Fossil field. Sports field. Tennis. Minigolf. Boules. Satellite TV. Internet facilities. WiFi (charged).

Key Features

 Pets Accepted

 Disabled Facilities

 Swimming Pool

 Play Area

 Bar/Restaurant

 Fishing

Scan me for more information.

Alan Rogers Code: FR40100
260 accommodations
190 pitches
GPS: 44.46052, -1.13065
Post Code: F-40600

Landes, Aquitaine

www.alanrogers.com/fr40100
info@larive.fr
Tel: 05 58 78 12 33
www.larive.fr

Open (Touring Pitches):
6 April - 1 September

Camping & Spa La Rive

Surrounded by pine woods, La Rive has a superb beach-side location on Lac de Sanguinet. With approximately 500 pitches (including mobile home accommodation), it provides 190 mostly level, numbered and clearly defined touring pitches of 80-100 sq.m. all with electricity connections (10A), 100 also with water and waste water. The swimming pool complex is wonderful with pools linked by water channels and bridges. There is also a jacuzzi, paddling pool and two large swimming pools all surrounded by sunbathing areas and decorated with palm trees. An indoor pool is heated and open all season. This is a friendly site with a good mix of nationalities.

Three good clean toilet blocks have washbasins in cabins and mainly British style toilets. Facilities for disabled visitors. Baby baths. Motorcaravan services. Shop with gas. New bar/restaurant complex with entertainment. Swimming pool complex (supervised July/Aug) with aquapark for children. Games room. Play area. Tennis. Bicycle hire. Boules. Fishing. Water-skiing. Watersports equipment hire. Tournaments (June-Aug). Skateboard park. Trampolines. Miniclub. No charcoal barbecues on pitches. Communal barbecue areas. WiFi throughout (charged).

Key Features

 Pets Accepted

 Disabled Facilities

 Swimming Pool

 Play Area

 Bar/Restaurant

 Bike Hire

 Fishing

 Sailing

Scan me for
more information.

LA RIVE

RESORT & SPA

★★★★★

In the heart of Les Landes and with direct access to the lake of Biscarrosse-Sanguinet.
La Rive Resort & Spa has the pleasure to welcome you for the new season in its new and modern reception.
You will discover a gigantic aquatic zone of 6500 M2, of which 3300 M2 covered and heated,
with a wave pool and Jacuzzi. Outside there is a new 30 meter long swimming pool, 200 meters of water slides
and a wild river, our great success. The children can enjoy the kid´s club while parents can relax at the Spa.
The entire family can enjoy a nice meal in the Bar-Restaurant or enjoy one of the activities and animations.
The innovative concept of our new accommodations ensures comfort and satisfaction.

40600 BISCARROSSE (France)
+33 (0)5 58 78 12 33
nfo@larive.fr   www.larive.fr

Alan Rogers Code: FR64250
130 accommodations
180 pitches
GPS: 43.41569, -1.61646
Post Code: F-64500

Pyrénées-Atlantiques, Aquitaine

www.alanrogers.com/fr64250
atlantica@cielavillage.com
Tel: +33 (0)5 59 47 72 44
www.atlantica.cielavillage.fr

Open (Touring Pitches):
05 April - 30 September

Camping Atlantica

Part of the Ciela Village group, this is a friendly, family run site with 180 shady and well kept grass pitches set amongst many shrubs, flowers and hedges. There are 50 pitches for touring, all with 6A electricity. The excellent swimming pool area is attractively landscaped with plenty of sunbeds. With a bar, restaurant and takeaway open April to September, the beach 600 m. and the cosmopolitan town of Saint Jean-de-Luz only 5 km. away, this site is suitable for families and couples of all ages. If excessively wet, motorcaravans are advised to call ahead to check availability.

Three immaculate toilet blocks include facilities for babies and campers with disabilities. Excellent laundry. Motorcaravan services. Shop, bar, restaurant and takeaway, heated outdoor swimming pool (all open all season). Games room. Multisports court. Bicycle hire. Modern, fenced play area. Family entertainment (July/Aug). WiFi throughout (charged).

Key Features

 Pets Accepted

 Disabled Facilities

 Swimming Pool

 Play Area

 Bar/Restaurant

 Bike Hire

Scan me for more information.

Alan Rogers Code: FR64330
72 accommodations
170 pitches
GPS: 43.46203, -1.56708
Post Code: F-64200

Pyrénées-Atlantiques, Aquitaine

www.alanrogers.com/fr64330
biarritz.camping@gmail.com
Tel: 05 59 23 00 12
www.biarritz-camping.fr

Open (Touring Pitches):
1 April - 29 September

Camping Biarritz

Nestled at the foot of the Pyrenees, this campsite in the heart of the Basque country, is ideally placed for you to visit Biarritz and experience all this culture-rich region has to offer. Biarritz Camping is just over 2km from the centre of town, only 700m from the sandy beach, and offers 170 pitches to campers. Pitches are large and partially in shade with electricity (10A) available. There are also mobile homes and bungalow tents available to rent. A bar serving snacks and takeaway food is on site and you'll find restaurants and cafés in easy walking distance. A shop on site sells essentials and fresh bread daily. Activities on site include petanque, table tennis and a children's playground as well as evening entertainment during July and August. Nearby, there is a surf school on the beach, an equestrian centre, golf and a number of thalassotherapy spas which have been popular in Biarritz for nearly 200 years.

Bright and comfortable shower and toilet blocks with facilities for families and disabled guests. Washing machine and dryer. Safety deposit boxes available to rent. Bar serving snacks and takeaway food. Shop selling essentials plus fresh bread daily and beach essentials. Petanque, Table tennis. Children's playground. Evening entertainment some evenings during July and August. WiFi (free).

Key Features

 Disabled Facilities

 Swimming Pool

 Play Area

 Bar/Restaurant

 Bike Hire

Scan me for more information.

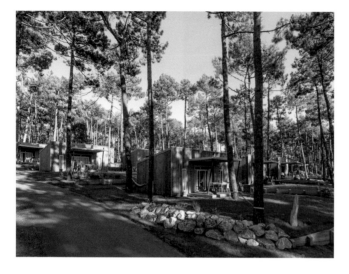

Alan Rogers Code: FR40060
131 accommodations
356 pitches
GPS: 43.95166, -1.35212
Post Code: F-40560

Landes, Aquitaine

www.alanrogers.com/fr40060
contact@camping-eurosol.com
Tel: 05 58 47 90 14
www.camping-eurosol.com

Open (Touring Pitches):
10 May - 18 September.

Camping Club Eurosol

Privately owned, Camping Club International Eurosol is an attractive, friendly and well maintained site extending over 15 hectares of undulating ground, amongst mature pine trees giving good shade. Of the 356 touring pitches, 231 have electricity (10A) with 120 fully serviced. A wide range of mobile homes and chalets, which are being updated, are available for rent. This is very much a family site with multi-lingual entertainers. Many games and tournaments are organised and a beach volleyball competition is held regularly in front of the bar. The adjacent boules terrain is floodlit. An excellent sandy beach 700 metres from the site has supervised bathing in high season and is ideal for surfing.

Four main toilet blocks and two smaller blocks are comfortable and clean with facilities for babies and disabled visitors. Motorcaravan services. Fridge rental. Well stocked shop and bar (all season). Restaurant, takeaway (1/6-7/9). Stage for live shows arranged in July/Aug. Outdoor swimming pool, paddling pool (all season) and heated, covered pool (May-July). Tennis. Multisports court. Bicycle hire. WiFi (charged). Charcoal barbecues are not permitted.

Key Features

 Pets Accepted

 Disabled Facilities

 Swimming Pool

 Play Area

 Bar/Restaurant

 Bike Hire

Scan me for more information.

Alan Rogers Code: FR46010
166 accommodations
294 pitches
GPS: 44.94542, 1.44137
Post Code: F-46200

Lot, Midi-Pyrénées

www.alanrogers.com/fr46010
info@lapaillebasse.com
Tel: 05 65 37 85 48
www.lapaillebasse.com

Open (Touring Pitches):
6 April - 14 September

Domaine de la Paille Basse

Castel Domaine de la Paille Basse was originally a medieval hamlet made up of three abandoned farmsteads which a British lady lovingly restored at the end of the 70's. Emphasis was laid on keeping the former aspects of the buidings, along with treasuring the unspoilt nature around. Today, the 3rd generation looks after this jewel, making sure the guests have the most enjoyable stay. Domaine de la Paille Basse is set in a rural location some 9 km from Souillac and stretches over a crest, 250m above sea level, offering wonderful views over the surrounding landscape. It is easily accessible from the A20 and well placed to take advantage of excursions into the Dordogne and it is part of a large domaine of 80 hectares, all available to campers for walks and recreation.

Key Features

 Pets Accepted

 Disabled Facilities

 Swimming Pool

 Play Area

 Bar/Restaurant

 Bike Hire

Three main toilet blocks have modern equipment and are kept very clean. There is also a cabin for disabled visitors and a baby area. Laundry. Small shop with a large selection of wine (seasonal). Restaurant, bar (open late in high season), terrace, pizza takeaway. Crêperie. Two swimming pools, paddling pool (unheated), water slides. Sun terrace. Soundproofed disco (seasonal). TV (with satellite). Cinema below the pool area. Tennis. Football pitch. Basketball pitch. Petanque pitch. Beach-volley pitch. Play areas. Table tennis. Library. WiFi in bar area (charged). Mini farm. Entertainment for all (seasonal). Electric barbecues are not permitted.

Scan me for more information.

Alan Rogers Code: FR31060
28 accommodations
117 pitches
GPS: 42.80814, 0.59725
Post Code: F-31110

Haute-Garonne, Midi-Pyrénées

www.alanrogers.com/fr31060
camping.pradelongue@wanadoo.fr
Tel: 05 61 79 86 44
www.camping-pradelongue.com

Open (Touring Pitches):
1 April - 1 October

Camping Pradelongue

Located within a half hour walk of Bagneres-de-Luchon, this green and pleasant site provides an ideal base for touring. Of the 135 pitches, 117 are for touring with the remainder being occupied by mobile homes for rent. The grassy pitches are level and separated by a mixture of hedges and small trees. Shade is provided by large mature trees. All have electricity (2–10A) and 18 also have water and waste water drainage. Just inside the gate is a tarmacked area for motorcaravans. This very well maintained site, situated in the Luchon valley, is surrounded by the Pyrenean mountains. Two guided walks are organised each week in July and August, and there are opportunities for paragliding, fishing, climbing and rafting nearby.

Key Features

 Pets Accepted

 Disabled Facilities

 Swimming Pool

 Play Area

Three toilet and shower blocks, one heated, some en-suite cabins all with high quality fittings. Facilities for children and disabled visitors. Washing machines and dryers. Fridge hire. Motorcaravan services. Heated swimming pool (1/6-30/9). Paddling pool. Football pitch. Boules. Volleyball. Basketball. New multisports area. Good play areas. Trampoline. Adult exercise equipment. Games room with pool and table football. Two TV rooms. Small library. WiFi over site (30 mins. free daily). Mobile homes to rent.

Scan me for more information.

Alan Rogers Code: FR12080
80 accommodations
163 pitches
GPS: 44.18933, 2.76693
Post Code: F-12410

Aveyron, Midi-Pyrénées

www.alanrogers.com/fr12080
contact@camping-les-genets.fr
Tel: 05 65 46 35 34
www.camping-les-genets.fr

Open (Touring Pitches):
6 May - 17 September.

Camping les Genêts

This family run site is on the shores of Lac de Pareloup and offers both family holiday and watersports facilities. The 163 pitches include 80 grassy, mostly individual pitches for touring units. These are in two areas, one on each side of the entrance lane, and are divided by hedges, shrubs and trees. All have 6A electricity, water and waste water drainage. The site slopes gently down to the beach and lake with facilities for all watersports including water-skiing. There is also a full entertainment and activities programme available in high season.

Two sanitary blocks are equipped with showers, one with suite for disabled guests. Nursery. Washing machines and dryers. Well stocked shop. Bar. Restaurant and takeaway. Refurbished heated outdoor pools. Sandy lake beach and lake with facilities for all watersports including water-skiing. Kinder play area. Mini-golf. Mini sport area. A full entertainment and activities programme is organised in high season and there is much to see and do in this very attractive corner of Aveyron. Bicycle hire. Boat, pedalo, canoe, kayak and paddles hire. Fishing on lake. TV in the bar. Free WiFi on all site.

Key Features

 Pets Accepted

 Disabled Facilities

 Swimming Pool

 Play Area

 Bar/Restaurant

 Bike Hire

 Fishing

 Sailing

Scan me for more information.

Alan Rogers Code: FR09170
18 accommodations
46 pitches
GPS: 42.99762, 1.87201
Post Code: F-09600

Ariège, Midi-Pyrénées

www.alanrogers.com/fr09170
contact@camping-la-serre.com
Tel: 05 61 03 06 16
www.camping-la-serre.com

Open (Touring Pitches):
19 March - 30 October.

Camping la Serre

A beautiful site set in ten hectares of gentle hillside and run by Corinne and Patrick, a hardworking and very friendly French couple. There are 66 spacious pitches, 46 for touring, all with electricity (5/10A). Most are on well drained grass with shade and privacy, some are on hardstanding and there is additional hardstanding for motorcaravans in wet weather. There is a small, friendly bar and the site takes pride in not having a disco or karaoke, but preferring to enjoy and respect nature – there are superb views towards the Pyrenees. A range of well specified chalets are available for hire.

Two main modern sanitary blocks and one small block. Good facilities for disabled campers. Child sized toilets, Baby room. Family shower rooms. Washing machines and dryers. Motorcaravan services. Bar, takeaway and outdoor swimming pool (July/Aug). Tennis. Volleyball. Pétanque. Mountain bike track. Extensive play area. Observation telescope. Small film theatre. Farming museum. Bicycle hire. Free WiFi over part of site. Telephone kiosk. Nature trail. Orchid and butterfly fields.

Key Features

 Pets Accepted

 Disabled Facilities

 Swimming Pool

 Play Area

 Bar/Restaurant

Scan me for more information.

Alan Rogers Code: FR30290
45 accommodations
75 pitches
GPS: 43.76579, 4.09743
Post Code: F-30250

Gard, Languedoc-Roussillon

www.alanrogers.com/fr30290
camping@massereau.com
Tel: 04 66 53 11 20
www.massereau.com

Open (Touring Pitches):
2 April - 29 October

Domaine de Massereau

Two brothers, one a wine producer and one an hotelier, opened Domaine de Massereau in August 2006. It is set within a 50-hectare vineyard dating back to 1804, and the idea was to promote their wine, so tours are arranged and they now produce their own olive oil as well. There are 149 pitches, with 75 available for touring units, all with electricity (45 with 16A electricity, water and drainage). Pitch sizes range from 150-250 sq.m. but the positioning of trees on some of the pitches could limit the usable space. The area is lightly wooded and most pitches are now hedged with flowering shrubs. The other pitches are used for chalets and mobile homes to rent. The site is a member of the Castels Group and good English is spoken.

Key Features

 Pets Accepted

 Disabled Facilities

 Swimming Pool

 Play Area

 Bar/Restaurant

 Bike Hire

The modern toilet block incorporates excellent facilities for children and disabled visitors. Laundry area. Motorcaravan services. Well stocked shop and newspapers. Restaurant, bar, pizzeria and outdoor grill, takeaway, (all season). Heated swimming pool with slide (all season). Paddling pool. Sauna, steam bath, jacuzzi and massage. Play area. Trampoline. Minigolf. Bicycle hire. Multisports area. Fitness trail. Pétanque. Short tennis. TV room. Barbecue hire. Fridge hire. Tent hire (2 person). Gas. WiFi (charged). Charcoal barbecues are not allowed.

Scan me for more information.

Alan Rogers Code: FR34110
459 accommodations
233 pitches
GPS: 43.17270, 3.25070
Post Code: F-34450

Hérault, Languedoc-Roussillon

www.alanrogers.com/fr34110
info@farret.com
Tel: 04 67 21 64 45
www.camping-farret.com/en

Open (Touring Pitches):
13 April - 28 September

Yelloh! Village Club Farret

An excellent site for families, well maintained and attractively landscaped with flowering shrubs, giving a truly Mediterranean feel. The main area has beach frontage and touring pitches, the other half, across a lane, has high quality mobile homes. Staff are helpful and everywhere is neat and tidy. It is a large, busy site but well organised with a relaxed atmosphere. There are 692 good sized, level, grassy pitches, with 233 for touring (10A electricity) with some shade from many trees. Both areas have impressive pool complexes, the newest has a pool bar. The safe beach is alongside the site, so some pitches have sea views as does the restaurant high above the pool. Evening entertainment and cultural visits are arranged.

Very clean toilet blocks (one heated) have facilities for children (including a baby bath) and disabled visitors. Washing machines. Dog shower. Motorcaravan services. Well stocked supermarket. Hairdresser. Bars with pizzas, snacks, takeaway. Restaurant. Heated swimming pool complex (1,000 sq.m) monitored all season. Indoor aquatic area with slides. Wellness centre with sauna, steam room, jacuzzi etc. Gym. Excellent play areas. Miniclub (5-12 yrs). Teenagers' club (13-17 yrs, only in July and August). Programme of sports and activities. Bicycle hire. WiFi (charged). New fitness room with cardio-training equipment. New multisports area and a padel-tennis.

Key Features

 Pets Accepted

 Disabled Facilities

 Beach Access

 Swimming Pool

 Play Area

 Bar/Restaurant

 Bike Hire

Sailing

Scan me for
more information.

Alan Rogers Code: FR34785
142 accommodations
50 pitches
GPS: 43.29416, 3.40818
Post Code: F-34450

Hérault, Languedoc-Roussillon

www.alanrogers.com/fr34785
info@domainesaintececile.fr
Tel: 04 67 21 63 70
www.camping-sainte-cecile.com

Open (Touring Pitches):
13 April - 22 September

Domaine Sainte Cécile

Enjoy the simple joys of nature at Yelloh! Village Domaine Sainte Cécile. Situated close to the beach and near the Canal du Midi, the Domaine Sainte Cécile is a family campsite that greets you under the Mediterranean sun and is cradled by the cicada song in a 4 hectare wooded and shaded park. The site offers 50 touring pitches and also various accommodation types to rent. Children will particularly love the waterslide and splashpad, whilst the adults can take advantage of the daily activities including aqua fitness.

Bar & restaurant. Swimming pool (heated during low season), waterslide and splashpad. Playgrounds, multisports field, beach volley, fitness trail. Daily animation programme including aqua fitness, aerobics, tennis and boules tournaments. Motorhome service area.

Key Features

 Swimming Pool

 Bar/Restaurant

 Golf

Scan me for more information.

Alan Rogers Code: FR34350
20 accommodations
645 pitches
GPS: 43.23467, 3.26867
Post Code: F-34350

Hérault, Languedoc-Roussillon

www.alanrogers.com/fr34350
contact@camping-plageetmer.com
Tel: 04 67 37 34 38
www.camping-plageetmer.com

Open (Touring Pitches):
1 June - 8 September.

La Plage & du Bord de Mer

A very impressive entrance leads you to this large site beside the beach, yet close to all the amenities of Valras-Plage with its own 'centre commercial.' There 670 level pitches on rough sandy grass with very little shade, 500 with electricity (6A/10A) and a further 60 with water and drain. There are just 20 private mobile homes which makes a pleasant change in this day and age. This is very much a seaside site, busy in high season, with three gates to the beach. It also has a good sea food restaurant that is popular with the public. An impressive swimming pool opened recently.

Six fully equipped toilet blocks with facilities for disabled visitors and babies. Laundry. Motorcaravan services. Range of shops, bar and restaurant. Takeaway (1/7-8/9). Tennis. Minigolf. Play area. Entertainment (July/Aug). No dogs or barbecues allowed.

Key Features

 Disabled Facilities

 Beach Access

 Play Area

 Bar/Restaurant

 Bike Hire

Scan me for
more information.

Alan Rogers Code: FR34070
493 accommodations
899 pitches
GPS: 43.26308, 3.31976
Post Code: F-34410

Hérault, Languedoc-Roussillon

www.alanrogers.com/fr34070
info@leserignanplage.com
Tel: 04 67 32 35 33
www.leserignanplage.com

Open (Touring Pitches):
19 April - 30 September

Camping le Sérignan-Plage

Yelloh! Village le Sérignan-Plage is a lively and vibrant site with direct access onto a superb 600 m. sandy beach (including a naturist section), plus two swimming pool complexes and an indoor pool, this is a must for a Mediterranean holiday. It is a busy, friendly, family orientated site with a very comprehensive range of amenities and activities for children. There are now over 1,300 pitches with 899 for touring units. They are fairly level, on sandy soil and all have 10A electricity. The collection of spa pools (balnéo) built in Romanesque style with colourful terracing and columns is overlooked by a very smart restaurant, Le Villa, available to use in the afternoons (used by the adjacent naturist site in the mornings).

Seven modern individually designed sanitary blocks with good amenities including showers with WC and washbasins. Facilities for people with reduced mobility. Baby bathroom. Automatic laundromat. Motorcaravan services. Supermarket, bakery and newsagent. Other shops (2/6-14/9). ATM. Restaurants, bars and takeaway. Hairdresser. Balnéo spa (afternoons). Gym. Indoor heated pool. Outdoor pools, water playground and waterslides (all season). Tennis court. Multisport courts. Playgrounds. Trampolines. Children's clubs. Evening entertainment. Sporting activities. Bike rental. Bus to Sérignan village (Jul/Aug). Beach (lifeguards 15/6-15/9). WiFi on site (charged). gas barbecues only.

Key Features

 Pets Accepted

 Disabled Facilities

 Beach Access

 Swimming Pool

 Play Area

 Bar/Restaurant

 Bike Hire

Scan me for more information.

Alan Rogers Code: FR11240
124 accommodations
236 pitches
GPS: 43.13270, 3.13890
Post Code: F-11430

Aude, Languedoc-Roussillon

www.alanrogers.com/fr11240
infos@
loisirs-vacances-languedoc.com
Tel: 04 68 49 81 59
www.camping-soleil-mer.com

Open (Touring Pitches):
24 March - 12 November

Camping Les Ayguades

Sites with direct access to the sea are popular, particularly those with a long season. Camping LVL Les Ayguades is situated between Gruissan Plage and Narbonne Plage and is overlooked by the Montagne de la Clape. The site is owned by an association which has recently updated the facilities and is committed to preserving the environment running the site with this in mind. There are 236 sandy pitches of various sizes, all with 10A electricity. The pitches are hedged and there is some shade. The site also has 70 chalets and mobile homes to rent, plus 15 privately owned. An upstairs restaurant has panoramic views of the sea.

Two fully equipped toilet blocks have been renovated and include facilities for disabled visitors. Launderette. Motorcaravan services. Shop, bar and takeaway (286-31/8). Restaurant (15/4-10/11). Play area and skate park. Fitness room. Children's club. Evening entertainment in high season. Direct access to the Beach. Heated swimming pool with Jaccuzi . Free WiFi.

Key Features

 Naturist Site

 Pets Accepted

 Disabled Facilities

 Beach Access

 Swimming Pool

 Play Area

 Bar/Restaurant

Scan me for
more information.

Alan Rogers Code: FR11080
90 accommodations
270 pitches
GPS: 43.14696, 3.00439
Post Code: F-11100

Aude, Languedoc-Roussillon

www.alanrogers.com/fr11080
info@campinglanautique.com
Tel: 04 68 90 48 19
www.campinglanautique.com

Open (Touring Pitches):
1 March - 31 October.

Camping la Nautique

This well established site is owned and run by a friendly Dutch family. It is an extremely spacious site situated on the Etang de Bages, where flat water combined with strong winds make it one of the best windsurfing areas in France. La Nautique has 390 huge, level pitches, 270 for touring, all with 10A electricity and fully equipped individual sanitary units. Six or seven overnight pitches with electricity are in a separate area. A range of mobile homes are available to rent. The flowering shrubs and trees give a pleasant feel while providing some shade. Hedges separate the pitches making some quite private and providing shade. The ground is quite hard and stony.

Each pitch has its own fully equipped sanitary unit. Extra facilities for disabled visitors. Laundry. Motorcaravan services. Shop. Bar/restaurant with terrace, TV, and takeaway (all 1/5-30/9). Snack bar (July/Aug). Outdoor heated swimming pool, water slide and paddling pool (1/5-30/9). Play areas. Tennis. Minigolf. Pétanque. Miniclub (high season). Games room. Bicycle hire. WiFi (charged). Only electric barbecues are permitted. Torch useful.

Key Features

 Pets Accepted

 Disabled Facilities

 Swimming Pool

 Play Area

 Bar/Restaurant

 Bike Hire

Scan me for more information.

Alan Rogers Code: FR11070
124 accommodations
130 pitches
GPS: 43.13662, 3.02562
Post Code: F-11100

Aude, Languedoc-Roussillon

www.alanrogers.com/fr11070
info@lesmimosas.com
Tel: 04 68 49 03 72
www.camping-les-mimosas.fr

Open (Touring Pitches):
6 April - 15 October

Camping les Mimosas

Six kilometres inland from the beaches of Narbonne and Gruissan, Yelloh! Village les Mimosas is a family owned site which benefits from a less hectic situation than others by the sea. Set amongst the vineyards, it is welcoming, peaceful in low season, but lively in July and August with plenty to amuse and entertain the younger generation, including a separate paddling pool for toddlers, but still offering facilities for the whole family. A free club card is available in July/August for use at the children's club, gym, sauna, tennis, minigolf, billiards etc. There are 266 pitches, 130 for touring, hedged and on level grass, and of a very good size, most with 6/10A electricity. There are a few 'grand confort' pitches with reasonable shade, mostly from two metre high hedges.

Sanitary buildings refurbished to a high standard include a baby room. Washing machines. Shop and restaurant (all season, incl. breakfast). Takeaway. Bar (low season only at w/ends). Small lounge, amusements (July/Aug). Landscaped heated pool with slides and islands (12/4-mid Oct), plus the original large pool and excellent new paddling pool and play room. Play area. Minigolf. Mountain bike hire. Tennis. Wellness area with massage, beauty treatments and sauna. Gym. Children's activities, sports, entertainment (high season). Bicycle hire. Multisports court. WiFi throughout (charged).

Key Features

 Pets Accepted

 Disabled Facilities

 Swimming Pool

 Play Area

 Bar/Restaurant

 Bike Hire

Scan me for more information.

Alan Rogers Code: FR66050
19 accommodations
100 pitches
GPS: 42.57581, 2.96481
Post Code: F-66690

Pyrénées-Orientales,
Languedoc-Roussillon

www.alanrogers.com/fr66050
contact@camping-le-haras.com
Tel: 04 68 22 14 50
www.camping-le-haras.com

Open (Touring Pitches):
1 April - 30 September

Le Haras

Situated in the mature grounds of an old hunting lodge, later developed into an arboretum, le Haras is a rather special site. The 131 pitches are in bays of four arranged amidst an amazing variety of trees and shrubs that provide colour and shade for 100 touring units and some 34 mobile homes (16 to rent). All the touring pitches have 10A electricity, 29 are fully serviced. Some of the access roads are narrow. Under the same family management as Ma Prairie at Canet Village (FR66020), this is a comfortable site popular with British visitors. Rail noise is possible, although the line is screened by large trees.

Fully equipped toilet blocks. Facilities for disabled visitors. Washing machines. Motorcaravan services. Fridge hire. Bar, restaurant and takeaway (all 5/4-25/9). Swimming and paddling pools (1/4-30/9). Play area. No charcoal barbecues. Max. 1 dog. WiFi throughout (1 hour per day free).

Key Features

 Pets Accepted

 Disabled Facilities

 Swimming Pool

 Play Area

 Bar/Restaurant

 Skiing

 Golf

 Sailing

Scan me for
more information.

Alan Rogers Code: FR66215
522 pitches
GPS: 42.62050, 2.99646
Post Code: 66750

Languedoc-Roussillon,
Pyrenees-Orientales

www.alanrogers.com/fr66215
lesoleildelamediterranee@orange.fr
Tel: 04 68 21 07 97
www.camping-soleil-mediterranee.
com/en

Open (Touring Pitches):

Le Soleil de la Méditerranée

Camping le Soleil de la Méditerranée in Saint Cyprien, just
1km from a long sandy beach, is an ideal base for exploring
the Pyrénées-Orientales area of sun, beach and blue waters.
The site has 50 touring pitches available which are grassy,
measure between 60 and 100 sq.m., have access to electricity
and some have shade and flowering borders. There is also
accommodation to rent on site. A large outdoor and indoor
swimming pool complex with water slides and a Hammam
is a great way to entertain the kids and satisfy the parents
who want to relax. There is a bar with a restaurant serving
excellent food either inside or outside on a large terrace and
entertainment is provided a few nights a week and during
the day in high season. Sports activities include tournaments
in high season and cover beach volleyball, beach football,
waterpolo and petanque and you'll find bicycle hire and
classes in aqua-aerobics and Zumba on site too.

Key Features

 Disabled Facilities

 Swimming Pool

 Play Area

 Bar/Restaurant

 Bike Hire

Heated toilet and shower facilities with child and disabled
facilities. Laundry facilities. Grocery shop. Hair and beauty salon
offering massage and solarium. Bar with restaurant and terrace
plus snacks and takeaway. Kid's club. Children's playground.
Waterpark with indoor and outdoor pools and waterslides.
Hammam. Jacuzzi. Dogs welcome. Games room with TV. Beach
volleyball. Beach football. Waterpolo. Petanque. Bicycle hire.
Aqua-aerobics. Zumba. Beach 1km and site runs land train shuttle.

Scan me for
more information.

Alan Rogers Code: FR66070
289 accommodations
705 pitches
GPS: 42.70830, 3.03552
Post Code: F-66141

Pyrénées-Orientales,
Languedoc-Roussillon

www.alanrogers.com/fr66070
info@lebrasilia.fr
Tel: 468802382
www.brasilia.fr

Open (Touring Pitches):
13 April - 5 October

Yelloh Village Le Brasilia

Situated across the yacht harbour from the resort of Canet-Plage, le Brasilia is an impressive, well managed family site directly beside the beach. The state-of-the-art reception incorporates an information centre. Although large, it is pretty, neat and well kept with an amazingly wide range of facilities – indeed, it is camping at its best. The touring pitches are neatly hedged, all with electricity (6-10A) and 304 with water and drainage. They vary in size from 80 to 120 sq.m. and some of the longer pitches are suitable for two families together. There is a variety of shade from pines and flowering shrubs, with less on pitches near the beach. A member of Yelloh! Village and Leading Campings group.

Nine modern sanitary blocks are very well equipped and maintained, with British style WCs and washbasins in cabins. Good facilities for children and for disabled campers. Laundry room. Motorcaravan services. Range of shops. Gas supplies. Bars and restaurant. Renovated pool complex (heated). New wellness centre including jacuzzi, massage and beauty rooms. Play areas. Sports field. Tennis. Sporting activities. Library, games and video room. Hairdresser. Internet café and WiFi. Daily entertainment programme. Bicycle hire. Fishing. Post office. Weather forecasts. No charcoal barbecues. Free WiFi in bar.

Key Features

 Pets Accepted

 Disabled Facilities

 Beach Access

 Swimming Pool

 Play Area

 Bar/Restaurant

 Bike Hire

Scan me for
more information.

Alan Rogers Code: FR66190
250 accommodations
450 pitches
GPS: 42.76750, 3.02972
Post Code: F-66440

Pyrénées-Orientales, Occitanie

www.alanrogers.com/fr66190
contact@lestropiques.fr
Tel: 04 68 28 05 09
www.campinglestropiques.com

Open (Touring Pitches):
20 April - 15 October.

Camping Les Tropiques

Camping Yelloh! Village les Tropiques is a very attractive site with a large pool complex, only 400 metres from a sandy beach. It will provide families with children of all ages with an ideal seaside holiday. There are 450 pitches with 78 for touring units, all with 10A electricity. Pleasant pine and palm trees with other Mediterranean vegetation give shade and provide a pleasant environment. Activities are provided for all including a large range of sports, activities, cabarets and shows. The pool complex at les Tropiques is very impressive with four pools, two heated with good provision for children, including a range of toboggans, all surrounded by spacious sunbathing terraces with loungers and parasols. Two play areas are provided – one for smaller children, the other with bridges and slides for the older ones.

Modern, fully equipped sanitary facilities, provision for disabled visitors. Launderette. Shop. Bar and restaurant. Takeaway and Pizzeria (1/7-31/8). Swimming pool and water slides. Paddling pool. Wellness centre. Outdoor fitness equipment. Tennis (floodlit). Multisports area (basketball, football, volleyball). Pétanque. Archery (1/7-31/8). TV/billiards room. Play area. Disco (every evening). Miniclub (6-12 yrs and teenagers' club for 13-17 yrs July/Aug). Bicycle hire (all season). WiFi throughout.

Key Features

 Pets Accepted

 Disabled Facilities

 Swimming Pool

 Play Area

 Bar/Restaurant

 Bike Hire

 Horse Riding

Scan me for more information.

Alan Rogers Code: FR66290
352 accommodations
140 pitches
GPS: 42.77855, 3.03010
Post Code: F-66420

Pyrénées-Orientales,
Languedoc-Roussillon

www.alanrogers.com/fr66290
contact@floride.fr
Tel: 04 68 86 11 75
www.floride.fr/en

Open (Touring Pitches):
29 March - 4 November

Le Floride & L'Embouchure

A well established and multi-lingual, family run enterprise, Campsite Resort Le Floride & L'Embouchure is really two sites in one – l'Embouchure the smaller one with direct access to the beach and le Floride on the opposite side of the road. Fifty pitches have their own individual sanitary facility and in total the site offers 632 reasonably sized pitches, 140 for touring, all with 10A electricity. A good range of chalets and mobile homes are available for rent, including a recent Polynesian-style village. It is relatively inexpensive, especially outside the July/August peak period and the majority of the comprehensive facilities are open from end of March until the beginning of November.

Four fully equipped toilet blocks on le Floride and two on l'Embouchure where 50 pitches near the beach have individual facilities. Facilities for babies and disabled visitors. Family shower room. Motorcaravan services. Grocery store. Souvenir shop. Bar and restaurant (from 10/4), takeaway (15/6-5/9). Excellent pool complex with indoor heated pool (all season). Beauty Centre. Hammam. Hairdressers. Excellent play area. Day care for kids. Multisports court. Gym. Tennis. Multilingual entertainment and sports programmes (1/5-30/9). Bicycle hire. Charcoal barbecues are not permitted. Max. 1 dog. WiFi over site (free).

Key Features

 Pets Accepted

 Disabled Facilities

 Swimming Pool

 Play Area

 Bar/Restaurant

 Skiing

Scan me for more information.

Alan Rogers Code: FR66200
260 accommodations
587 pitches
GPS: 42.56378, 3.03407
Post Code: F-66702

Pyrénées-Orientales,
Languedoc-Roussillon

www.alanrogers.com/fr66200
lesmarsouins@cielavillage.com
Tel: 04 68 81 14 81
www.lesmarsouins.cielavillage.com

Open (Touring Pitches):
12 April - 30 September

Camping les Marsouins

Now part of the Ciela Village group, Les Marsouins is a large site situated 800m from the sandy beach. There are 587 pitches in total. The good size, grassy, level touring pitches, all with electricity (5A), divided by hedging and tall trees, are providing some shade. There are also 260 mobile homes. An outdoor entertainment area is located at the entrance beside the bar and restaurant. In the 1-hectare pool area, you can sunbathe and relax underneath the palm trees. There are five water slides.

Fully equipped toilet blocks, one of them is heated. Washing machines. Motorhome services. Shop. Bakery. Bar. Restaurant and takeaway. Bike Rental. Free shuttle bus from the campsite to the beach. Kids club and teenagers club (high season). Heated swimming pool with waterslides. Play area. Organised activities for all ages (high season). Foam parties. Evening entertainment.

Key Features

 Swimming Pool

 Play Area

 Bar/Restaurant

 Bike Hire

Scan me for
more information.

Alan Rogers Code: FR66560
500 accommodations
10 pitches
GPS: 42.57093, 3.02906
Post Code: F-66702

Pyrénées-Orientales,
Languedoc-Roussillon

www.alanrogers.com/fr66560
contact@camping-lasirene.fr
Tel: 04 68 81 04 61
www.camping-lasirene.fr

Open (Touring Pitches):
20 April - 28 September.

Camping Club la Sirène

From the moment you step into the hotel-like reception area you realise that this large site offers the holidaymaker everything they could want, including a super pool complex, in a well managed and convenient location close to Argelès-sur-Mer and the beaches. There are 740 pitches over the 17-hectare site, and 520 mobile homes and chalets. They are modern in design, all less than five years old, and laid out in pretty avenues with flowering shrubs and shade from tall trees. There are now just ten touring pitches, with 16A electricity and water, and some 200 taken by tour operators. All the shops and amenities are near reception making the accommodation areas quite peaceful and relaxing.

Two well equipped toilet blocks with facilities for babies and disabled visitors (key access). Laundry. Traditional restaurant and fast food bar, bar and takeaway, large shop and bazaar, large aqua park, paddling pools, slides, jacuzzi (all season). Games room. Two play areas. Multisports field. Four tennis courts. Archery. Minigolf. Football. Theatre, evening entertainment, discos, show time spectacular. Riding. Bicycle hire. Watersports. WiFi throughout (free). Gas and electric barbecues only.

Key Features

 Pets Accepted

 Disabled Facilities

 Swimming Pool

 Play Area

 Bar/Restaurant

 Bike Hire

 Horse Riding

Scan me for more information.

Alan Rogers Code: FR84290
16 accommodations
66 pitches
GPS: 44.24496, 5.07851
Post Code: F-84110

Vaucluse, Provence

Du Théatre Romain

www.alanrogers.com/fr84290
info@camping-theatre.com
Tel: 04 90 28 78 66
www.camping-theatre.com

Open (Touring Pitches):
15 March - 5 November

This family friendly site is ideally situated within easy walking distance of the delightful town of Vaison and its excellent tourist office, shops, restaurants and museums. There are 66 level pitches and these all have electricity (5/10A), water and drainage and are of a good size (100 sq.m). Most pitches are part grass and part gravel and are generally separated by hedges and mature trees, giving partial shade. The site also has 16 mobile homes for rent. This is a quiet site with no organised entertainment, perfect for a relaxing holiday and a good base for exploring the surrounding Provençal countryside.

Key Features

 Pets Accepted

 Disabled Facilities

 Swimming Pool

 Play Area

Two heated sanitary blocks include facilities for babies and disabled visitors. Launderette. Fresh bread daily. Pizza van twice a week. Hot and cold drinks machine. Heated outdoor swimming pool (1/4-31/10). Play area. Table football. Snooker. Pétanque. WiFi throughout (free).

Scan me for
more information.

Alan Rogers Code: FR84190
41 accommodations
134 pitches
GPS: 44.00635, 5.03877
Post Code: F-84210

Vaucluse, Provence

www.alanrogers.com/fr84190
contact@campingfontaines.com
Tel: 04 90 46 82 55
www.campingfontaines.fr

Open (Touring Pitches):
1 May - Mid September.

Camping les Fontaines

A warm welcome awaits visitors to the peaceful and rustic setting of Camping les Fontaines. It is a small, family run site set in three and a half hectares, with magnificent views of Mont Ventoux and the mountains of the Vaucluse. There are 90 level, grassy pitches, 60 for tourers, all with 6A electricity and some shade from mature trees. They are separated by hedging and flowering shrubs. On-site amenities include a 200 sq.m. lagoon-style pool, an excellent restaurant and a bar with a large terrace overlooking the pool complex. New for 2017 is the creation of 43 premium sites named 'Grand Confort' which will provide between 90 and 110 m2 of space.

The modern, very clean, heated central toilet block has facilities for babies and disabled visitors. Laundry. Motorcaravan services. Small shop selling basics and fresh bread. Bar, restaurant, takeaway (all May-Sept). Lagoon-style pool with large 'beach' area (all season). Play area. Free WiFi. Twin-axle caravans are not accepted.

Key Features

 Pets Accepted

 Disabled Facilities

 Swimming Pool

 Play Area

 Bar/Restaurant

Scan me for more information.

185

Alan Rogers Code: FR04010
265 accommodations
177 pitches
GPS: 44.10462, 6.01688
Post Code: F-04290

Alpes-de-Haute-Provence,
Provence

Sunêlia L'Hippocampe

www.alanrogers.com/fr04010
camping@l-hippocampe.com
Tel: 00 33 4 92 33 50 00
www.l-hippocampe.com

Open (Touring Pitches):
27 April - 13 September

Sunêlia L'Hippocampe is a friendly, family run, all action, riverside site (no swimming), with families in mind, situated in a beautiful area of France. The perfumes of thyme, lavender and wild herbs are everywhere and the higher hills of Haute-Provence are not too far away. There are 447 level, numbered pitches (177 for touring units), medium to very large (130 sq.m) in size. All have 10A electricity and 140 have water and drainage, most being separated by bushes and cherry trees. Some of the best pitches border the lake or are in the centre of the site. The waterpark, restaurant, bar, takeaway and shop have all been completely renewed. Games, aerobics, competitions, entertainment and shows, plus a daily club for younger family members are organised in July and August and organised activities also at Easter and Whitsun.

Four refurbished toilet blocks, all with good clean facilities that include washbasins in cabins. Washing machines. Motorcaravan services. Shop (July/Aug). Restaurant, bar, snacks and bread (27/4-13/9). Large, heated pool complex (all season) with waterslides, Jacuzzi, children's pool. Animation (July-Aug). Children's clubs. Tennis. Fishing. Canoeing. Boules. Bicycle hire. Several sports facilities (some with free instruction). Charcoal barbecues are not permitted. WiFi throughout (charged).

Key Features

 Pets Accepted

 Disabled Facilities

 Swimming Pool

 Play Area

 Bar/Restaurant

 Bike Hire

 Fishing

Scan me for
more information.

Alan Rogers Code: FR05110
50 accommodations
190 pitches
GPS: 44.65854, 6.63816
Post Code: F-05600

Hautes-Alpes, Provence

www.alanrogers.com/fr05110
guillestre@aol.com
Tel: 04 92 45 02 15
www.campingguillestre.com

Open (Touring Pitches):
5 May - 16 October

Camping la Rochette

At a height of 800 metres, this attractive municipal site looks fresh and well kept. Located in a beautiful mountainous region, it is run under contract by a very welcoming young couple who are fully responsible for the day-to-day running of the site. There are 190 grassy pitches, separated by trees that give welcome shade, with 180 for touring; all have 4-10A electricity. The excellent, clean facilities are immaculately kept. Although there are few amenities on site, most can be found in the town, only ten minutes' walk away. The Monday market is well worth a visit. English and Dutch are spoken.

Three well appointed toilet blocks are clean and modern. Facilities for disabled visitors. Small shop, snack bar/takeaway and restaurant (end Jun - end Aug). Heated outdoor swimming pool (July/Aug). Play area. Boules. Bicycle hire. Only gas and electric barbecues are permitted. Internet access and WiFi throughout (free).

Key Features

 Pets Accepted

 Swimming Pool

 Play Area

 Bar/Restaurant

Scan me for more information.

Alan Rogers Code: FR83170
380 accommodations
200 pitches
GPS: 43.39880, 6.67542
Post Code: F-83520

Var, Côte d'Azur

Domaine de la Bergerie-Var

www.alanrogers.com/fr83170
info@domainelabergerie.com
Tel: 04 98 11 45 45
www.domainelabergerie.com

Open (Touring Pitches):
30 March - 4 November

Castel Camping Domaine de la Bergerie is an excellent site near the Côte d'Azur which will take you away from all the bustle of the Mediterranean to total relaxation amongst the cork, oak, pine and mimosa in its woodland setting, whilst only ten minutes away from the sea. The 60-hectare site is well spread out with semi-landscaped areas for mobile homes and 200 separated pitches for touring caravans and tents. All pitches average over 80 sq.m. and have electricity, with one area also having water and drainage. Eight premium pitches with cabins equipped with kitchenette and bathroom have been added. The restaurant/bar, a converted farm building, is surrounded by shady patios, inside it oozes character with beams and archways leading to intimate corners.

Key Features

 Pets Accepted

 Disabled Facilities

 Swimming Pool

 Play Area

 Bar/Restaurant

 Bike Hire

Fishing

Four toilet blocks are kept clean and include washbasins in cubicles, facilities for babies & disabled visitors. Supermarket. Bar/restaurant/takeaway (seasonal). Indoor heated pool with Jacuzzi, sauna and steam bath. Outdoor pool complex, aquagym, slides & paddling pools. Fitness centre. Bicycle hire. Tennis. Archery. Roller skating. Minigolf. English-speaking childrens & teenagers clubs. Minifarm. Fishing. Paintball (July/Aug). WiFi throughout (charged). Only gas barbecues permitted.

Scan me for more information.

Alan Rogers Code: FR83120
173 accommodations
1320 pitches
GPS: 43.11779, 6.35176
Post Code: F-83230

Var, Côte d'Azur

www.alanrogers.com/fr83120
mail@campdudomaine.com
Tel: 04 94 71 03 12
www.campdudomaine.com

Open (Touring Pitches):
8 April - 31 October.

Camp du Domaine

Camp du Domaine, 3 km. south of Le Lavandou, is a large, attractive, beachside site with 1,173 touring pitches set in 45 hectares of pinewood, yet surprisingly it does not give the impression of being so big. The pitches are large and most are reasonably level; 957 have 10/16A electricity. The most popular pitches are beside the beach, but those furthest away are generally larger and have more shade. Amongst the trees, many pitches are more suitable for tents. There are also 147 mobile homes to rent, located on the hillside with super sea views. The beach is the attraction and everyone tries to get close. American motorhomes are accepted.

Ten modern, well used but clean toilet blocks. Facilities for disabled visitors. Baby room with showers, WC and changing facilities. Washing machines. Fridge hire. Well stocked supermarket, bars, pizzeria (all open all season). No swimming pool, but direct beach access. Several excellent play areas for all ages. Activities and entertainment for children and teenagers (July/Aug). 6 tennis courts. Kayaks and paddle boards for hire. Wide range of watersports. Water games. New gym. Multisports courts (one indoor for wet or hot weather) for football, basketball. Only gas and electric barbecues are allowed. Direct beach access. Dogs not accepted 16/7-13/8. Free WiFi at tennis bar.

Key Features

 Pets Accepted

 Disabled Facilities

 Beach Access

 Play Area

 Bar/Restaurant

 Skiing

 Fishing

 Sailing

Scan me for
more information.

Alan Rogers Code: FR06030
16 accommodations
434 pitches
GPS: 43.71174, 7.09050
Post Code: F-06140

Alpes-Maritimes, Côte d'Azur

www.alanrogers.com/fr06030
info@camping-domainedelabergerie.com
Tel: 04 93 58 09 36
camping-domainedelabergerie.com

Open (Touring Pitches):
25 March - 15 October

Domaine de la Bergerie-Vence

La Bergerie is a quiet, family owned site, situated in the hills about 3km from Vence and Saint Paul de Vence. 10km from the sea at Cagnes sur Mer. This extensive, lightly wooded site has been left very natural and is in a secluded position about 300m above sea level. Because of the trees most of pitches are shaded and all are of a good size. It is a large site but because it is so extensive it does not give that impression. There are 434 pitches, 300 with electricity (66 also with water and drainage) and 4 of them with private sanitary. Ther are also various types of accommodation to rent including the new Mobile Home Malaga Duo. Because of the nature of this site some pitches are a litle distance from the toilet blocks.

Key Features

 Pets Accepted

 Disabled Facilities

 Swimming Pool

 Play Area

 Bar/Restaurant

Refurbished toilet blocks are centrally positioned and include excellent provision for disabled visitors (pitches near the block are reserved for disabled visitors). Good shop. Small bar/restaurant, takeaway (all 1/5-30/9). Large swimming pool, smaller pool and spacious sunbathing area (1/5-30/9). Tennis court. Table tennis. Pétanque courts. Playground for children. Outdoor fitness area. Charcoal barbecues are not permitted. Two mobile homes and new camping pods to rent.

Scan me for more information.

Alan Rogers Code: FR06220
6 accommodations
50 pitches
GPS: 43.81612, 7.34324
Post Code: F-06390

Alpes-Maritimes, Côte d'Azur

La Ferme Riola

www.alanrogers.com/fr06220
contact@campinglafermeriola.com
Tel: 04 93 79 03 02
www.campinglafermeriola.com

Open (Touring Pitches):
1 April - 30 September

La Ferme Riola is a very small site with just 50 pitches for touring and six gîtes attractively dispersed amongst olive trees around the four-hectare terrain. Areas for touring units are spread all around the site, mostly situated on the terraces. Pitches are large and generally well shaded. All are equipped with electrical connections. Leisure facilities include a swimming pool, a volleyball court and a children's playground. This is a working farm and fresh produce including olives, olive oil and fresh eggs, is available at the site's small shop.

Key Features

 Pets Accepted

 Disabled Facilities

 Swimming Pool

 Play Area

Two sanitary blocks have preset pushbutton showers and include a family shower room, baby room and facilities in one block for disabled visitors. Laundry. Small shop (bread to order in July/Aug). Swimming pool (April-Sept). Volleyball pitch. Games room. Play area. Large communal barbecue area. Sporting competitions and organised walks in high season. Free WiFi around reception area.

Scan me for
more information.

Capital Berlin
Currency Euro (€)
Language German
Telephone country code 00 49
Time Zone CET (GMT/UTC+1)
Tourist Office germany-tourism.co.uk

Climate Temperate climate. In general, winters are a little colder and summers a little warmer than in the UK.

Germany

With its wealth of scenic and cultural interests, Germany is a land of contrasts. From the flat lands of the north to the mountains in the south, with forests in the east and west, regional characteristics are a strong feature of German life, and present a rich variety of folklore and customs.

Each region in Germany has its own unique identity. Home of lederhosen, beer and sausages is Bavaria in the south, with small towns, medieval castles and Baroque churches. In the south-west, Baden Württemberg is famous for its ancient Black Forest and its spas, and boasts the most hours of sunshine. Further west is the stunningly beautiful Rhine Valley, where the river winds through steep hills dotted with castles, ruins and vineyards. Eastern Germany is studded with lakes and rivers, and undulating lowlands that give way to mountains. The north has busy cities such as Bremen and Hamburg as well as traditional North Sea family resorts. The capital city of Berlin, situated in the north-east of the country, and once divided by the Berlin Wall, is an increasingly popular tourist destination, with its blend of old and modern architecture, zoos and aquariums, museums, green spaces and lively nightlife

Shops Opening hours vary throughout the year. In high-season 9.30am to 8pm Monday to Saturday.

Banks 9am to 4pm weekdays, extended hours on Tuesdays and Thursdays, and some open Saturday.

Travelling with Children A very children-friendly country with lots to do for all ages from fairy tale castles to huge theme parks. The Black Forest in the south is great for sports activities including kayaking and swimming in Lake Constance. Neuscwanstein Castle in Bavaria is the ultimate fairy tale castle. Northern Germany has some great sandy beaches. Berlin and other large cities have a plethora of museums, zoos and other cultural and historical attractions, most of which are free for under 18s. Public transport is usually half price for children. Many restaurants offer a kids menu but children are also expected to behave.

Public Holidays New Year's Day, Good Friday, Easter Monday, Labour Day, Ascension, Whit Monday, Day of German Unity 3 Oct, Christmas Day, Boxing Day. Epiphany, Corpus Christi, Assumption, Reformation Day, All Saints' and Repentance Day are regional public holidays.

Motoring An excellent network of (toll-free) motorways (autobahns) exists in the West and the traffic moves fast. Remember in the East a lot of road building is going on, amongst other works, so allow plenty of time when travelling and be prepared for poor road surfaces.

See campsite map page 479.

Alan Rogers Code: DE30230
300 accommodations
200 pitches
GPS: 54.12923, 10.45504
Post Code: D-24306

Augstfelde/Plön, Schleswig-Holstein

www.alanrogers.com/de30230
info@augstfelde.de
Tel: 04522 8128
www.augstfelde-camping.de

Open (Touring Pitches):
1 April - 26 October.

Campingpark Augstfelde

Campingpark Augstfelde is a spacious site with plenty of good sport and leisure facilities. The site borders a lake and is next to an 18-hole golf course in this picturesque region of hills, forests and lakes. Two hundred of the 500 pitches are reserved for touring, 145 are fully serviced and all have 16A Europlug. Undulating in some areas, the grassed site offers some tree shade, with hedges and bushes providing pitch separation in places. The sandy beaches along the sites 800 m. long bank with the lake are a popular sunbathing area and playground for children. With its lakeside location in a nature park and with a wealth of on and off-site facilities, there is lots to offer to all age groups. There are plenty of activities for children and family pets are well catered for.

Sanitary blocks with showers on payment (€ 0.75) and bathrooms to rent. Washing machines and dryers. Restaurant. Shop. Motorcaravan services. Dog shower. Separate beach for dogs. Sauna, fitness, massage. Four playgrounds. Activity programmes. Theatre club with cinema and disco in high season. Sailing. Windsurfing. Fishing. Canoe, boat and bicycle hire. Football. Basketball. Volleyball. WiFi. Quick stop facility at entrance.

Key Features

 Pets Accepted

 Disabled Facilities

 Play Area

 Bar/Restaurant

 Bike Hire

 Fishing

 Horse Riding

 Sailing

Scan me for more information.

Alan Rogers Code: DE30030
160 accommodations
372 pitches
GPS: 54.40805, 11.17374
Post Code: D-23769

Wulfen auf Fehmarn, Schleswig-Holstein

Camping Wulfener Hals

www.alanrogers.com/de30030
info@wulfenerhals.de
Tel: 043 718 6280
www.wulfenerhals.de

Open (Touring Pitches):
All year.

This is a top class, all year round site suitable as a stopover or as a base for a longer stay. Attractively situated by the sea, it is large, mature (34 hectares) and well maintained. It has over 800 individual pitches (372 for touring) of up to 160 sq.m. in glades. Some are separated by bushes providing shade in the older parts, less so in the newer areas nearer the sea. There are many hardstandings and all pitches have electricity (16A), water and drainage. Some new rental accommodation has been added, including a 'honeymoon mobile home'. A member of Leading Campings group.

Key Features

 Open All Year

 Pets Accepted

 Disabled Facilities

 Beach Access

 Swimming Pool

 Play Area

 Bar/Restaurant

 Bike Hire

Five heated sanitary buildings have first class facilities including showers and both open washbasins and private cabins. Family bathrooms to rent. Facilities for disabled visitors. Beauty and cosmetic facilities (all year), wellness (all year). Laundry. Motorcaravan services. Shop, bar, restaurants and takeaway (April-Oct). Swimming pool (May-Oct). Sauna. Solarium. Jacuzzi. Sailing, catamaran, windsurfing and diving schools. Boat slipway. Golf courses (18 holes, par 72 and 9 holes, par 3). Riding. Fishing. Archery. Well organised and varied entertainment programmes for all ages. Bicycle hire. Catamaran hire. WiFi over part of site (charged).

Scan me for more information.

Alan Rogers Code: DE30080
6 accommodations
120 pitches
GPS: 53.96142, 10.33737
Post Code: D-23795

Klein Rönnau, Schleswig-Holstein

www.alanrogers.com/de30080
info@kluethseecamp.de
Tel: 045 518 2368
www.kluethseecamp.de

Open (Touring Pitches):
All year except February.

Klüthseecamp Seeblick

Klüthseecamp Seeblick is a modern, family run site situated on a small hill between two lakes. It is an ideal location for a family holiday with activities on site for all ages and a useful base to explore the region. The large, open grass, touring part of the site has sunny, shaded and semi-shaded areas on offer. There are 120 touring pitches on fairly level ground, all with electricity (10/16A) and 30 with water and drainage, and pitches for tents in natural surroundings. Klüthseecamp offers wellness, a swimming pool, food and drink, organised entertainment for young and old, and a sandy lakeside beach.

Two modern, heated sanitary blocks, some washbasins in cabins, five bathrooms to rent and free showers. Facilities for children and disabled visitors including electric vehicle. Attractive baby room. Motorcaravan services. Gas supplies. Laundry. Shop with breakfast service. Bar and café in main building, additional beer garden and restaurant by the lake. Outdoor swimming pool (heated May-Sept). Wellness. Sauna, steam bath, massage. Play room/kindergarten. Bouncy castle. Three outside play areas. Large LCD0 projected TV. Bicycle hire. Go-kart hire. Minigolf. Way-marked paths around lake. Kids' and teenagers' clubs including weekly disco. Free WiFi at small restaurant.

Key Features

 Pets Accepted

 Disabled Facilities

 Swimming Pool

 Play Area

 Bar/Restaurant

 Bike Hire

 Fishing

 Sailing

Scan me for more information.

Alan Rogers Code: DE38200
70 accommodations
320 pitches
GPS: 53.30517, 13.00133
Post Code: D-17237

Gross Quassow, Mecklenburg-
West Pomerania

www.alanrogers.com/de38200
info@haveltourist.de
Tel: 039 812 4790
www.haveltourist.de

Open (Touring Pitches):
All year.

Ferienpark Havelberge

The Müritz National Park is a very large area of lakes and marshes, popular for birdwatching as well as watersports, and Havelberge is a large, well equipped site to use as a base for enjoying the area. It is quite steep in places with many terraces, most with shade, and views over the lake. There are 415 pitches in total with 320 good sized, numbered touring pitches (all with 16A Europlug electrical connections) with many of the pitches on a newly developed area to the rear of the site with water and drainage. Pitches on the new field are level and separated by low hedges and bushes but have no shade. A member of Leading Campings group.

Four sanitary buildings (one new and of a very high standard) provide very good facilities, with private cabins, showers on payment and large section for children. Fully equipped kitchen and laundry. Motorhome services. Small shop, modern restaurant, bar, takeaway and wellness (open seasonally). The lake provides fishing, swimming from a small beach and boats can be launched (over 5 hp requires a German boat licence). Rowing boats, windsurfers and bikes can be hired. Canoe centre with beginners' courses and canoe hire. Accompanied canoe, cycle and walking tours. Play areas and entertainment for all the family in high season. Teepee village. Tree walkway (2.5 m. high with safety wires). WiFi (charged).

Key Features

 Open All Year

 Pets Accepted

 Disabled Facilities

 Play Area

 Bar/Restaurant

 Bike Hire

 Fishing

Scan me for more information.

Alan Rogers Code: DE37780
100 accommodations
250 pitches
GPS: 54.37964, 12.66177
Post Code: D-18356

Pruchten, Mecklenburg-West
Pomerania

www.alanrogers.com/de37780
info@naturcamp.de
Tel: 0049(0)38231 2045
www.naturcamp.de

Open (Touring Pitches):
1 April - 31 October

Naturcamp Pruchten

On the shore of Barther Bodden, a shallow lagoon separated
from the Baltic Sea by the narrow Zingst Peninsula,
Naturcamp Pruchten is a family run campsite in the southern
part of the National Park 'Vorpommersche Boddenlandschaft'.
There are 250 level pitches with a scattering of mature trees
providing some shade; some are occupied by holiday homes
and log cabins for hire, the remainder are for touring units,
with 16A electrical connections available. A short walk away
is the gently-sloping beach on the lagoon, ideal for swimming
and with several playgrounds. An easy ride or drive takes you
to a sandy Baltic Sea beach.

Three heated sanitary blocks with baby room and family
bathroom. Laundry room with washing machines and dryers.
Motorhome services. Restaurant with bar and terrace (seasonal).
Mini-market (all season). Volleyball court. Barbecue area. 3D
cinema room. Bicycle hire. Log cabins, holiday homes and
apartments for hire. Leisure and sporting activities for children
and families in high season. WiFi throughout (charged).

Key Features

 Pets Accepted

 Disabled Facilities

 Beach Access

 Play Area

 Bar/Restaurant

 Bike Hire

 Fishing

Scan me for
more information.

Alan Rogers Code: DE38265
50 accommodations
249 pitches
GPS: 52.65482, 12.42967
Post Code: D-14715

Ferchesar, Brandenburg

www.alanrogers.com/de38265
campingpark-buntspecht@web.de
Tel: 03387 490072
www.campingpark-buntspecht.de

Open (Touring Pitches):
15 April - 15 October.

Campingpark Buntspecht

Campingpark Buntspecht is a high quality, well maintained site 85 km. west of Berlin, lying alongside the large Ferchesarer lake and surrounded by the Brandenburg Forest and a large nature reserve. The pitches (90-120 sq.m) are laid out on grass in a parkland setting with tall pine trees offering some shade. There are 249 pitches, with 155 average size, fully serviced pitches for touring (16A electricity). Sixteen are alongside the lake and seven are for short stays. The large lake has a sandy beach and is ideal for swimming, boating and fishing, with a range of boats for hire.

Two well equipped, modern sanitary blocks with all necessary facilities including those for babies and disabled campers. Dog showers and walking area. Washing machines and dryers. Shop with basics. Bar with terrace. Restaurant. Football. Volleyball. Badminton. Adventure playground with large sand pit. Petting zoo. Bouncy castle. Bicycle and children's go-kart hire. WiFi throughout (charged).

Key Features

 Pets Accepted

 Disabled Facilities

 Play Area

 Bar/Restaurant

 Skiing

 Bike Hire

 Fishing

Scan me for more information.

Alan Rogers Code: DE38300
250 accommodations
180 pitches
GPS: 52.37012, 13.68435
Post Code: D-12527

Berlin, Berlin

www.alanrogers.com/de38300
info@campingplatz-krossinsee.de
Tel: 03067 58687
www.campingplatz-berlin.de

Open (Touring Pitches):
All year.

Campingplatz Krossinsee

Am Krossinsee is an efficiently run site and a good base for visiting the capital of Germany. The Krossinsee itself is one of many clean lakes in the southeast of Berlin and is suitable for swimming, fishing and boating, with access by key through a gate from the woodland site. 180 of the some 450 pitches here are for tourers and are of varying but reasonable size, mainly with some degree of slope, most with 10A electrical connections and a fair amount of shade. A separate area is set aside for tents. For visits in high season, you should try to arrive as early as possible as reservations are not taken.

The sanitary facilities are of above average quality for a city site, situated in a modern building with plenty of private cabins, smallish showers (token from reception), hand and hair dryers, a baby room and a well equipped unit for disabled visitors. Kitchen. Laundry. Lake swimming, fishing, boating (hire facilities), watersports, windsurfing school and woodland walks. Motorhome services. Bicycle hire. WiFi.

Key Features

 Open All Year

 Disabled Facilities

 Play Area

Scan me for
more information.

Alan Rogers Code: DE38620
36 accommodations
151 pitches
GPS: 50.98160, 13.92504
Post Code: D-01796

Pirna, Saxony

www.alanrogers.com/de38620
waldcamping@stadtwerke-pirna.de
Tel: 03501 523 773
www.waldcamping-pirna.com

Open (Touring Pitches):
30 March - 2 November.

Waldcamping Pirna-Copitz

In wooded countryside southeast of Dresden, close to the border with the Czech Republic, Waldcamping Pirna-Copitz lies on the shore of a small lake, surrounded by forest. There are 151 touring pitches (80-100 sq.m) in two areas; all have electricity connections (16A, Europlug) and 90 also have individual water taps and waste water drains. There are 13 caravans and chalets for hire. You can relax on the sandy beach, swim in the lake or stroll through the woods. The historic city of Dresden, capital of Saxony, is an easy drive away.

The central sanitary building includes facilities for babies, children and disabled visitors. Washing machines and dryers. Table tennis and ball games. Swimming in lake. Fishing. Bicycle hire. Programme of activities and entertainment for children and families (Tues. and Thurs. in July/Aug); these include geocaching (digital treasure hunt), felting, creating ships using cork, designing storm lanterns and carving soapstone. WiFi throughout (free).

Key Features

 Pets Accepted

 Disabled Facilities

 Play Area

 Bike Hire

 Fishing

Scan me for more information.

Alan Rogers Code: DE38330
40 accommodations
238 pitches
GPS: 51.12040, 13.98010
Post Code: D-01900

Dresden, Saxony

www.alanrogers.com/de38330
info@luxoase.de
Tel: 03595 256666
www.luxoase.de

Open (Touring Pitches):
All year excl. February.

Camping LuxOase

This is a well organised and quiet site located just north of Dresden, with easy access from the autobahn. The site has very good facilities and is arranged on grassland beside a lake, which is reached from the site through a gate. Although the site is fairly open, trees do provide shade in some areas. There are 238 large touring pitches (plus 40 seasonal in a separate area), marked by bushes or posts on generally flat or slightly sloping grass. All have 10/16A electricity and 132 have water and drainage. At the entrance is an area of hardstanding (with electricity) for late arrivals. A member of Leading Campings group. You may swim, fish or use inflatables in the lake (at your own risk). A wide entertainment programme is organised for children in high season.

Two excellent buildings provide modern, heated facilities with private cabins, a family room, baby room, units for disabled visitors and eight bathrooms for hire. Special facilities for children with novelty showers and washbasins. Kitchen. Gas supplies. Motorcaravan services. Shop and bar plus restaurant (open seasonally). Lake swimming. Jacuzzi. Sauna. Fitness room. Fishing. Play area. Sports field. Minigolf. Train, bus and theatre tickets from reception. Regular guided bus trips to Dresden, Prague etc. Bicycle hire. Internet point. WiFi throughout (charged).

Key Features

 Pets Accepted

 Disabled Facilities

 Play Area

 Bar/Restaurant

 Bike Hire

 Fishing

Scan me for more information.

Alan Rogers Code: DE38550
9 accommodations
150 pitches
GPS: 50.73367, 10.75667
Post Code: D-99330

Frankenhain, Thuringia

www.alanrogers.com/de38550
info@oberhofcamping.de
Tel: 03620 576518
www.oberhofcamping.de

Open (Touring Pitches):
All year.

Oberhof Camping

Beside a lake, at an altitude of 700 metres and quietly hidden in the middle of the Thüringer forest, Oberhof Camping has seen many changes since the departure of its former owners, the East German secret police. There are 150 touring pitches, all with electricity (10A Europlug), 20 with water and drainage. From this fairly open site there are views of the surrounding forests and of the lake, which is bordered by wide grass areas ideal for a picnic or for just lazing around and enjoying the view. The site is very quiet and has direct access to marked routes for rambling and cycling in the forest. Nine small cottages are also available to rent on site.

Two sanitary blocks with all usual facilities including free hot water, plus 15 bathrooms to rent. Facilities for disabled visitors in one block. Baby room. Laundry. Motorcaravan services. Gas sales. Modern reception building with shop and attractive restaurant and takeaway (open seasonally). Shop with fresh bread (all year). Children's club room. Play area. On the lake: fishing (licence required), swimming and boating. WiFi (charged).

Key Features

 Open All Year

 Pets Accepted

 Disabled Facilities

 Play Area

 Bar/Restaurant

 Skiing

 Bike Hire

 Fishing

Scan me for more information.

Alan Rogers Code: DE40290
2 accommodations
100 pitches
GPS: 49.86116, 10.91535
Post Code: D-96049

Bamberg/Bug, Bavaria (N)

www.alanrogers.com/de40290
buero@campinginsel.de
Tel: 09515 6320
www.campinginsel.de

Open (Touring Pitches):

Camping Insel

This pleasant campsite is located on the banks of the river Regnitz in the Bavarian region of Germany. The pitches are spacious and delimited with a good range of shade provided by the beautiful old trees growing around the campsite. There is a good quality restaurant on site providing Franconia specialties and a pleasant beer garden where you can enjoy a local Bamberg Beer. There are various cycle routes on site with bikes available to hire and you can swim nearby in the river. Children have a large playground on site and there is a table tennis table for use.

First class, well maintained new sanitary block with spacious shower cubicles. Fresh warm bread can be ordered from reception the day before. Washing machines and sinks can be found in both sanitary areas. Baby playground and children's play area with old tractors, ping pong tables, trampolines and plenty of space to run and play. BBQs allowed however open fires are prohibited. Wifi service (charged). Bike hire. Dogs are accepted in a special area allocated on site. 3km from the nearest supermarkets.

Key Features

 Open All Year

 Pets Accepted

 Play Area

 Bar/Restaurant

 Bike Hire

 Fishing

Scan me for more information.

Alan Rogers Code: DE36980
25 accommodations
330 pitches
GPS: 48.41526, 13.13005
Post Code: D-94137

Bayerbach, Bavaria (S)

www.alanrogers.com/de36980
info@vitalcamping-bayerbach.de
Tel: 08532 927 8070
www.vitalcamping-bayerbach.de

Open (Touring Pitches):
All year.

Vital Camping Bayerbach

Vital Camping Bayerbach opened in 2011 and is situated between the rivers Danube, Rott and Inn, in one of the most picturesque regions of Bavaria. It is convenient for popular tourist destinations such as Munich and Passau in southern Germany, and Salzburg in Austria. There are 330 grass and gravel pitches (90-130 sq.m) for touring, all are serviced with 16A electricity, water and drainage. In addition, there are 6 apartments and 14 cottages available to rent. The focal point of this site is, without doubt, its wellness centre with its indoor thermal pool, themed saunas, oriental bath, swimming pools and cosmetic studio. Whether you come for the traditional 'cure' or just to unwind and pamper yourself, there is a wide range of treatments on offer by fully qualified staff, with a range of prices to suit.

Two modern sanitary blocks with hot showers and washbasins in cabins, family shower room and facilities for children. Both blocks have excellent units for disabled visitors. Private bathrooms (charged). Dog shower. Laundry room. Motorhome service points. Shop. Restaurant and takeaway with beer garden. Indoor heated swimming pool. Large wellness and spa facility. Play area. Activity programme for adults and children (high season). Twin-axle caravans and large motorhomes are accepted. Bicycle store. Dogs (1 max) are welcomed on specific pitches. WiFi on part of site (charged).

Key Features

 Open All Year

 Pets Accepted

 Disabled Facilities

 Swimming Pool

 Play Area

 Bar/Restaurant

Scan me for more information.

205

Alan Rogers Code: DE36500
310 accommodations
349 pitches
GPS: 47.58331, 9.68331
Post Code: D-88131

Lindau (Bodensee), Bavaria (S)

www.alanrogers.com/de36500
info@gitzenweiler-hof.de
Tel: 08382 94940
www.gitzenweiler-hof.de

Open (Touring Pitches):
All year.

Gitzenweiler Hof

Gitzenweiler Hof is a really well equipped, first-class site with quality amenities, close to the Swiss and Austrian borders. Set in the countryside with 349 pitches for touring units, this site is arranged in rows with access roads, all are numbered and have 6/16A electricity. A separate open area is for tents with electrical connections; many of the pitches have water, drainage and TV connections. A large outdoor swimming pool has attractive surrounds with seats. This is a pleasant, friendly, well-run site with lots of activities for children and also space for those seeking peace and quiet.

The toilet blocks have been beautifully renovated and include some washbasins in cabins, a children's bathroom and baby bath. Laundry facilities. Motorhome service points. Shop (limited hours in low season). Two restaurants with takeaway. Large, heated, outdoor swimming pool in summer (33x25 m). Three playgrounds, one with water, and play room with entertainment during the holidays. Organised activities. Small animals and ponies for children. Fishing in lake. Minigolf. Cinema. Club room with arcade games, library and WiFi (charged). American-style motorhomes accepted up to ten tonnes. Overnight parking for motorhomes outside all year.

Key Features

 Open All Year

 Pets Accepted

 Disabled Facilities

 Swimming Pool

 Play Area

 Bar/Restaurant

 Bike Hire

 Fishing

Scan me for more information.

Alan Rogers Code: DE36960
5 accommodations
230 pitches
GPS: 48.43518, 13.10942
Post Code: D-84364

Bad Birnbach, Bavaria (S)

www.alanrogers.com/de36960
info@arterhof.de
Tel: 08563 96130
www.arterhof.de

Open (Touring Pitches):
All year.

Camping Arterhof

Based around a Bavarian farmstead, Gutshof-Camping Arterhof is an excellent site combining the charm of the old together with the comfort of the new. An attractive courtyard at the front of the site houses reception, a farm shop and a café with a flower decked terrace. To the rear is a tropical indoor pool containing soft water at a comfortable 30°C as well as a sauna, solarium, fitness room and much more. The 230 touring pitches with some hedge separation, on grass or pebble standing, all have TV, electricity, fresh and waste water connections, and 12 have their own pitch-side sanitary facilities. For winter camping, 50 of the pitches have a gas supply.

Modern, attractive, well maintained sanitary blocks with heated floor, free showers, washbasins in cabins, hairdryers and bathrooms to rent. Hairdressing salon, cosmetic studio. Laundry facilities. Motorcaravan services. Swimming pools. Wellness centre. Traditional restaurant serving southern Bavarian dishes with meat from the farm's own Aberdeen Angus cattle. Play area. Live music Fridays. WiFi.

Key Features

 Open All Year

 Pets Accepted

 Disabled Facilities

 Swimming Pool

 Play Area

 Bar/Restaurant

 Bike Hire

Scan me for more information.

Alan Rogers Code: DE36420
50 pitches
GPS: 48.43759, 10.92937
Post Code: D-86444

Affing-Mühlhausen bei
Augsburg, Bavaria (S)

www.alanrogers.com/de36420
info@lech-camping.de
Tel: 08207 2200
www.lech-camping.de

Open (Touring Pitches):
14 April - 17 September.

Lech Camping

Situated just north of Augsburg, this beautifully run site with its own small lake, is a pleasure to stay on. Gabi Ryssel, the owner, spends her long days working very hard to cater for every wish of her guests – from the moment you arrive and are given the key to one of the cleanest toilet blocks we have seen, plus plenty of tourist information, you are in very capable hands. The 50 level, grass and gravel pitches are roomy and have shade from pine trees. Electricity connections are available (10/16A Europlug). This is an immaculate site with a separate area for disabled visitors to park near the special facilities provided. The site is located beside a busy main road. A key (deposit payable) is needed to access washrooms and water points.

The new toilet block (cleaned several times daily) provides British style WCs and good showers with seating area and non-slip flooring. Baby room. Separate family bathroom to rent. Five star facilities for disabled visitors. Separate room with washing machine and laundry sinks. Motorcaravan services. Small shop, lakeside restaurant/bar/takeaway (all season). Small playground (partially fenced). Bicycle hire. Free WiFi. Trampolines. Surf boards and rowing boats (free).

Key Features

 Pets Accepted

 Disabled Facilities

 Play Area

 Bar/Restaurant

 Bike Hire

Scan me for more information.

Alan Rogers Code: DE36020
4 accommodations
100 pitches
GPS: 49.43950, 10.04211
Post Code: D-97993

Creglingen-Münster, Baden-Württemberg

www.alanrogers.com/de36020
camping.hausotter@web.de
Tel: 07933 20289
camping-romantische-strasse.de

Open (Touring Pitches):
15 March - 15 November.

Romantische Strasse

This popular tourist area can become very busy during summer when Romantische Strasse will be greatly appreciated for its peaceful situation in a wooded valley just outside the small village of Münster. There are 100 grass touring pitches (out of 140), many level, others with a small degree of slope. They are not hedged or fenced, in order to keep the natural appearance of the woodland. All the pitches have electricity (6A), some shade and are situated either side of a stream (fenced off from a weir at the far end of the site). Twenty-seven fully serviced pitches are on higher ground near reception.

The two main sanitary blocks are of good quality with free hot water. A third unit further into the site is due for refurbishment. Launderette. Motorcaravan services. Small shop (1/4-9/11). Gas supplies. Large, pleasant bar/restaurant at the entrance (1/4-9/11, closed Mon). Barbecue and covered sitting area. Heated indoor swimming pool (caps required) and sauna. Minigolf. Play area. Bicycle hire. Four mobile homes for hire. WiFi (charged).

Key Features

 Pets Accepted

 Disabled Facilities

 Swimming Pool

 Play Area

 Bar/Restaurant

 Bike Hire

Scan me for more information.

Alan Rogers Code: DE34400
20 accommodations
362 pitches
GPS: 47.96042, 7.95083
Post Code: D-79199

Kirchzarten, Baden-Württemberg

www.alanrogers.com/de34400
info@camping-kirchzarten.de
Tel: 076 619 040910
www.camping-kirchzarten.de

Open (Touring Pitches):
All year.

Camping Kirchzarten

Set in a green valley among the foothills of the Black Forest, this family managed site is well placed for visiting the popular Titisee, Feldberg and Totdnau areas, and is only 8 km. from Freiburg. It is divided into 486 numbered pitches, 362 of which are for touring, all with electricity (16A Europlug). Most pitches, which are side by side on gently sloping ground, are of reasonable size and clearly marked out, though there is nothing to separate them. There are increasing numbers of hardstanding pitches suitable for motorhomes. From about late June to mid-August, this site becomes very busy, and booking is advised.

The superb main sanitary building includes a large, central section for children, private cabins (some for hire) and a laundry room. The sanitary block near reception has been rebuilt to exemplary standards. Cooking stoves. Washing machines, dryers and irons (all on payment by meter) are available among the other buildings. Motorcaravan services. New bar/restaurant and takeaway (all year). Shop (15/4-31/10). Swimming pool complex (15/5-15/9). Wellness. TV room, play room and youth room. Large playground. Bicycle hire (electric). WiFi over site (charged). Children's activities in season.

Key Features

 Open All Year

 Pets Accepted

 Disabled Facilities

 Swimming Pool

 Play Area

 Bar/Restaurant

 Skiing

Scan me for more information.

Alan Rogers Code: DE34670
3 accommodations
50 pitches
GPS: 47.67828, 10.03035
Post Code: D-88316

Isny, Baden-Württemberg

www.alanrogers.com/de34670
info@waldbad-camping-isny.de
Tel: 07562 2389
www.camping-isny.de

Open (Touring Pitches):
1 March - 1 November.

Waldbad Camping Isny

Isny is a delightful spot for families and others looking for a peaceful stay in a very well managed environment. The site has been developed to a high standard and lies just south of the village in a wood, by a lake. In an open area, there are 50 individual 100 sq.m. hardstanding pitches (all with 16A electricity) with a circular access road. A further area is on a terrace just above. A café with light snacks during the week and meals at the weekends is open long hours in high season. It has a terrace that overlooks the lake, which is used for swimming (unsupervised). A low metal rail marks the area for non-swimmers, and there is a large grass sunbathing area. The site also offers a large family play area and fly fishing for trout in September and October.

The main sanitary unit is first class and has automatic toilet seat cleaning. There are cabins as well as vanity style washbasins, large controllable showers, with full curtain, token operated. Further facilities near the reception house showers, WCs, washbasins and a good unit for disabled visitors. Laundry. Basic motorcaravan services. Café/bar. Reception keeps a few basic supplies. Bicycles to borrow. WiFi throughout (charged).

Key Features

 Pets Accepted

 Swimming Pool

 Play Area

 Bar/Restaurant

 Skiing

 Bike Hire

Scan me for
more information.

Alan Rogers Code: DE35510
201 pitches
GPS: 50.36622, 7.60377
Post Code: D-56070

Koblenz, Rhineland Palatinate

www.alanrogers.com/de35510
koblenz@knauscamp.de
Tel: 02618 2719
www.knauscamp.de

Open (Touring Pitches):
10 February - 8 January.

Knaus Koblenz

One of the Knaus Group sites, Rhein-Mosel Koblenz overlooks the confluence of the Rhine and Mosel rivers where the city of Koblenz has stood since Roman times. One of the most visited cities in Germany, it is well served by this large, busy and efficient site. Unusually, there are no seasonal pitches here, leaving the whole site available for touring units and tents. All pitches have 16A electricity. There is some shade from young trees, but the site has an open feel with views of the rivers, the Kaiser Wilhelm Monument and the Ehrenbreitstein Fortress. There is some noise from rail and river traffic, but our sleep was not disturbed.

Key Features

 Pets Accepted

 Disabled Facilities

 Play Area

 Bar/Restaurant

Two excellent toilet blocks with free showers. One block has a baby bathing and changing room, whilst the other has a suite for disabled visitors. Washing machine and dryer at each block. Electric hotplates at each block (slot meters). Motorcaravan services. Small restaurant with sensibly priced family fare. Small playground. Boules. Dog bath. WiFi throughout (charged). Twelve overnight motorcaravan stands outside the barrier (charged).

Scan me for more information.

Alan Rogers Code: DE32420
400 pitches
GPS: 50.10600, 7.56750
Post Code: D-56291

Hausbay, Rhineland Palatinate

www.alanrogers.com/de32420
info@countrycamping.de
Tel: 06746 800 5440
www.countrycamping.de

Open (Touring Pitches):
All year.

Camping Schinderhannes

About 35 km. south of Koblenz, between Rhine and Mosel, and an ideal base from which to visit these regions, this site is set on a south-facing slope that catches the sun all day. With trees and parkland all around, it is a peaceful and picturesque setting. There are 150 permanent caravans in a separate area from 90 short stay touring pitches on hardstanding. For longer stays, an area around the lake has a further 160 numbered pitches. These are of over 100 sq.m. on grass, some with hardstanding and all with 8A electricity. You can position yourself for shade or sun. The lake is used for inflatable boats and fishing. English is spoken by the helpful reception staff. Country Camping could be a useful transit stop en route to the Black Forest, Bavaria, Austria and Switzerland, as well as a family holiday.

The sanitary buildings, which can be heated, are of a high standard with one section in the reception/shop building for the overnight pitches and the remainder close to the longer stay places. Facilities for disabled visitors and families. Laundry. Bar. Restaurant with takeaway. TV area. Skittle alley. Shop (all amenities 1/3-31/10 and Xmas). Tennis. Fishing. Play area. Rallies welcome. Torches useful. WiFi in restaurant and reception areas (charged). Some breeds of dog not accepted.

Key Features

 Open All Year

 Pets Accepted

 Disabled Facilities

 Play Area

 Bar/Restaurant

 Bike Hire

Scan me for more information.

Alan Rogers Code: DE32580
6 accommodations
154 pitches
GPS: 49.35174, 7.78066
Post Code: D-67705

Trippstadt, Rhineland Palatinate

www.alanrogers.com/de32580
info@saegmuehle.de
Tel: 06306 92190
www.saegmuehle.de

Open (Touring Pitches):
All year excl. 1 November - 11
December.

Camping Sägmühle

Freizeitzentrum Sägmühle is peacefully situated beside a lake, in a wooded valley in the heart of the Palatinate Nature Park, and there are many kilometres of walks to enjoy, as well as castles to explore. There are 303 pitches in total, of which 154 are available for touring, at least 80 sq.m. or more on flat grass, each with electricity (4/16A). Fifty of these are fully serviced and some have hardstanding. One area is close to the lake and it is a pleasant change to find a site that keeps the lakeside pitches for touring units.

Each area has its own sanitary facilities, which feature private cabins, baby bathroom, facilities for disabled visitors, launderette. Motorcaravan services. Restaurant serving local specialities and takeaway (lunchtime and evening). Bread available in high season. Solarium. Tennis. Play areas. Boules. Minigolf. Lake fishing. Beach volleyball. Entertainment daily in high season. Guided tours for ramblers and mountain bikers. Electric barbecues are not permitted. WiFi on part of site (charged).

Key Features

 Pets Accepted

 Disabled Facilities

 Play Area

 Bar/Restaurant

 Golf

Scan me for
more information.

Alan Rogers Code: DE35670
7 accommodations
140 pitches
GPS: 50.58688, 8.03488
Post Code: D-56479

Seck, Rhineland Palatinate

www.alanrogers.com/de35670
info@camping-park-weiherhof.de
Tel: 026 648 555
www.camping-park-weiherhof.de

Open (Touring Pitches):
1 March - 31 October.

Weiherhof am See

Camping Park Weiherhof is a family run site in the Hoher Westerwald, an attractive nature protected area of meadows, forests and streams with over 250 km. of maintained trails, ideal for those who enjoy rambling or cycling, or simply to relax. Eight years ago Birgit and Helmut Stelzen took over the site and have developed it into a prize-winning environmentally friendly site. Of the 340 pitches, 140 are available to visitors, all with electricity (10-16A). They are gently sloping, on grass/gravel with some tree shade and hedge separation, 80 are fully serviced and some have a lakeside location. In places the Hoher Westerwald rises to over 650 metres and with its network of cycling and walking trails is ideal for those who enjoy a leisurely walk in natural surroundings or something more strenuous.

Four well maintained sanitary blocks, some washbasins in cabins, showers upon payment, facilities for children and disabled visitors. Baby room. Washing machine and dryers. Shop (15/3-31/10). Restaurant with terrace and lake view. Snack bar (high season). Sunbathing area beside lake and small beach. Play areas, indoor activity room, table tennis, animation in high season. Swimming and boating on small lake. Wellness centre. Rambling/cycling directly from site. Bicycle and E-bicycle hire (battery charging stations in Westerwald). Overnight pitches outside barrier (€10).

Key Features

 Pets Accepted

 Disabled Facilities

 Play Area

 Bar/Restaurant

 Skiing

 Bike Hire

 Fishing

 Scan me for more information.

Alan Rogers Code: DE32800
10 accommodations
250 pitches
GPS: 51.17550, 8.89067
Post Code: D-34516

Vöhl-Herzhausen, Hessen

www.alanrogers.com/de32800
info@camping-teichmann.de
Tel: 05635 245
www.camping-teichmann.de

Open (Touring Pitches):
All year.

Camping Teichmann

Situated near the eastern end of the 27 km. long Edersee and the Kellerwald-Edersee National Park, this attractively set site is surrounded by wooded hills and encircles a six-hectare lake, which has separate areas for swimming, fishing and boating. Of the 500 pitches, 250 are for touring; all have 10A electricity, and 50 have fresh and waste water connections. The pitches are on level grass, some having an area of hardstanding, and are separated by hedges and mature trees. At the opposite side of the lake from the entrance, there is a separate area for tents with its own sanitary block. The adjoining national park, a popular leisure attraction, offers a wealth of holiday/sporting activities including walking, cycling (there are two passenger ferries that take cycles), boat trips, cable car and much more. Full details are available at the friendly reception. For winter sports lovers, the ski centre at Winterberg is only 30 km. away from this all-year-round site.

Three good quality sanitary blocks can be heated and have free showers, washbasins (open and in cabins), baby rooms and facilities for wheelchair users. Laundry. Motorcaravan services. Café and shop (both summer only). Restaurant by entrance open all day (closed Feb). Watersports. Boat and bicycle hire. Lake swimming. Fishing. Minigolf. Playground. Sauna. Solarium. Disco (high season). Internet access.

Key Features

 Open All Year

 Pets Accepted

 Disabled Facilities

 Play Area

 Bar/Restaurant

 Skiing

 Bike Hire

 Fishing

Scan me for more information.

Alan Rogers Code: DE31970
26 accommodations
150 pitches
GPS: 50.41508, 6.71869
Post Code: D-53945

Blankenheim/Freilingen, North
Rhine-Westphalia

Eifel-Camp

www.alanrogers.com/de31970
info@eifel-camp.de
Tel: 02697 282
www.eifel-camp.de

Open (Touring Pitches):
All Year

This delightful campsite offers spaciously arranged pitches on terraces set amongst lush greenery. All pitches are equipped with 220V/16 A electricity connection and the long-term pitches have access to the community antenna/common aerial. You will also find a drain and service-station for caravans and campervans, as well as well-grounded pitches for campervans. Located in the northern Eifel, Eifel-Camp is situated only a few kilometres away from Blankenheim and close to Lake Freilingen in the countryside. Situated within half an hour coming from the direction of Cologne, from Aachen, Bonn and Koblenz in less than an hour, and driving from Trier will take around 1.5 hours.

Key Features

 Open All Year

 Pets Accepted

 Play Area

 Bar/Restaurant

 Bike Hire

Enjoy the comforts of this award-winning camping-site with facilities including a disabled bathing unit, spacious and superb bathroom/sanitary facilities with centrally heated showers providing free unlimited hot water. You may also book individual bathing units with washbasin, shower and toilet. Washing machines and tumble dryers. The popular "Waldläufer" restaurant with sun terrace. On-site kiosk offering fresh rolls and croissants in the morning, as well as basic necessities. Playground. Leisure club " Geißbock-Stadel" on the first floor of the sanitary building offering various options for guests, e.g. as a lounge or recreation room, but it can also be used for mini-club activities, the mini-disco, indoor sports activities or cinema shows. An open barbecue facility with a separate fireplace on the outskirts of the campsite, or a small complete BBQ-cabin in the upper part of the "mountain pasture" offering room for up to 24 people. There are also two BBQ-cabins (additional-charge).

Scan me for
more information.

Alan Rogers Code: DE31490
35 accommodations
50 pitches
GPS: 51.13694, 7.93984
Post Code: D-57439

Attendorn, North Rhine-
Westphalia

www.alanrogers.com/de31490
info@biggen.de
Tel: 02722 95530
www.biggen.de

Open (Touring Pitches):
All year.

Camping Hof Biggen

Camping Hof Biggen is a well-established site in the heart of the Sauerland region, close to the city of Attendorn, just 4 km. away from the Biggesee. It is set amidst beautiful green countryside, and a large touring area at the top of the site offers a great view over woods, meadows and the Burg Schnellenberg castle. There are 350 pitches, 50 for tourers, all equipped with 16A electricity, in addition to 50 for tents on the slightly sloping ground. There are 25 caravans for hire. The site can become a suntrap in hot weather. This area of Sauerland is characterised by Lake Biggesee, where there are numerous opportunities for watersports and swimming. Nature lovers can enjoy the many walking routes through the Ebbe Mountains National Park, and days out include the medieval village of Attendorn (for shopping), the Atta Höhle Caves and the castle.

Key Features

 Open All Year

 Pets Accepted

 Disabled Facilities

 Play Area

 Bar/Restaurant

 Skiing

 Bike Hire

Three older style toilet blocks of varying sizes are clean and well maintained, with showers and washbasins in cubicles. Car wash area. Waste disposal station. Laundry. Camp kitchen. Self-service supermarket, restaurant with adjoining terrace (both open all year). Large screen TV. Bowling alley. Play areas. Football field. Volleyball court. Outdoor board games. Games room. Children's entertainment (July/Aug). Bicycle hire. Free cars available for motorcaravanners.

Scan me for
more information.

Alan Rogers Code: DE31260
2 accommodations
40 pitches
GPS: 52.05163, 9.10140
Post Code: D-32699

Extertal, North Rhine-Westphalia

www.alanrogers.com/de31260
info@campingpark-extertal.de
Tel: 05262 3307
www.campingpark-extertal.de

Open (Touring Pitches):
All year.

Campingpark Extertal

Campingpark Extertal is a well maintained site located in the Weser mountains, 20 km. west of Hameln. Many pitches here have permanent caravans but around 40 terraced pitches are reserved for tourers. All pitches have 16A electricity, water, drainage and cable TV connections. Pitches are generally grassy and of a good size. On-site amenities include a bar/snack bar, TV/games room and small shop (fresh bread available daily). There is also a small fishing lake. A range of shops and restaurants are available in the village of Extertal, to the north.

Heated, modern sanitary building with separate facilities for children and wheelchair accessible bath. Washing machine, dryer and ironing board. Kitchen with sink, hotplates and microwave. Small lake (fishing). Sports field. TV/games room. Mobile homes to rent (1/4-31/10). Shop, restaurant with bar (1/4-31/10). Motorcaravan service point. Children's playground. Dog shower. WiFi (free).

Key Features

 Open All Year

 Pets Accepted

 Disabled Facilities

 Play Area

 Bar/Restaurant

 Skiing

 Fishing

Scan me for more information.

Alan Rogers Code: DE30390
150 pitches
GPS: 51.49139, 9.76123
Post Code: D-37127

Dransfeld, Lower Saxony

www.alanrogers.com/de30390
mail@campingplatz-dransfeld.de
Tel: 05502 2147
www.campingplatz-dransfeld.de

Open (Touring Pitches):
All year excl. November.

Am Hohen Hagen

This family run campsite is on the edge of the small town of Dransfeld in the heart of Lower Saxony. There are over 300 pitches of which 150 are for touring units, all with 16A electrical connections and 20 also have water and waste water connections. One touring section offers superb views over the surrounding countryside. The site is quiet and relaxing in low season, becoming more lively during the main holiday period with a range of activities and entertainment provided. Shops and restaurants are within walking distance, whilst the old town of Göttingen is an easy drive away and provides a wider range of shops, bars and restaurants.

Three sanitary blocks with free hot showers. Heated outdoor swimming pool (June-Oct). Shop (mornings). Restaurant with terrace. Laundry. Kitchen. Playground. Football field. Beach volleyball. Basketball. Minigolf. Wellness and sauna. Fitness equipment. Entertainment and activities for all ages (holiday periods). Free loan of city and mountain bikes. Six caravans for hire. Motorcaravan services. WiFi throughout (charged).

Key Features

 Pets Accepted

 Disabled Facilities

 Swimming Pool

 Play Area

 Bar/Restaurant

 Bike Hire

Scan me for
more information.

Alan Rogers Code: DE28355
30 pitches
GPS: 53.52107, 8.23484
Post Code: D-26969

Eckwarderhörne, Lower Saxony

www.alanrogers.com/de28355
eckwarderhoerne@knauscamp.de
Tel: 04736 1300
www.knauscamp.de

Open (Touring Pitches):
All year.

Knaus Eckwarderhörne

Knaus Campingpark Eckwarderhörne is directly on the Wadden Sea National Park. This is an excellent area to enjoy the North Sea beaches and watch the tides change. It has 180 pitches, of which just 30 are for tourers, on flat and open grassy fields right behind the dyke. There are two pitches for very large units and 16 hardstandings. All are fully serviced with water, waste water and 16A electricity. Being small, it is much quieter than many of the sites along this stretch of coast. Over 250 km. of cycle routes have been laid out in the vicinity, and of course one can try the famous Wad Walking (bring your oldest clothes) to get as close as possible to the wildlife. On the Butjadingen peninsula, time seems to slow down, making this a great spot for a relaxing holiday surrounded by nature.

One central toilet block with open style washbasins, controllable hot showers and facilities for disabled visitors. Washing machine and dryer. Playground. Playing field. Games room with billiards, library and TV. Activity programme (July/Aug). Boat launching. WiFi (charged).

Key Features

 Open All Year

 Pets Accepted

 Disabled Facilities

 Beach Access

 Play Area

 Fishing

Scan me for more information.

Alan Rogers Code: DE30250
16 accommodations
750 pitches
GPS: 52.48555, 7.99003
Post Code: D-49597

Rieste, Lower Saxony

Alfsee Ferien & Erholungspark

www.alanrogers.com/de30250
info@alfsee.de
Tel: 054 649 2120
www.alfsee.de

Open (Touring Pitches):
All Year

Alfsee has plenty to offer for the active family and children of all ages. It is a really good base for enjoying the many recreational activities available here on the lake. The smaller lake has a 780 m. water ski cableway (on payment) and there is also a separate swimming area with a sandy beach. The Alfsee itself is now a nature reserve. Many birdwatching excursions are organised by the site. Improvements to this already well equipped site continue. There are now over 750 pitches (many long stay but with 375 for touring units) on flat grass, all with 16A electricity, with some shade for those in the original area. A new camping area provides 290 large pitches. A member of Leading Campings group.

Five excellent heated sanitary blocks with family bathrooms (to rent), baby rooms and laundry facilities. Cooking facilities. Dishwashers. Motorcaravan services. Gas supplies. Shop, restaurants and takeaway (high season). Watersports. Playground, new indoor play centre (on payment) and entertainment for children. Entertainment hall. Grass tennis courts. Trampoline. Minigolf. Go-kart track. Games room. Fishing. Bicycle and E-bike hire. Free WiFi throughout.

Key Features

 Open All Year

 Pets Accepted

 Disabled Facilities

 Swimming Pool

 Play Area

 Bar/Restaurant

 Bike Hire

 Fishing

Scan me for more information.

Alan Rogers Code: DE30210
168 pitches
GPS: 53.11483, 8.83247
Post Code: D-28359

Bremen, Bremen

www.alanrogers.com/de30210
info@hansecamping.de
Tel: 0421 3074 6825
www.hansecamping.de

Open (Touring Pitches):
All year.

Hanse Camping

Formerly known as Camping am Stadtwaldsee, this well designed and purpose built campsite overlooking a lake is ideally placed for those travelling to northern Europe and for people wishing to visit Bremen and places within the region. There is a bus stop outside the site. Of the 220 level pitches 168 are for touring units, standing on grass with openwork reinforcements at the entrances. All have electricity (16A), water and drainage. The pitches are positioned around the spacious grass-roofed sanitary block and are laid out in areas separated by trees and hedges. A restaurant/cafeteria with open-air terrace overlooks the lake.

Modern sanitary block with free hot showers, facilities for disabled visitors, five private bathrooms for rental. Washing machines and dryers. Motorcaravan services. Large, modern kitchen. Sitting/dining room with LCD projector facilities. Small supermarket (1/3-31/12). Lakeside café/restaurant with terrace. Play room. Play area. Lake swimming, windsurfing, fishing and scuba diving (air tank refill facility on site). Tents for hire. WiFi (charged). Bicycle and go-kart hire.

Key Features

 Open All Year

 Pets Accepted

 Disabled Facilities

 Play Area

 Bar/Restaurant

 Bike Hire

Scan me for more information.

Capital London
Currency British Pound (£)
Language English
Telephone country code 00 44
Time Zone GMT/UTC
Tourist Office visitbritain.com

Climate Maritime climate. Varied and hard to predict but generally mild in the summer with temperatures into the high 20s and cooler and wetter in the winter months.

Great Britain

The United Kingdom offers a wealth of extraordinary landscapes set against the backdrop of a rich and vibrant history. In terms of character and stunning scenery it offers an unsurpassed choice of holiday activities from coast to country.

Northern England A beautiful and varied region of rolling hills and undulating moors, along with a wealth of industrial heritage and undiscovered countryside. The Yorkshire moors, the Cumbrian lakes, -the Northumbrian ancient forts and fairytale castles, these are all highlights not to be missed.

Southern England Rich in maritime heritage and historical attractions, the southern region comprises tranquil English countryside replete with picture postcard villages, ancient towns, formidable castles and grand stately homes, coupled with a beautiful coastline, white-faced cliffs and lively seaside resorts.

Heart of England Spanning central England, from the ancient borders of Wales in the west across to Lincolnshire on the east coast, the Heart of England is rich in glorious rolling countryside, magnificent castles and fine stately homes.

Eastern England A perfect mix of gentle countryside and sleepy storybook villages, it's an unspoilt region with endless skies, inland waterways and traditional beach resorts.

Western England A region of contrasts, with windswept moorlands and dramatic cliffs towering above beautiful sandy beaches.

Wales Land of ancient myths and Celtic legends, Wales boasts a diverse landscape, from lakes and mountains, rivers and valleys to beautiful coastlines and rolling wooded countryside.

Scotland From gentle rolling hills and rugged coastlines, to dramatic peaks punctuated with beautiful lochs, Scotland is an untamed land steeped in history.

Northern Ireland With a diversity of unspoilt landscapes, from wild coastlines to green valleys, rugged mountains and shimmering lakes, to the natural phenomenon of the Giant's Causeway, Northern Ireland is crammed full of sights.

Public Holidays New Year's Day, Good Friday, Easter Monday, Early May Bank Holiday 6 May, Spring Bank Holiday 27 May, Summer Bank Holiday 26 August, Christmas Day, Boxing Day.

Motoring Driving is on the left and the imperial system for road signs is used. Speed limits are 30 mp\h in residential areas and 70mp/h on motorways. When using motorways never use the hard shoulder unless instructed to or if you break down (in this situation turn on your hazard lights). Tailgating is illegal as is drink driving and using your mobile phone whilst driving unless it is hands-free.

See campsite map page 480.

Alan Rogers Code: UK0320
7 accommodations
31 pitches
GPS: 50.37722, -4.41850
Post Code: PL13 1QS

Cornwall, South West

www.alanrogers.com/uk0320
info@looecountrypark.co.uk
Tel: 01503 240265
www.looecountrypark.co.uk

Open (Touring Pitches):
All Year

Looe Country Park

Looe Country Park is a lovely all year site, which will appeal to those who prefer a quiet, well kept small family site to the larger ones with many on-site activities. With good countryside views, 31 touring units can be accommodated on well-tended grass. Good sized pitches are marked with some hedging between pairs of pitches to give privacy, and most have electricity connections. There are several hardstandings and 12 fully serviced pitches. Five mobile homes (2x new 3 bedroom and 3x 2 bedroom, including 2 dog-friendly) and two camping pods are available to rent. The owners, Rob and Jill, live on the park and make everyone very welcome, creating a relaxed and happy atmosphere. The nearest beach is a 15-20 minute walk from a gate in the corner of the park. This is a good area for walking with links to the coastal path through Duchy woodlands. The Monkey Sanctuary is also nearby.

Laminated teak with chrome fittings and black surfaces make an unusual but stylish and fully equipped, heated sanitary block. Family room. Laundry room. Shop (open on demand.) for gas and basics, and some camping accessories. New play area planned for spring 2019. Tourist information in reception. WiFi (free - conditions apply).

Key Features

 Open All Year

 Pets Accepted

 Play Area

Scan me for
more information.

Alan Rogers Code: UK0681
7 accommodations
110 pitches
GPS: 51.20484, -4.06417
Post Code: EX34 9SH

Devon, South West

Mill Park

www.alanrogers.com/uk0681
enquiries@millpark.com
Tel: 01271 882647
www.millpark.com

Open (Touring Pitches):
31 March - 31 October

Mill Park is a sheltered touring caravan and camping site set in an attractive wooded valley on the North Devon Coast. It has a shop, a takeaway, games room, laundry, and has many other useful facilities such as gas-changing and ice pack freezing. There is also an on-site pub. It's surrounded by attractive woodland and is an ideal family site as it's just a short walk to quiet beaches, both sand and pebble. Equally close by is the unspoilt and breathtaking beauty of Exmoor and the nearest village, Berrynarbor is just a five minute walk from the site. This village dates back from the sixteenth century and earlier. There is a quaint old country pub, village stores and post office. Buses also pass by the site regularly. They cater very well for families and couples and they do all possible to create a friendly relaxed atmosphere.

Key Features

 Pets Accepted

 Disabled Facilities

 Play Area

 Bar/Restaurant

 Fishing

2 Separate shower blocks - both recently refurbished and kept impecably clean, onsite bar, well stocked shop, fishing lake, small river flowing through the park, childrens play area, games room, book swap, games library, free Internet in bar and games room. Close to beaches, secluded and quiet, very peaceful.

Scan me for
more information.

Alan Rogers Code: UK0745
12 accommodations
52 pitches
GPS: 51.02918, -3.82347
Post Code: EX36 3HQ

Devon, South West

www.alanrogers.com/uk0745
relax@exmoorriverside.co.uk
Tel: 01769 579269
www.exmoorriverside.co.uk

Open (Touring Pitches):
All year

Riverside Park Exmoor

A very impressive purpose built campsite beside the River Mole, Riverside is set in 70 acres of meadow and ten acres of woodland. There are 54 pitches with hardstanding, 16A electricity connection, water, drainage and TV aerial socket and some large tent pitches with or without electricity. Neat grass, tarmac roads and growing trees and hedges contribute to the attractive, overall impression. The heated toilet block gleams and visitors will appreciate the hairdryers, hand-dryers and shaver points. The owners, Joe and Nicky Penfold, are not resting on their laurels and have developed fishing lakes with specimen carp down by the river, a play area on the opposite bank and a new 9 bedroom luxurious leisure facility, offering high quality south facing rooms with glass fronted balconies and views overlooking the landscaped parkland. They also have a few mobile homes for rental.

Key Features

 Open All Year

 Pets Accepted

 Disabled Facilities

 Play Area

 Bar/Restaurant

 Fishing

Two modern, fully equipped and heated toilet blocks accessed by code. Facilities for disabled visitors. Family shower room. Laundry room. Shop (limited hours in low season). New 9 bedroom luxurious leisure facility is an exciting addition to the park, with high quality south facing rooms with glass fronted balconies and views overlooking the landscaped parkland. Play area. New modern bar with wide screen TV & pool table. Restaurant. Entertainment (B.Hs and high season). Fishing. Caravan storage. Swimming in river. WiFi throughout (free). Accommodation to rent. Dog friendly.

Scan me for more information.

Alan Rogers Code: UK1690
165 pitches
GPS: 51.19053, -2.27835
Post Code: BA12 7NL

Wiltshire, South West

www.alanrogers.com/uk1690
UKSitesBookingService@camc.com
Tel: 01985 844663
www.caravanclub.co.uk/site-search/?q=longleat

Open (Touring Pitches):
20 March - 4 January.

Longleat CAMC Site

The site is well managed by Caravan & Motorhome Club (CAMC) wardens and is situated in ten acres of lightly wooded, level grassland within walking distance of the house and gardens. What a magnificent situation in which to find a caravan park, next to Longleat House, gardens and Safari Park. There are 165 generous pitches (151 with hardstanding and ten on grass), all with 16A electricity connections. Water points and recycling bins are neatly walled with low night lighting. Two new buildings provide immaculate facilities, while an amenity block houses a family room and tourist information. Tents are not accepted (except trailer tents). Admission charges now apply to all of the Longleat attractions and grounds. Discounts are available to Caravan & Motorhome Club members.

Key Features

 Pets Accepted

 Disabled Facilities

 Play Area

Two heated toilet blocks provide washbasins in cubicles, controllable showers and a vanity section with mirrors and hairdryers. Baby/toddler room, suite for disabled visitors, laundry room and a family room with a DVD player. Two motorcaravan service points. Play area. Office is manned 09.00-17.30 and stocks basic food items, papers can be ordered and gas is available. Paperback exchange library. Fish and chip van calls some evenings. WiFi over site (charged). Late arrivals area with hook-up.

Scan me for more information.

Alan Rogers Code: UK3210
17 accommodations
34 pitches
GPS: 51.75374, 0.00013
Post Code: EN11 0AS

Hertfordshire, London

Dobbs Weir

www.alanrogers.com/uk3210
dobbsweircampsite@leevalleypark.
org.uk
Tel: 03000 030 619
www.visitleevalley.org.uk/wheretostay

This large (27-acre) camping park is ideally situated in the Lee Valley for fishing, walking and cycling activities. It is divided into two sections: one for private static caravans with a large fenced caravan storage area, the other for touring. The 34 level touring pitches are numbered, but not separated; all have 10A electricity and 22 are hardstanding. There is an area for tents with a field adjacent to the River Lee for tents requiring electricity. The whole complex is very flat with little shade. There is no public transport, but a 25-minute walk along a towpath takes you to Broxbourne railway station for travel along the Lee Valley to London.

Open (Touring Pitches):
1 March - 31 January

Key Features

 Pets Accepted

 Disabled Facilities

 Play Area

 Fishing

One modern, heated toilet block with controllable showers, open washbasins and facilities for disabled campers. Washing machines and dryers. Motorcaravan services. Small shop (open all season). Small play area. River fishing. Bicycle hire. WiFi over site (charged).

Scan me for more information.

Alan Rogers Code: UK3055
300 pitches
GPS: 51.20073, 0.39333
Post Code: TN12 6PY

Kent, South East

www.alanrogers.com/uk3055
touring@thehopfarm.co.uk
Tel: 01622 870838
www.thehopfarm.co.uk

Open (Touring Pitches):
1 March - 30 September.

The Hop Farm Campsite

Set in 400 acres of the Garden of England, The Hop Farm Touring & Camping Park is a popular family visitor attraction. There are plenty of activities to entertain children including adventure play areas (indoor and outdoor), a driving school, funfair rides, the Magic Factory and the Great Goblin Hunt. This is also the venue for many special events throughout the summer including music festivals, shows and other gatherings. To one side, and overlooking all this activity and the attractive cluster of oasts, is the touring park which provides over 300 grass and hardstanding pitches on flat, open fields. Electricity (16A) and water are available. There is also plenty more space for tents.

Brand new state-of-the-art shower and washrooms have been added to the site to enhance guest experiences, providing a luxurious touch to their stay. Small shop (in reception) for essentials. Free entry for campers and caravanners to the Family Park with restaurant and café. Nature walks. Boat launching. Fishing. Dogs accepted but not permitted inside the visitor attraction. Activities and entertainment at the visitor attraction.

Key Features

 Pets Accepted

 Disabled Facilities

 Play Area

 Bar/Restaurant

 Fishing

Scan me for more information.

Alan Rogers Code: UK3400
65 pitches
GPS: 52.85804, 0.97583
Post Code: NR21 0NL

Norfolk, East of England

www.alanrogers.com/uk3400
enquiries@old-brick-kilns.co.uk
Tel: 01328 878305
www.old-brick-kilns.co.uk

Open (Touring Pitches):
All year excl. 2 January - 14 March.

The Old Brick Kilns

This is an excellent tranquil, family run park and a friendly, helpful atmosphere prevails. The park's development on the site of old brick kilns has resulted in land on varying levels. This provides areas of level, well drained pitches with many on hardstanding. There are 65 pitches in total, all with 16A electricity and 30 are fully serviced. A wide range of trees and shrubs provide shelter and are home for a variety of wildlife. There are garden areas, including a butterfly garden, and a conservation pond is the central feature. There is a large, comfortable bar area and restaurant open five days a week. A member of the Best of British group.

Very good heated toilet blocks provide very clean facilities. Baby room. Facilities for disabled guests (Radar key). Laundry room. Motorcaravan services. Good shop with gas supplies. Bar/restaurant (5 days a week, April-Oct) and takeaway (July/Aug) with patio area outside. TV/games room. Giant chess. Small library. Fenced play area. Fishing. WiFi (charged). B&B also available. Caravan storage.

Key Features

  Pets Accepted

 Disabled Facilities

 Play Area

 Bar/Restaurant

Fishing

Scan me for more information.

Alan Rogers Code: UK5360
87 pitches
GPS: 53.58880, -3.04400
Post Code: PR8 3ST

Mersey, North West

Willowbank Touring Park

www.alanrogers.com/uk5360
info@willowbankcp.co.uk
Tel: 01704 571566
www.willowbankcp.co.uk

Open (Touring Pitches):
14 February - 31 January.

Well situated for the Sefton coast and Southport, Willowbank Holiday Home & Touring Park is set on the edge of sand dunes amongst mature, wind swept trees. Entrance to the park is controlled by a barrier, with a pass-key issued at the excellent reception building which doubles as a sales office for the substantial, high quality caravan holiday home development. There are 79 touring pitches, 30 on gravel hardstandings, 16 on grass and a further 33 pitches, all with 10A electricity; these are on grass hardstanding using an environmentally friendly reinforcement system. Large units are accepted by prior arrangement.

The purpose built, heated toilet block is of a high standard including an excellent bathroom for disabled visitors, although the showers are rather compact. Baby room. Laundry. Motorcaravan services. Play area. Field for ball games. Beauty treatments. WiFi throughout (charged).

Key Features

 Pets Accepted

 Disabled Facilities

 Play Area

Scan me for more information.

Alan Rogers Code: UK3640
5 accommodations
28 pitches
GPS: 53.50273, -0.39363
Post Code: LN7 6RX

Lincolnshire, Heart of England

www.alanrogers.com/uk3640
info@caistorlakes.co.uk
Tel: 01472 859626
www.caistorlakes.co.uk

Open (Touring Pitches):
1 January - 31 December.

Caistor Lakes

Caisor Lakes offers 28 hardstanding pitches, each with electrical hook-up facility. Each pitch has a double wide gravel area, perfect for parking your caravan or motorhome and your car. The adjacent grassed area is ideal for your awning and allows ample space for relaxation. On-site they have fresh water points, waste water and chemical disposal, motorhome drop point and pot washing facilities, as well as 5-star toilet and shower blocks. Pitches start from £22 per night, which incudes two adults, up to two well behaved pets, car and awning. A £20 deposit for electric is taken upon checking in, and any monies not used will be unded at the end of the stay. A £5 fully refundable deposit for a Gate fob which allows 24 hour access to the site for residents is also taken upon check in, and is refunded upon return of the fob.

Ladies and Gentlemen toilets with showers, cubicles and sinks. Disabled toilet facilities with toilet, sink and shower. Onsite bait shop for all bait needs. Multi-award winning 100 seater restaurant with ample outdoor seating area and food delivery service to pitch or peg.

Key Features

 Adults Only

 Open All Year

 Pets Accepted

 Disabled Facilities

 Bar/Restaurant

 Fishing

 Scan me for more information.

Alan Rogers Code: UK4715
2 accommodations
61 pitches
GPS: 54.11311, -2.51066
Post Code: LA2 7FJ

North Yorkshire, Yorkshire

www.alanrogers.com/uk4715
info@riversidecaravanpark.co.uk
Tel: 01524 261272
www.riversidecaravanpark.co.uk

Open (Touring Pitches):
1 March - 2 January.

Riverside Park Bentham

The pretty, tree-lined approach to Riverside leads into an attractive park, owned by the Marshall family since the late 1960s. Nestling in beautiful countryside, alongside the River Wenning, the park has easy access to the Yorkshire Dales and the Lake District. For touring units there are 12 fully serviced pitches, 15 on hardstanding and 30 grass pitches. All have 16A electricity and TV hook-ups. An area has been developed for 50 seasonal pitches on gravel. Located away from the touring area are 206 privately owned holiday homes. Tents are not accepted. The smart reception building includes a small shop selling caravan accessories.

The modern toilet block with underfloor heating is centrally situated. Washbasins in cubicles. Unisex showers in a separate area. Toilet and shower room for disabled visitors (Radar key). Family shower/bathroom (charged). Motorcaravan services. Shop (all season). Play area for younger children. Large field for ball games. Family games room. The river can be used for fishing (permit from reception) swimming and small boats. Caravan storage. WiFi (free).

Key Features

 Pets Accepted

 Disabled Facilities

 Play Area

 Fishing

Scan me for more information.

Alan Rogers Code: UK5650
25 pitches
GPS: 54.31313, -2.67500
Post Code: LA8 0AS

Kendal, Cumbria

www.alanrogers.com/uk5650
ashescaravanpark@gmail.com
Tel: 01539 731833
www.ashescaravanpark.co.uk

Open (Touring Pitches):
1 March - 1 November.

Ashes Adult Only Park

The Ashes is a small, friendly, adults only park in an extremely peaceful setting in the rolling Cumbrian countryside, yet less than three miles from the M6, and only slightly further from Kendal. Thus it is not only a convenient night stop, but also a useful base from which to explore the Lake District and the Yorkshire Dales. A very tidy park, the central grass area is attractively planted with shrubs and bushes and there is an open vista (with little shade). There are 25 hardstanding gravel pitches, all with 10A electrical connections. These are neatly placed around the perimeter with an oval access road. The whole area slopes gently down from the entrance, with some pitches fairly level and others with a little more slope (levelling system for caravans on all pitches). No tents are accepted other than trailer tents.

A small, purpose built stone building with a slate roof houses two unisex shower rooms (underfloor heating) and the washing and toilet facilities. New facilities for disabled visitors. No shop. New electronic barrier. TV signal booster. Dog exercise area. WiFi (charged).

Key Features

(18+) Adults Only

Pets Accepted

Disabled Facilities

Scan me for more information.

Alan Rogers Code: UK5520
8 accommodations
97 pitches
GPS: 54.41715, -2.99528
Post Code: LA22 0HX

Ambleside, Cumbria

Skelwith Fold

www.alanrogers.com/uk5520
info@skelwith.com
Tel: 01539 432277
www.skelwith.com

Open (Touring Pitches):
1 March - 15 November.

Skelwith Fold has been developed in the extensive grounds of a country estate taking advantage of the wealth of mature trees and shrubs. Over 300 privately owned caravan holiday homes and 97 touring pitches are absorbed into this unspoilt natural environment, sharing it with red squirrels and other wildlife in several discrete areas branching off the central, mile-long main driveway. Touring pitches (no tents) are on gravel hardstanding and metal pegs will be necessary for awnings. Electricity hook-ups (10-16A) and basic amenities are available in all areas. Youngsters, and indeed their parents, will find endless pleasure exploring over 90 acres of wild woodland and, if early risers, it is possible to see deer, foxes, etc. at the almost hidden tarn deep in the woods.

Key Features

 Pets Accepted

 Disabled Facilities

 Play Area

Three toilet blocks, well situated to serve all areas, have the usual facilities including laundry, drying and ironing rooms. Facilities for disabled visitors. Motorcaravan services. Well stocked, licensed shop. Battery charging, gas and caravan spares and accessories. Adventure play area. Astroturf sports pitch. Library with computer. E-bicycle hire. Family recreation area with picnic tables and goal posts in the Lower Glade. WiFi. New for 2019 - Dishwashing facilities by EasyBe

Scan me for more information.

Alan Rogers Code: UK6670
90 pitches
GPS: 52.99788, -2.96632
Post Code: LL13 0SP

Wrexham, North Wales

www.alanrogers.com/uk6670
enquiries@plassey.com
Tel: 01978 780277
www.plassey.com

Open (Touring Pitches):
8 February - 4 January.

Plassey Leisure Park

Plassey Leisure Park has been carefully developed over the past 50 years. Improvements include landscaping, car parking and low level lighting installed around the park. An area for privately owned holiday homes has been recently created. Originally a dairy farm, the park is set in 247 acres of the Dee Valley and offers an extensive range of activities. It has been divided into discreet areas with 120 pitches around the edges. There are 90 touring pitches with 16A electrical connections, 30 pitches are fully serviced, and 50 have hardstanding. Five further areas accommodate 120 seasonal caravans. There is much to do and to look at in the rural setting at Plassey. A member of the Best of British group.

Some refurbished toilet facilities are supplemented by a newer heated block with individual washbasin cubicles, a room for families and disabled visitors. Laundry. Motorcaravan services. Shop (with gas). Club room with games room for children. Heated indoor pool with sunbed, sauna and viewing area (charged). Adventure play area. 9-hole golf course. Fishing lakes. Wildlife meadow and countryside footpaths. Bicycle hire. No skateboards or footballs permitted. Winter caravan storage. Luxury holiday home for hire. WiFi throughout (charged).

Key Features

 Pets Accepted

 Disabled Facilities

 Swimming Pool

 Play Area

 Bar/Restaurant

 Bike Hire

 Fishing

 Golf

Scan me for more information.

Alan Rogers Code: UK6689
65 pitches
GPS: 53.28485, -3.59384
Post Code: LL22 8ET

Conwy,

www.alanrogers.com/uk6689
booking@manorafon.co.uk
Tel: 01745 833237
www.manorafon.co.uk

Open (Touring Pitches):
01 March - 30 September

Manorafon Farm Camping

Manorafon Farm Touring & Camping is situated on the north Wales coast and boasts beautiful views of the countryside and coastline with the backdrop of Gwrych Castle; all this within a short walk from the town of Abergele which can offer all of the facilities associated with a small but lively town. The campsite is set within the Gwrych Castle Estate and neighbouring Abergele Golf Club's rolling lawns. This delightful site offers 65 pitches, modern facilities and is just a short stroll away from local inns, eateries and grocery stores. You'll also reach the lovely beach within 15 minutes' walk and there are woodland walks directly from the site. For those wanting to visit Farm Park, you can also purchase discounted tickets.

Heated sanitary block equipped with showers, toilets and baby changing/baby bathroom. Dishwashing facilities. Icepack freezer. Laundry facilties. Tourist information. Free WiFi throughout the site. Beautiful woodland walks from the site which take in views of Gwrych Castle, the coastline and vast woodland. Ajoining the site is an extensive farm park (additional entrance charge).

Key Features

 Pets Accepted

 Disabled Facilities

Scan me for
more information.

239

Alan Rogers Code: UK6015
35 accommodations
130 pitches
GPS: 52.18798, -4.35402
Post Code: SA44 6NL

Ceredigion, West Wales

www.alanrogers.com/uk6015
holidays@pencnwc.co.uk
Tel: 01545 560479

Open (Touring Pitches):
1 March - 31 October.

Pencnwc Holiday Park

Pencnwc Holiday Park is a family owned holiday park with a wide range of recreational facilities, close to the Cardigan Bay coastline and only two miles from the seaside town of New Quay. There are 414 pitches, 130 for touring, of which 74 are fully serviced seasonal pitches, 13 are fully serviced daily pitches and 43 are hardstanding 16A hook-up pitches. They are in the centre of the site, away from the static and seasonal vans.

Toilet blocks throughout are clean and have facilities for disabled visitors. Launderette. Two bars (entertainment centre with top class singers etc.) and a smaller, quiet bar. Fish and chip shop. Amusement arcade. Indoor heated swimming pool and paddling pool (small charge). Kids' club. Coarse fishing lake. Free WiFi in clubhouse. Dogs are not accepted at Bank Holidays.

Key Features

 Pets Accepted

 Disabled Facilities

 Swimming Pool

 Play Area

 Bar/Restaurant

 Fishing

Scan me for more information.

Alan Rogers Code: UK5995
25 accommodations
107 pitches
GPS: 51.87298, -5.25690
Post Code: SA62 6QT

Pembrokeshire, West Wales

www.alanrogers.com/uk5995
info@caerfaibay.co.uk
Tel: 01437 720274
www.caerfaibay.co.uk

Open (Touring Pitches):
1 March - 11 November

Caerfai Bay

Caerfai Bay Caravan & Tent Park is about as far west as one can get in Wales. Located near to St Davids, Britain's smallest city, noted for its cathedral and Bishop's Palace. This cliff-top park, just a 15 minute walk from St Davids, has direct access to the Pembrokeshire Coastal Path and a magnificent sandy beach. Family-run with an emphasis on peace, quiet and relaxation, the perfect spot for walkers, rock climbers, water sports enthusiasts, star gazers & wildlife lovers. There are 107 touring pitches (inc.78 for tents) and 59 electric hook-ups (10A), & 33 hardstandings. The site is spread over three open fields with magnificent seaviews, one for caravans and motorhomes with hardstanding and electric as well as accommodation to rent; two for tents with some electric points. Main access roads are tarmac.

Key Features

 Pets Accepted

 Disabled Facilities

Three main buildings house the sanitary facilities (two are heated), one by reception contains facilities for disabled visitors and families, dishwashing, laundry, cooking facilities (hot plate, microwave and fridge). A small block offers 3 unisex cubicles (WC and basin). The third, in the tent field, includes 4 family rooms, dishwashing, microwave, fridge, toaster, wet suit washing and drying area. Motorcaravan services. Bicycle storage. Gas. Dog walking area (there is a non-dog camping area in tent field 3). WiFi (charged). Secure charging points for phones/tablets. Lounge with tourist information, maps & book exchange.

Scan me for more information.

Alan Rogers Code: UK6945
58 accommodations
21 pitches
GPS: 54.89502, -3.84256
Post Code: DG7 1PF

Dumfries and Galloway,
Lowlands

www.alanrogers.com/uk6945
info@gillespie-leisure.co.uk
Tel: 01557 870267
www.barlochancaravanpark.co.uk

Open (Touring Pitches):
Easter/1 April - 31 October.

Barlochan Caravan Park

Barlochan Caravan Park is situated on a hillside overlooking the Urr Estuary on the Solway Coast close to Dalbeattie and Castle Douglas, with the small village of Palnackie being a short walk away. Set on terraces, level, marked and numbered, most of the touring and tent pitches are on grass with a limited number of hardstandings available. There are 16 with 16A electrical connections. In addition, there are two hikers' pods and around 60 holiday homes (with eight available for hire) are positioned on terraces high above the touring areas and screened by mature shrubs and trees. Just to the left of the entrance, there is a minigolf course and an adventure play area screened from the park with mature trees. The small sheltered outdoor swimming pool is popular.

The heated sanitary facilities are kept spotlessly clean. Shower cubicles have recently been made larger, suitable for wheelchair entry, but if required there is also a separate unit with WC and basin. Fully equipped laundry with outside drying area. Reception and well stocked shop. Heated small outdoor swimming pool and terrace. Large games room and TV room. Minigolf.

Key Features

 Pets Accepted

 Disabled Facilities

 Swimming Pool

 Play Area

Scan me for more information.

Alan Rogers Code: UK7740
4 accommodations
105 pitches
GPS: 57.48570, -6.43020
Post Code: IV51 9PS

Isle of Skye, Highlands and
Islands

www.alanrogers.com/uk7740
skye.site@
campingandcaravanningclub.co.uk
Tel: 01470 582230
campingandcaravanningclub.co.uk/
skye

Open (Touring Pitches):
1 April - 4 October

Skye C&C Club Site

The Skye Camping & Caravanning Club (C&C) site can be found on the banks of Loch Greshornish, the location of this site is both scenic and peaceful. The owners look after the site themselves and everything is very well cared for, clean and attractive. There are 105 pitches, 85 with 16A electricity and of these, 46 are on hardstanding. Most pitches are level and have loch views. The site also has two Camping Pods and Two Yurts. The atmosphere is very welcoming, from the first greeting at reception to the wave goodbye. Facilities are modern, warm and clean. There is much wildlife in the area and we were lucky enough to see and hear a golden eagle just above the site. The site owns the adjoining loch shore, which is fenced and gated, so fishing (without a licence) is possible.

Key Features

 Pets Accepted

 Disabled Facilities

 Fishing

Well maintained sanitary block with underfloor heating in the cooler months, separate provision for campers with disabilities, and a separate family room. Small laundry. Dog shower. Motorcaravan services. Camper's shelter with seating, cooking and eating area. Good shop with bread and fresh eggs. Gas. Fishing. Island trips. Two camping pods and two yurts to rent. WiFi throughout (charged).

Scan me for
more information.

Alan Rogers Code: UK7325
32 accommodations
154 pitches
GPS: 56.69614, -3.72559
Post Code: PH16 5NA

Perth and Kinross, Heart of Scotland

Milton of Fonab

www.alanrogers.com/uk7325
info@fonab.co.uk
Tel: 01796 472882
www.fonab.co.uk

Open (Touring Pitches):

The quite caravan park, Milton of Fonab is located on the banks of the River Tummel, just south of the Highland town of Pitlochry. The site accommodates tents, caravans and motorhomes, all with electric hook up available. The site also has around 30 static caravan, holiday homes for hire which are set around a central green. The site is very well maintained, with large pitches, modern washrooms and a small, but well stocked shop which is open every day. Booking in advance is essential during the Highland Games.

Key Features

 Pets Accepted

 Bar/Restaurant

Site shop open daily from 9am to 9pm, Gas available, Laundry available, Electric hook up on all pitches, dogs accepted (must be kept on a lead) free WiFi throughout the site.

Scan me for more information.

Alan Rogers Code: UK7535
350 accommodations
101 pitches
GPS: 57.72126, -3.33506
Post Code: IV31 6SP

Moray, Grampian

www.alanrogers.com/uk7535
info@silver-sands.co.uk
Tel: 01343 813262
www.silver-sands.co.uk

Open (Touring Pitches):
1 April - 31 October.

Silver Sands Holiday Park

Silver Sands is in a peaceful location on the Moray Firth in the north east of Scotland. It is close to the seaside town of Lossiemouth, which has a bustling marina and a good selection of shops and restaurants. This popular holiday park has a wealth of amenities, including a heated indoor pool, playground and games arcade, restaurant, fish and chip shop and plenty of entertainment for the whole family. There is a choice of grass or hardstanding touring pitches, many fully serviced. With direct access to a beautiful sandy beach, this is a good choice for a lively family holiday. The site is very close to an RAF base, so some aircraft noise can be expected.

Sanitary block with hot showers. Launderette. Shop stocks essentials. Bar. Café. Restaurant. Fish and chips to take away. Heated indoor swimming pool with sauna and steam room. Gym. Playground. Children's club. Games room. Activity and entertainment programme. WiFi. Direct beach access.

Key Features

 Pets Accepted

 Disabled Facilities

 Beach Access

 Swimming Pool

 Bar/Restaurant

Scan me for more information.

Alan Rogers Code: UK7710
7 accommodations
68 pitches
GPS: 57.93397, -5.19702
Post Code: IV26 2TN

Highland, Highlands and Islands

www.alanrogers.com/uk7710
sales@ardmair.com
Tel: 01854 612054
www.ardmair.com

Open (Touring Pitches):
1 April - late September, depending
on the weather.

Ardmair Point Caravan Park

This spectacularly situated park, overlooking the little Loch Kanaird, just around the corner from Loch Broom, has splendid views all round. It is now run by new people who are really making a difference. The 68 touring pitches are arranged mainly on grass around the edge of the bay, in front of the shingle beach. Electricity hook-ups (10A) are available and some gravel hardstandings are on the other side of the access road, just past the second toilet block. Tent pitches, together with cheaper pitches for some touring units are in a large field behind the other sanitary facilities. Scuba diving is popular at Loch Kanaird because the water is so clear.

Two toilet blocks, both with good facilities. One block has wonderful views from the large windows in the launderette and dishwashing rooms. Large en-suite rooms for disabled visitors. Motorcaravan services. Shop. Ardmair Bay Café in reception area serves breakfast and light meals (9.00-16.30; open to public). Play area. Fishing. Sailing and boating (with your own boat).

Key Features

 Pets Accepted

 Disabled Facilities

 Beach Access

 Play Area

 Fishing

 Sailing

Scan me for
more information.

Alan Rogers Code: UK8330
37 pitches
GPS: 54.71533, -6.23375
Post Code: BT41 4DG

Antrim, Co. Antrim

Six Mile Water

www.alanrogers.com/uk8330
sixmilewater@antrim.gov.uk
Tel: 028 9446 4963
www.antrimandnewtownabbey.gov.uk

Open (Touring Pitches):
6 February - 29 November.

Six Mile Water is located at the Lough Shore Park and is adjacent to the Antrim Forum leisure complex, a major amenity area that includes swimming pools, a bowling green, an adventure playground for children, fitness and health gyms and sports fields. Managed by Antrim Borough Council, the park is easily accessible when travelling to and from the ports of Belfast and Larne, making it perfect for stopovers. There are now 37 pitches with 13A electricity, arranged in a herringbone layout of hardstandings with grass for awnings, a grass area for eight tents to one side, plus picnic and barbecue areas. Advance booking is advisable.

The small, modern toilet block provides toilets, washbasins and showers and facilities for disabled campers. Baby changing unit. Laundry room. Restaurant and takeaway. TV lounge and games room. Fishing and boat launching. WiFi throughout.

Key Features

 Pets Accepted

 Disabled Facilities

 Bar/Restaurant

 Fishing

 Sailing

Scan me for
more information.

Capital Athens
Currency Euro (€)
Language Greek
Telephone country code 00 30
Time Zone Eastern European Standard Time (GMT/UTC+2)
Tourist Office visitgreece.gr

Climate Greece has a Mediterranean climate with plenty of sunshine, mild temperatures and limited amount of rainfall.

Greece

Greece is made up of clusters of islands with idyllic sheltered bays and coves, golden stretches of sand with dunes, pebbly beaches, coastal caves with steep rocks and volcanic black sand and coastal wetlands. Its rugged landscape is a monument to nature with dramatic gorges, lakes, rivers and waterfalls.

Nestling between the waters of the Aegean, Ionian and Mediterranean seas, Greece has over 13,000 km of coastline. A largely mountainous country, its backbone is formed from the Pindus range, which extends as far as Crete, the largest of Greece's 6,000 islands, themselves peaks of the now submerged landmass of Aegeis.

Mount Olympus in the north of the country, known from Greek mythology as the abode of the gods, is the highest mountain (2,917 m).

The Greek islands have something to offer every visitor – the vibrant nightlife of Mykonos, the 'honeymoon' island of Santorini; Rhodes, where the modern city sits alongside the medieval citadel, and Corfu with its Venetian and French influences. The mainland is home to some of the most important archaeological sites, including the Acropolis, the Parthenon and Delphi.

Shops Opening hours vary throughout the year. In high-season 8am to 2pm Monday, Wednesday and Saturday, 8am to 2pm and 5pm to 9pm Tuesday, Thursday and Friday.

Banks 8.30am to 2.30pm Monday to Thursday, 8am to 2pm Friday.

Travelling with Children Greece doesn't cater to children as much as other European countries but children will be welcomed wherever they go. Athens is great for kids with lots of big parks, gardens and historical attractions. Crete is great for its sandy beaches. The Greek culture is all about sharing so restaurants will always be accommodating towards children. Overall Greece is a safe country to travel to with children but make sure you bring mosquito repellant.

Public Holidays New Year's Day, Epiphany, Clean Monday 11 Mar, Greek Independence Day 25 Mar, Orthodox Good Friday, Easter Monday, May Day 1 May, Whit Monday, Assumption, Ohi Day 28 Oct, Christmas Day, Boxing Day. Many historical sites offer free entry on the first Sunday of each month with the exception of Jul and Aug.

Motoring Speed limits are 100-120 km/h on highways unless otherwise posted; 50 km/h in residential areas unless otherwise marked. An international driver's licence is required. Road signs are written in Greek and repeated phonetically in English. Road tolls exist on two highways in Greece, one leading to Northern Greece and the other to the Peloponnese.

See campsite map page 481.

Alan Rogers Code: GR8235
2 accommodations
67 pitches
GPS: 39.47378, 20.24082
Post Code: GR-46100

Epirus, Centre

www.alanrogers.com/gr8235
info@campingkalamibeach.gr
Tel: 266 507 1211
www.campingkalamibeach.gr

Open (Touring Pitches):
20 March - 15 October.

Camping Kalami Beach

Set in a bay, this colourful, attractive, family run site leads down to a beach and the crystal clear waters of the Ionian Sea. Colour comes mainly from the beautiful bougainvillaea plants that clad many of the buildings, and ample shade for the 67 level, terraced pitches, all with 4A electricity, is provided by olive and eucalyptus trees. From the lower pitches there are panoramic views of the island of Corfu from which, at night, lights reflect across the open water. The construction of the site with natural stone paving and a generous display of plants is entirely in keeping with its well-chosen setting. A flight of steps and a small slipway lead down to the beach and the sea, which is perfect for swimming. The site owners can arrange water-skiing with a local company for those interested in more active watersports.

One sanitary block with British style WCs, washbasins and large showers. Second block has showers and washbasins in cabins. Laundry room with sinks, washing machines and dryer (token operated). Motorcaravan services. Shop. Bar and restaurant, takeaway (1/5-15/10). Beach. WiFi over site (free).

Key Features

 Pets Accepted

 Disabled Facilities

 Beach Access

 Bar/Restaurant

Scan me for more information.

Alan Rogers Code: GR8225
20 accommodations
150 pitches
GPS: 39.28172, 20.43395
Post Code: GR-48060

Epirus, Centre

Camping Enjoy Lichnos

www.alanrogers.com/gr8225
holidays@enjoy-lichnos.net
Tel: 268 403 1171
www.enjoy-lichnos.net

Open (Touring Pitches):
1 May - 31 October.

This is a quiet campsite with attractive views of the Ionian Sea and the coastlines towards Preveza and Parga. The site has been created on a steep incline with extensive terraces and pitches under constructed shade, all with 16A electricity. The ground levels out in front of the beach and pitches here have sea views. There are 150 touring pitches and a large area for tents under the shade of the 500-year-old olive trees. The sandy beach is the site's main attraction, and various water-based activities are available. The nearby resort of Parga is a lively place of narrow streets and a wealth of tavernas. It can be reached using one of the many water taxis which frequent the area throughout the day.

Key Features

 Pets Accepted

 Disabled Facilities

 Beach Access

 Play Area

 Bar/Restaurant

 Sailing

Unisex toilet blocks in small units are situated on each terrace with washbasins (cold water only) and solar-heated showers. Main sanitary facilities at base of site, two blocks, one with wheelchair access. Washing machine and ironing. Motorcaravan services. Shop. Bar and beach bar. Restaurant with children's menu (discount for campsite visitors). Playground. WiFi over part of site (charged). English is spoken.

Scan me for more information.

Alan Rogers Code: GR8525
10 accommodations
70 pitches
GPS: 38.47243, 22.45915
Post Code: GR-33054

Central Greece, Centre

www.alanrogers.com/gr8525
info@chrissacamping.gr
Tel: 226 508 2050
www.chrissacamping.com

Open (Touring Pitches):
All year.

Chrissa Camping

From this well kept site a free road train takes guests to Delphi, which was once sacred to the god Apollo and is now the setting for some of the most important monuments of ancient Greek civilisation. The site's situation on a hill ensures stunning views across a vast olive grove to the Gulf of Corinth beyond. There are 70 pitches with electricity connections (10A). They are well shaded and mostly terraced, which means that everyone can enjoy the views. The site is attractively landscaped with lots of flowers, and round wooden cabins for rent blend in very well with the natural environment. An evening meal on the restaurant's terrace is a must.

Modern, well maintained toilet block with British style WCs, open washbasins and controllable showers. Family shower rooms. Motorcaravan services. Laundry room with sinks, washing machine and dryer. Shop (1/4-30/10). Bar, restaurant and takeaway (weekends only in winter). Outdoor pool and paddling pool. Barbecues are not allowed. Internet point. WiFi (charged).

Key Features

 Open All Year

 Pets Accepted

 Swimming Pool

 Play Area

 Bar/Restaurant

 Skiing

Scan me for more information.

Alan Rogers Code: GR8145
27 accommodations
130 pitches
GPS: 40.02418, 23.81595
Post Code: GR-63081

Central Macedonia, North and East

Camping Areti

www.alanrogers.com/gr8145
info@areti-chalkidiki.gr
Tel: 237 507 1430
www.areti-campingandbungalows.gr

Open (Touring Pitches):
1 May - 31 October.

If you imagine a typical Greek campsite as being set immediately behind a small sandy beach in a quiet cove with pitches amongst pine and olive trees that stretch a long way back to the small coast road, then you have found your ideal site. Camping Areti is beautifully located just off the beaten track on the peninsula of Sithonia. It has 130 pitches for touring units. The olive groves at the rear provide hidden parking spaces for caravans and boats, and small boats can be launched from the beach. The Charalambidi family maintain their site to very high standards and visitors will not be disappointed.

Three excellent toilet blocks include showers, WCs and washbasins. Kitchen with sinks, electric hobs and fridges. Laundry with washing machines. Small shop and restaurant. Sandy beach. Fishing, sailing and swimming. Communal barbecues. Free WiFi over part of site. Bungalows to rent. Dogs are not allowed on the beach, max. 1 per pitch.

Key Features

 Pets Accepted

 Beach Access

 Play Area

 Bar/Restaurant

 Fishing

 Sailing

Scan me for more information.

Alan Rogers Code: GR8705
8 accommodations
70 pitches
GPS: 36.94764, 21.70618
Post Code: GR-24001

Peloponnese, South

Camping Navarino Beach

www.alanrogers.com/gr8705
info@navarino-beach.gr
Tel: 272 302 2973
www.navarino-beach.gr

Open (Touring Pitches):
1 April - 31 October.

Situated directly on the beach in the historic Bay of Navarino, there can be very few sites that occupy the fantastic position that Camping Navarino Beach has. There are around 70 pitches, most facing the beach, with 30 being directly situated alongside. All have electricity (10A) and most have good shade. They are arranged in rows to ensure that all have beach access. The facilities are adequate and cleaned regularly. The staff are friendly and efficient, and there is a very good restaurant with a terrace directly by the beach. The light wind in the morning, which strengthens on some afternoons, makes it a great windsurfing location and boats can be moored by the shore. The site is split into two, with the section across the road used mainly for tents or as the overspill. There is plenty of shade. The beach is sandy and shelves gently making it incredibly safe for children. This site is highly recommended.

Key Features

 Pets Accepted

 Beach Access

 Bar/Restaurant

The five toilet blocks are well situated and, even in high season, were kept very clean and never became overcrowded. Open washbasins, hot water to showers, and communal refrigerators and freezers. Washing machine. Small shop sells basic provisions (May-Oct). Other shops within walking distance. Snack bar/restaurant. Communal barbecue. WiFi over site (free).

Scan me for more information.

Alan Rogers Code: GR8325
55 accommodations
90 pitches
GPS: 37.89920, 21.11650
Post Code: GR-27050

Peloponnese, South

www.alanrogers.com/gr8325
fournia@otenet.gr
Tel: 262 309 5095
www.fourniabeach.gr

Open (Touring Pitches):
1 April - 20 October.

Camping Fournia Beach

The village of Kastros, and the Chlemoutsi castle that towers above it can be seen for miles across the flat landscape towards the coast. Camping Fournia Beach is owned by the four Lefkaditis brothers, and their wives have ensured that this new site is awash with flowering shrubs. The site offers 90 first class pitches and modern facilities, and the bar and restaurant sit in a landscaped area high above the beach with spectacular views across the sea to Zakynthos. Steps to the beach provide private access to the sandy cove below. The castle is being restored and is now used for summer concerts. Nearby are the Kyllini baths dating from Roman times, where the benefits of a mud bath can still be enjoyed.

Two modern toilet blocks include showers, WCs and washbasins and good facilities for disabled visitors. Laundry with washing machines, sinks and hot water. Kitchen with hobs, fridge and freezer. Shop. Restaurant and bar overlooking the sea and the island of Zakinthos. Outdoor swimming pool (15/5-15/10). Play area. Accommodation to rent.

Key Features

 Pets Accepted

 Disabled Facilities

 Swimming Pool

 Play Area

 Bar/Restaurant

Scan me for more information.

Alan Rogers Code: GR8625
21 accommodations
100 pitches
GPS: 37.61855, 23.15639
Post Code: GR-21052

Peloponnese, South

Camping Bekas

www.alanrogers.com/gr8625
info@bekas.gr
Tel: 275 309 9930
www.bekas.gr

Open (Touring Pitches):
1 April - 20 October.

Just 60 kilometres south of Corinth you will find the town of Ancient Epidavros, and just south of that is Camping Bekas. With 150 pitches (100 for touring, 6-10A electricity available) set amongst the trees, there is shade and a quiet atmosphere. Arranged along a small sand and shingle beach, the site offers opportunities for swimming, sailing and fishing. The Argolid region of the Peloponnese has much to offer the curious tourist. About 12 km. south is the sanctuary of Asclepios. On a hillside lies the theatre, the most famous and best preserved of all the ancient theatres in Greece. Built in the 4th century BC, the limestone theatre can seat 12,000 spectators. Every summer, in July and August, there are various orchestral and theatrical performances, and attendance at one of these has been described as an almost mystical experience.

Key Features

 Pets Accepted

 Disabled Facilities

 Bar/Restaurant

 Fishing

Three toilet blocks with a mixture of British and Turkish style WCs, hot showers, some washbasins in cubicles (cold water), facilities for babies and shower rooms for disabled visitors. Laundry with washing machine. Shop. Bar. Restaurant (20/5-20/9). Internet access. TV room. Sand and shingle beach. Apartments to rent.

Scan me for more information.

Alan Rogers Code: GR8695
15 accommodations
80 pitches
GPS: 36.80282, 21.78105
Post Code: GR-24006

Peloponnese, South

www.alanrogers.com/gr8695
info@finikescamping.gr
Tel: 272 302 8524
www.finikescamping.gr

Open (Touring Pitches):
All year.

Camping Finikes

This site offers 80 level pitches with good shade and great views. It also has 15 apartments to rent. Some pitches have high reed screens that give good protection from the blazing Greek sun, while the turquoise sea is excellent for swimming, windsurfing and sailing and generally cooling off. The site is at the western corner of Finikounda Bay and has direct access to the sandy beach by crossing small natural dunes. The facilities are excellent, and in low season, when there are 18 or fewer campers, each is given the keys to a WC and shower for their personal use. The small picturesque village, three kilometres to the east, is at the back of the bay. Caiques and fishing boats are drawn up all along the sandy shore here, while tavernas serve their fresh catch along the water's edge.

The good toilet block includes showers, WCs and washbasins. Facilities for disabled visitors. Kitchen includes sinks, electric hobs and fridges. Laundry. Bar, small shop and restaurant (1/4-31/10). Library. Play area. WiFi over site (free). Accommodation to rent.

Key Features

 Open All Year

 Pets Accepted

 Disabled Facilities

 Play Area

 Bar/Restaurant

 Scan me for more information.

Capital Dublin
Currency Euro (€)
Language English and Irish
Telephone country code 00 353
Time Zone GMT/UTC
Tourist Office ireland.com

Climate Oceanic climate. Summers are cool to mild with temperatures rarely exceeding 25C. Winters are cold but not freezing, and often rainy.

Ireland

Ireland is made up of four provinces: Connaught, Leinster, Munster and Ulster, comprising 32 counties, 26 of which lie in the Republic of Ireland.

Famed for its folklore, traditional music and friendly hospitality, the Republic of Ireland offers spectacular scenery contained within a relatively compact area. With plenty of beautiful areas to discover, and a relaxed pace of life, it is an ideal place to unwind.

Ireland is the perfect place to indulge in a variety of outdoor pursuits while taking in the glorious scenery. There are plenty of waymarked footpaths which lead through woodlands, across cliffs, past historical monuments and over rolling hills. The dramatic coastline, with its headlands, secluded coves and sandy beaches, is fantastic for watersports: from sailing to windsurfing, scuba diving and swimming; or for just simply relaxing and watching the variety of seabirds that nest on the shores.

The Cliffs of Moher, in particular, is a prime location for birdwatching and Goat Island, just offshore, is where puffins make their nesting burrows. Fishing is also popular with plenty of opportunity in the numerous streams, rivers, canals and hidden lakes.

In the south the beautiful Ring of Kerry is one of the most visited regions. This 110 mile route encircles the Inveragh Peninsula and is surrounded by mountains and lakes. Other sights include the Aran Islands, home to some of the most ancient Christian and pre-Christian remains in Ireland, the Rock of Cashel and the bustling cities of Dublin, Galway and Cork.

Shops 9.30am to 6pm Monday to Saturday (to 8pm Thursday in cities), noon to 6pm Sunday.

Banks 10am to 4pm weekdays (to 5pm Thursday).

Travelling with Children Although children are welcomed in Ireland, family facilities aren't always accessible in rural spots. Most restaurants accept children although some high-end establishments may not. Entertainment-wise Ireland is well placed with a plethora of kid-friendly museums and attractions. Children under five travel free on all public transport.

Public Holidays New Year's Day, St Patrick's Day 17 Mar, Easter Monday, May Day 6 May, June Bank Holiday 3 Jun, August Bank Holiday 5 Aug, October Bank Holiday 28 Oct, Christmas Day, Boxing Day.

Motoring Driving is on the left-hand side and roads are generally well maintained. Tolls exist in the Republic, generally paid at the barrier. Speed limits are 50 kp/h in built-up areas, 120 kp/h on motorways. Signposts are in both Gaelic and English in most areas (where Irish is the primary language signage is in Gaelic).

See campsite map page 480.

Ireland

Alan Rogers Code: IR9100
1 accommodations
113 pitches
GPS: 53.30445, -6.41533

Co. Dublin, Dublin

Camac Valley Camping

www.alanrogers.com/ir9100
reservations@camacvalley.com
Tel: 014 640 644
www.camacvalley.com

Open (Touring Pitches):
All year.

Opened in 1996, this campsite is not only well placed for Dublin, but also offers a welcome stopover if travelling to the more southern counties from the north of the country, or vice versa. Despite its close proximity to the city, and the constant noise from the dual carriageway, being located in the 300-acre Corkagh Park gives it a 'heart of the country' atmosphere. There are 113 pitches on hardstanding for caravans, laid out in bays and avenues, all fully serviced (10A Europlug). Maturing trees and shrubs separate pitches and roads are of tarmac. Beyond the entrance gate and forecourt stands an attractive, timber-fronted building housing the site amenities.

Heated sanitary facilities include good sized showers (token). Facilities for disabled visitors. Baby room. Laundry. Shop (for basics) and coffee bar. Playground with wooden play frames and safety base. Fishing. Electronic gate controlled from reception and 24-hour security. WiFi (free).

Key Features

 Open All Year

 Pets Accepted

 Disabled Facilities

 Play Area

 Bar/Restaurant

 Fishing

 Scan me for more information.

Alan Rogers Code: IR9040
30 pitches
GPS: 53.00820, -7.37208

Co. Laois, Heart

Laois Camping

www.alanrogers.com/ir9040
ti.brenn1@gmail.com
Tel: 086 339 0867

Open (Touring Pitches):
March - September.

Opened in 2011 and set on a family run farm, this small site is conveniently situated for the Dublin to Limerick M7 motorway. It is less than 15 km. from the Slieve Bloom mountains, a Mecca for walkers, and 6 km. from the centre of Portlaoise. There are seven touring pitches with hardstanding, 16A electricity and water set to one edge of a camping field. Children can enjoy farm animals such as sheep, goats, chickens and pigs, and perhaps help feed lambs, and find eggs (even chocolate ones at Easter). There is some distant noise from the motorway, and mainline trains pass behind the farm. It would make a good stopover between Dublin and Cork or Limerick.

Key Features

 Pets Accepted

 Disabled Facilities

A new timber-clad toilet block is tiled and heated, and has three family rooms with WC and shower. One also has a bath and is equipped for disabled visitors. Laundry room. Kitchen/lounge with cooking and dishwashing facilities, satellite TV, extensive library, comfortable seating and table tennis. Motorcaravan services.

Scan me for
more information.

Alan Rogers Code: IR9150
17 accommodations
160 pitches
GPS: 52.88840, -6.14528

Co. Wicklow, Heart

River Valley Holidays

www.alanrogers.com/ir9150
info@rivervalleypark.ie
Tel: 040 441 647
www.rivervalleypark.ie

Open (Touring Pitches):
11 March - 4 November

In the small country village of Redcross, in the heart of County Wicklow, you will find River Valley Caravan & Camping Park, a first rate, family run park. It is within easy reach of beauty spots such as the Vale of Avoca (Ballykissangel), Glendalough and Powerscourt, plus the safe beach of Brittas Bay. The 160 touring pitches are divided into separate, well landscaped areas with an adults-only section. All have 6/10A electricity connections and offer a choice of hardstanding or grass – you select your pitch. A late arrivals area has electricity hook-ups, water and night lighting.

All sanitary blocks are of the highest quality, modern and well designed. Excellent facilities for disabled visitors. Showers are on payment (€1 token). Laundry area. Campers' kitchen. Motorcaravan services. Gas supplies. Full bar and restaurant. Entertainment twice per week. TV and games room. Three tennis courts. Beer garden with entertainment for children (July/Aug). Sports complex. Foot-golf course. Go-kart track. Remote control boats and cars. Movie nights. Adventure and toddlers' playgrounds. Caravan storage. WiFi (free). Archery range. Mini wildlife walk. New for 2019 Ireland's first Glampotel onsite.

Key Features

 Pets Accepted

 Disabled Facilities

 Play Area

 Bar/Restaurant

 Golf

Scan me for more information.

Alan Rogers Code: IR9340
40 pitches
GPS: 52.14763, -7.17274

Co. Waterford, South East

Newtown Cove Camping

www.alanrogers.com/ir9340
info@newtowncove.com
Tel: 051 381 979
www.newtowncove.com

Open (Touring Pitches):
2-6 April and 1 May - 27 September.

Well run and friendly, this very attractive small park is only five minutes walk from the beautiful Newtown Cove. It offers views of the famous and historic Metal Man and is 2.5 km. from Tramore beach and 11 km. from Waterford. Neatly set out on gently sloping grass are 40 pitches, with the abundance of shrubs and bushes reflecting the efforts of the owners. All pitches have 10A Europlug, 30 with hardstanding also, and access is by well lit, tarmac roads. There are around 56 privately owned caravan holiday homes. A modern building at the entrance houses reception, the amenities and additional sanitary facilities.

Key Features

 Pets Accepted

 Play Area

The main sanitary block at the bottom end of the site provides good, clean facilities including a bathroom. Showers on payment (token from reception). Additional toilet facilities in reception. Excellent motorcaravan services. Campers' kitchen with cooking facilities, sheltered eating area, lounge and small laundry. Small shop (July/Aug). TV room. Games room. Small play area. WiFi throughout (charged).

Scan me for more information.

Alan Rogers Code: IR9400
1 accommodations
42 pitches
GPS: 52.41998, -8.18787

Co. Tipperary, Shannon

www.alanrogers.com/ir9400
rdrew@tipperarycamping.com
Tel: 062 565 55
www.tipperarycamping.com

Open (Touring Pitches):
All year.

The Glen of Aherlow

The owners of one of Ireland's newest parks, George and Rosaline Drew, are campers themselves and have set about creating an idyllic park in an idyllic location. This three-hectare park is set in one of Ireland's most picturesque valleys and is open all year. There are beautiful views of the wooded and hilly areas of Slievenamuck and the Galtee Mountains. There are 42 large and level touring pitches, on both hardstanding and grass, each pair sharing a double 10A Europlug post and water point. The Drew family is happy to welcome large groups and rallies, and large units can be accommodated. The new stone-built reception and shop beside the gate is a super addition to the site and includes a coffee shop. The excellent facilities are located in a purpose-built toilet block.

The modern toilet block includes free showers and facilities for disabled visitors. Motorcaravan services. Laundry room with ironing. Campers' kitchen. Recreation and TV rooms. Shop. Coffee shop. Bicycle hire (delivered to site). WiFi (free).

Key Features

 Open All Year

 Pets Accepted

 Disabled Facilities

 Bar/Restaurant

Scan me for more information.

Alan Rogers Code: IR9465
3 accommodations
99 pitches
GPS: 53.01677, -9.40200

Co. Clare, Shannon

Nagle's Doolin Camping Park

www.alanrogers.com/ir9465
ken@doolincamping.com
Tel: 065 707 4458
www.doolincamping.com

Open (Touring Pitches):
Mid March - mid October.

This neat and tidy seaside site is located just one kilometre from the cliffs of Moher, and a short ferry ride from the sparsely populated Aran Islands. The nearby village of Doolin, famed for its traditional music, has a good range of shops, restaurants and pubs. The four-hectare site, which enjoys spectacular views over the bay to Conemara, has 99 pitches, including 76 level hardstandings (all with 10A electricity, and 21 also with water and drainage) and grass pitches for tents. They are not separated by hedges, but the site is divided into bays by limestone walls. Three new camping pods are available for hire. There is excellent WiFi coverage over the whole site.

Key Features

 Pets Accepted

 Disabled Facilities

 Play Area

 Skiing

One modern, well equipped toilet block is unheated but has good facilities including hot showers (€ 1) and en-suite unit for disabled visitors. Laundry facilities (charged). Kitchen with cooking rings (charged), fridge/freezer and sinks with hot water. Motorcaravan services. Shop (June-Aug). Gas. Games room. Play area. WiFi throughout.

Scan me for
more information.

Alan Rogers Code: IR9510
125 pitches
GPS: 51.71833, -9.45528

Co. Cork, South West

www.alanrogers.com/ir9510
eaglepointcamping@eircom.net
Tel: 027 506 30
www.eaglepointcamping.com

Open (Touring Pitches):
17 April - 21 September.

Eagle Point Camping

Midway between the towns of Bantry and Glengarriff, the spectacular peninsula of Eagle Point juts into Bantry Bay. The first impression is of a spacious country park rather than a campsite. As far as the eye can see this 20-acre, landscaped, part-terraced park, with its vast manicured grass areas separated by mature trees, shrubs and hedges, runs parallel with the shoreline providing lovely views. Suitable for all ages, this is a well run park mainly for touring units, with campers pitched mostly towards the shore. It provides 125 pitches with 6A electricity, although many are seasonally occupied.

Three well maintained, well designed toilet blocks are of a high standard. Laundry. Motorcaravan services. Play area. Tennis. Football field, well away from the pitches. Fishing. Boat launching. Supermarket at park entrance. Dogs are not accepted. WiFi on part of site.

Key Features

 Beach Access

 Play Area

 Fishing

 Sailing

Scan me for more information.

Alan Rogers Code: IR9620
6 accommodations
66 pitches
GPS: 52.05595, -9.47458

Co. Kerry, South West

www.alanrogers.com/ir9620
info@killarneycamping.com
Tel: 064 663 1590
www.killarneycamping.com

Open (Touring Pitches):
13 March - 26 October.

Fleming's White Bridge

The main road from Cork to Killarney (N22) runs through the gentle valley of the River Flesk. Between the two sits Fleming's White Bridge camping park. Its ten-hectare site is within comfortable walking distance of Killarney centre. Surrounded by mature, broad-leafed trees, the park is flat, landscaped and generously adorned with flowers and shrubs. It comprises 92 pitches, the majority for touring caravans, on well-kept grass pitches with electricity hook-ups, although some have concrete hardstanding and some pitches are reserved for tents. Well distributed around the park are three well-appointed toilet blocks. This is a site of which the owners are very proud. Hillary, Moira and Breda Fleming personally supervise the reception and grounds, maintaining high standards of hygiene, cleanliness and tidiness. In the main season, they even find time to organise on-site activities that keep children happy and parents relaxed. The park's location so close to Ireland's premier tourism centre makes it an ideal base to explore Killarney and the southwest.

Three toilet blocks are of a high standard. Motorcaravan services. Campers' drying room and two laundries. Small shop (1/6-1/9). Two TV rooms and a games room. Fishing (advice and permits provided). Canoeing (own canoes). Bicycle hire. Woodland walks. WiFi.

Key Features

 Pets Accepted

 Disabled Facilities

 Play Area

 Bike Hire

 Fishing

Scan me for
more information.

267

Alan Rogers Code: IR9570
5 accommodations
20 pitches
GPS: 51.75562, -9.76193

Co. Kerry, South West

Creveen Lodge Camping Park

www.alanrogers.com/ir9570
info@creveenlodge.com
Tel: 064 668 3131
www.creveenlodge.com

Open (Touring Pitches):
Easter - 30 September.

The Healy Pass is the well known scenic summit of the R574 road that crosses the Beara Peninsula, shortening the original journey from Kenmare Bay in the north to Bantry Bay in the south by nearly 70 km. As this narrow coast road starts to climb steeply, on the mountain foothills, you will arrive at Creveen Lodge, a working hill farm with a quiet, homely atmosphere. The park provides 20 attractive pitches, 10 with 10A electricity and an area of hardstanding for motorhomes. To allow easy access, the steep farm track is divided into a simple one-way system. Creveen Lodge, commanding views across Kenmare Bay, is split between three gently sloping fields separated by trees. The park is carefully tended with neat rubbish bins and rustic picnic tables informally placed. Although not so famed as the Iveragh Peninsula, around which runs the Ring of Kerry, the northern Beara is a scenically striking area of County Kerry. This is walking and climbing countryside or, of interest close by, is Derreen Gardens.

Key Features

 Pets Accepted

 Play Area

Well appointed and maintained, the small toilet block provides token operated showers (€1). Communal room with cooking facilities, a fridge, freezer, TV, ironing board, fireplace, tables and chairs. Reception is in the farmhouse. Play area. Accommodation (3 cottages, 2 caravans) to rent. WiFi available outside the reception area.

Scan me for more information.

Alan Rogers Code: IR8780
12 accommodations
70 pitches
GPS: 53.79391, -8.91387

Co. Mayo, West

Knock Camping Park

www.alanrogers.com/ir8780
caravanpark@knock-shrine.ie
Tel: 094 938 8100
www.knock-shrine.ie

Open (Touring Pitches):
1 April - 31 October.

This park is in a sheltered, landscaped area immediately south of the world famous Shrine that receives many visitors. Comfortable and clean, the park has neatly trimmed lawns with tarmac roads and is surrounded by clipped trees. The 70 touring pitches are of an average size on hardstanding, and 52 have 15A electricity connections. There is also an overflow field. Because of the religious associations of the area, the site is jam-packed in August, and indeed there are unlikely to be any vacancies at all for 14-16 August. Besides visiting the Shrine and Knock Museum, it is also a good centre for exploring scenic County Mayo. Nearby are Ashford Castle and the picturesque village of Cong (location for the film Quiet Man), while Connemara National Park, Achill Island and Galway are possible days out.

Two heated toilet blocks, one dated, have good facilities for disabled visitors and a nice sized rest room attached, hot showers and adequate washing and toilet facilities. Laundry room. Gas supplies. TV rooms. Playground. Free WiFi over site.

Key Features

 Pets Accepted

 Disabled Facilities

 Play Area

 Bar/Restaurant

Scan me for more information.

Capital Rome
Currency Euro (€)
Language Italian. Some German is
spoken near the Austrian border.
Telephone country code 00 39
Time Zone CET (GMT/UTC+1)
Tourist Office enit.it

Climate The south enjoys extremely
hot summers and mild, dry winters,
whilst the mountainous regions of the
north are cooler with heavy snow in
winter.

Italy

Italy, once the capital of the Roman Empire, was unified as recently as 1861, thus regional customs and traditions have not been lost. Its enviable collections of art, literature and culture have had worldwide influence and continue to be a magnet for visitors who flock to cities such as Venice, Florence and Rome.

In the north, the vibrant city of Milan is the fashion capital of the world and home to the famous opera house, La Scala, as well as Da Vinci's 'The Last Supper'. It is also a good starting-off point for the Alps; the Italian Lake District, incorporating Lake Garda, Lake Como and Lake Maggiore; the canals of Venice and the lovely town of Verona.

The hilly towns of central Italy are especially popular, with Siena, San Gimignano and Assisi among the most visited. The historic capital of Rome with its Colosseum and Vatican City is not to be missed.

Naples is an ideal base for visiting Pompeii and the breathtaking scenery of the Amalfi coast but the city also has a charm of its own – winding narrow streets and crumbling façades inset with shrines sit alongside boutiques, bars and lively street markets, amid chaotic traffic and roaring scooters

Shops Opening hours vary throughout the year. In high-season 9am to 1pm and 3.30pm to 7.30pm Monday to Saturday, some also open Sunday.

Banks 8.30am to 1.30pm and 2.45pm to 4.30pm weekdays.

Travelling with Children Italy is the kid-friendly capital of Europe. Its mix of historical and cultural sights and breathtaking natural landscapes means there is always something to do. In Rome, the Roman ruins and world-class museums are great for older children. Naples and the ancient city of Pompeii are good for all ages. Italy's beaches are generally safe. State-run attractions are often free to EU citizens under 18 years of age. Italian families tend to eat later meaning few restaurants open before 7.30pm. Pizzerias usually open earlier. The south can get very hot in the summer months.

Public Holidays New Year's Day, Epiphany, Liberation Day 25 Apr, Easter Monday, Labour Day, Republic Day 2 Jun, Assumption, All Saints' 1 Nov, Immaculate Conception 8 Dec, Christmas Day, Boxing Day.

Motoring Tolls are payable on the autostrada network. If travelling distances, save time by purchasing a 'Viacard' from pay booths or service areas. An overhanging load, e.g. a bicycle rack, must be indicated by a large red/white hatched warning square. Failure to do so will result in a fine.

See campsite map page 482.

Alan Rogers Code: IT62160
2 accommodations
95 pitches
GPS: 45.81840, 7.22891
Post Code: I-11014

Etroubles, Valle d'Aosta

www.alanrogers.com/it62160
info@campingtunnel.it
Tel: 016 578 292
www.campingtunnel.it

Open (Touring Pitches):
Year round with seasonal closures

Camping Tunnel

This is a small, friendly site located near the southern exit of the Gran San Bernardo tunnel. The views from the site are really very pleasant with green hills and towering peaks all around. There is a distinct Italian feel about it and the young English-speaking owners, Silvia and Roberto, are most welcoming and helpful. The site sits on two sides of a quiet road and steady improvements are being made. There are 95 pitches, with 45 of mixed size for touring units, plus a special overnight area for motorcaravans, opposite the main gate. All have electricity (6A Europlug) with drainage and water taps nearby. Gas connections are also available. Some have shade and most are on terraces or gentle slopes. Two fully equipped, air-conditioned mobile homes are available to rent.

The main toilet block is beneath the restaurant building and has recently been refurbished, while the smaller block is central to the upper part of the site. WCs are mixed British and Turkish styles. Showers are modern in one block, outdoor in the other. Good facilities for disabled visitors. Laundry room with washer/dryer and baby changing. Motorcaravan services. Bar and restaurant (1/6-15/9 and 26/12-6/1). New lounge with TV, games and library. Torches and long leads useful. Playground. Pétanque. Communal barbecue. WiFi (free). Nightstop area for motorcaravans with electricity and access to toilets. A small outdoor swimming pool with a hydro-massage bench.

Key Features

 Pets Accepted

 Disabled Facilities

 Swimming Pool

 Play Area

 Bar/Restaurant

 Skiing

Scan me for
more information.

Alan Rogers Code: IT62419
20 pitches
GPS: 45.82331, 8.41398
Post Code: I-28028

Pettenasco, Piedmont

Camping Royal

www.alanrogers.com/it62419
info@campingroyal.com
Tel: 0323 888 945
www.campingroyal.com

Open (Touring Pitches):
1 March - 30 November.

It would be difficult to find a more beautiful lake than Orta, surrounded by wooded hills and mountains and fringed with ancient towns and villages. Camping Royal, family owned and run, sits on a hillside overlooking the lake. There are 60 pitches, 20 for touring, set on level terraces, each with 5A Europlug and a water point nearby. Although professionally managed, this site has maintained the typical relaxed informality for which Italy is famous. Popular with campers from all over Europe, many return year after year. Nothing seems to be too much trouble to ensure a memorable stay.

Key Features

 Pets Accepted

 Disabled Facilities

 Swimming Pool

 Play Area

 Bar/Restaurant

 Skiing

 Bike Hire

Refurbished toilet block has hot showers (20c tokens) and a mixture of British and Turkish style toilets. New wet room for disabled campers by reception. Washing machine and dryer. Laundry and dishwashing sinks. Fridges. Shop with takeaway pizzas. Bar. New swimming pool. Playground. Football field. Room with games, library, cooking hobs and TV. Children's activities (daily in July/August) and some entertainment for adults. Shuttle bus to San Giulio in season (€2 return). Bicycle, scooter and car hire arranged. Internet cabin. WiFi (charged).

Scan me for
more information.

Alan Rogers Code: IT62455
20 accommodations
80 pitches
GPS: 45.93923, 8.48577
Post Code: I-28924

Fondotoce di Verbania,
Piedmont

www.alanrogers.com/it62455
info@campinglidotoce.eu
Tel: 0323 496 220
www.campinglidotoce.eu

Open (Touring Pitches):
Mid March - mid October.

Camping Lido Toce

This small family owned site is the type that some will love — camping as a back-to-nature experience. The facilities here are of a very high quality and the Perucchini family team, with 50 years' experience, are all very keen to make your stay enjoyable. The 80 touring pitches are between 80-140 sq.m, with 6A electricity and larger outfits can access the site easily. There is plenty of shade and greenery, and the beach frontage is attractive with excellent views. There is much to do in the local area. Near the entrance is a pleasant bar and snack bar which has a terrace and offers simple fare at reasonable prices. All the buildings here are bright and clean, and the atmosphere is really enjoyable.

Two sanitary blocks with spotless, modern facilities. Good showers. Baby room. Facilities for disabled visitors. Washing machines. Motorcaravan services. Small shop. Bar. Takeaway (from April). Play area with climbing frames. Beach frontage onto lake. River alongside (through small wood). WiFi over part of site (charged).

Key Features

 Pets Accepted

 Disabled Facilities

 Play Area

 Bar/Restaurant

 Fishing

 Sailing

Scan me for more information.

Alan Rogers Code: IT62460
218 accommodations
420 pitches
GPS: 45.93835, 8.50008
Post Code: I-28924

Fondotoce di Verbania,
Piedmont

www.alanrogers.com/it62460
info@isolino.com
Tel: 0323 496 080
www.isolino.it

Open (Touring Pitches):
23 March - 19 September.

Camping Village Isolino

Lake Maggiore is one of the most attractive Italian lakes and Isolino is an impressive site and one of the largest in the region. Most of the 442 touring pitches have shade from a variety of trees. They vary in size, all have 6A electrical connections, 216 with water, drainage and satellite TV, some with lake views. The bar and restaurant terraces overlook the very large, lagoon-style swimming pool with its island sun deck area, water games and a canyon river, and stunning views across the lake to the fir-clad mountains beyond. Often the social life of the campsite is centred around the large bar/terrace which has a small stage inside, sometimes used for musical entertainment.

Six well built toilet blocks have hot water for showers and washbasins but cold for dishwashing and laundry. Good baby room. Laundry facilities. Motorcaravan services. Supermarket, bar and takeaway (all season). Boutique. Gelateria. Swimming pool (23/4-18/9). Animation (23/4-11/9). Amphitheatre. Football field. Tennis court. Table tennis. Fishing. Watersports. Boat launching. Bicycle hire and guided mountain bike tours. Long beach. WiFi on part of site (charged). Good English is spoken. Bookings for dogs must be made in high season.

Key Features

  Pets Accepted

 Disabled Facilities

 Swimming Pool

 Play Area

 Bar/Restaurant

 Bike Hire

Fishing

Scan me for
more information.

Alan Rogers Code: IT64107
215 pitches
GPS: 44.14906, 8.26856
Post Code: I-17027

Pietra Ligure, Ligúria

www.alanrogers.com/it64107
info@piandeiboschi.it
Tel: 0196 254 25
www.piandeiboschi.it

Open (Touring Pitches):
Easter - end September.

Camping Pian dei Boschi

Camping Pian dei Boschi can be found on the Ligurian Riviera, 700 m. from the sea, close to the resort of Pietra Ligure. There are 215 pitches available for touring. They are well shaded, and most have electrical connections (5-6A). A number of mobile homes are available for rent, as well as apartments (for 4-6 people). There is a large swimming pool surrounded by a wide sun terrace, with a paddling pool adjacent. The campsite restaurant includes a wood-fired pizza oven and offers an enticing range of Mediterranean cuisine. Other on-site amenities include a tennis court and sports field. An entertainment and activity programme is organised in peak season and includes evening entertainment.

Two sanitary blocks with mainly Turkish style toilets, some hot water to open style washbasins, preset showers (token). Facilities for disabled visitors. Washing machines. Motorcaravan services. Shop. Bar/restaurant/pizzeria. Takeaway. Swimming pool (caps compulsory). Paddling pool. Play area. Tennis. Sports field. Entertainment and activity programme. Mobile homes and apartments for rent.

Key Features

 Pets Accepted

 Swimming Pool

 Play Area

 Bar/Restaurant

Scan me for
more information.

Alan Rogers Code: IT64015
4 accommodations
80 pitches
GPS: 43.89457, 7.64691
Post Code: I-18035

Isolabona, Ligúria

www.alanrogers.com/it64015
info@campingdellerose.eu
Tel: 0184 208 130
www.campingdellerose.eu

Open (Touring Pitches):
21 March - 6 November.

Camping Delle Rose

Camping Delle Rose is close to the French border, and a few miles inland from the Italian Riviera. This is a peaceful spot, set deep in the Maritime Alps, with many unspoilt medieval towns, picturesque churches and bustling markets. This is a friendly, family site where Lorena, Mauro and Lorenzo will guarantee a warm welcome. The site is located on a steeply terraced hillside, surrounded by eucalyptus and mimosa. The 80 touring pitches are 40-80 sq.m, and most have 3A electricity connections. A number of mobile homes and apartments are available for rent. Many improvements are being made to the site and those already completed are of a high standard.

One basic toilet block has been recently refurbished and provides some washbasins with hot water, pushbutton showers (no dividers) and baby changing mat. No facilities for disabled visitors. Swimming pools (15/6-15/9). New bar (15/6-15/9). Restaurant and pizzeria (July/Aug). Small play area. Animation for children and live music for adults (high season). Communal barbecues only. Mobile homes and chalets for rent. Torch useful. WiFi (charged in high season).

Key Features

 Pets Accepted

 Disabled Facilities

 Swimming Pool

 Play Area

 Bar/Restaurant

 Fishing

Scan me for more information.

Alan Rogers Code: IT62610
157 accommodations
149 pitches
GPS: 45.65708, 10.03740
Post Code: I-25049

Iseo, Lombardy

www.alanrogers.com/it62610
info@campingdelsole.it
Tel: 0309 802 88
www.campingdelsole.it

Open (Touring Pitches):
16 April - 25 September.

Camping del Sole

Camping del Sole is, in our opinion, one of Italy's best family sites. It lies on the southern edge of Lake Iseo, just outside the pretty lakeside town of Iseo. The site has 306 pitches, of which 149 are for touring, all with 3A electricity and some fine views of the surrounding mountains and lake. Pitches are generally flat and of a reasonable size, but cars must park in the car park. The site has a wide range of excellent leisure amenities, including a large swimming pool. There is a bar and restaurant with a pizzeria near the pool and an entertainment area.

Sanitary facilities are modern and well maintained, including special facilities for children and disabled visitors. Washing machines and dryers (€ 4). Bar, restaurant, pizzeria, snack bar and excellent shop. Motorcaravan services. Bicycle hire. Swimming pool with children's pool (21/5-10/9). Tennis. Football pitch. Fitness area. Canoe and pedal boat hire. WiFi. Dog exercise area. Entertainment in high season.

Key Features

 Pets Accepted

 Disabled Facilities

 Swimming Pool

 Play Area

 Bar/Restaurant

 Bike Hire

 Fishing

Scan me for
more information.

Alan Rogers Code: IT62595
70 pitches
GPS: 45.66667, 10.06694
Post Code: I-25049

Iseo, Lombardy

www.alanrogers.com/it62595
info@campingcovelo.it
Tel: 0309 8213 05
www.campingcovelo.com

Open (Touring Pitches):
1 April – 31 October.

Camping Covelo

Covelo has a superb lakeside location and is one of the friendliest family sites we have visited in Italy. It is three hundred metres long, with grassy pitches and mature trees. The average sized, level pitches are in rows parallel with the shores of the lake. As the site is just four pitches deep, all have excellent access to the water plus brilliant views of the mountains across the lake and the tree-clad escarpment to the rear of the site. The owners take great pride in their site, insisting on high levels of simple family-style enjoyment for their guests. Although the site is small, the creative owners of Covelo have worked wonders in getting the maximum from their site for their guests to feel relaxed and have an enjoyable holiday.

Three refurbished sanitary blocks of differing sizes provide pleasant facilities including those for disabled visitors. Baby cubicle. Motorcaravan services. Shop. Bar. Restaurant. Small play area. Entertainment. TV room. Big screen movies at night. Free bicycles for guests. Fishing. Boat launching. Buoys for boats. Free WiFi.

Key Features

 Pets Accepted

 Disabled Facilities

 Play Area

 Bar/Restaurant

 Bike Hire

 Fishing

 Horse Riding

Scan me for more information.

Alan Rogers Code: IT62390
20 accommodations
90 pitches
GPS: 46.03886, 8.73473
Post Code: I-21010

Maccagno, Lombardy

Maccagno Lagocamp

www.alanrogers.com/it62390
maccagno@lagocamp.com
Tel: 0332 560 203
www.lagocamp.com

Open (Touring Pitches):
18 March - 13 November.

Parkcamping Maccagno Lagocamp is a delightful small site with immediate access to the shores of Lake Maggiore and a shingle beach. With hills on each side, the views over the lake are spectacular. There is no entertainment or infrastructure, so the site will suit those who just wish to relax on a traditional style campsite. The 90 pitches vary in size (40-80 sq.m), are relatively flat, most have been re-turfed and many have shade. They are numbered but demarcation is somewhat informal. The bar and shop were completely refurbished in 2015, with a few snacks added to the menu. There are restaurants close by. English, German and Dutch are spoken and the site management is keen to assist you in having a pleasant holiday.

Key Features

 Pets Accepted

 Disabled Facilities

 Play Area

 Bar/Restaurant

 Fishing

 Sailing

The toilet block is old but has been re-fitted inside to provide clean and modern facilities including those for babies (in ladies' toilet) and disabled visitors (key). Laundry facilities. Motorcaravan services. Newly refurbished bar and shop selling bread and basics. Terrace seating. Basic snacks. Simple play areas and sandpit. WiFi around reception area (charged).

Scan me for more information.

Alan Rogers Code: IT62040
3 accommodations
150 pitches
GPS: 46.53344, 11.53335
Post Code: I-39050

Völs am Schlern, Trentino - Alto Adige

www.alanrogers.com/it62040
info@camping-seiseralm.com
Tel: 0471 706 459
www.camping-seiseralm.com

Open (Touring Pitches):
20 December - 2 November.

Camping Seiser Alm

What an amazing experience awaits you at Seiser Alm! Elisabeth and Erhard Mahlknecht have created a superb site in the magnificent Südtirol region of the Dolomite mountains. Towering peaks provide a wonderful backdrop when you dine in the charming, traditionally styled restaurant on the upper terrace. Here you will also find the bar, shop and reception. The 150 touring pitches have 16A electricity, gas, water, drainage, satellite connection and WiFi. Guests were delighted with the site when we visited, many coming to walk or cycle, some just to enjoy the surroundings. There are countless things to see and do here, including a full entertainment programme and a brilliant new pool.

One spotless, luxury underground block is in the centre of the site. 16 private units are available. Excellent facilities for disabled visitors. Fairy tale facilities for children. Infrared sensors, underfloor heating and gently curved floors to prevent slippery surfaces. Washing machines and large drying room. Sauna. Supermarket. Quality restaurant and bar with terrace. Swimming pool (heated in cool weather). Entertainment programme six days a week. Miniclub. Children's adventure park and play room. Rooms for ski equipment. Animal enclosure. WiFi (charged). Apartments, mobile homes and maxi-caravans for rent.

Key Features

 Pets Accepted

 Disabled Facilities

 Swimming Pool

 Play Area

 Bar/Restaurant

 Skiing

 Bike Hire

 Golf

Scan me for more information.

Alan Rogers Code: IT62310
115 pitches
GPS: 46.02773, 11.23144
Post Code: I-38057

Pergine, Trentino - Alto Adige

www.alanrogers.com/it62310
info@campingpuntaindiani.it
Tel: 046 154 8062
www.campingpuntaindiani.it

Open (Touring Pitches):
29 April - 30 September.

Punta Indiani

Punta Indiani is on a small peninsula on the northwestern shore of Lake Caldonazzo, one of the smaller and most easterly of the Italian lakes. This simple, family run campsite is split into three camping areas. Two are split by a railway line (the trains only run during the day – great for train spotters). There are 115 pitches here which vary in size, all with 3/4A electricity, some with shade. Many have a superb position being right on the shores of this beautiful lake. There are limited amenities on the site, but a rear gate gives access to the town which has all the usual facilities and these compensate for the site's simplicity. This site is very popular with windsurfers and offers uncomplicated camping at reasonable prices for all.

Two modernised toilet blocks with mixed British and Turkish style toilets and hot water. Washing machine and dryer. Freezer. High season family activities including al fresco eating. Simple play area. Beach. Dogs accepted by prior arrangement only.

Key Features

 Pets Accepted

 Disabled Facilities

 Play Area

 Bar/Restaurant

 Fishing

Scan me for
more information.

Alan Rogers Code: IT62000
8 accommodations
230 pitches
GPS: 46.73445, 12.19427
Post Code: I-39034

Toblach, Trentino - Alto Adige

www.alanrogers.com/it62000
info@camping-olympia.com
Tel: 0474 972 147
www.camping-olympia.com

Open (Touring Pitches):
All year.

Camping Olympia

In the Dolomite mountains, Camping Olympia continues to maintain its high standards. The 300 pitches are set out in a regular pattern and the tall pine trees, shrubs and hedges make this a very pleasant and attractive site. There are tree-clad hills on either side and craggy mountains beyond. The 230 mainly level touring pitches all have 6-16A electricity and a TV point. There are 63 fully serviced pitches with water, waste water, gas (21), telephone and satellite TV points. Some accommodation is available to rent, and there are 62 seasonal caravans which are mainly grouped at one end of the site.

The toilet block is of a very high standard. Rooms with WC, washbasin and shower to rent. Baby room. Facilities for disabled visitors. Two small blocks provide further WCs and showers. Motorcaravan services. Shop. Attractive bar, restaurant and pizzeria (all year). Second bar with grill and terrace by pool (10/6-30/9; 20/12-Easter). Heated swimming pool (20/5-15/9). Sauna, solarium, steam bath and whirlpools. Massage and Kneipp treatments. Fishing. Bicycle hire. Play area. WiFi throughout (free). Programme of activities and excursions. Entertainment in high season.

Key Features

 Open All Year

 Pets Accepted

 Disabled Facilities

 Swimming Pool

 Play Area

 Bar/Restaurant

 Skiing

Bike Hire

Scan me for more information.

Alan Rogers Code: IT62850
38 accommodations
209 pitches
GPS: 45.53967, 10.55595
Post Code: I-25080

Manerba del Garda, Lake Garda

Camping Zocco

www.alanrogers.com/it62850
info@campingzocco.it
Tel: 036 555 1605
www.campingzocco.it

Open (Touring Pitches):
22 April - 3 October.

Camping Zocco is an excellent, professionally run site in a quiet, scenic location sloping gently down towards the lake where there is a jetty, buoys for your boat and a long pleasant shingle beach with a bar. The Sandrini family, who run this site, give British and Dutch visitors a warm welcome and English is spoken. There are 209 pitches for touring units, all with 6A electricity either on slightly sloping ground or terraced. The position and quality of the facilities make Zocco a most attractive option if you prefer a smaller, quieter site which improves year on year. A variety of trees give shade in some parts. These include olives, which provide oil for the owners and may be bought in attractive personalised bottles as a souvenir. The site has a pool and children's pool, a smart reception and late arrivals area. Watersports can be enjoyed on the lake and boats may be launched from the site. Mobile homes to rent.

Key Features

 Pets Accepted

 Disabled Facilities

 Swimming Pool

 Play Area

 Bar/Restaurant

 Bike Hire

 Fishing

Three tiled sanitary blocks, clean and well cared for, are well spaced around the site. Two are very modern with spacious showers and toilets (some Turkish). Facilities for disabled visitors. Washing machines. Motorcaravan services. Well stocked shop. Bar overlooking beach (reduced hours in low season), good restaurant/pizzeria with terrace and bar. Pool complex with jacuzzi (22/4-3/10). Fishing. Tennis. Play area. Bocce. Children's entertainment (July/Aug). Bicycle hire arranged. No electric barbecues. WiFi on part of site (first hour free daily).

Scan me for
more information.

Alan Rogers Code: IT63015
49 accommodations
133 pitches
GPS: 45.46472, 10.71476
Post Code: I-37017

Lazise, Lake Garda

www.alanrogers.com/it63015
info@lepalmecamping.it
Tel: 0457 590 019
www.lepalmecamping.it

Open (Touring Pitches):
4 April - 27 October.

Camping Le Palme

On the southern shore of Lake Garda, Le Palme is a quiet site on the attractive Riviera degli Olivi, yet within easy reach of numerous attractions including several theme parks. There are 133 touring pitches, all with electricity (6-10A), water and waste water connections. Trees provide some shade throughout and a few pitches have spectacular views across the lake, for which a supplement is payable. Some mobile homes and chalets are available for hire. Nearby Lazise and Peschiera del Garda are both attractive towns with plenty of history, as well as shops, bars and restaurants. The ancient city of Verona is an easy drive away.

Three heated sanitary blocks provide hot showers, baby and laundry rooms. Motorcaravan services. Swimming pool with terrace, bar, slides and children's pool. Restaurant, pizzeria and bar with entertainment in high season. Shop with bazaar. Playground. Football. Volleyball. Rent of bicycles, fridges, private bathrooms, boat moorings and parking for boat trailers. WiFi throughout (charged). Underground carpark available. Doctor daily in middle and high season. Direct lake access.

Key Features

 Pets Accepted

 Disabled Facilities

 Swimming Pool

 Play Area

 Bar/Restaurant

 Bike Hire

 Fishing

Scan me for more information.

285

Alan Rogers Code: IT62630
492 accommodations
400 pitches
GPS: 45.44165, 10.67920
Post Code: I-37019

Peschiera del Garda, Lake Garda

www.alanrogers.com/it62630
info@camping-bellaitalia.it
Tel: 045 640 0688
www.camping-bellaitalia.it

Open (Touring Pitches):
12 March - 23 October.

Camping Bella Italia

Peschiera is a picturesque village on the southern shore of Lake Garda, and Camping Bella Italia is a very attractive, large, well organised and very busy site in the grounds of a former farm, just west of the centre of the village. Half of the 1,200 pitches are occupied by the site's own mobile homes and chalets and by tour operators; there are some 400 touring pitches, most towards the lakeside and reasonably level on grass under trees. All have 16A electricity, water and waste water and are separated by shrubs. There are some fine views across the lake to the mountains beyond. A superb promenade allows direct access to the town.

Six modern toilet blocks have British style toilets, washbasins and showers. Baby rooms and facilities for disabled visitors. Washing machines. Motorcaravan services. Infirmary. Shops. Gelateria. Bars. Waiter service restaurant and terrace and two other restaurants (one in the old farm building). Swimming pools. Tennis. Archery. Playgrounds (small). Games room. Watersports. Fishing. Bicycle hire. Organised activities and entertainment. Mini club. WiFi over part of site (charged). ATMs. Dogs are not accepted.

Key Features

 Disabled Facilities

 Swimming Pool

 Play Area

 Bar/Restaurant

 Bike Hire

 Sailing

Scan me for more information.

Alan Rogers Code: IT62830
25 accommodations
180 pitches
GPS: 45.56118, 10.56383
Post Code: I-25080

Manerba del Garda, Lake Garda

www.alanrogers.com/it62830
info@laroccacamp.it
Tel: 0365 551 738
www.laroccacamp.it

Open (Touring Pitches):
15 April - 28 September.

Camping la Rocca

Set high on a peninsula, on the quieter western shore of Lake Garda, La Rocca is an amiable, family orientated campsite. The 180 attractive touring pitches enjoy shade from the tree canopy, and 20 are on open terraces with lake views. Also, there are 25 mobile homes to rent. Visitors have the choice of two pebble lakeside beaches with a jetty. The beaches can be accessed from the site, and there is a pleasant pool complex. The site has all modern amenities without losing its distinctive Italian ambience with an open feel. Nothing is too much trouble for the management. The owner, Livio, is charming and very engaging with his pleasant, halting English. The restaurant offers a selection of dishes and pizzas, and there is a selection of sports activities. It is close to traditional Italian villages, modern theme parks and all manner of watersports. The beach is accessed via a tunnel beneath the road.

Two sanitary blocks with smart new units for disabled campers and baby changing areas which are kept in a clean condition at all times. Washing machines. Small shop. Bar with terrace also offers basic meals. Swimming pools. Tennis. Play area. Fishing (permit). Boat launching. Music in the evenings. Miniclub (high season). Torches required on beach steps and tunnel. WiFi in some areas (free).

Key Features

 Pets Accepted

 Disabled Facilities

 Swimming Pool

 Play Area

 Bar/Restaurant

 Fishing

Scan me for more information.

Alan Rogers Code: IT62700
20 accommodations
25 pitches
GPS: 45.57861, 10.55388
Post Code: I-25010

San Felice del Benaco, Lake Garda

www.alanrogers.com/it62700
info@baiaholiday.com
Tel: 0365 559 240
www.campinglagardiola.com

Open (Touring Pitches):
1 April - 12 October.

Villaggio La Gardiola

Located at the end of a narrow lakeside road, this small neat site has just 25 touring pitches; five are fully serviced. The touring pitches are close to the lake with mobile homes on the slope above. The bar, café and reception area is modern but small and simple in keeping with the private feel to the campsite. The café terrace overlooks the lake. The sanitary amenities are of a high standard and discretely built underground, preventing any intrusion on the beautiful views. We found this a delightful, friendly site with cheerful staff who give you a chance to practise your Italian. The lakeside beach is just five metres from the closest pitches and is brilliant for peaceful picnics in sight of your pitch. The road alongside the site has very little traffic and is quiet. It is a boutique type site which is part of the Baia Holiday group, the high standards here are a reflection of all the sites we have visited in the group.

The sanitary block is just below ground level and has a mixture of Turkish and British style WCs. Lift system for disabled visitors. The facilities are quite small but are adequate. Hot water is free throughout. Laundry. Motorcaravan services. Small kiosk with terrace for coffee and snacks. Small playground. Fishing. Diving. Bicycle hire. WiFi (charged).

Key Features

 Pets Accepted

 Disabled Facilities

 Play Area

 Bar/Restaurant

 Fishing

Scan me for more information.

Alan Rogers Code: IT60200
285 accommodations
2200 pitches
GPS: 45.46788, 12.53037
Post Code: I-30013

Cavallino-Treporti, Veneto

www.alanrogers.com/it60200
info@unionlido.com
Tel: 041 257 5111
www.unionlido.com

Open (Touring Pitches):
21 April - 3 October.

Camping Union Lido Vacanze

This amazing site is very large, offering absolutely everything a camper could wish for. It is extremely professionally run and we were impressed with the whole organisation. It lies along a 1.2 km. long, broad sandy beach which shelves very gradually and offers a huge number of sporting activities. The site itself is regularly laid out with parallel access roads under a covering of poplars, pine and other trees. There are 2,200 pitches for touring units, all with 6/10/16A electricity and 1,969 also have water and drainage. Because of the size of the site, there is an internal road train and amenities are repeated across the site (cycling is permitted on specific roads). A member of Leading Campings group.

Fourteen superb, fully equipped toilet blocks; 11 have facilities for disabled visitors. Launderette. Motorcaravan services. Gas supplies. Comprehensive shopping areas set around a pleasant piazza (all open till late). Eight restaurants each with a different style plus 11 pleasant and lively bars (all services open all season). Impressive aqua parks (all season). Tennis. Riding. Minigolf. Skating. Bicycle hire. Archery. Two fitness tracks in 4 ha. natural park with play area and supervised play. Diving centre and school. Windsurf school in season. Exhibitions. Boat excursions. Recreational events. Hairdressers. Internet cafés. ATM. Dogs are accepted in designated areas. Free WiFi throughout.

Key Features

 Pets Accepted

 Disabled Facilities

 Beach Access

 Swimming Pool

 Play Area

 Bar/Restaurant

 Bike Hire

 Horse Riding

Scan me for more information.

Alan Rogers Code: IT60590
70 pitches
GPS: 44.84613, 12.46330
Post Code: I-45010

Bonelli di Porto Tolle, Veneto

Villaggio Barricata

www.alanrogers.com/it60590
info@villaggiobarricata.com
Tel: 0426 389 198
www.villaggiobarricata.com

Open (Touring Pitches):
15 May - 20 September.

Villaggio Barricata is a pleasant site located within the large nature reserve at the mouth of the Po Delta. A drive through many rows of mobile homes brings you to 70 touring pitches, all with 6A electricity and water connections, and protected in the main by expensive artificial shading. On-site amenities are impressive and include a fabulous swimming pool complex, a bar/restaurant and a well stocked supermarket. A lively entertainment and activity programme is on offer during the peak season, including a children's club. A short walk leads to a long, gently shelving sandy beach.

Heated sanitary facilities include provision for disabled visitors. Laundry. Bazaar. Bar. Restaurants. Takeaway. Shop. Swimming pools. Pool bar. Children's pool and lagoon. Wellness and spa. Aerobics. Tennis. Miniclub. Entertainment. Disco. Dancing classes. Play area. TV/games room. Bicycle hire. Riding. Archery. 5-a-side football. Canoeing. Dog beach. Accommodation and glamping. Max. 1 dog.

Key Features

 Pets Accepted

 Disabled Facilities

 Beach Access

 Swimming Pool

 Play Area

 Bar/Restaurant

 Bike Hire

 Horse Riding

Scan me for more information.

Alan Rogers Code: IT60220
302 accommodations
422 pitches
GPS: 45.55357, 12.76752
Post Code: I-30020

Eraclea Mare, Veneto

www.alanrogers.com/it60220
info@portofelice.it
Tel: 0421 664 11
www.portofelice.it

Open (Touring Pitches):
7 May - 18 September.

Camping Village Portofelice

Portofelice is an efficient and attractive coastal site, with a sandy beach which is a short walk through a protected pine wood. The excellent beach is very safe and has lifeguards. There are a total of 422 pitches, half of which are available for touring. These flat and shady pitches have 6/8A electricity (70 also have water, drainage and TV sockets), are well kept and cars are parked separately. Some 302 pitches are dedicated to rental accommodation. The social life of the site is centred around the stunning pool complex where the shops, pizzeria, bar, café and restaurant are also located. This is a tremendous family site.

Three modern sanitary blocks have the usual facilities with slightly more Turkish style toilets than British. Baby room and excellent children's block (0-12 yrs). Facilities for disabled campers. Very large supermarket and bazaar. Pizzeria and takeaway. Bar/restaurant with terraces and waiter service. American diner. Gelateria. Crêperie. Three superb pools with waterfalls, slides and an area specifically equipped for disabled guests, hydro-massage and sunbathing. Playgrounds. Go-kart track. Pedalos. Water dodgems. Tennis. 5-a-side football. Basketball. Volleyball. Sandy beach. Bicycle hire. ATM. Organised activity and entertainment programmes. Miniclub. WiFi throughout (charged). Internet room. Dogs are not accepted.

Key Features

 Disabled Facilities

 Beach Access

 Swimming Pool

 Play Area

 Bar/Restaurant

 Bike Hire

Scan me for more information.

Alan Rogers Code: IT60330
240 accommodations
220 pitches
GPS: 45.52410, 12.70040
Post Code: I-30016

Lido di Jesolo, Veneto

www.alanrogers.com/it60330
info@campingmalibubeach.com
Tel: 042 136 2212
www.campingmalibubeach.com

Open (Touring Pitches):
7 May - 18 September.

Camping Malibu Beach

This is a family site which has direct access to a beach. There are 220 pitches for touring units, all with 6A electricity. Some are well shaded by pine trees and there are some fully serviced pitches. The beach is of soft sand, shelves gently and has lifeguards plus sunshades and loungers for hire. The central complex incorporates a bright, cheery self-service restaurant topped by a very smart restaurant and cocktail patio with views. A large entertainment theatre offers all manner of delights in high season. Other amenities include a large swimming pool, plus a paddling pool with slide and fountains. Everything around this site was clean and smart and the visitors we spoke to were happy.

Three very clean blocks provide very good facilities with some Turkish style toilets. Facilities for disabled visitors and children. Bar, self-service restaurant and formal restaurant and cocktail patio. Pizzeria. Shop. Games room. Fitness centre. Hairdresser. Massage. Swimming pool, jacuzzi and paddling pool (hats compulsory). Playground. Miniclub. Entertainment programme. Direct beach access. Fridge box hire. WiFi throughout (charged). Dogs are not accepted.

Key Features

   Disabled Facilities

   Beach Access

   Swimming Pool

   Play Area

   Bar/Restaurant

   Bike Hire

Fishing

Scan me for more information.

Alan Rogers Code: IT60030
523 accommodations
800 pitches
GPS: 45.57312, 12.81248
Post Code: I-30021

Caorle, Veneto

Pra' Delle Torri

www.alanrogers.com/it60030
info@pradelletorri.it
Tel: 042 129 9063
www.pradelletorri.it

Open (Touring Pitches):
21 April - 25 September.

Pra' Delle Torri is a superb Italian Adriatic site which has just about everything! Pitches for camping, hotel accommodation and two very large, superbly equipped pool complexes, which may be rated among the best in the country. There is also a full-size golf course. Of the 1,000 pitches, 800 are available for touring and are arranged in zones, with 5A electricity and shade. There is an amazing choice of quality restaurants, bars, shops and services placed strategically around an attractive square. Although a very large site, there is a great atmosphere here that families will enjoy.

Sixteen high quality, spotless toilet blocks with excellent facilities including very attractive children's bathrooms. Units for disabled visitors. Laundry facilities. Motorcaravan services. Large supermarket and wide range of shops, restaurants, bars and takeaways. Indoor and outdoor pools. Disco with music selected by mobile phone app. Tennis. Minigolf. Fishing. Watersports. Archery. Diving. Fitness programmes and keep fit track. Crèche and supervised play area. Bowls. Mountain bike track. Wide range of organised sports and entertainment. Road train to town in high season. Dogs are not accepted.

Key Features

 Disabled Facilities

 Beach Access

 Swimming Pool

 Play Area

 Bar/Restaurant

 Bike Hire

 Golf

Horse Riding

Scan me for
more information.

Alan Rogers Code: IT60440
256 accommodations
800 pitches
GPS: 45.44543, 12.46127
Post Code: I-30013

Ca'Savio, Veneto

www.alanrogers.com/it60440
info@casavio.it
Tel: 0419 660 17
www.casavio.it

Open (Touring Pitches):
26 April - 2 October.

Camping Ca'Savio

Ca'Savio is a very large, family owned site of almost 50 years standing. It is in traditional Italian style and is set on a wide, sandy, Blue Flag beach which is safe for swimming. The beach is separated from the pitches by a pleasant open area and a row of bungalows. There are many activities here, some requiring additional payment. There are 800 touring pitches (all with 10A electricity), 256 mobile homes/bungalows and around 400 tour operator pitches. Rows of pitches lead off a very busy central avenue and they are shaded, mostly flat and varying in size (90-100 sq.m). Many are a long way from water and sanitary facilities. Customers are left to find their own pitches, so leave someone there while you fetch your unit!

Three large toilet blocks include many shower, toilet and washbasin units. The toilets are in cabins with showers and washbasins, so at busy periods there may be a long wait. Supermarket, bazaar and other shops. Restaurants, pizzeria, café and pub. Two very large pool complexes (free). Miniclub. Bicycle hire. Minigolf. Good adventure style playground. Car hire. Internet and WiFi (at the restaurant; charged). Dogs are not accepted.

Key Features

 Disabled Facilities

 Beach Access

 Swimming Pool

 Play Area

 Bar/Restaurant

 Bike Hire

Scan me for more information.

Alan Rogers Code: IT60070
179 accommodations
900 pitches
GPS: 45.72867, 13.40109
Post Code: I-33051

Grado, Friuli - Venézia Giúlia

www.alanrogers.com/it60070
info@belvederepineta.it
Tel: 0431 910 07
www.belvederepineta.com

Open (Touring Pitches):
29 April - 30 September.

Belvedere Pineta

Belvedere Pineta is situated on the edge of an almost entirely land-locked lagoon, 5 km. from Grado on the northern Adriatic Sea. A minor road runs between the site and the lagoon and a bridge over this connects the site with the beach of fine sand. It is a large site with 900 touring pitches arranged in regular rows with most under shade provided by the many tall pine trees which cover the site. Most are of reasonable size and all have electricity. An area of accommodation to let is to one side of the camping area. In high season a large programme of sport and entertainment for children and adults is organised. With two pools, an area for ball games, tennis courts, minigolf and the beach there are plenty of activities to enjoy. In nearby Aquileia, once the fourth city of the Roman Empire, is one of the world's most magnificent mosaic floors. Excursions can be made by rail to Venice and other places in the region.

Most of the six toilet blocks have been refurbished to a good standard with all the usual facilities including some for children and free hot water in all washbasins, showers and sinks. Facilities for disabled visitors. Motorcaravan services. Range of shops. Restaurant, pizzeria and takeaway. Swimming pools. Sports facilities. Play areas. Organised entertainment in high season. Bicycle hire. WiFi (charged).

Key Features

 Pets Accepted

 Disabled Facilities

 Beach Access

 Swimming Pool

 Play Area

 Bar/Restaurant

 Bike Hire

 Fishing

Scan me for more information.

295

Alan Rogers Code: IT60065
100 accommodations
582 pitches
GPS: 45.70510, 13.46400
Post Code: I-34073

Grado, Friuli - Venézia Giúlia

www.alanrogers.com/it60065
info@tenuta-primero.com
Tel: 0431 896 900
www.tenuta-primero.com

Open (Touring Pitches):
21 April - 23 September

Camping Tenuta Primero

Tenuta Primero is a large, attractive, well run, family owned site with direct access to its own private beach, marina and golf course. It offers a wealth of facilities and activities and caters for all members of the family. All of the pitches are all level, with 6A electricity, some separating hedges and ample tree shade. The site has several restaurants and bars, and the large, elevated, flower decked Terrazza Mare, overlooking the sea, is great for eating and drinking whilst enjoying views over the romantic Adriatic.

Nine traditional sanitary blocks, seven with facilities for disabled visitors. Washing machines and dryers. Motorcaravan services. Swimming pools and paddling pool. Shop, bars and restaurants, pizzeria, takeaway (all May-Sept). Beauty salon. Aerobics. Water gymnastics. Football pitch. Tennis. Boules. Skateboarding. Play areas. Windsurfing. Marina, sailing, boat launching and boat hire. Bicycle hire. Children's and family entertainment. Live music, disco, dancing. Private beach with sunshades, deck chairs and jetty. Internet corner and WiFi (free). Dogs are not accepted. Courses now available for many activities.

Key Features

 Disabled Facilities

 Beach Access

 Swimming Pool

 Play Area

 Bar/Restaurant

 Bike Hire

 Fishing

 Golf

Scan me for
more information.

Alan Rogers Code: IT60080
293 accommodations
974 pitches
GPS: 45.68198, 13.12577
Post Code: I-33054

Lignano Sabbiadoro, Friuli - Venézia Giúlia

www.alanrogers.com/it60080
campsab@lignano.it
Tel: 043 171 455
www.campingsabbiadoro.it

Open (Touring Pitches):
28 March - 9 October.

Camping Sabbiadoro

Sabbiadoro is a large, top quality site that caters very well for children. It is divided into two parts with separate entrances and efficient receptions. It has 974 touring pitches and is ideal for families who like all their amenities to be close by. The level, grassy pitches vary in size, are shaded by attractive trees and have electricity (6-10A) and TV connections. The facilities are all in excellent condition and well thought out, especially the pool complex, and everything here is very modern, safe and clean. The site's private beach (with 24-hour guard) is only 250 m. away and has its own showers, toilets and baby rooms.

Well equipped sanitary facilities with free showers includes superb facilities for disabled visitors. Washing machines and dryers. Motorcaravan services. Huge supermarket (all season). Bazaar. Good restaurant, snack bar and takeaway. Heated outdoor pool complex with separate fun pool area, slides and fountains (all season). Heated indoor children's pool. Swimming courses. Play areas. Tennis. Fitness centre. Boat launching. Windsurfing school. Activity centre for children with well organised entertainment (high season) and language school. WiFi throughout (charged). Bicycle hire. Excursions to Venice.

Key Features

 Pets Accepted

 Disabled Facilities

 Beach Access

 Swimming Pool

 Play Area

 Bar/Restaurant

 Bike Hire

 Scan me for more information.

Alan Rogers Code: IT60900
26 accommodations
230 pitches
GPS: 44.80621, 10.00980
Post Code: I-43039

Tabiano di Salsomaggiore Terme,
Emília-Romagna

www.alanrogers.com/it60900
info@camping-arizona.it
Tel: 0524 565 648
www.camping-arizona.it

Open (Touring Pitches):
1 April - 15 October.

Camping Arizona

Camping Arizona is a green site with a zero carbon rating, set on steep slopes, and 500 m. from the pretty town of Tabiano, with its thermal springs dating back to the Roman era. The focus on water is continued within this pleasant, family run site by a complex of four large pools, long water slides into a plunge pool, a jacuzzi and play area, all set in open landscaped grounds with superb views (open to the public). The 300 level pitches with electricity (3A solar-generated on site) vary from 50-90 sq.m. Those on terraced pitches enjoy shade from mature trees, others have no shade. Cars must be parked in the large adjacent car park under a solar panel array.

Two modern toilet blocks provide good facilities including some for disabled visitors. Solar-heated water. Washing machines and dryers. Small, well stocked shop, bar/restaurant with patio (all 1/4-6/10). Swimming pools, slides and jacuzzi (16/5-15/9, also open to the public but free for campers). Tennis. Boules. Large play centre. WiFi throughout (charged).

Key Features

 Pets Accepted

 Disabled Facilities

 Swimming Pool

 Play Area

 Bar/Restaurant

 Horse Riding

Scan me for more information.

Alan Rogers Code: IT60650
150 accommodations
450 pitches
GPS: 44.73457, 12.22178
Post Code: I-44020

Lido delle Nazioni - Comacchio,
Emília-Romagna

Camping Tahiti

www.alanrogers.com/it60650
info@campingtahiti.com
Tel: 053 337 9500
www.campingtahiti.com

Open (Touring Pitches):
12 May - 18 September.

Tahiti is an excellent, extremely well run, family owned site, thoughtfully laid out 800 m. from the sea (a continuous, fun road-train link is provided). An abundance of flowers and shrubs enhance its appearance. The 450 touring pitches are of varying sizes, back to back from hard roads, defined by trees with shade in most areas and all with 10A electricity. There are six types, from a basic pitch to those with kitchens plus a shower. Several languages, including English, are spoken by the friendly staff. The Thermal Oasis is luxurious and there is a 50% discount for campers. This award-winning site has a great atmosphere and everyone was cheerful when we visited.

Key Features

 Pets Accepted

 Disabled Facilities

 Swimming Pool

 Play Area

 Bar/Restaurant

 Bike Hire

 Horse Riding

All toilet blocks are of a very high standard. British and Turkish style WCs. Baby room. Large supermarket, two restaurants, bar, pizzeria, takeaway, heated swimming pools (all season). Thermal Oasis (charged). Fitness and beauty centre. Several playgrounds and miniclub. Gym. Tennis. Floodlit sports area. Minigolf. Riding. Bicycle hire. Entertainment and excursions (high season). 'Disco-pub'. ATM. WiFi on part of site (charged). Free transport to beach. Torches needed in some areas. Archery. Bowls. Dogs are only accepted from 12/5-19/6 and 28/8-18/9.

Scan me for more information.

Alan Rogers Code: IT66210
200 accommodations
200 pitches
GPS: 44.16597, 12.43196
Post Code: I-47043

Gatteo a Mare, Emília-Romagna

www.alanrogers.com/it66210
info@villaggiorose.com
Tel: 0547 862 13
www.villaggiorose.com

Open (Touring Pitches):
1 May - 19 September.

Villaggio Delle Rose

On the Cesanatico coastline of Emilia-Romagna, this site is unusually located in a shaded park area just 450 m. from the beautiful sandy beach. It is a site with a very Italian flavour and when we visited we were made very welcome. The 200 touring pitches, with 3/10A electricity, are cosily positioned and most have shade. There is a large swimming pool and paddling pool and an ambitious programme of activities and entertainment takes place throughout the day and during the evening. The bar and restaurant facilities on site are very good, as is the pool bar.

Modern sanitary facilities are very clean and well spaced around the site. Motorcaravan services. Shop. Restaurant, pizzeria and snack bar with takeaway (all 1/5-20/9). Swimming pool with pool bar (30/5-13/9). Paddling pool. Hydro-massage. Playgrounds. Games room. TV room. Children's club and entertainment programme. Sports field. Free shuttle bus and use of bicycles to beach. WiFi on part of site (free).

Key Features

 Pets Accepted

 Disabled Facilities

 Swimming Pool

 Play Area

 Bar/Restaurant

 Bike Hire

Scan me for more information.

Alan Rogers Code: IT66090
53 accommodations
240 pitches
GPS: 43.72187, 11.22058
Post Code: I-50023

Firenze, Tuscany

www.alanrogers.com/it66090
internazionale@florencevillage.com
Tel: 055 237 4704
www.florencevillage.com

Open (Touring Pitches):
19 March - 3 November.

Camping Village Firenze

Camping Village Internazionale Firenze is set in the hills about 5 km. south of Florence. This is a well shaded, terraced site with 240 informal touring pitches set around the top of a hill. Although it is a very green site, the camping area is somewhat more open with two electricity pylons at the top of the hill and some noise from the busy motorway which is below and next to the site. It is often lively at night with many young people from tour groups. There is a small restaurant half way up the slope of the site with a reasonable menu. A well located site for visiting Florence rather than for extended stays.

Two traditional toilet blocks include free hot showers. Laundry. Some kitchen facilities. Motorcaravan services. Shop. New bar and restaurant at the lower level. Evening entertainment. Two swimming pools. Swim cap compulsory. Playground. WiFi over part of site (charged). Gas and electric barbecues only.

Key Features

 Pets Accepted

 Disabled Facilities

 Swimming Pool

 Bar/Restaurant

Scan me for more information.

Alan Rogers Code: IT66080
51 accommodations
220 pitches
GPS: 43.72520, 10.38190
Post Code: I-56122

Pisa, Tuscany

www.alanrogers.com/it66080
info@campingtorrependente.com
Tel: 0505 617 04
www.campingtorrependente.it

Open (Touring Pitches):
1 April - 15 October.

Camping Torre Pendente

Torre Pendente is a most friendly site, efficiently run by the Signorini family who speak good English and make everyone feel welcome. It is amazingly close to the famous leaning tower of Pisa and therefore busy throughout the main season. It is a medium sized site with 220 touring pitches, all with 5A electricity, on level, grassy ground with some shade from trees and lots of artificial shade. Fifty bungalows are also available for hire. The excellent site facilities are near the entrance including a most pleasant restaurant, swimming pool complex with a pool bar and a large terrace. Here you can relax after hot days in the city and enjoy drinks and snacks or find more formal fare in the restaurant with a reasonable à la carte menu. This is a very busy site in high season with many nationalities discovering the delights of Pisa. It is ideal for exploring the fascinating leaning tower and other attractions. It is very close to the railway stations for travel to Lucca and Florence.

Three toilet blocks are very clean and smart with British style toilets and good facilities for disabled campers. Private cabins for hire. Hot water at sinks. Washing machines. Motorcaravan services. Well stocked supermarket. Pleasant restaurant, bar and takeaway. Swimming pool with pool bar, paddling pool and spa. Playground. Boules. Entertainment in high season. WiFi over site (charged). Bungalows for hire.

Key Features

 Pets Accepted

 Disabled Facilities

 Swimming Pool

 Play Area

 Bar/Restaurant

 Bike Hire

Scan me for more information.

Alan Rogers Code: IT66050
95 accommodations
250 pitches
GPS: 43.96148, 11.31030
Post Code: I-50038

Scarperia e San Piero, Tuscany

Camping Mugello Verde

www.alanrogers.com/it66050
mugelloverde@florencevillage.com
Tel: 055 848 511
www.campingmugelloverde.com

Open (Touring Pitches):
16 March - 3 November

Mugello Verde is a country, hillside site with 250 good sized pitches for motorhomes and caravans and smaller pitches for tents. All have 6A electricity. Some are on flat ground; others are on steep terraces where mature trees provide shade. The big attraction here is the site's proximity to the international Mugello racing track, just 5 km. away. It is used by Ferrari for practice runs and is also an international car and motorcycling track. The site has a pleasant, open feel and the accommodation for hire does not impinge on the touring area. The on-site restaurant serves food at reasonable prices, and the large terrace overlooks the pool which is also used by locals. The bar has a TV, and the local racing is covered fairly constantly. English is spoken at reception where much tourist information is available. A good site, particularly for motor racing enthusiasts.

Two toilet blocks are well positioned and the facilities are clean with mixed British and Turkish style WCs. Hot water throughout. Facilities for disabled visitors. Laundry facilities. Shop. Restaurant/bar and pizzeria (all season). Swimming pool (25/5-22/9; no paddling pool). Play area. Tennis. Free WiFi on part of site.

Key Features

 Pets Accepted

 Disabled Facilities

 Swimming Pool

 Play Area

 Bar/Restaurant

Scan me for more information.

Alan Rogers Code: IT66540
59 accommodations
260 pitches
GPS: 43.18103, 12.01630
Post Code: I-06061

Castiglione del Lago, Umbria

www.alanrogers.com/it66540
info@badiaccia.com
Tel: 075 965 9097
www.badiaccia.com

Open (Touring Pitches):
1 April - 30 September.

Camping Badiaccia

A lakeside site, Camping Badiaccia has excellent views of the surrounding hills and the islands of the lake. Being directly on the lake, with a long sandy beach, gives an almost seaside atmosphere. Unusually, the site uses a birdcage as the post box! The 260 numbered and well-tended pitches (4-12A electricity) vary in size and are shaded and separated by trees and bushes. Badiaccia has a relaxed atmosphere enhanced by a variety of plants and flowers, and English is spoken by the friendly staff. A very pleasant, large pool is by the restaurant, and a children's pool is in the beach area. There is a protected swimming area along the beach with lots of sunbathing space and sun loungers with some reed areas close by, a jetty for fishing and a protected mooring for small boats. The site offers a good selection of sporting opportunities with special staff in high season to organise activities for children and adults.

Key Features

 Pets Accepted

 Swimming Pool

 Play Area

 Bar/Restaurant

 Bike Hire

Three top quality, heated sanitary blocks with sliding doors include hot showers, provision for children and superb units for disabled visitors. Washing machines and dryer. Motorcaravan services. Gas supplies. Restaurant, snack bar and shop. Health and wellness centre. Swimming and paddling pools (15/5-30/9). Play areas. Tennis. Fitness room. Bicycle hire. Boules. Minigolf. Watersports. Fishing. Boat hire. Entertainment and excursions in high season. Free WiFi over part of site. Barbecue area by lake. Torches required in places. Boat trips around the lake.

Scan me for more information.

Alan Rogers Code: IT66550
20 accommodations
100 pitches
GPS: 43.07510, 12.57440
Post Code: I-06081

Assisi, Umbria

www.alanrogers.com/it66550
info@greenvillageassisi.it
Tel: 075 816 816
www.greenvillage-camping-hotel-assisi.com

Open (Touring Pitches):
12 April - 3 November.

Green Village Assisi

Green Village Assisi is an excellent site situated on the west side of Assisi and provides a green environment and tranquillity. Situated on a 30.000 Sqm green area of pinewood forest, it is a good base to visit both Saint Francis' city, only 3.5 km away, and nearby Perugia and Lake Trasimeno. The flat grassy pitches, with 6A electricity, vary in size and some are specifically for motorhomes overlooking the hills to Assisi. It can be very hot in this part of Italy, and a welcome relief is a large pool and shady pitches. The excellent restaurant serves reasonably priced meals, ranging from pizzas to local Umbrian dishes. A large terrace can be completely enclosed. A daily shuttle bus service is available to the city, which is lit up in the evenings, providing a beautiful backdrop from some areas of the site. An ideal place for families with children to enjoy safely the spacious playground and swimming pool.

Key Features

 Pets Accepted

 Disabled Facilities

 Swimming Pool

 Play Area

 Bar/Restaurant

 Bike Hire

The neat and clean toilet block is central and provides free hot showers, mainly Turkish style WCs (only four British style in each block) and facilities for disabled visitors. Washing machine. Gas supplies. Motorcaravan services. Campers' kitchen. Restaurant/pizzeria with self-service section. Bar with snacks. Shop. Swimming pool, jacuzzi and circular paddling pool (1/6-5/9, charged, caps mandatory). Bicycle hire. Tennis. Five-a-side. Volleyball. No charcoal barbecues on pitches. Communal barbecue. WiFi throughout (free).

Scan me for more information.

Alan Rogers Code: IT67800
230 accommodations
100 pitches
GPS: 41.88770, 12.40420
Post Code: I-00165

Roma, Lazio

www.alanrogers.com/it67800
campingroma@ecvacanze.it
Tel: 0666 230 18
www.humancompany.com

Open (Touring Pitches):
All year.

Camping Village Roma

Perched high on a hilltop on the edge of Rome, the site is owned by the Cardini/Vanucchi family, who have other quality city sites in Italy. The diverse range of facilities are designed in particular to meet the needs of young travellers and the aim here is to provide a friendly helpful service all year round. There are 100 touring pitches of varying sizes on level terraces. Motorhomes are mostly placed in a separate area where 20 pitches are fully serviced. There is a new swimming pool and a jacuzzi on a terrace with beach volleyball on soft sand, and relaxation areas with a barbecue. The modern bar (nightclub) has a huge TV screen and a terrace to relax and enjoy the cool evening breezes and the views. We visited on a Saturday when there was a superb cheap buffet prepared in the large, well appointed, Italian-themed restaurant. A vibrant site where all can have fun and get good value for money, but the many young people can be noisy after hours.

Key Features

 Open All Year

 Pets Accepted

 Disabled Facilities

 Swimming Pool

 Play Area

 Bar/Restaurant

Two toilet blocks with British style WCs and showers. Good facilities for disabled visitors and children. Baby baths. Washing machines. Motorcaravan services. Well stocked supermarket (closed in winter). Large restaurant/late night bar with DJ plus pizzeria with terrace and poolside bar (high season). Swimming pool and jacuzzi. Huge TV screen. Evening entertainment/disco and regular themed parties. Play area. Free WiFi over site. Travel information.

Scan me for more information.

Alan Rogers Code: IT67850
22 accommodations
50 pitches
GPS: 42.14472, 12.26865
Post Code: I-00069

Trevignano Romano, Lazio

www.alanrogers.com/it67850
camping.village@gmail.com
Tel: 0699 850 32
www.campingvillagebracciano.com

Open (Touring Pitches):
29 March - 30 September.

Lago di Bracciano

Lago di Bracciano is just 47 km. from the centre of Rome. The site is of a size that provides excellent opportunities for watersports and is inevitably very popular with windsurfers. With some pitches alongside a private little beach, the site provides 110 pitches of which about 50 are for touring units. Our pitch had a full view of the lake, and the gentle breeze made the temperature at the end of June quite bearable. Some shade is provided by large trees. A bar and restaurant near the entrance are behind the site's small swimming pool and play area. The local bus has a regular service to Rome, and the nearby train station has a direct line to Rome. There are various opportunities for excursions that the site owners will be pleased to tell you about. This site would be a good choice for long or short stays, especially in low season.

Two toilet blocks are clean and have open style washbasins, preset showers and facilities for disabled visitors (key). Washing machine. Motorcaravan services. There is no shop on site, but the nearest Carrefour supermarket is just 4.5km away. Bar and restaurant/pizzeria. Small saltwater swimming pool (15/5-15/9). Play area. Beach volleyball court. Free WiFi and Internet access. Mobile homes to rent.

Key Features

 Pets Accepted

 Disabled Facilities

 Swimming Pool

 Play Area

 Bar/Restaurant

 Bike Hire

 Fishing

Scan me for more information.

Alan Rogers Code: IT67980
171 accommodations
189 pitches
GPS: 42.88010, 13.92050
Post Code: I-64014

Martinsicuro, Abruzzo

www.alanrogers.com/it67980
emanuele.dionisi@rivanuova.it
Tel: 086 179 7515
www.rivanuova.com

Open (Touring Pitches):
1 May - 18 September.

Camping Riva Nuova

Situated at the south end of the small town of Martinsicuro on the Adriatic coast, this excellent site offers a first-class camping experience with a great ambience. Set in pleasant, neat, landscaped gardens and obviously well planned, there are 334 pitches for touring units varying in size from 60 to 120 sq.m. There are 140 pitches with water, drainage and electricity and a further 23 with a private bathroom on the pitch. Across a beach road is a long beach of soft sand and a promenade with the usual seaside facilities. This is a great site for low or high season, especially for families with children. Riva Nuova has something for everyone. A bonus is the backdrop of the Gran Sasso d'Italia (highest peak 2,912 m). The site nestles between the Parco Nazionale d'Abruzzo and the turquoise Adriatic. Abruzzo, dominated by the Apennines, is a brooding, introspective land of shepherds. There is much to explore here including Atri, Lanciano and Sulmona.

Key Features

 Disabled Facilities

 Beach Access

 Swimming Pool

 Bar/Restaurant

An exceptional, central sanitary block provides everything to the highest standard. Ample toilets, showers and washbasins. Children's bathroom. Facilities for disabled visitors. Private bathrooms to rent. Laundry facilities. Bar, restaurant and shop. Swimming pool (extra daily charge) and sunbathing area. Gym. Boules. Tennis. Entertainment in high season. Bicycle hire. Sailing. ATM. WiFi (charged). Dogs are not accepted.

Scan me for more information.

Alan Rogers Code: IT68000
170 accommodations
40 pitches
GPS: 42.56738, 14.09247
Post Code: I-64028

Silvi, Abruzzo

www.alanrogers.com/it68000
info@europegarden.it
Tel: 085 930 137
www.europegarden.it

Open (Touring Pitches):
18 May - 14 September.

Camping Europe Garden

This site is 13 kilometres northwest of Pescara and lies just back from the coast about 2 km. up a long and very steep hill from where it has great views over the Adriatic sea. The site predominantly consists of bungalows and chalets for hire, with around 40 pitches at the top of the site available for smaller touring units (with 6A electricity). These are mainly on level terraces, but access to some may be difficult. If the installation of caravans is a problem, a tractor is available to help. The site is not suitable for disabled or infirm visitors as the roads are extremely steep. The swimming pool at the bottom of the site includes a small bar that overlooks the sea. During high season an entertainment programme is run on a small stage and associated area within the pool boundary. There is a very large air-conditioned reception area where it is possible to book a wide range of activities taking place both on and off-site.

The toilet block provides a mixture of British and Turkish style WCs. Hot showers. Washing machines. Shop, bar, restaurant, takeaway (all season). Swimming pool (May-Sept. 300 sq.m; caps compulsory), small paddling pool and jacuzzi. Tennis. Playground. Entertainment programme. Free weekly excursions (15/6-8/9). Free shuttle bus service (18/5-7/9) to site's own private beach. Free WiFi. Dogs are not accepted. Barbecues are not allowed on pitches.

Key Features

 Swimming Pool

 Play Area

 Bar/Restaurant

 Skiing

 Bike Hire

Scan me for more information.

Alan Rogers Code: IT68340
150 accommodations
500 pitches
GPS: 40.62753, 14.35736
Post Code: I-80067

Sorrento, Campania

www.alanrogers.com/it68340
info@santafortunata.eu
Tel: 081 807 3574
www.santafortunata.eu

Open (Touring Pitches):
1 April - 25 October

Santa Fortunata

Village Camping Santa Fortunata is situated on the hillside just outside Sorrento among olive and lemon groves. There is plenty of shade but low hanging branches make some of the pitches unsuitable for larger units. There is a steep tarmac approach to some but the stunning views over the bay more than compensate. Pitches are of average size with several spaces for larger units and there is a feeling of spaciousness as many are separated by trees and shrubs intersected with wooden constructed walkways. Two small beaches can be reached via long steep inclines. A daily excursion to Capri (well worth taking) departs from one of the beaches. The good sized pool, terrace and bar are especially welcome after a day's sightseeing.

Five sanitary blocks with adjustable hot showers. Hot water for dishwashing but not laundry sinks. Washing machines and dryers. Good restaurant/bar. Small well stocked shop. Swimming pool. Disco bar (high season). Mini farm. Boules pitch. Football and basketball court. Excursions. Bicycle and scooter hire. Car hire. WiFi.

Key Features

 Pets Accepted

 Beach Access

 Swimming Pool

 Play Area

 Bar/Restaurant

 Bike Hire

 Sailing

Scan me for
more information.

Alan Rogers Code: IT68410
60 accommodations
480 pitches
GPS: 40.49117, 14.94458
Post Code: I-84025

Eboli Mare, Campania

www.alanrogers.com/it68410
info@campingpaestum.it
Tel: 082 869 1003
www.campingpaestum.it

Open (Touring Pitches):
15 May - 10 September

Camping Village Paestum

This large, family owned site is set some way back from the beach near Paestum and the important ancient Greek temples of ancient Poseidon, built by the Greeks in the sixth century BC and taken by the Romans and renamed in 273 BC. Fast becoming a popular tourist resort, the town of Paestum is some way south of the site which enjoys a quiet, rural environment. With 480 level and well defined pitches, it has 200 allocated for international touring units and these are sited in a special area maintained for non-Italian guests on the basis that they prefer more peace and quiet.

Five toilet blocks are well finished and provide 75% Turkish and 25% British style WCs. Free hot showers and hot and cold to washbasins. Facilities for disabled visitors. Motorcaravan services. Washing machines. Small shop. Bar and restaurant. Swimming pool, children's pool and slide (swimming caps compulsory). Tennis. Entertainment and children's club. Disco. Shuttle bus to beach. WiFi (charged). Bungalows to rent. Pets are not accepted.

Key Features

 Disabled Facilities

 Swimming Pool

 Play Area

 Bar/Restaurant

 Bike Hire

Scan me for more information.

Alan Rogers Code: IT69170
13 accommodations
250 pitches
GPS: 37.43830, 13.24515
Post Code: I-92016

Ribera, Sicily

www.alanrogers.com/it69170
info@kamemivillage.com
Tel: 092 569 212
www.kamemivillage.com

Open (Touring Pitches):
All year.

Camping Kamemi

Camping Kamemi can be found close to Ribera in Sicily's southwest corner, just 300 m. from the sea. There are 250 pitches here (electricity 6A Europlug) – some are shaded, others make use of artificial screening. Thirteen mobile homes are available for rent. There is a typically Sicilian restaurant (with some excellent local fish cuisine) and a pizzeria. A snack bar incorporates an ice cream parlour with typical Sicilian ice creams. Other on-site amenities include two swimming pools, a tennis court and a football pitch. In high season, a lively activity and entertainment programme is on offer, including Latin American music and a summer carnival.

Two new blocks have small shower cubicles (token), open style washbasins with cold water, but no toilets - these are in pool area. En-suite unit for disabled visitors (key). Laundry. Shop (1/5-30/9). Restaurant (1/6-15/9). Outdoor swimming pools (10/5-15/9, hats compulsory). Tennis. Football pitch. Playground. Activity and entertainment programme (July/Aug). Diving trips arranged. Mobile homes for rent. WiFi (charged).

Key Features

 Open All Year

 Pets Accepted

 Disabled Facilities

 Swimming Pool

 Bar/Restaurant

Scan me for more information.

Alan Rogers Code: IT69970
150 accommodations
450 pitches
GPS: 40.59457, 8.29152
Post Code: I-07041

Alghero, Sardinia

www.alanrogers.com/it69970
info@campeggiocalik.it
Tel: 079 930 111
www.campinglagunablu.com

Open (Touring Pitches):
1 April - 31 October.

Camping Laguna Blu

Camping Village Laguna Blu is a large site, pleasantly placed between the sea and a huge lagoon, the beach being directly across the road from the site. Most of the 600 pitches (450 for touring units) have 6A electricity and are shaded with pine and eucalyptus trees. Some pitches are in the trees; others are on level ground in long rows, the end ones enjoying lagoon-side positions. A considerable number are fully serviced. On-site amenities are close to the entrance and include a novel white, canvas-roofed restaurant/pizzeria plus a self-service restaurant. The site offers an ambitious entertainment programme and many watersports, notably windsurfing and sailing. It is also a good base for exploring northern Sardinia. One of the most popular excursions is to the beautiful Grotte di Nettuno (Neptune's Grotto). The site is a member of the Baia Group and reflects its high standards.

Four renovated sanitary blocks provide a high standard of facilities. Units for disabled campers. Restaurant/pizzeria. Self-service restaurant. Takeaway. Supermarket. Play area. Activity and entertainment programme. Bicycle hire. Boat launching. Internet and WiFi (payment). Watersports. Sea fishing. Mobile homes and chalets to rent.

Key Features

 Pets Accepted

 Disabled Facilities

 Beach Access

 Play Area

 Bar/Restaurant

 Bike Hire

 Sailing

Scan me for
more information.

Capital Luxembourg City
Currency Euro (€)
Language Letzeburgesch. French and
German also spoken.
Telephone country code 00 352
Time Zone CET (GMT/UTC+1)
Tourist Office luxembourg.co.uk

Climate A temperate climate prevails,
the summer often extending from May
to late October.

Luxembourg

The Grand Duchy of Luxembourg is a sovereign state, lying between Belgium, France and Germany. Divided into two areas: the spectacular Ardennes region in the north and the rolling farmlands and woodland in the south, bordered on the east by the wine growing area of the Moselle Valley.

Most attractions are within easy reach of Luxembourg's capital, Luxembourg-Ville, a fortress city perched dramatically on its rocky promontory overlooking the Alzette and Petrusse Valleys. The verdant hills and valleys of the Ardennes are a maze of hiking trails, footpaths and cycle routes – ideal for an activity holiday. The Moselle Valley, famous for its sweet wines, is just across the river from Germany; its charming hamlets can be discovered by bicycle or by boat. Popular wine tasting tours take place from late spring to early autumn. Echternacht is a good base for exploring the Mullerthal region, known as 'Little Switzerland'. Lying on the banks of the River Sûre, its forested landscape is dotted with curious rock formations and castle ruins, notably those at Beaufort and Larochette. The pretty Schießentümpel cascade is worth a visit.

Shops Opening hours vary throughout the year. In high-season 10am to 5pm Monday to Saturday, some shops in Luxembourg City open on Sunday.

Banks 8.30am to 4.30pm weekdays, with an hour's break for lunch. Some open Saturday morning.

Travelling with Children Luxembourg is a very family-friendly country with good facilities and accessibility. Many attractions are free for under 26s. Most restaurants will cater for children. Currently public transport is free for those aged under 20, however, Luxembourg is set to become the first country in the world to make all it's public transport free (from summer 2019). Children under 12 must sit in the back of the car.

Public Holidays New Year's Day, Easter Monday, May Day 1 May, Ascension, Whit Monday, Grand Duke's Birthday 23 Jun, Assumption, All Saints' 1 Nov, Christmas Day, Boxing Day.

Motoring Many holidaymakers travel through Luxembourg to take advantage of the lower fuel prices, thus creating traffic congestion at petrol stations, especially in summer. A Blue Zone area exists in Luxembourg City and various parts of the country (discs from tourist offices) but meters are also used.

See campsite map page 473.

Alan Rogers Code: LU7680
20 accommodations
80 pitches
GPS: 50.01602, 6.13600
Post Code: L-9838

Eisenbach, Diekirch

www.alanrogers.com/lu7680
kohnenhof@pt.lu
Tel: 929 464
www.campingkohnenhof.lu

Open (Touring Pitches):
1 April - 31 October.

Camping Kohnenhof

Nestling in a valley with the River Our running through it, Camping Kohnenhof offers a delightful location for a relaxing family holiday. From the minute you stop at the reception you are assured of a warm and friendly welcome. There are 105 pitches, 80 for touring, all with 6/16A electricity. Numerous paths cross through the wooded hillside, so this could be a haven for walkers. A little bridge crosses the small river over the border to Germany. The river is shallow and safe for children (parental supervision essential). A large sports field and play area with a selection of equipment caters for younger campers. During the high season, an entertainment programme is organised for parents and children. The owner arranges special golf weeks with games on different courses and discounts have been agreed at several local courses (contact the site for details). The restaurant is part of an old farmhouse and offers a wonderful ambience to enjoy a meal.

Heated sanitary block with showers and washbasins in cabins. Facilities for disabled visitors. Motorcaravan services. Laundry. Bar, restaurant, takeaway (open all season). Baker calls daily. TV room. Sports field with play equipment. Boules. Bicycle hire. Golf weeks. Discounts on six local 18-hole golf courses. WiFi over site. Apartments to rent.

Key Features

 Pets Accepted

 Disabled Facilities

 Play Area

 Bar/Restaurant

 Bike Hire

 Fishing

Scan me for more information.

Alan Rogers Code: LU7810
20 accommodations
85 pitches
GPS: 49.83910, 6.22500
Post Code: L-9366

Ermsdorf, Diekirch

www.alanrogers.com/lu7810
info@camping-neumuhle.lu
Tel: 879 391
www.camping-neumuhle.lu

Open (Touring Pitches):
15 March - 31 October.

Camping Neumuhle

Camping Neumuhle is located at Ermsdorf, at the heart of Luxembourg close to Diekirch. It is surrounded by the Mullerthal and some delightful countryside, known as Little Switzerland. Pitches here are spacious and all have electricity. This is great walking country and the long-distance hiking track GR5 (North Sea-Riviera) passes close to the site. Walking maps are available for loan at reception. There are 85 touring pitches all with 6A electricity and 20 chalets to rent. The site is terraced with level grass pitches separated by small hedges. The restaurant and covered terrace overlook the swimming pool and a small shop sells all basic provisions. Other on-site amenities include a large adventure playground. A children's club is organised in high season.

The central sanitary block is modern and clean. No facilities for disabled visitors. Restaurant with covered terrace and snack bar. Takeaway (July/Aug). Shop (July/Aug). Swimming pool (May-Aug). Boules. Adventure play area. Entertainment and activity programme. Children's club (high season). Bicycle hire. Mobile homes to rent. Free WiFi over site.

Key Features

 Pets Accepted

 Swimming Pool

 Play Area

 Bar/Restaurant

 Bike Hire

Scan me for more information.

Alan Rogers Code: LU7840
108 accommodations
190 pitches
GPS: 49.83990, 6.28945
Post Code: L-6310

Beaufort, Grevenmacher

www.alanrogers.com/lu7840
camplage@pt.lu
Tel: 836 099 300
www.campingplage.lu

Open (Touring Pitches):
All year.

Camping Plage Beaufort

Plage Beaufort is an all-year-round site run by the Syndicat d'Initiative et du Tourisme. It is a little off the main tourist route but there is some nice countryside in the area known as Little Switzerland. The site has 298 pitches, 108 of which are taken by privately owned mobile homes and chalets, leaving around 190 for touring units. The terrain is undulating with some terracing and some pitches are hidden away in quiet corners. Pitch sizes do vary but all have 10A electricity. In summer, the area provides for cycling, tennis and other sporting facilities, with the main attraction of the site being the excellent municipal swimming pool adjacent (included in price).

Four toilet blocks, some heated, provide an interesting mix of facilities with baby room and facilities for disabled visitors. All are spotlessly clean. Motorcaravan services. Recycling. Snack bar. Several small rather basic playgrounds. Bicycle hire. Internet access.

Key Features

 Open All Year

 Pets Accepted

 Disabled Facilities

 Swimming Pool

 Play Area

 Bike Hire

Scan me for more information.

Alan Rogers Code: LU7640
18 accommodations
180 pitches
GPS: 49.79992, 6.19817
Post Code: L-7633

Larochette-Medernach, Diekirch

www.alanrogers.com/lu7640
info@kengert.lu
Tel: 837 186
www.kengert.lu

Open (Touring Pitches):
1 March - 8 November.

Camping Auf Kengert

A friendly welcome awaits you at this peacefully situated, family run site, 2 km. from Larochette, which is 24 km. northeast of Luxembourg City, providing 180 individual pitches, all with electricity (16A Europlug). Some in a very shaded woodland setting, on a slight slope with fairly narrow access roads. There are also eight hardened pitches for motorcaravans on a flat area of grass, complete with motorcaravan service facilities. Further tent pitches are in an adjacent and more open meadow area. There are also site owned wooden chalets to rent. This site is popular in season, so early arrival is advisable, or you can reserve.

Key Features

 Pets Accepted

 Disabled Facilities

 Swimming Pool

 Play Area

 Bar/Restaurant

The well maintained sanitary block in two parts includes a modern, heated unit with some washbasins in cubicles, and excellent, fully equipped cubicles for disabled visitors. The showers, facilities for babies, additional WCs and washbasins, plus laundry room are located below the central building which houses the shop, bar and restaurant. An additional block is planned for 2015. Motorcaravan services. Gas supplies. Indoor and outdoor play areas. Solar heated swimming pool (Easter-30/9). Paddling pool. WiFi (free).

Scan me for more information.

Alan Rogers Code: LU7620
32 accommodations
359 pitches
GPS: 49.78472, 6.16519
Post Code: L-7465

Nommern, Luxembourg District

www.alanrogers.com/lu7620
info@nommerlayen-ec.lu
Tel: 878 078
www.nommerlayen-ec.lu

Open (Touring Pitches):
1 March - 6 November.

Europacamping Nommerlayen

Situated at the end of its own road, in the lovely wooded hills of central Luxembourg, this is a top quality site with fees to match, but it has everything! A large, central building housing most of the services and amenities opens onto a terrace around an excellent swimming pool complex with a large fun pool and an imaginative water playground. The 359 individual pitches (100 sq.m) are on grassy terraces, all have access to electricity (2/16A) and water taps. Pitches are grouped beside age-appropriate play areas and the facilities throughout the campsite reflect the attention given to families in particular. Interestingly enough, the superb sanitary block is called Badtemple, (having been built in the style of a Greek temple). A member of Leading Campings group.

A large, high quality, modern sanitary unit provides some washbasins in cubicles, facilities for disabled visitors, family and baby rooms and a sauna. Twelve private bathrooms for hire. Laundry. Motorcaravan services. Supermarket. Restaurant. Snack bar. Bar (all 19/3-6/11). Excellent swimming pool complex and new heated pool with sliding roof (1/5-15/9). Fitness programmes. Bowling. Playground. Large screen TV. Entertainment in season. Bicycle hire. WiFi (free over part of site).

Key Features

 Pets Accepted

 Disabled Facilities

 Swimming Pool

 Play Area

 Bar/Restaurant

 Bike Hire

Scan me for more information.

Alan Rogers Code: LU7910
36 accommodations
100 pitches
GPS: 49.84607, 6.08202
Post Code: L-9022

Ettelbruck, Diekirch

www.alanrogers.com/lu7910
ellen.ringelberg@gmx.de
Tel: 812 185
www.campingettelbruck.com

Open (Touring Pitches):
1 April - 15 October.

Camping Ettelbruck

This agreeable, good value municipal site is situated on a hilltop overlooking the town. It is quietly located about 1 km. from the centre of Ettelbruck, with a nice atmosphere and well-tended gardens and grass. The modern main building includes reception, an excellent restaurant and a 'salle de séjour' (with library and TV). The 136 marked pitches, 100 for touring, are accessed from tarmac roads and have electricity available (16A). Reception provides good tourist information and English is spoken. There is a welcome cup of coffee on arrival.

A new sanitary unit using solar energy provides washbasins in cabins and hot showers. Provision for disabled campers. Laundry. Dishwasher. Motorcaravan services. Restaurant. Snack bar and takeaway (evenings). Breakfasts can also be served. Baker calls daily at 09.00 (order day before). Playground. Entertainment in season. Daily baking session for children and afternoon tea twice a week for parents. Electric car hire. WiFi (charged).

Key Features

 Pets Accepted

 Disabled Facilities

 Play Area

 Bar/Restaurant

Scan me for more information.

Alan Rogers Code: LU7450
17 accommodations
70 pitches
GPS: 49.90516, 5.95631
Post Code: L-9659

Heiderscheidergrund, Diekirch

www.alanrogers.com/lu7450
info@camping-bissen.lu
Tel: 839 004
www.camping-bissen.lu

Open (Touring Pitches):
1 April – 2 October.

Camping Bissen

Camping Bissen is a family owned site on two levels, stretching along the banks of the River Sûre, within the idyllic upper-Sûre nature park. The higher level contains privately owned static caravans, with the 70 touring pitches (10A electricity) on the lower level immediately adjacent to the river. There is a well stocked shop and a new building houses a bar/snack bar with a terrace overlooking the river. A restaurant, owned by the same family, is just across the road and offers a comprehensive menu. During high season a six-day activity programme has something for all the family, while the nature park with its large lake offers opportunities for swimming, canoeing and fishing. The access roads could prove challenging for large units, particularly in poor weather, due to a very tight and narrow u-bend at the entrance.

Three heated sanitary blocks with free hot water to showers and sinks. Good facilities for children and disabled visitors in two blocks. Family shower room. Laundry area with washing machine and tumble dryer. Well stocked shop. Bar and snack bar with terrace. Grass area for ball games. New indoor and outdoor play areas. Entertainment (July/Aug). Free WiFi.

Key Features

 Pets Accepted

 Disabled Facilities

 Play Area

 Bar/Restaurant

 Bike Hire

 Fishing

Scan me for
more information.

Alan Rogers Code: LU7830
18 accommodations
200 pitches
GPS: 49.95387, 6.02730
Post Code: L-9663

Kautenbach, Diekirch

www.alanrogers.com/lu7830
campkaut@pt.lu
Tel: 00352950303
www.campingkautenbach.lu

Open (Touring Pitches):
20 January - 16 December

Camping Kautenbach

Kautenbach is situated in the heart of the Luxembourg Ardennes and was established over 60 years ago. Although in an idyllic location, it is less than a mile from a railway station with regular trains to Luxembourg City to the south. There are 200 touring pitches here, mostly of a good size and with reasonable shade. All pitches have electrical connections (10A). This is excellent walking country with many tracks around the site. The site managers will be happy to recommend walks for all abilities. Kautenbach has an attractive bistro style restaurant specialising in local cuisine, as well as a large selection of whiskies!

Key Features

 Pets Accepted

 Disabled Facilities

 Play Area

 Bar/Restaurant

 Fishing

Three toilet blocks with open style washbasins and showers, baby changing. Facilities for disabled visitors (key). Laundry. Shop for basics (1/4-31/10, bread to order). Restaurant, bar/snack bar (all season). Direct river access. Fishing. Play area. Mobile homes, safari tents and camping pods for rent. Internet café.

Scan me for more information.

Capital Amsterdam
Currency Euro (€)
Language Dutch. English is widely spoken, as is German and French.
Telephone country code 00 31
Time Zone CET (GMT/UTC+1)
Tourist Office holland.com/uk

Climate Temperate with mild winters and warm summers.

Netherlands

With vast areas of the Netherlands reclaimed from the sea, nearly half of the country lies at or below sea level. The result is a flat, fertile landscape criss-crossed with rivers and canals. Famous for its windmills and bulb fields, it also boasts some of the most impressive coastal dunes in Europe.

No visit to the Netherlands would be complete without experiencing its capital city, Amsterdam, with its maze of canals, bustling cafés, museums and summer festivals.

The fields and gardens of South Holland are an explosion of colour between March and May when the world's biggest flower auction takes place at Aalsmer. The Netherlands offers all manner of holiday, from lively seaside resorts to picturesque villages, idyllic old fishing ports and areas of unspoiled landscape.

The Vecht valley and its towns of Dalfsen, Ommen and Hardenberg are best explored by bicycle, while Giethoorn, justly dubbed the 'Venice of Holland' has to be seen from a boat. The Kinderdijk windmills on the Alblasserwaard polder are a UNESCO World Heritage Site.

The islands of Zeeland are home to beautiful old towns such as Middelburg, the provincial capital, Zierikzee, with its old harbour and the quaint old town of Veere.

Shops Opening hours vary throughout the year. In high-season 10am or noon to 6pm Tuesday to Friday, 10am to 5pm Saturday and Sunday, noon to 5pm Monday although shops sometimes close on Mondays. Supermarkets 8am to 8pm.

Banks 9am to 4pm weekdays and some open Saturday mornings.

Travelling with Children The Netherlands is very tolerant towards children and you'll find that locals are very welcoming. Amsterdam is one of Europe's most child friendly cities although we recommend you stay clear of the Red Light District. Most of the larger cities have attractions to suit all ages. Away from the cities, Friesland is a hot spot for Dutch holiday-makers with sandy beaches, cycling paths and watersports activities. Many restaurants will accept children and nearly all offer childrens menus and colouring crayons.

Public Holidays New Year's Day, Good Friday, Easter Monday, King's Day 27 Apr, Liberation Day 5 May, Ascension, Whit Monday, Christmas Day, Boxing Day.

Motoring There is a comprehensive motorway system but due to the high density of population, all main roads can become very busy, particularly in the morning and evening rush hours. There are many bridges which can cause congestion. There are no toll roads but there are a few toll bridges and tunnels, notably the Zeeland Bridge, Europe's longest across the Oosterschelde.

See campsite map page 483.

Alan Rogers Code: NL5570
7 accommodations
100 pitches
GPS: 51.57840, 3.69642
Post Code: NL-4493 NC

Kamperland, Zeeland

www.alanrogers.com/nl5570
info@demolenhoek.com
Tel: 0113 371 202
www.demolenhoek.com

Open (Touring Pitches):
19 March - 28 October.

Camping De Molenhoek

This rural, family run site makes a pleasant contrast to the livelier coastal sites in this popular holiday area. There is an emphasis on catering for the users of the 300 permanent or seasonal holiday caravans and 100 tourers. Eighty of these have 6A electricity, water and drainage. The site is neat and tidy with surrounding hedges and trees giving privacy and some shade, and electrical connections are available. A large outdoor pool area has ample space for swimming, children's play and sun loungers. Entertainment, including dance evenings and bingo, is organised in season.

Two very clean and well appointed sanitary blocks include some washbasins in cabins and facilities for children. Toilet and shower facilities for disabled visitors and for babies. Laundry facilities. Motorcaravan services. Bar/restaurant with terrace and large TVs and LCD projection. Snack bar. Heated outdoor swimming pool (15/5-15/9). Playground. Bicycle hire. Pool tables. Sports field. Entertainment for children and teenagers. WiFi over site (charged).

Key Features

 Pets Accepted

 Disabled Facilities

 Swimming Pool

 Play Area

 Bar/Restaurant

Scan me for more information.

Alan Rogers Code: NL5502
105 accommodations
110 pitches
GPS: 51.36613, 3.38583
Post Code: NL-4525 LW

Retranchement, Zeeland

www.alanrogers.com/nl5502
info@cassandriabad.nl
Tel: 0117 392 300
www.cassandriabad.nl

Open (Touring Pitches):
27 March - 30 October.

Camping Cassandria Bad

Cassandria Bad was established in 1992, lying very close to the Belgian border and the resort of Cadzand Bad, just under 2 km. from the nearest North Sea beach. Pitches are grassy and spacious; some are privately let for the full season. All pitches are equipped with 10A electricity and free cable TV connections. Except for loading and unloading, cars are not allowed in the camping area, but a large parking area is provided. On-site amenities include a bar, snack bar, shop services and games room. During the peak season, a variety of activities are organised, including karaoke, bingo and sports tournaments.

Two clean and well maintained sanitary units with free showers, and two family bathrooms in the main block. Good laundry facilities. Small shop (fresh bread daily). Bar with LCD projector and screen. Snack bar. Sports fields with volleyball and 2 football pitches. Games room with table football, air hockey and electronic games. Trampoline. Several well appointed and interesting play areas including an indoor play area. Bicycle hire. WiFi over site (charged). 1 dog allowed per pitch.

Key Features

 Pets Accepted

 Play Area

 Bar/Restaurant

 Bike Hire

Scan me for more information.

Alan Rogers Code: NL5630
48 accommodations
200 pitches
GPS: 52.20012, 4.45623
Post Code: NL-2231 NW

Rijnsburg, Zuid-Holland

www.alanrogers.com/nl5630
info@koningshofholland.nl
Tel: 0714 026 051
www.koningshofholland.com

Open (Touring Pitches):
15 March - 31 October

Vakantiepark Koningshof

This popular site is run in a personal and friendly way. The 200 pitches for touring units (some with hardstandings for larger units) are laid out in small groups, divided by hedges and trees and all with 10A electrical connections. Cars are mostly parked in areas around the perimeter and 100 static caravans, confined to one section of the site, are entirely unobtrusive. Reception, a pleasant, good quality restaurant, bar and a snack bar are grouped around a courtyard-style entrance which is decorated with seasonal flowers. The site has a small outdoor, heated pool (13.5x7 m) with a separate paddling pool and imaginative children's play equipment. A member of the Holland Tulip Parcs Group.

Three well-maintained toilet blocks, two with underfloor heating, with washbasins in cabins and provision for disabled visitors. Laundry facilities. Motorcaravan services. Gas supplies. Restaurant, snacks, takeaway, bar and supermarket on site (5 April -26 October). Small outdoor pool (unsupervised; 15/5-15/9). Indoor pool. Adventure playground and sports area. Outdoor gym and skateboard ramps. Tennis. Fishing pond (free). Bicycle hire. Entertainment in Dutch school holidays. Room for shows. Max. 1 dog, accepted in a limited area of the site. WiFi over site (free 1 GB per stayed night).

Key Features

 Pets Accepted

 Disabled Facilities

 Swimming Pool

 Play Area

 Bar/Restaurant

 Bike Hire

 Fishing

Scan me for more information.

Netherlands

Alan Rogers Code: NL5695
9 accommodations
22 pitches
GPS: 51.90114, 5.02646
Post Code: NL-4243 JS

Nieuwland, Zuid-Holland

www.alanrogers.com/nl5695
receptie@degrienduil.nl
Tel: +31(0)183 351 512
www.degrienduil.nl

Open (Touring Pitches):
All Year

Camping de Grienduil

A compact, family run site located in the area known as The Green Heart of the Netherlands. You should expect a heart warming welcome from the enthusiastic owner at de Grienduil, which has a total of 22 touring pitches ranging in size from 100 to 120 sq. metres and with computer controlled current (6-16A) to the electricity hook-ups. Your unit will be placed on site by the owner, as cars are left outside the campsite. There is a choice of rental accommodation, including a luxury Romany-style caravan. Be sure to arrive before Friday to take advantage of the 'all you can eat' pizza experience, where you roll your own dough base! This is a perfect place to experience the green agricultural heart of the Netherlands.

One central, heated sanitary block has unisex facilities, with open washbasins, coin-operated showers (€ 0.50) and hot water for dishwashing (€ 0.20). Motorcaravan services. Pizza oven and terrace. Takeaway. Ice-cream, drinks and essentials. Bread to order. Breakfast service. Adventure-style playground. WiFi over site (free).

Key Features

 Open All Year

 Pets Accepted

 Swimming Pool

 Play Area

 Bar/Restaurant

 Bike Hire

 Fishing

Scan me for more information.

Alan Rogers Code: NL5600
42 accommodations
160 pitches
GPS: 52.01767, 4.37908
Post Code: NL-2616 LJ

Delft, Zuid-Holland

www.alanrogers.com/nl5600
info@delftsehout.nl
Tel: 0152 130 040
www.delftsehout.nl

Open (Touring Pitches):
25 March - 1 November.

Vakantiepark Delftse Hout

Pleasantly situated in Delft's park and forest area on the eastern edge of the city, is this well run, modern site. It has 160 touring pitches quite formally arranged in groups of four to six and surrounded by attractive trees and hedges. All have sufficient space and electrical connections (10A Europlug). Modern buildings near the entrance house the site amenities. A good sized first floor restaurant serves snacks and full meals and has an outdoor terrace overlooking the swimming pool and pitches. Walking and cycling tours are organised and there is a recreation programme in high season.

Modern, heated toilet facilities include a spacious family room and children's section. Facilities for disabled visitors. Laundry. Motorcaravan services. Shop for basic food and camping items (all season). Restaurant, takeaway and bar (1/4-1/10). Small heated outdoor swimming pool (mid May - mid Sept.) Adventure playground. Recreation room. Bicycle hire. Gas supplies. Max. 1 dog. WiFi (100mb/day included).

Key Features

 Pets Accepted

 Disabled Facilities

 Swimming Pool

 Play Area

 Bar/Restaurant

 Bike Hire

Scan me for more information.

De Achterste Hoef

Alan Rogers Code: NL6710
2 accommodations
390 pitches
GPS: 51.34406, 5.22694
Post Code: NL-5531 NA

Bladel, Noord-Brabant

www.alanrogers.com/nl6710
info@achterstehoef.nl
Tel: 0497 381 579
www.achterstehoef.nl

Open (Touring Pitches):
4 April - 26 October.

This quite large campsite is to be found off the N284 at Bladel in Noord-Brabant. It is an ideal location for cycling and walking and is close to the Belgian border. A family oriented site, it offers good quality facilities which are well maintained and kept very clean. There are 390 touring pitches, all fully serviced and 22 with their own sanitation, sited near the lake. The touring pitches are 80-150 sq.m. in size with many amongst the trees, but some are on open meadows and some divided by young shrubs. There are also seasonal and static caravan places, but these are kept apart and mostly in one area.

Four sanitary blocks have showers, washbasins, both open and in cabins, a bathroom and a baby bath. Washing machine and dryer. Motorcaravan services. Supermarket, restaurant/bar and snack bar (18/4-28/9). Heated indoor (5/4-28/9) and outdoor (26/4-31/8) swimming pools. Disco. Recreation room. Football. Tennis. Nine hole golf course, school and driving range. Bicycle hire. Watersports. Play areas (including indoor). Animal corner. Internet access and WiFi throughout (charged). Organised activities in July/Aug. Max. 2 dogs.

Key Features

 Pets Accepted

 Disabled Facilities

 Swimming Pool

 Play Area

 Bar/Restaurant

 Bike Hire

 Golf

Scan me for more information.

Alan Rogers Code: NL6750
160 accommodations
117 pitches
GPS: 51.39494, 5.41200
Post Code: NL-5504 PZ

Veldhoven, Noord-Brabant

Camping 't Witven

www.alanrogers.com/nl6750
info@witven.nl
Tel: 0402 300 043
www.witven.nl/vakantiepark

Open (Touring Pitches):
1 April - 25 September.

Vakantiepark 't Witven is situated in Veldhoven in North Brabant and is located by a delightful recreational lake which is perfect for swimming. The campsite pitches are well marked out – some with shade, without shade, or partial shade. They also have bungalows for rent. Enjoy waking up to bird song in this peaceful nature reserve, which is also located close to a sandy beach. For the sporty holidaymaker, the campsite has various cycle routes, and for those not wishing to cook, there is a snack bar and a restaurant. Whilst the facilities here are vast, the campsite still has an intimate feel. Vakantiepark 't Witven offers you a unique spectrum of possibilities and is closer to Germany than you think.

Modern sanitary facilities including hot showers, washing cabins, wash basins with hot/cold water, toilets and laundry facilities. Shower for disabled visitors. Recreational lake for swimming. Children's playground. Children's entertainment available during the school holidays. Sports field. Restaurant. Snack bar. Bakery. Free WiFi.

Key Features

 Pets Accepted

 Disabled Facilities

 Play Area

 Bar/Restaurant

 Bike Hire

 Fishing

Scan me for more information.

Alan Rogers Code: NL6790
84 accommodations
160 pitches
GPS: 51.57755, 5.44682
Post Code: NL-5491 TE

Sint-Oedenrode, Noord-Brabant

www.alanrogers.com/nl6790
kienehoef@ardoer.com
Tel: 0413 472 877
www.kienehoef.nl

Open (Touring Pitches):
28 March - 28 October.

Camping De Kienehoef

Camping De Kienehoef is located at Sint-Oedenrode in Noord-Brabant, which boasts many historical sights, including two castles. This site is well cared for and attractively laid out with the reception to the right of the entrance and the site facilities to the left. Behind this area is a heated swimming pool. The generous pitches are mostly laid out in bays and placed between trees and shrubs to the right of a long avenue leading through the site. The touring pitches are on three separate fields amongst pitches used for caravan holiday homes. There are some 40 serviced pitches with electricity, water, and drainage.

Two modern, clean and well maintained toilet blocks include preset showers and some shower/wash cubicles, also family and baby rooms. Laundry area with iron and board. Motorcaravan services. Shop, restaurant/bar and snacks (all 1/5-15/9). Heated outdoor pool (1/5-15/9). Lake fishing. Bicycle hire. Sports field. Tennis. Dogs and other pets are not accepted.

Key Features

 Swimming Pool

 Play Area

 Bar/Restaurant

 Bike Hire

 Fishing

Scan me for more information.

Alan Rogers Code: NL6650
600 accommodations
440 pitches
GPS: 51.49139, 4.89646
Post Code: NL-4861 RC

Chaam, Noord-Brabant

De Flaasbloem

www.alanrogers.com/nl6650
reservation@rcn.eu
Tel: +31 85 0400 700
www.rcn.nl/flaasbloem

Open (Touring Pitches):
23 March - 5 November

This is a large (100 hectares) friendly and quiet campsite set well out in the countryside. It would suit those who prefer to stay in a countryside environment, on a site providing very good facilities to keep children busy and happy. Like all successful sites it is continually developing and the latest addition is the Wildenberg, a large, vehicle-free area for tents with three Finnish nomadic huts. The level touring pitches are set on grass among hedges and tall trees, and all have 10A electricity. They are spacious and shady, with a number of more open, landscaped pitches on grassy fields.

Good sanitary facilities including those for disabled visitors. Launderette. Supermarket, bar, snack bar and bakery, restaurant with indoor garden (all open all season). Small covered pool, outdoor children's pool with water games, recreational lake. Games room. Library. One large and several small play areas. Mini train around the site. Multisports terrain. Tennis. Children's farm. Bicycle and go-kart hire. Mobile homes and chalets to rent (some adapted for visitors with disabilities). WiFi (free).

Key Features

 Pets Accepted

 Disabled Facilities

 Swimming Pool

 Play Area

 Bar/Restaurant

 Bike Hire

 Fishing

Scan me for more information.

Alan Rogers Code: NL6550
52 accommodations
650 pitches
GPS: 51.27411, 5.93197
Post Code: NL-6088 NT

Roggel, Limburg

www.alanrogers.com/nl6550
info@leistert.nl
Tel: 0475 493 030
www.leistert.nl

Open (Touring Pitches):
3 April - 30 September
(accommodation to 3 November).

Recreatiepark De Leistert

This large, long established site in the wooded Limburg province of south Holland provides 1,200 pitches, of which 650 are touring pitches. With its varied amenities, the site would be a good choice for families with small children and teenagers. Most of the pitches are not separated, but are arranged in hedged groups with tall, mature trees. They are serviced with electricity (4-16A), cable TV connections, water and drainage. A recreation programme is organised for all ages in high season.

Five toilet blocks are fully equipped, with good facilities for children. Covered plaza with supermarket, bar, restaurant, snack bar, games and TV room and disco, indoor pool. Outdoor pool (both pools with lifeguard). Minigolf. Tennis. Adventure playground. Rowing, fishing and sandy beach. Bicycle hire with plentiful racks all over the site. Go-Kart track. Skateboarding ramps. Mini zoo. Gas refill at supermarket. Recreation programme (high season). WiFi over site (charged). Chalets to rent. Dogs welcomed in a designated area.

Key Features

 Pets Accepted

 Disabled Facilities

 Swimming Pool

 Play Area

 Bar/Restaurant

 Bike Hire

 Fishing

Scan me for more information.

Alan Rogers Code: NL6525
130 accommodations
370 pitches
GPS: 51.34897, 5.96101
Post Code: NL-5981 NX

Panningen, Limburg

www.alanrogers.com/nl6525
info@beringerzand.nl
Tel: 0773 072 095
www.beringerzand.nl

Open (Touring Pitches):
24 April - 2 October.

Camping Beringerzand

The history of this friendly site dates back more than 100 years to when it was established as a holiday resort for members of the Lazarist religious congregation. The park and its historic building (now the Patershof restaurant) have, for the last 40 years, been developed as a holiday paradise for young families. Beringerzand is set amongst the lovely villages and small lakes of the wooded area between the De Peel Natural Park and the Muse river. The 21-hectare site offers 370 spacious touring pitches, all with electricity (10A), TV, water and wastewater, arranged around the edges of green fields. There are currently also 130 privately owned chalets. The fields have been very well designed and include various activity areas appropriate to different age groups.

Four heated toilet blocks include bathrooms for children and a fully equipped launderette. Well stocked supermarket, bar, restaurant and takeaway (all open all season). Games and TV rooms. Indoor and outdoor swimming pools (not guarded). Tennis. Minigolf. Pétanque. Adventure play areas. Bicycle hire. Small BMX track. Outdoor chess. Riding. Fishing. Children's club and evening entertainment. WiFi throughout (charged). Max. 2 dogs per pitch.

Key Features

 Pets Accepted

 Disabled Facilities

 Swimming Pool

 Play Area

 Bar/Restaurant

 Bike Hire

 Fishing

 Horse Riding

Scan me for more information.

Alan Rogers Code: NL6530
120 accommodations
266 pitches
GPS: 50.80673, 5.89413
Post Code: NL-6271 NP

Gulpen, Limburg

www.alanrogers.com/nl6530
info@gulperberg.nl
Tel: 0434 502 330
www.campinggulperberg.nl

Open (Touring Pitches):
Easter - 31 October.

Gulperberg Panorama

Gulperberg Panorama is just three kilometres from the attractive village of Gulpen, midway between the interesting cities of Maastricht and Aachen. The 266 touring pitches are large and flat on terraces overlooking the village on one side and open countryside on the other. Many have full services. English is spoken in reception, although all written information is in Dutch (ask if you require a translation). Gulperberg Panorama is a haven for children. During the high season there is a weekly entertainment programme to keep them occupied. The site is not suitable for visitors with disabilities. Dogs are restricted to one section of the campsite. Visitors are assured of a warm welcome and if arriving (or leaving) on a Saturday are welcomed (or bade farewell) by the Aartje Twinkle.

Four sanitary blocks have good facilities. Family shower room and baby room. Laundry. Shop (27/4-31/8). Bar. Takeaway. New restaurant with terrace. Swimming pool (29/4-15/9). Three play areas. Bouncy cushion. TV and games room. Extensive entertainment programme for children plus family entertainment. WiFi over site (charged).

Key Features

 Open All Year

 Pets Accepted

 Swimming Pool

 Play Area

 Bar/Restaurant

Scan me for
more information.

Alan Rogers Code: NL5890
120 accommodations
135 pitches
GPS: 51.63848, 6.00380
Post Code: NL-5851 AG

Afferden, Limburg

www.alanrogers.com/nl5890
info@kleincanada.nl
Tel: 0485 531 223
www.kleincanada.nl

Open (Touring Pitches):
All year.

Klein Canada

Following the war, the family who own this site wanted to emigrate to Canada – they didn't go but instead created this attractive site with the maple leaf theme decorating buildings, pool and play equipment. There are three touring areas, one on an island surrounded by an attractive, landscaped moat used for fishing, the other on flat ground on the other side of the entrance. They provide 135 large, numbered touring pitches, all with electricity (6-10A), water, drainage and TV connections. Some places have hardstanding for motorhomes. The newest area offers 45 pitches, each with its own sanitary unit and car park space.

Mixed toilet facilities are partially refurbished and include some with washbasins in cubicles, family facilities in a tiled and heated room and a separate children's section. Some pitches have individual units. Motorcaravan services. Gas supplies. Supermarket and restaurant (24/4-31/8). Bar, snack bar and takeaway (all Easter-31/10). Outdoor pool (1/5-1/9). Indoor pool (31/3-1/11). Sauna and solarium. Tennis. Fishing. Playground. Animal enclosure. Bicycle hire. WiFi over site (charged). Gas barbecues only. Max. 2 dogs.

Key Features

 Open All Year

 Pets Accepted

 Disabled Facilities

 Swimming Pool

 Play Area

 Bar/Restaurant

 Bike Hire

 Fishing

Scan me for more information.

Alan Rogers Code: NL6528
25 accommodations
57 pitches
GPS: 51.20970, 5.82972
Post Code: NL-6037 NR

Kelpen-Oler, Limburg

www.alanrogers.com/nl6528
info@geelenhoof.nl
Tel: 0495 651 858
www.geelenhoof.nl

Open (Touring Pitches):
1 March - 31 October.

Camping Geelenhoof

Camping Geelenhof is a small, family site located between Roermond and Weert, in the heart of Limburg, Belgium and Germany are both half hour drive away. All the pitches are comfortable, spacious and grassy and have 6A (for 120m²) or 10A (for 160m²/200m²) electricity, water, drainage and recycling bin. The pitches are arranged in rows separated by hedges. Visitors can order bread for the next day and buy drinks at the reception. This site is ideal for small children and has a number of indoor and outdoor play areas including a sandpit, trampoline and Beugelen (a medieval Dutch folk game - a cross between bowling and croquet.) There is also an activity centre where you can play Boerenweigolf (golf with a clog), Jack darts (a curious combination of javelin and darts) and indoor minigolf. Camping Geelenhoof is surrounded by two National Parks: Groote Peel and Meinweg. Here are many opportunities to cycle, walk or ride.

Sanitary block with hot showers, some washbasins in cabins, baby room and facilities for disabled visitors. Indoor and outdoor play areas. Boules. Minigolf. Go-karts. Bicycle hire. Cable TV and WiFi connections. Fishing on site.

Key Features

 Disabled Facilities

 Play Area

 Bar/Restaurant

 Bike Hire

 Fishing

Scan me for more information.

Alan Rogers Code: NL6828
97 accommodations
270 pitches
GPS: 52.05612, 5.31372
Post Code: NL-3941 ZK

Doorn, Utrecht

www.alanrogers.com/nl6828
reservation@rcn.eu
Tel: +31 85 0400 700
www.rcn.nl/het-grote-bos

Open (Touring Pitches):
23 April - 5 November

RCN Het Grote Bos

Het Grote Bos (the large forest) is ideally located for a tranquil woodland holiday, but is also an ideal base to explore the western part of the Netherlands, or for visits to Amsterdam, Utrecht and Amersfoort. The site is located in the grounds of a former estate called Hydepark, and the prevailing atmosphere still reflects this parkland setting. Touring fields with 270 pitches are surrounded by high trees and are marked out by shrubs and hedges. Leisure amenities include attractive play areas, a heated outdoor pool complex (with slides and a children's pool) and a multisports terrain. A survival course has been built in the trees around the site.

Six toilet blocks around the site. Launderette. Restaurant, café/bar, takeaway. Bakery and supermarket. Motorcaravan services. Heated outdoor pool with lazy river, water slides, children's pool and sunbathing area. Sports hall. Picnic area. Various themed play areas (such as a butterfly garden). Fitness trail. Tennis courts. Minigolf. Basketball. Bicycle and go-kart hire. Mobile homes and chalets to rent. WiFi throughout (charged). Torches useful.

Key Features

 Pets Accepted

 Disabled Facilities

 Swimming Pool

 Play Area

 Bar/Restaurant

 Bike Hire

Scan me for more information.

Alan Rogers Code: NL6837
18 accommodations
97 pitches
GPS: 52.49659, 5.83779
Post Code: NL-8251 PX

Dronten, Utrecht

www.alanrogers.com/nl6837
info@campingderuimte.nl
Tel: 0321 31 64 42
www.campingderuimte.nl

Open (Touring Pitches):
1 April - 30 September.

Camping De Ruimte

Camping De Ruimte is a family run site with 97 spacious touring pitches. Of these, 14 are serviced with fresh water and sewerage connections. The site extends to over six hectares with open spaces and wooded areas. It is possible to pitch in either the wooded parts or in open fields with play areas in the centre. The campsite also offers well equipped wooden bungalow style accommodation and pre-erected family size tents. A small shop, dining area and cosy bar cater for most needs. Children will be well entertained by the recreation team.

Centrally located, modern and heated sanitary facilities. Good facilities for disabled visitors. Café and bar. Wet and dry play areas. Bicycle hire. Accommodation to rent. Free WiFi.

Key Features

 Pets Accepted

 Disabled Facilities

 Play Area

 Bar/Restaurant

 Bike Hire

Scan me for more information.

Alan Rogers Code: NL6872
1400 accommodations
337 pitches
GPS: 52.56140, 4.63310
Post Code: NL-1901 NZ

Castricum aan Zee, Noord-Holland

Duincamping Bakkum

www.alanrogers.com/nl6872
info@campingbakkum.nl
Tel: 0251 661 091
www.campingbakkum.nl

Open (Touring Pitches):
24 March - 30 October.

Kennemer Duincamping Bakkum lies in a wooded area in the centre of a protected dune reserve. There are over 1,700 pitches of which 337 are used for touring units. These pitches are spacious and 300 are equipped with electricity (10A Europlug). Mobile homes and seasonal units use the remaining pitches in separate areas of the site. For safety and tranquillity the majority of the site is kept free of cars. Family activities and special entertainment for children are arranged in high season. The dunes are accessible from the site and offer plenty of opportunities for walking and cycling with the beach a walk of only 25 minutes.

Three toilet blocks for tourers with toilets, washbasins in cabins, free, controllable showers and family shower rooms. Facilities for disabled visitors. Laundry area. Excellent supermarket, baker, pizza, fish and chicken takeaways. Snack bar and restaurant. Gas supplies. Play area. Sports pitch. Tennis. Bicycle hire. Activities for children and teens. WiFi over part of site (charged). Motorbikes and dogs are not accepted.

Key Features

 Disabled Facilities

 Play Area

 Bar/Restaurant

 Bike Hire

Scan me for more information.

Alan Rogers Code: NL6862
390 accommodations
295 pitches
GPS: 52.53038, 4.64839
Post Code: NL-1901 NH

Castricum, Noord-Holland

www.alanrogers.com/nl6862
info@geversduin.nl
Tel: 0251 661 095
www.campinggeversduin.nl

Open (Touring Pitches):
24 March - 30 October.

Duincamping Geversduin

The comfortable, family site of Geversduin lies in an area of forests and sand dunes. The site offers 685 pitches of which 295 are for touring units and 31 for accommodation to rent. They have good shade and privacy, and all pitches have 4-16A electricity connections. The pitches without electricity have a unique location and cars must be parked elsewhere. In high season, many activities are organised for youngsters including the unusual opportunity to join a forestry worker for the day. The beach is only 4 km. away and is easily accessible by bike or on foot.

Four sanitary blocks with WCs, open style washbasins, preset hot showers and family shower rooms including baby room. Facilities for disabled visitors. Laundry with washing machines and dryers. Supermarket. Snack bar and café for meals with large terrace (weekends only in low season). Recreation area. Sports pitch. Play area. Bicycle hire. WiFi (free). Safes. Only gas barbecues are permitted.

Key Features

 Pets Accepted

 Disabled Facilities

 Play Area

 Bar/Restaurant

 Skiing

 Bike Hire

Scan me for
more information.

Alan Rogers Code: NL5670
350 pitches
GPS: 52.31222, 4.99139
Post Code: NL-1108 AZ

Amsterdam, Noord-Holland

www.alanrogers.com/nl5670
info@gaaspercamping.nl
Tel: 0206 967 326
www.gaaspercamping.nl/en

Open (Touring Pitches):
15 March - 1 November

Gaasper Camping

Amsterdam is probably the most popular destination for visits in the Netherlands and Gaasper Camping Amsterdam is on the southeast side, a short walk from a Metro station with a direct 15-minute service to the centre. The site is well kept and neatly laid out on flat grass with attractive trees and shrubs. There are touring pitches in two main areas – one more open and grassy, mainly kept for tents, the other more formal with numbered pitches mainly divided by shallow ditches or good hedges. Areas of hardstanding are available and all caravan pitches have electrical connections (10A).

Three modern, clean toilet blocks (one unisex) for the tourist sections are an adequate provision. A number of cabins with basin and shower. Hot water for showers and some dishwashing sinks on payment. Facilities for babies. Washing machine and dryer. Motorcaravan services. Gas supplies. Supermarket, café/bar/restaurant plus takeaway (all 1/4-1/11). Play area on grass. WiFi over site (charged).

Key Features

 Pets Accepted

 Play Area

 Bar/Restaurant

 Bike Hire

Scan me for
more information.

Alan Rogers Code: NL6412
8 accommodations
100 pitches
GPS: 51.95214, 6.73690
Post Code: NL-7115 AG

Winterswijk, Gelderland

www.alanrogers.com/nl6412
info@hetwinkel.nl
Tel: 0543 513025
www.hetwinkel.com

Open (Touring Pitches):
All year.

Recreatiepark Het Winkel

Recreatiepark Het Winkel is a friendly family campsite in the middle of unspoilt countryside, surrounded by woodland in the Achterhoek region. The generous pitches (100 for touring) are serviced with 10A electricity, water and drain. Some meadow areas (without electricity) are only used for tents. Eight chalets are available to rent. There are large open spaces for leisure and sporting activities and a wide range of facilities for all the family. Cycling, running and walking routes start from the site. The Achterhoek region has the most extensive network of cycle paths in the Netherlands.

Eight modern sanitary units and a beautifully presented block for children. Private en-suite facilities to rent for 8 touring pitches. Shop and bar (both open all year). Restaurant/takeaway (1/4-30/9). Swimming and paddling pools (heated 1/5-15/9) with water slide, sauna and solarium. Indoor play area for children. Bicycle hire. Tennis. Volleyball. Basketball. Terrace. Small animal park. WiFi (charged).

Key Features

 Open All Year

 Pets Accepted

 Disabled Facilities

 Swimming Pool

 Play Area

 Bar/Restaurant

 Bike Hire

Scan me for more information.

Alan Rogers Code: NL6425
71 accommodations
350 pitches
GPS: 51.94961, 6.64770
Post Code: NL-7109-AH

Winterswijk, Gelderland

www.alanrogers.com/nl6425
info@detweebruggen.nl
Tel: 0543 565 366
www.detweebruggen.nl

Open (Touring Pitches):
All year.

De Twee Bruggen

De Twee Bruggen is a spacious recreation park set in the Achterhoek countryside. The 350 touring pitches (all with 10/16A electricity) are divided between several fields of varying sizes. Although the fields are surrounded by tall trees, the ground is open and sunny. Beyond the touring area, 71 chalets set in well tended grounds, are for rent. Indoor and outdoor swimming pools can be enjoyed by children and adults. At the indoor pool there is a covered terrace and, for relaxation, a sauna and jacuzzi. Adjacent to the pool is a small, open-air theatre, where shows are staged in high season.

Three modern, well maintained sanitary buildings include showers and washbasins in private cabins. Fourteen pitches have private sanitary facilities. Washing machines and dryers. Motorcaravan services. Supermarket, bar, restaurant and takeaway (all year). Heated outdoor pool (30/4-15/9). Heated indoor pool (all year). Paddling pool. Sauna. Jacuzzi. Solarium. Sports field. Tennis courts. Bicycle hire. Minigolf. Bowling. Playground. Bouncy castle. Deer field. Free WiFi over site. Max. 2 dogs.

Key Features

 Open All Year

 Pets Accepted

 Swimming Pool

 Play Area

 Bar/Restaurant

 Bike Hire

Scan me for more information.

Netherlands

Alan Rogers Code: NL5840
10 accommodations
280 pitches
GPS: 52.11885, 5.90569
Post Code: NL-7351 TN

Hoenderloo, Gelderland

www.alanrogers.com/nl5840
info@veluwevakantieparken.nl
Tel: 0553 781 760
www.pampel.nl

Open (Touring Pitches):
All year.

Camping De Pampel

Camping De Pampel has the most congenial atmosphere and caters both for families (great facilities for children) and for those seeking peace and quiet. This is enhanced by its situation deep in the forest, with nine hectares of its own woods to explore. There are 280 pitches (20 seasonal) with 6-16A electricity. You can choose to site yourself around the edge of a large, open field with volleyball in the middle, or pick one of the individual places which are numbered, divided by trees and generally quite spacious.

Toilet facilities are excellent and the Sani Plaza is outstanding. Laundry. Well stocked shop (1/4-1/10). Restaurant. Snack bar (July/Aug, otherwise weekends only). Swimming pool and new fun paddling pool with water canon (heated by solar panels; open 1/4-31/10). Play area. Pets' corner. Sports area. Indoor play area. Barbecues by permission only, no open fires. Dogs are not accepted. WiFi throughout (free).

Key Features

 Open All Year

 Swimming Pool

 Play Area

 Bar/Restaurant

 Bike Hire

Scan me for more information.

Alan Rogers Code: NL6337
8 accommodations
130 pitches
GPS: 52.18756, 5.63098
Post Code: NL-3781 NJ

Voorthuizen, Gelderland

www.alanrogers.com/nl6337
info@deboshoek.nl
Tel: 0342 471 297
www.deboshoek.nl

Open (Touring Pitches):
23 March - 27 October.

Recreatiepark De Boshoek

Camping de Boshoek is a spacious, family oriented campsite, which forms a part of a large leisure park which includes bungalows to rent and private chalets. There are 130 touring pitches of 100-120 sq.m., all equipped with 10A electricity, water, drainage and cable TV connections. They are in various fields, each with its own play area and including two car-free areas, with a central area for general use. There are eight pitches reserved for campers. Rented accommodation includes comfortable safari tents equipped with kitchen, terrace and a private bathroom. Children will enjoy the playground with its giant 7.5-metre slide. There is also a pony club and a children's farm.

One clean, heated toilet block has free showers and some washbasins in cubicles. Good facilities for children and disabled visitors. Some private sanitary facilities to rent on pitches. Shop. Restaurant, bar, snack bar. Large swimming complex. Sauna and Turkish steam bath. Large adventure play area. Pony riding and lessons. Minigolf. 10-pin bowling. Short golf. Tennis. Football. Basketball. Children's farm. Entertainment and children's club. Hairdresser. Bicycle hire. WiFi over part of site (charged).

Key Features

 Pets Accepted

 Disabled Facilities

 Swimming Pool

 Play Area

 Bar/Restaurant

 Bike Hire

 Horse Riding

Scan me for more information.

Alan Rogers Code: NL6487
50 accommodations
100 pitches
GPS: 52.43990, 6.34616
Post Code: NL-8151 PP

Lemelerveld, Overijssel

www.alanrogers.com/nl6487
info@campingheidepark.nl
Tel: 0572 371 525
www.campingheidepark.nl

Open (Touring Pitches):
1 April - 1 October.

Camping Heidepark

Camping Heidepark is centrally located in Overijssel, near the Salland Ridge, and convenient for excellent hiking and cycling routes. This southern tip of the Overijssels Vecht valley has a great deal to offer holidaymakers. Heidepark is a car-free site, set in spacious, landscaped parkland. There are 100 touring pitches (all with 6/10A electricity, water, drainage and TV connections) spread across eight camping fields. Pitches are arranged around the edge of the grassy fields and are bordered by thick woods. A large, indoor activity room will appeal to all children, including teenagers. There is plenty of space for children to play safely in the middle of each field.

Two modern toilet blocks with baby room. Family shower room and facilities for children. Laundry. Shop. Terrace bar. Heated swimming and paddling pools with terrace. Natural swimming pool adjacent. Play areas. Play attic for children. Indoor playground. Tennis. Football. Library. Bicycle and go-kart hire. Separate fields for dog owners. WiFi throughout (charged).

Key Features

 Pets Accepted

 Swimming Pool

 Play Area

 Bar/Restaurant

 Bike Hire

Scan me for more information.

Alan Rogers Code: NL5980
12 accommodations
275 pitches
GPS: 52.51075, 6.51506
Post Code: NL-7736 PJ

Beerze-Ommen, Overijssel

www.alanrogers.com/nl5980
info@campingderoos.nl
Tel: 0523 251 234
www.campingderoos.nl

Open (Touring Pitches):
15 April - 2 October.

Camping De Roos

De Roos is a family run site in an Area of Outstanding Natural Beauty, truly a nature lovers' campsite, immersed in an atmosphere of tranquillity. It is situated in Overijssel's Vecht Valley, a unique region set in a river dune landscape on the River Vecht. The river and its tributary wind their way unhurriedly around and through this spacious campsite. It is a natural setting that the owners of De Roos have carefully preserved. The 275 pitches and necessary amenities have been blended into the landscape with great care. Pitches, most with electricity hook-up (6A Europlug), are naturally sited, some behind blackthorn thickets, in the shadow of an old oak or in a clearing scattered with wild flowers.

Four well maintained sanitary blocks are kept fresh and clean. The two larger blocks are heated and include baby bath/shower and wash cabins. Launderette. Motorcaravan services. Gas supplies. Health food shop and tea room serving snacks (30/4-4/9). Bicycle hire. Boules. Several small playgrounds and field for kite flying. Sports field. Football. Volleyball. River swimming. Fishing. Internet access (charged). WiFi in tearoom 09.00-12.00 (free). Dogs are not accepted (and cats must be kept on a lead!). Torch useful. Bungalows for rent (all year).

Key Features

 Play Area

 Bar/Restaurant

 Bike Hire

 Fishing

Scan me for more information.

Alan Rogers Code: NL6470
100 accommodations
245 pitches
GPS: 52.39200, 7.04900
Post Code: NL-7591 NH

Denekamp, Overijssel

www.alanrogers.com/nl6470
info@depapillon.nl
Tel: 0541 351 670
www.depapillon.nl

Open (Touring Pitches):
29 March - 1 October.

Camping De Papillon

De Papillon is perhaps one of the best and most enjoyable campsites in the Netherlands. All 245 touring pitches are spacious (120-160 sq.m), all have electricity (4/10/16A), and TV; a further 220 have water and drainage. An impressive, new sanitary block has state-of-the-art equipment and uses green technology. There is a new entertainment centre with an outdoor auditorium for children, and the water play area by the adventure playground and covered, heated pool are among the most imaginative and exciting we have seen, making it ideal for families. The restored heathland area offers opportunities for nature lovers; there is also a large fishing lake and a swimming lake with beach area and activities. A member of Leading Campings group.

Two large sanitary buildings with showers, toilets, washbasins in cabins, facilities for babies and for disabled visitors. Laundry room. Spacious reception area with supermarket, restaurant, bar and takeaway. Heated pool with children's pool and sliding roof. Lake swimming with sandy beach. New modern adventure play area and smaller play areas. Pétanque. Bicycle hire. Fishing pond. Tennis. Pets to stroke. Max. 2 dogs. Luxury bungalows to rent (good views). New water spray park for children up to 13 yrs. Free WiFi over the whole site. Motorhome Friendly.

Key Features

 Pets Accepted

 Disabled Facilities

 Swimming Pool

 Play Area

 Bar/Restaurant

 Bike Hire

 Fishing

Scan me for
more information.

Alan Rogers Code: NL6004
110 accommodations
341 pitches
GPS: 52.58694, 6.53049
Post Code: NL-7797 HH

Rheezerveen-Hardenberg,
Overijssel

www.alanrogers.com/nl6004
info@stoetenslagh.nl
Tel: 0523 638 260
www.stoetenslagh.nl

Open (Touring Pitches):
1 April - 30 September.

Het Stoetenslagh

Arriving at Het Stoetenslagh and passing reception, you reach the pride of the campsite; a large natural lake with several little beaches. Many hours can be spent swimming, canoeing or sailing a dinghy here. There are 341 spacious grass touring pitches (120-140 sq.m) divided between several fields and arranged around clean sanitary buildings. Each field also has a small volleyball area and climbing frames. You may choose between nature pitches, standard pitches or serviced pitches with water, drainage, 10A electricity and cable connection. There are climbing frames for children, much space for playing, a children's club and, particularly popular with little ones, a small animal farm.

Three toilet blocks include private cabins, baby facilities, family showers and facilities for disabled visitors. Beach shower. Washing machines and dryers. Motorcaravan services. Shop. Restaurant with bar. Snack bar with takeaway. Disco, bowling, curling and archery (all indoor). New indoor pool. Natural pool with sandy beaches. Canoeing. Play areas. Fishing. Bicycle hire. Activities for children and teenagers. Bouncy castle. Free WiFi over site.

Key Features

 Pets Accepted

 Disabled Facilities

 Swimming Pool

 Play Area

 Bar/Restaurant

 Bike Hire

 Fishing

Scan me for
more information.

Alan Rogers Code: NL6065
431 accommodations
375 pitches
GPS: 52.93832, 6.34158
Post Code: NL-8426 GK

Appelscha, Friesland

De Roggeberg

De Roggeberg may prove a good choice for families with children who love outdoor activities. There is an impressive paddling pool here, with all manner of water features (including fountains and water games). Older children will enjoy the 15 m. climbing wall with six different ascent routes, as well as the 80 m. long climbing track. Specialist instructors are on hand to teach the basics of climbing. This is a spacious site with large, grassy pitches (around 20 with electricity, water and drainage) scattered across a number of small fields. Many are sunny, but some are backed with high hedges and are rather more shaded. A good range of modern mobile homes and chalets are available to rent and are located close to the main amenities area. This secluded, wooded region in southeast Friesland has no large cities close at hand, but a visit to Giethoorn is highly recommended; known locally as 'the Venice of the North' and was founded in 1230. Transport around the village is only possible by boat or bicycle.

Good toilet facilities. Laundry. Restaurant, bar/café, takeaway. Bakery. Supermarket. Heated outdoor children's pool with water slides and fountains. Play area and adventure track. Sports hall. 9-hole golf course. Sports field. Tennis courts. 5-a-side football. Bicycle and go-kart hire. Minigolf. Climbing wall. 80 m. zip wire. Mobile homes and chalets to rent. Free wifi.

www.alanrogers.com/nl6065
reservation@rcn.eu
Tel: +31 85 0400 700
www.rcn.nl/roggeberg

Open (Touring Pitches):
All Year

Key Features

 Open All Year

 Pets Accepted

 Disabled Facilities

 Swimming Pool

 Play Area

 Bar/Restaurant

 Bike Hire

 Golf

Scan me for more information.

Alan Rogers Code: NL6027
150 accommodations
40 pitches
GPS: 52.94651, 5.62768
Post Code: NL-8551 NW

Woudsend, Friesland

www.alanrogers.com/nl6027
info@derakken.nl
Tel: 0514 591525
www.derakken.nl

Open (Touring Pitches):
All year.

Aquacamping De Rakken

Located between the three largest Frisian lakes, Slotermeer, Heegermeer and Sneekermeer, De Rakken is a great choice for both nature and watersports enthusiasts. Just two minutes on foot from the site, Woudsend is a good watersports resort with a wealth of catering facilities and places of interest (including mills and churches). The site offers boat moorings as well as bicycle, electric boat and car hire. The 40 touring pitches are of a reasonable size and all have 6-16A electricity, with 15 on hardstanding (20 with drainage). Accommodation to rent on site includes hikers' cabins and attractive chalets. De Rakken is open all year.

Four heated toilet blocks include preset hot showers, open style washbasins, a baby room and facilities for disabled visitors. Play area with volleyball. Petting zoo. Tennis. Fishing. Marina. Boat launching. Electric boats to rent. Hiker cabins and chalets to rent. WiFi.

Key Features

 Open All Year

 Pets Accepted

 Disabled Facilities

 Play Area

 Bike Hire

 Fishing

 Sailing

Scan me for more information.

Alan Rogers Code: NL5760
233 accommodations
310 pitches
GPS: 52.90250, 5.46620
Post Code: NL-8723 CG

Koudum, Friesland

www.alanrogers.com/nl5760
info@kuilart.nl
Tel: 0514 522 221
www.kuilart.nl

Open (Touring Pitches):
All year.

Camping De Kuilart

De Kuilart is a well run, modern and partly car-free site by Friesland's largest lake. With its own marina and many facilities, it attracts many watersports enthusiasts. There are around 543 pitches, 310 for touring units, all with electricity (6/16A), water, drainage, WiFi and TV connections, and 34 pitches with private sanitary facilities. The restaurant provides beautiful views over Lake Fluessen. The marina provides windsurfing and sailing lessons and boat hire, and there are special rates at the site for groups and sailing clubs. However, the site also has an excellent indoor swimming pool, as well as an area for lake swimming and on land, there are sports facilities and woods for cycling and walking. It may also, therefore, appeal for a relaxing break in a pleasant area not much visited by British campers.

Four modern, heated sanitary blocks well spaced around the site with showers on payment and most washbasins (half in private cabins) have only cold water. Launderette. Motorcaravan services. Gas supplies. Restaurant/bar, supermarket, indoor pool with 3 sessions daily (all open 30/3-4/11). Sauna and solarium. Sports field. Play areas. Tennis. Bicycle hire. Fishing. Animation team (high season). Internet access. Lake swimming area. Marina. Windsurfing, boat hire and boat shop. Car hire. WiFi over site (charged).

Key Features

 Open All Year

 Pets Accepted

 Disabled Facilities

 Swimming Pool

 Play Area

 Bar/Restaurant

 Bike Hire

 Fishing

Scan me for more information.

Alan Rogers Code: NL6150
52 accommodations
334 pitches
GPS: 52.70300, 6.37640
Post Code: NL-7932 PX

Echten, Drenthe

www.alanrogers.com/nl6150
info@westerbergen.nl
Tel: 0528 251 224
www.westerbergen.nl

Open (Touring Pitches):
26 March - 29 October (mobile home accommodation, all year).

Vakantiepark Westerbergen

Vakantiepark Westerbergen is beautifully situated in the picturesque region of Drenthe. The campsite is divided into two different areas, the campsite itself and the residential park. There are 386 pitches of which 334 are for touring. All pitches have electricity (6-16A), and most are equipped with water, drainage and cable TV connections. Mostly on a separate field, the marked pitches are of a good size. In the centre of the site, there is a fishing pond. During holiday times an entertainment team organises activities, for example, survival exercises, children's theatre, treasure hunts, discos and much more. The site's swimming pool is heated and covered. There is also an outside water play area for little ones. There are many things to do and places to see in the surrounding area, and the friendly reception staff are happy to provide information.

One new and two renovated toilet blocks are clean and neat with hot showers, toilets and individual washbasins. One block provides facilities for disabled visitors and for babies. Washing machines and dryer. Motorcaravan services. Shop (April-Oct). Restaurant. Snack bar. Attractive bar and terrace. Indoor swimming pool. Indoor and outdoor play areas. Multisports court. Minigolf. Laser game. Archery. Tennis. Bicycle hire. Fishing. WiFi throughout (charged).

Key Features

 Pets Accepted

 Disabled Facilities

 Swimming Pool

 Play Area

 Bar/Restaurant

 Bike Hire

 Fishing

Scan me for more information.

Alan Rogers Code: NL6124
32 accommodations
110 pitches
GPS: 52.97652, 6.75608
Post Code: NL-9462 TB

Gasselte, Drenthe

www.alanrogers.com/nl6124
info@delentevandrenthe.nl
Tel: 0599 564 333
www.lentevandrenthe.nl

Open (Touring Pitches):
29 March - 25 October.

De Lente van Drenthe

De Lente van Drenthe is located on the edge of the Gieten-Borger forest. Along with its attractive situation amidst forests and moorland, it is also just a short walk (200 m.) from 't Nije Hemelriek. This is a large lake, with a maximum depth of 1.3 m, crystal clear water and a fine sandy beach. There is direct access to the many cycle, mountain bike and walking routes in the area. There are around 100 pitches for touring units here, all with 6A electricity and cable TV connections. The pitches are of a good size (a minimum of 100 sq.m). Electricity, water and drainage are available on 25 touring pitches. Enjoyable excursions for children are the Sprookjeshof in Zuidlaren and Kabouterland in Exloo. Close by are two sub-tropical pools.

Good modern toilet blocks, including a family shower room. Basic essentials from reception. Small restaurant, bar, snack bar (1/4-15/9). Heated outdoor swimming pool (1/5-15/9). Playground. Sports field. Tennis. Minigolf. Bicycle and go-kart hire. Nordic walking classes. Games room. Entertainment for children (high season). Max. 2 dogs. Internet corner. WiFi throughout (charged).

Key Features

 Pets Accepted

 Disabled Facilities

 Swimming Pool

 Play Area

 Bar/Restaurant

 Bike Hire

 Scan me for more information.

357

Alan Rogers Code: NL6120
9 accommodations
180 pitches
GPS: 53.15278, 6.19138
Post Code: NL-9865 VP

Opende, Groningen

Camping 't Strandheem

www.alanrogers.com/nl6120
info@strandheem.nl
Tel: 0594 659 555
www.strandheem.nl

Open (Touring Pitches):
25 March - 25 September.

Camping 't Strandheem has 330 quite large, numbered pitches (110 sq.m) some with hardstanding and suitable for motorcaravans. All with electricity (4/10A), there are 180 used for touring units, partly separated by low hedges but without much shade. Of these, 45 pitches have water points, drainage and cable TV connections. The Bruinewoud family will give you a warm welcome. The reception building houses an attractive bar, a full restaurant, a disco for teenagers and a shop. The site has a lot to offer, especially for youngsters with a full entertainment programme in high season with water games in the lake next to the site, a games area and an indoor pool.

Two modern toilet buildings have washbasins, controllable showers, child size toilets and washbasins, a good baby room and fully equipped bathroom. Facilities for disabled campers. Launderette. Motorcaravan service. Shop. Restaurant and bar. Café and snack bar. Covered swimming pool (5x5 m) with separate paddling pool, slide and sun terrace. Playgrounds. Indoor play hall. Minigolf. Fishing. Bicycle hire. Boules. Lake with beach (€ 1 p/p per day). Extensive recreation programme (July/Aug). Film and card nights. WiFi on part of site (charged).

Key Features

 Pets Accepted

 Disabled Facilities

 Swimming Pool

 Play Area

 Bar/Restaurant

 Bike Hire

 Fishing

Scan me for more information.

Alan Rogers Code: NL6090
10 accommodations
250 pitches
GPS: 53.40205, 6.21732
Post Code: NL-9976 VS

Lauwersoog, Groningen

www.alanrogers.com/nl6090
info@lauwersoog.nl
Tel: 0519 349 133
www.lauwersoog.nl

Open (Touring Pitches):
All year.

Camping Lauwersoog

The focus at Camping Lauwersoog is very much on the sea and watersports. One can have sailing lessons or hire canoes and there is direct access to the beach from the site. There are 450 numbered pitches with 250 for tourers; 140 have water, drainage, electricity and cable connections. The pitches are on level, grassy fields (some beside the beach), partly separated by hedges and some with shade from trees (cars parked separately). A building in the marina houses a restaurant, bar, shop, laundry and an adventure playground. It also provides beautiful views over the Lauwersmeer. The site's restaurant specialises in seafood and even the entertainment programmes for all ages have a water theme.

The two toilet blocks for touring units provide washbasins, preset showers and child size toilets. Facilities for disabled visitors. Laundry. Campers' kitchen. Ice pack service. Motorcaravan service. Shop. Restaurant (all year), bar and snack bar including takeaway service (1/4-1/10). Play area with bouncy castle. Minigolf at the beach. Sailing school. Canoe hire. Surfing lessons (July/Aug). Riding. Bicycle and go-kart hire. Boules. WiFi. Extensive entertainment programme for all ages in high season. Communal barbecue. Torch useful.

Key Features

 Open All Year

 Pets Accepted

 Disabled Facilities

 Beach Access

 Play Area

 Bar/Restaurant

 Bike Hire

 Fishing

Scan me for more information.

Capital Oslo
Currency Norwegian Krone (NOK)
Language Norwegian
Telephone country code 00 47
Time Zone CET (GMT/UTC+1)
Tourist Office visitnorway.com

Climate Winters are mild on the coast, cold and snowy inland and extemely cold in the north with 24hr daylight. Summers are hot and dry.

Norway

A land full of contrasts, from magnificent snow-capped mountains, dramatic fjords, vast plateaux with wild untamed tracts, to huge lakes and rich green countryside. With nearly one-quarter of the land above the Arctic Circle, Norway has the lowest population density in Europe.

Norway is made up of five regions. In the heart of the eastern region, Oslo has everything one would expect from a major city, and is the oldest of the Scandinavian capitals. The west coast boasts some of the world's most beautiful fjords, with plunging waterfalls and mountains.

Trondheim, in the heart of central Norway, is a busy university town with many attractions, notably the Nidarosdomen Cathedral. The sunniest region is the south, its rugged coastline with white wooden cottages is popular with Norwegians and ideal for swimming, sailing, scuba diving and fishing.

The north is the Land of the Midnight Sun and the Northern Lights. It is home to the Sami, the indigenous people of Norway, whose traditions include fishing, hunting and reindeer herding. The scenery varies from forested valleys and narrow fjords to icy tundra, and there are several cities worth visiting including Tromsø, with the Fjelheisen cable car, Polaria aquarium with bearded seals, and the Arctic Cathedral.

Shops Opening hours vary throughout the year. In high-season 10am to 5pm Monday to Saturday, some open late until 7pm on Thursday. Supermarkets 9am to 11pm weekdays and until 10pm Saturday.

Banks 8am to 4pm weekdays.

Travelling with Children A great country to travel to with children however distances between towns and cities are huge so be sure to put in some careful planning. Oslo is home to many parks and museums but not all attractions are children-friendly. Attractions are often free for under 6s and discounted for under 16s.

Public Holidays New Year's Day, Maundy Thursday, Good Friday, Easter Monday, Labour Day 1 May, Constitution Day 17 May, Ascension, Whit Monday, Christmas Day, Boxing Day.

Motoring Roads are generally uncrowded around Oslo and Bergen but be prepared for tunnels and hairpins bends. Certain roads are forbidden to caravans or best avoided (check the Visit Norway website). Vehicles must have sufficient road grip and in winter it may be necessary to use winter tyres with or without chains. Vehicles entering Bergen on weekdays must pay a toll and other tolls are levied on certain roads.

See campsite map page 486.

Alan Rogers Code: NO2425
19 accommodations
40 pitches
GPS: 71.11217, 25.82177
Post Code: N-9763

Finnmark, North

www.alanrogers.com/no2425
kipo@kirkeporten.no
Tel: 78 47 52 33
www.kirkeporten.no

Open (Touring Pitches):
1 May - 1 October.

Kirkeporten Camping

This is the most northerly mainland campsite in the world (71° 06) and considering the climate and the wild, unspoilt location it has to be one of the best sites in Scandinavia and also rivals the best in Europe. The 40 touring pitches, 32 with 16A electricity, are on grass or gravel hardstanding in natural tundra terrain beside a small lake, together with room for 40 tents. There are also 16 cabins to rent and five rooms in the old barn. We advise you to pack warm clothing, bedding and maybe propane for this location. Note: Although overnighting at Nordkapp Centre is permitted, it is on the very exposed gravel carpark with no electric hook-ups or showers. Sea fishing and photographic trips by boat can be arranged, and buses run four times a day to Honningsvåg or the Nordkapp Centre. We suggest you follow the marked footpath over the hillside behind the campsite, from where you can photograph Nordkapp at midnight if the weather is favourable. A bonus is that the reindeer often come right into the campground to graze.

Key Features

 Pets Accepted

 Bar/Restaurant

Excellent modern sanitary installations in two underfloor heated buildings. They include a sauna, two family bathrooms, baby room, and excellent unit for disabled visitors. Laundry. Kitchen with hot plates, sinks and a dining area. Motorcaravan services. Shop, restaurant and takeaway (15/5-15/9). TV. WiFi.

Scan me for more information.

Alan Rogers Code: NO2487
61 accommodations
190 pitches
GPS: 65.83417, 13.22025
Post Code: N-8657

Nordland, North

www.alanrogers.com/no2487
post@mosjoenhotell.no
Tel: 75 17 79 00
www.mosjoenhotell.no

Open (Touring Pitches):
All year.

PlusCamp Mosjoen

This campsite off the E6 near Mosjøen, allows access to 'The World's Most Beautiful Journey'. The Kystriksveien (RV17) runs north to Bodø and south to Steinkjer, however this site offers more to the traveller than a simple stopover or change of route. Complete with a six-lane, ten-pin bowling alley, games rooms, food and bar, it has both entertainment and mountain views with forested valley slopes. It has modern, well equipped sanitary facilities. The 190 terraced pitches are level with electricity (16A), some on tarmac and gravel and others are on grass with a pleasant separate area for tents.

Two heated sanitary units are linked together in the centre of the site. The newer unit offers up-to-date facilities for all, with family rooms and disabled access. Motorcaravan services (ask at reception). Good size kitchen and dining area. Laundry. Restaurant. Café/bar. Heated outdoor swimming pool with slide. 10-pin bowling alley with bar. Pool table and video games. TV room. WiFi (charged). Access to large ball games area. Autogas/LPG filling station off main car park.

Key Features

 Open All Year

 Pets Accepted

 Disabled Facilities

 Swimming Pool

 Play Area

 Bar/Restaurant

 Skiing

Scan me for more information.

Norway

Alan Rogers Code: NO2500
22 accommodations
30 pitches
GPS: 63.34686, 9.96234
Post Code: N-7354

Sør Trøndelag, North

www.alanrogers.com/no2500
post@trasavika.no
Tel: 72 86 78 22
www.trasavika.no

Open (Touring Pitches):
1 May - 20 September.

Tråsåvika Camping

On a headland jutting into the Trondheimfjord, some 40 km. from Trondheim, Tråsåvika commands an attractive position. For many, this compensates for the extra distance into town. The 30 touring pitches with fjord views (some slightly sloping), all with electricity connections (10/16A), are on an open grassy field at the top of the site, or on a series of terraces below. These run down to the small sandy beach, easily accessed via a well-designed gravel service road. To one side, on a wooded bluff at the top of the site, are 19 cabins (open all year), many in the traditional style. The smart reception complex also houses a small shop, licensed café with a lounge area and a terrace overlooking the entire panorama.

The neat, fully equipped, sanitary unit includes two controllable hot showers per sex (on payment). Water for touring pitches is also accessed from this block. Hot water (on payment) in kitchen and laundry. Shop. Café (sells beer, wine and food, 1/6-20/8). TV/sitting room. Play area. Jetty and boat hire. Free fjord fishing with catches of good sized cod from the shore. Free WiFi on touring pitches.

Key Features

 Pets Accepted

 Play Area

 Bar/Restaurant

 Fishing

 Sailing

Scan me for more information.

Alan Rogers Code: NO2390
14 accommodations
100 pitches
GPS: 61.21157, 7.12110
Post Code: N-6856

Sogn og Fjordane, Western Fjords

www.alanrogers.com/no2390
camping@kjornes.no
Tel: 97 54 41 56
www.kjornes.no

Open (Touring Pitches):
All year.

Kjørnes Camping

Kjørnes Camping is idyllically situated on the Sognefjord, three kilometres from the centre of Sogndal. It occupies a long open meadow which is terraced down to the waterside. The site has 100 pitches for camping units (all with electricity), 14 cabins and two apartments for rent. Located at the very centre of the 'fjord kingdom' by the main no. 5 road, this site is the ideal base from which to explore the Sognefjord. You are within a short drive (maximum one hour) from all the major attractions including the Jostedal glacier, the Nærøyfjord, the Flåm Railway, the Urnes Stave Church and Sognefjellet. This site is ideal for those who enjoy peace and quiet, renowned local walks, lovely scenery or a spot of fishing with a bonus of evening sunshine. Local activities include organised guided walks on glaciers, access to several stave churches and a goat farm in the mountains.

A modern, high quality sanitary building has washbasins in cubicles and a feature children's room. Baby room. Facilities for disabled visitors. Kitchen with cooking facilities, dishwasher, a dining area overlooking the fjord and laundry facilities. Motorcaravan services. Small shop (10/6-20/8). Satellite TV, WiFi over site (free). Cabins and apartments for hire.

Key Features

 Open All Year

 Pets Accepted

 Disabled Facilities

 Play Area

 Skiing

 Fishing

Scan me for more information.

Alan Rogers Code: NO2375
29 accommodations
100 pitches
GPS: 61.10037, 7.46986
Post Code: N-6886

Sogn og Fjordane, Western Fjords

Lærdal Ferie & Fritidspark

www.alanrogers.com/no2375
info@laerdalferiepark.com
Tel: 57 66 66 95
www.laerdalferiepark.com

Open (Touring Pitches):
10 January - 15 December

This site is beside the famous Sognefjord, the longest fjord in the world. It is ideally situated if you want to explore the glaciers, fjords and waterfalls of the region. The 100 pitches (all with 16A electricity) are level with well-trimmed grass, connected by tarmac roads and are suitable for tents, caravans and motorhomes. The fully licensed restaurant serves traditional, locally sourced meals as well as snacks and pizzas. The pretty little village of Laerdal, only 400 m. away, is well worth a visit. A walk among the old, small wooden houses is a pleasant and exciting experience. You can hire boats on the site for short trips on the fjord. Guided hiking, cycling and fishing trips are also available, with waymarked cycling and walking trails running through the park. Climbing excursions can be arranged on request. The site also provides 29 traditional Norwegian cabins, flats and rooms to rent, plus a motel, all very modern and exceptionally tastefully designed.

Key Features

 Pets Accepted

 Disabled Facilities

 Play Area

 Bar/Restaurant

 Bike Hire

 Fishing

Sailing

Two modern and well decorated sanitary blocks with washbasins (some in cubicles), showers on payment, and toilets. Facilities for disabled visitors. Children's room. Washing machine and dryer. Kitchen. Motorcaravan services. Small shop, bar, restaurant and takeaway (all 1/5-30/9). TV room. Playground. Fishing. Motorboats, rowing boats, canoes, bicycles and pedal cars for hire. Go-kart sales. Free WiFi over site.

Scan me for more information.

Alan Rogers Code: NO2590
12 accommodations
150 pitches
GPS: 59.98923, 8.81810
Post Code: N-3650

Telemark, South

Sandviken Camping

www.alanrogers.com/no2590
post@sandviken-camping.no
Tel: 35 09 81 73
www.sandviken-camping.no

Open (Touring Pitches):
All year.

Sandviken is a delightful, family run site in a scenic location, suitable for exploring Hardangervidda. Remote, yet with good access by road, it has its own shingle beach at the head of the beautiful Tinnsjo Lake. It provides 150 grassy, mostly level pitches, many with spectacular views along the lake. Most have electricity (10/16A), and there is an area for tents along the waterfront. Activities on site naturally include swimming, fishing and excellent facilities for launching boats. The modern reception building houses a small shop selling confectionery and essential supplies. Bread can be ordered daily and takeaway food is available.

Two heated sanitary blocks include some washbasins in cubicles, showers on payment, sauna, solarium and a dual-purpose disabled/family bathroom with ramped access and baby changing. Kitchen and laundry rooms (hot water on payment). New, smaller unit with kitchen, TV and dining area overlooking the lake also have en-suite family rooms adapted for disabled visitors. Motorcaravan services. Reception with kiosk, bar and takeaway snacks. Two playgrounds. TV and games room. Minigolf. Trampoline. Beach volleyball. Mini football. Fishing and watersports. Boat hire.

Key Features

 Open All Year

 Pets Accepted

 Disabled Facilities

 Play Area

 Skiing

 Fishing

 Sailing

Scan me for more information.

Alan Rogers Code: NO2660
150 pitches
GPS: 58.99888, 6.09217
Post Code: N-4100

Rogaland, South

www.alanrogers.com/no2660
info@preikestolencamping.com
Tel: 48 19 39 50
www.preikestolencamping.com

Open (Touring Pitches):
All year.

Preikestolen Camping

Taking its name from one of Norway's best known attractions, the Preikestolen (Pulpit Rock) cliff formation, Preikestolen Camping is situated in the beautiful region of Rogaland, surrounded by high mountains and deep fjords. This is a site where you could easily stay a few days to explore the beautiful region. The friendly owners are happy to help with maps and guidance. The site is laid out in a relaxed way with an open, level grass area where trees and bushes create pleasant little 'rooms' for your tent, caravan or motorcaravan. There are 150 pitches, 56 with electricity (10/16A), water tap and waste water drainage. The famous and outstanding cliff of Preikestolen was probably formed by the action of frost over 10,000 years ago. From the cliff, 604 m. above fjord level, there are magnificent views over Lysefjorden with its green glacier water. Even the most experienced tourist must find this scenery breathtaking.

Key Features

 Open All Year

 Pets Accepted

 Disabled Facilities

 Play Area

 Bar/Restaurant

 Fishing

The modern heated sanitary block has showers, washbasins in cubicles and facilities for disabled visitors. Room with sinks but no cookers - all with free hot water. Washing machines and dryers. Motorcaravan services. Freezer. Small shop and craft shop (1/5-30/9). Restaurant and takeaway (1/5-30/9). Fishing. Play area. WiFi over part of site (free).

Scan me for
more information.

Alan Rogers Code: NO2606
5 accommodations
15 pitches
GPS: 58.18810, 8.19991
Post Code: N-4770

Aust-Agder, South

www.alanrogers.com/no2606
postmaster@isefjar.no
Tel: 37 27 49 90
www.isefjar.no

Open (Touring Pitches):
1 May - 1 September.

Sørlandets Naturist

Sørlandets is renowned for idyllic inlets and islands, and has a reputation as the 'Norwegian Riviera' with warm summer temperatures and sea water reaching over twenty degrees. An equally warm and enthusiastic welcome awaits naturists at Isefjær, where the 15 touring pitches and 5 rental accommodations are supported by basic but comfortable facilities. The site has been lovingly developed from an ex-military recreation camp by volunteers. It is secluded with access that may prove difficult for larger units. A limited number of camping pitches enjoy views over the fjord from the water's edge or from high above the site. A continuous programme of improvements has produced comfortable facilities inside the outer shell, and guests often become part of the group of volunteers, who are keen to share their way of life with others. A small church, part of the original camp, is in the fjord seaside camping area.

Key Features

 Naturist Site

 Pets Accepted

 Beach Access

 Bar/Restaurant

 Fishing

 Sailing

The clean sanitary blocks are typical of those found in many naturist sites, with open plan showers and washbasins. Sanitary facilities specially for children. Laundry facilities. Excellent communal kitchen and large outside barbecue area. Motorcaravan services. Restaurant with meals available three times a day. Hot tub (Sat.) Sauna. Large lounge area. TV room. Fishing. Boat launching. Fjord swimming. Diving platform. Free WiFi in lounge and reception. Accommodation to rent.

Scan me for
more information.

Capital Lisbon
Currency Euro (€)
Language Portuguese
Telephone country code 00 351
Time Zone GMT/UTC
Tourist Office visitportugal.com

Climate The country enjoys a maritime climate with hot summers and mild winters with comparatively low rainfall in the south, heavy rain in the north.

Portugal

Portugal is the westernmost country of Europe, situated on the Iberian peninsula, bordered by Spain in the north and east, with the Atlantic coast in the south and west. In spite of its relatively small size, the country offers a tremendous variety, both in its way of life and in its history and traditions.

Every year the Algarve is the destination for some ten million sunseekers and watersports enthusiasts who love its sheltered sandy beaches and clear Atlantic sea. In contrast, the lush hills and forests of central Portugal are home to historic buildings and monuments, in particular the capital city of Lisbon, adjacent to the estuary of the River Tagus. Lisbon's history can still be seen in the Alfama quarter, which survived the devastating earthquake of 1755; at night the city comes alive with vibrant cafés, restaurants and discos.

To the south-east of Lisbon, the land becomes rather impoverished, consisting of stretches of vast undulating plains, dominated by cork plantations. Most people head for Evora, a medieval walled town and UNESCO World Heritage Site. The Minho area in the north is said to be the most beautiful part of Portugal, home to the country's only National Park, and vineyards producing the famous Port wine.

Shops Opening hours vary throughout the year. In high-season 9.30am to noon and 2pm to 7pm weekdays, 10am to 1pm Saturday. Shopping centres 10am to 10pm.

Banks 8.30am to 3pm weekdays.

Travelling with Children For such a small country Portugal has a lot to offer children. Lisbon has a good choice of museums, castles, parks and an aquarium. The Algarve is one of the best destinations for kids with its long sandy beaches, zoos, water parks and boat trips.

Public Holidays New Year's Day, Good Friday, Liberation Day 25 Apr, Labour Day, National Day 10 Jun, Corpus Christi, Assumption, Republic Day 5 Oct, All Saints' Day 1 Nov, Independence Restoration Day 1 Dec, Immaculate Conception 8 Dec, Christmas Day.

Motoring The standard of roads is very variable, even some of the main roads can be very uneven. Tolls are levied on certain motorways (auto-estradas) out of Lisbon, and upon southbound traffic at the Lisbon end of the giant 25th Abril bridge over the Tagus. Parked vehicles must face the same direction as moving traffic.

See campsite map page 484.

Alan Rogers Code: PO8370
16 accommodations
200 pitches
GPS: 41.76310, -8.19050
Post Code: P-4840 030

Braga, Porto and The North

www.alanrogers.com/po8370
info@parquecerdeira.com
Tel: 253 351 005
www.parquecerdeira.com

Open (Touring Pitches):
All Year

Parque Cerdeira

Located in the Peneda-Gerês National Park, amidst spectacular mountain scenery, this excellent site offers modern facilities in a truly natural area. The national park is home to all manner of flora, fauna and wildlife, including the roebuck, wolf and wild boar. The well fenced, professional and peaceful site offers 200 good sized, unmarked, mostly level, grassy pitches in a shady woodland setting. Electricity (5/10A) is available for the touring pitches, though some long leads may be required. A very large timber complex, tastefully designed with the use of noble materials – granite and wood - provides a superb restaurant with a comprehensive menu.

Three very clean sanitary blocks provide mixed style WCs, controllable showers and hot water. Good facilities for disabled visitors. Laundry. Gas supplies. Shop. Restaurant/bar. Outdoor pool (15/6-15/9). Playground. TV room (satellite). Medical post. Good tennis courts. Minigolf. Adventure park. Car wash. Barbecue areas. Torches useful. English spoken. Attractive bungalows to rent. WiFi in reception/bar area.

Key Features

 Open All Year

 Pets Accepted

 Disabled Facilities

 Swimming Pool

 Play Area

 Bar/Restaurant

Scan me for
more information.

Alan Rogers Code: PO8377
3 accommodations
10 pitches
GPS: 41.46166, -8.01095
Post Code: P-4890-505

Braga, Porto and The North

Camping Quinta Valbom

www.alanrogers.com/po8377
info@quintavalbom.nl
Tel: 253 653 048
www.quintavalbom.nl

Open (Touring Pitches):
April - September.

Anyone who likes a simple, well-run campsite in the depths of the countryside will love Quinta Valbom. Surrounded by wooded slopes with mountains in the distance, the site has been created from a deserted wine-producing farmstead by its enthusiastic Dutch owners, Els and Herman. It is primarily a place for campers; of the 30 pitches, 20 are for campers. All pitches 10A electricity available, on several terraces reached by a steep cobbled road. Those on the upper terraces are suitable only for tents. There is space for nine caravans (maximum length 6 m) and one motorcaravan on the lower terraces (Herman will meet caravanners and tow you up the extremely steep approach road and onto your pitch).

Modern little toilet block tucked away behind a remnant of an old stone corn store; hot water to preset showers and open style washbasins. Washing machine. Rustic bar in former adega (wine-making cellar), opening onto an attractive terrace with amazing views. Set meals which Els provides twice or three times a week (all season, subject to demand). Delightful little swimming pool. Information about excursions. Contact site about dogs (max. 3 on site). WiFi in bar and on terrace (free).

Key Features

 Pets Accepted

 Swimming Pool

 Bar/Restaurant

Scan me for more information.

Alan Rogers Code: PO8150
190 accommodations
228 pitches
GPS: 38.65390, -9.23833
Post Code: 2825-450

Costa da Caparica, Lisbon

www.alanrogers.com/po8150
infocaparica@orbitur.pt
Tel: 212 901 366
www.orbitur.com

Open (Touring Pitches):
All Year.

Orbitur Costa da Caparica

This campsite is located in a spa town, 20 km from Lisbon. Given its proximity to the Portuguese capital, it has numerous permanent facilities and is perfect for weekends at any time of the year. Caparica campsite has a large leisure area, social hall, terraces, a mini-market and bar-restaurant. The beach is just 200m away. With relatively easy access to Lisbon via the motorway, by bus or even by bus and ferry, this site is situated near a small resort, favoured by the Portuguese themselves, which has all the usual amenities. Of the 440 pitches, 250 are for touring units, although some can only accommodate tents; all have 6A electrical connections available. A row of pitches close to the road can accommodate larger units. In addition, there are 90 permanent caravans and 90 chalets, tents and mobile homes to rent.

The three toilet blocks have mostly British style toilets, washbasins with cold water and some controllable showers, although these come under pressure when the site is full. Facilities for disabled visitors. Washing machines and dryer. Motorcaravan services. Supermarket and bar with snacks (23/3-30/9), small shop in reception in low season. Self-service restaurant and takeaway (1/6-20/9). TV room (satellite). Playground. Gas supplies. WiFi over part of site (free).

Key Features

 Open All Year

 Pets Accepted

 Disabled Facilities

 Play Area

 Bar/Restaurant

Scan me for more information.

Alan Rogers Code: PO8140
70 accommodations
171 pitches
GPS: 38.72477, -9.20737
Post Code: P-1400-061

Lisbon, Lisbon and Vale do Tejo

www.alanrogers.com/po8140
info@lisboacamping.com
Tel: 217 628 200
www.lisboacamping.com

Open (Touring Pitches):
All year.

Lisboa Camping & Bungalows

Arriving at this large site in the suburbs of Lisbon, first impressions are good. Beyond the wide entrance with its ponds and fountains, the trees, lawns and flowering shrubs lead up to the attractive swimming pool area. Positive impressions continue: on sloping ground, the site's many terraces are well shaded by trees and shrubs and all 171 touring pitches are on concrete hardstandings with grass and a picnic table. All have 10A electricity connections, water and a drain. There is a huge separate area for tents and 70 chalet-style bungalows are for hire. Central Lisbon is easily reached by bus with a regular service from near the gate.

Eight solar-powered toilet blocks are well equipped and kept clean, although in need of some refurbishment. Controllable showers and hot water to open style washbasins. Facilities for disabled visitors. Launderette. Motorcaravan services. Shop, bar and self-service restaurant with takeaway (all year). Swimming and paddling pools (lifeguard June-Sept). Tennis. Minigolf. Sports field. Playgrounds. Amphitheatre. Entertainment in high season. Games and TV rooms. Bicycle hire. Booking service for excursions. WiFi in restaurant area (free).

Key Features

 Open All Year

 Pets Accepted

 Disabled Facilities

 Swimming Pool

 Play Area

 Bar/Restaurant

 Skiing

 Bike Hire

Scan me for more information.

375

Alan Rogers Code: PO8040
35 accommodations
360 pitches
GPS: 40.55810, -8.74528
Post Code: 3840-254

Vagueira, Aveiro

www.alanrogers.com/po8040
infovagueira@orbitur.pt
Tel: 234 797 526
www.orbitur.com

Open (Touring Pitches):
All Year

Orbitur Vagueira

An urban campsite, although located in a pine forest 500 m from the Ria de Costa Nova, 1 km from Vagueira, 8 km from Vagos and 16 km from Aveiro and Ílhavo, that offers relaxing holidays. The nearest beaches are those of Vagueira and Areão, 1.5 km away, rich in natural attractions and which offer the chance of watching wild grey herons while you lie in the sun. These beaches are also widely appreciated by surfers and bodyboarders. You must not miss the Xávega Art, the region's traditional fishing and, in Vagos, we recommend a visit to the Sanctuary of Nossa Senhora de Vagos, the chapels of Senhora da Misericórdia, Santo António and the Torre Militar. The area's excellent gastronomy is another reason for a visit.

Seven modern sanitary buildings are kept clean but equipment is fairly basic; mainly British style WCs, open washbasins (some with warm water) and free showers. Facilities for disabled campers. Washing machines and dryer. Shop, bar/snacks and restaurant (newly franchised when we visited and not yet operating, probably March-Sept). Basic supplies from reception at other times. Outdoor disco (w/ends in high season). Games room. Playground. Tennis (charged). Satellite TV. WiFi throughout (free). Torches useful.

Key Features

 Open All Year

 Pets Accepted

 Disabled Facilities

 Beach Access

 Swimming Pool

 Play Area

 Bar/Restaurant

Scan me for more information.

Alan Rogers Code: PO8335
4 accommodations
150 pitches
GPS: 40.82270, -7.69609
Post Code: P-3560-043

Viseu, Beiras and The Centre

Camping Quinta Chave Grande

www.alanrogers.com/po8335
info@chavegrande.com
Tel: 232 665 552
www.chavegrande.com

Open (Touring Pitches):
15 March - 31 October.

Quinta Chave Grande is an attractive, good quality campsite where you will receive a friendly welcome from Jorge and Lidia who look after things for the Dutch and Portuguese owners. It is set in a rural valley with several marked walks, close to many charming old villages, yet only 25 km. from the provincial capital of Viseu with its museums, churches and beautiful old town centre. The spacious site offers 150 unmarked touring pitches, some defined by trees. Electricity (6A) is available to all but long leads may be required. There is a separate terraced area for tents. Torches are essential in some areas. For those who enjoy walking, there are eight marked walking tours starting from the campsite.

Key Features

 Pets Accepted

 Disabled Facilities

 Swimming Pool

 Play Area

 Bar/Restaurant

Two toilet blocks, one traditional with open-style washbasins and controllable showers, the other with four spacious en-suite units with separate toilet and washbasin and large shower room, two equipped for use by visitors with disabilities. Service wash. Water point for motorcaravans (full services planned for 2015). No shop but baker calls daily (excl. Sun) and greengrocer twice weekly. Bar (all season). Swimming and paddling pools (1/5-31/9). Fenced play area. Organised events for children and teenagers in July/Aug. Tennis. Boules. WiFi in bar area (free).

Scan me for more information.

Alan Rogers Code: PO8355
15 pitches
GPS: 39.41001, -7.34074
Post Code: 7330-204

Portalegre, Alentejo

www.alanrogers.com/po8355
gary-campingasseiceira@hotmail.com
Tel: 245 992 940
www.campingasseiceira.com

Open (Touring Pitches):
1 January - 31 October

Camping Asseiceira

Set amongst unspoilt mountain scenery in the spectacular Serra de São Mamede National Park, Camping Asseiceira is a British-owned site where visitors receive a warm welcome. The Spanish border is just eight kilometres. Arranged in a small olive grove are 15 touring pitches with 10A electricity available and 5 tent pitches. There are views rising up to the spectacular medieval castle and town of Marvão. This is a small, pleasant, well cared for site with few facilities, although the village of Santo António das Areias is only a few minutes' walk with shops, restaurants and a bank. There is plenty of cultural and historical sightseeing to be done in the surrounding area.

The shower block has been re-built and equipped to a high standard, using locally sourced materials. Hot water throughout. Baker calls daily. Swimming pool and terrace (May-Oct).

Key Features

 Pets Accepted

 Swimming Pool

 Bar/Restaurant

Scan me for more information.

Alan Rogers Code: PO8180
42 accommodations
540 pitches
GPS: 37.73190, -8.78301
Post Code: P-7645-300

Beja, Alentejo

Camping Milfontes

www.alanrogers.com/po8180
geral@campingmilfontes.com
Tel: 283 996 140
www.campingmilfontes.com

Open (Touring Pitches):
All year.

This popular site, with good facilities, has the advantage of being open all year and is within walking distance of the town and beach. As such, it makes a perfect base for those visiting out of main season, or for long winter stays when fees are heavily discounted. Well lit and fenced, it has around 500 shady pitches for touring units on sandy terrain, many marked out and divided by hedges. There is an area, mainly for motorcaravans, where you just park under the trees. Some pitches are small and cars may have to be parked in an internal car park. Electricity (6A) is available throughout.

Four clean and well maintained toilet blocks. Two have en-suite units for disabled visitors with ramped entrances. Mainly British style WCs, bidets, washbasins (some with hot water), controllable showers and limited facilities for children. Laundry. Motorcaravan services. Supermarket, bar, snacks and takeaway (all 15/4-30/9). Outdoor pool (15/6-30/9). TV room. Playground. Car wash. Gas supplies. WiFi throughout (free).

Key Features

 Open All Year

 Pets Accepted

 Disabled Facilities

 Swimming Pool

 Play Area

 Bar/Restaurant

Scan me for more information.

Alan Rogers Code: PO8354
33 pitches
GPS: 39.42777, -7.38561
Post Code: P-7330-013

Portalegre, Alentejo

www.alanrogers.com/po8354
info@campingbeiramarvao.com
Tel: 935 041 588
www.campingbeiramarvao.com

Open (Touring Pitches):
All Year

Beira-Marvao Alentejo

Beirã-Marvão is a family run campsite close to the Spanish border, in the Serra de São Mamede National Park. This is very much rural camping and the Dutch owners' aim is that the campsite should have a negligible impact on the surroundings. After the attractive traditional reception building, a rough track climbs to the hill-top where there are touring pitches on roughly-cut terraces between olive trees. The track then descends to an open field, with more olive trees, where there are further pitches. There is space for 20 touring units and 10 tents, with 30 electrical connections (6/10A) available; long cables, and possibly levelling blocks, may be needed in places. The surrounding National Park is a haven for walkers and birdwatchers, many rare raptors nest within the park and the owners will provide details of walks in the area that take advantage of viewing points.

Key Features

 Open All Year

 Pets Accepted

 Disabled Facilities

 Swimming Pool

 Bar/Restaurant

 Bike Hire

Modern shower block with spacious, controllable showers, open-style washbasins with cold water only (but hot tap outside). Service washes. Small bar and restaurant (1/4-31/12). Snacks from reception and take away meals (winter season). Two small pre-cast, no-frills pools - parental supervision of children essential (1/1-31-12). Car hire. Powerful telescope can be borrowed to study night sky. Charcoal barbecues not permitted. Bicycle hire. Max. 1 dog. WiFi at bar (free).

Scan me for more information.

Alan Rogers Code: PO8200
46 accommodations
700 pitches
GPS: 37.09940, -8.71750
Post Code: 8600-148

Lagos, Faro

www.alanrogers.com/po8200
infovalverde@orbitur.pt
Tel: 282 789 211
www.orbitur.com

Open (Touring Pitches):
All Year.

Orbitur Valverde

Just 1.5 km from Playa da Luz and 6 km from the town of Lagos, you will find the Orbitur Valverde campsite. It is large, with around 700 numbered pitches, a spacious area and ample shade. It has four showers blocks and swimming pools for adults and children, free to users, as well as a leisure centre, which is lit at night. It offers a wide choice of accommodation with modern facilities, social areas, bar and terraces, restaurant, self-service and a mini-market. A visit to Lagos is recommended - a historic city which was the centre of trade between Africa and Portugal, the marina, Sagres town and Cabo de São Vicente. Close to the village of Praia da Luz and its beach, this large, well-run site is certainly worth considering for your stay in the Algarve. It has pitches of varying sizes, either enclosed by hedges or on open, gently sloping ground.

Six large, clean, toilet blocks have controllable hot showers but only cold water to open style washbasins. Units for disabled campers. Laundry. Motorcaravan services. Supermarket, self-service restaurant and takeaway (1/6-30/9). Shop for basics and small bar/coffee bar in reception (1/10-31/5). Swimming pool (Easter-30/9) with paddling pool. Playground. Tennis. Lounge with TV. Games room. WiFi over part of site (free).

Key Features

 Open All Year

 Pets Accepted

 Disabled Facilities

 Beach Access

 Swimming Pool

 Play Area

 Bar/Restaurant

Scan me for more information.

Alan Rogers Code: PO8202
108 accommodations
240 pitches
GPS: 37.10111, -8.73278
Post Code: P-8600-109

Faro, Algarve

www.alanrogers.com/po8202
info@turiscampo.com
Tel: 282 789 265
www.turiscampo.com/en

Open (Touring Pitches):
All Year

Turiscampo Algarve

Yelloh! Village Turiscampo is an outstanding site which has been thoughtfully refurbished and updated since it was purchased by the friendly Coll family in 2003. The site provides 240 pitches for touring units, mainly in rows of terraces, 197 of which have 6/10A electricity, some with shade. There are 43 deluxe pitches with water and drain. The upper terraces are occupied by 132 bungalows for rent. Just down the road is the fashionable resort of Praia de Luz with a beach, shops, bars and restaurants. Head west and the road takes you to Sagres and the western tip of the Algarve. Portugal's 'Land's End' remains unspoilt and there are numerous rocky coves and little sandy beaches to explore. A member of Leading Campings group.

Two heated toilet blocks provide outstanding facilities. There is a third facility beneath the pool. Spacious controllable showers, hot water throughout. Children & baby room. Facilities for disabled visitors. Dog shower. Laundry facilities. Shop. Gas supplies. Modern restaurant/bar with buffet & some theme party dinners. Pizza bar & takeaway. Swimming pools (all year) with extensive terrace & Jacuzzi. Aquagym. Wellness facility. Bicycle hire. Entertainment on the bar terrace. Miniclub. Two playgrounds. Boules. Archery. Multisports court, WiFi (partial coverage) on payment.

Key Features

 Open All Year

 Pets Accepted

 Disabled Facilities

 Swimming Pool

 Play Area

 Bar/Restaurant

 Bike Hire

Scan me for more information.

OPEN ALL YEAR ● **HEATED INDOOR POOL** ● **OUTDOOR SWIMMING POOL** ● **SPA & GYM**

Turiscampo
camping bungalow park

LeadingCampings

yelloh! VILLAGE

E.N. 125, Km17 Espiche 8600-109 Lagos-Algarve-Portugal | T. +351 282 789 265 | info@turiscampo.com | www.turiscampo.com

Alan Rogers Code: PO8230
35 accommodations
800 pitches
GPS: 37.03528, -7.82250
Post Code: P-8700

Faro, Algarve

Camping Olhão

www.alanrogers.com/po8230
parque.campismo@sbsi.pt
Tel: 289 700 300
www.sbsi.pt/atividadesindical/
Servicos/ParquedeCampismo

Open (Touring Pitches):
All Year

The large, sandy beaches in this area are on offshore islands reached by ferry and are, as a result, relatively quiet. This site, on the edge of town, has around 800 pitches, all with 6A electrical connections available. Its many mature trees provide good shade. The pitches are marked in rows divided by shrubs, although levelling will be necessary in places and the trees make access tricky on some. There is a separate area for tents and places for very large motorcaravans. Seasonal units take up one fifth of the pitches, the touring pitches filling up quickly in July and August, so arrive early. The site has a relaxed, casual atmosphere, though there is some subdued noise in the lower area from an adjacent railway.

Key Features

 Open All Year

 Pets Accepted

 Disabled Facilities

 Swimming Pool

 Play Area

 Bar/Restaurant

 Bike Hire

Eleven sanitary blocks are adequate, kept clean even when busy and are well sited so that any pitch is close to one. Two blocks have facilities for disabled visitors. Laundry. Excellent supermarket. Kiosk. Restaurant/bar. Café and general room with cable TV. Playgrounds. Swimming pools (all year, charged in season). Tennis courts. Bicycle hire. Internet at reception and Free WI-FI

Scan me for more information.

Capital Ljubljana
Currency Euro (€)
Language Slovene
Telephone country code 00 386
Time Zone CET (GMT/UTC+1)
Tourist Office slovenia.info

Climate Cold, sometimes snowy winters and warm summers with highs of 21 degrees celcius. Coastal areas enjoy a submediterranean climate.

Slovenia

What Slovenia lacks in size it makes up for in exceptional beauty. Situated between Italy, Austria, Hungary and Croatia, it has a diverse landscape with stunning Alps, rivers, forests and the warm Adriatic coast.

Mount Triglav is at the heart of the snow-capped Julian Alps, a paradise for lovers of the great outdoors, with opportunities for hiking, rafting and mountaineering. From the Alps down to the Adriatic coast, the Karst region is home to the famous Lipizzaner horses, vineyards and myriad underground caves, including the Portojna and Skocjan Caves.

The tiny Adriatic coast has several bustling beach towns including Koper, Slovenia's only commercial port, whose 500 years of Venetian rule is evident in its Italianate style. Ljubljana, one of Europe's smallest capitals with beautiful baroque buildings, lies on the Ljubljanica river, spanned by numerous bridges, including Jože Plečnik's triple bridge.

The old city and castle sit alongside a thriving commercial centre. Heading eastwards, the hilly landscape is dotted with monasteries, churches and castles, including the 13th century Zuzemberk castle, one of Slovenia's most picturesque. The Posavje region produces cviček, a famous blend of white and red wines.

Shops Opening hours vary throughout the year. In high-season 8am to 7pm weekdays, to 1pm Saturdays.

Banks 8.30am to 12.30pm and 2pm to 5pm weekdays.

Travelling with Children Great for children during the summer months. The capital is full to the brim with things to do with little ones. Most regions have grand castles that children will love exploring. Locals are friendly and welcoming and distances are short. Most attractions won't charge for children under 7 years of age and those under 15 will pay a discounted fee. Most restaurants will cater for children.

Public Holidays New Year's Day, Preseren Day 8 Feb, Easter Monday, Resistance Day 27 Apr, May Day 1 May, Statehood Day 25 Jun, Assumption, Reformation Day 31 Oct, All Saints' 1 Nov, Christmas Day, Independence Day 26 Dec.

Motoring A small but expanding network of motorways. A 'vignette' system for motorway travel is in place. The cost is around €35 (for a six-month vignette) and they can be purchased at petrol stations and DARS offices in Slovenia and near the border. Winter driving equipment (winter tyres and snow chains) is mandatory between 15 No and 15 March. Headlights must be on at all times. You are also required to carry a reflective jacket, warning triangle and first aid kit in the vehicle. Do not drink and drive.

See campsite map page 474.

Alan Rogers Code: SV4410
150 accommodations
300 pitches
GPS: 46.67888, 16.22165
Post Code: SLO-9226

Moravske Toplice, Slovenia

www.alanrogers.com/sv4410
recepcija.camp2@terme3000.si
Tel: 025 121 200
www.terme3000.si

Open (Touring Pitches):
All year.

Camping Terme 3000

Camping Terme 3000 is a large site with over 400 pitches. Three hundred are for touring units (all with 16A electricity, 30 with hardstanding), the remaining pitches being taken by seasonal campers. On a grass and gravel surface (hard tent pegs may be needed), the level, numbered pitches are of 50-100 sq.m. The site is part of an enormous thermal spa and fun pool complex (free entry to campers) under the same name. There are over 5,000 sq.m. of water activities – swimming, jet streams, waterfalls, water massages, four water slides (the longest is 170 m.) and thermal baths.

Modern and clean toilet facilities provide British style toilets, open washbasins and controllable, free hot showers. Laundry facilities. Football field. Tennis. Water gymnastics. Daily activity programme for children. Golf. WiFi (charged).

Key Features

 Open All Year

 Pets Accepted

 Swimming Pool

 Play Area

 Bar/Restaurant

 Bike Hire

 Golf

Scan me for more information.

Kamp Koren

Alan Rogers Code: SV4270
8 accommodations
100 pitches
GPS: 46.25100, 13.58680
Post Code: SI-5222

Kobarid, Slovenia

www.alanrogers.com/sv4270
info@kamp-koren.si
Tel: 053 891 311
www.campingslovenia.com

Open (Touring Pitches):
All Year

Kamp Koren is situated in picturesque valley by the Soča river, 500 m from historical town Kobarid. A unique campsite and sole holder of the eco certificates: EU Ecolabel and Ecocamping. Its policy is to keep the environment clean and have minimum effect on nature. Slovenia's first ecological site is in a quiet location above the emerald coloured river, within easy walking distance of Kobarid. The site has slightly sloping pitches, all with 6/16A electricity and ample tree shade. It is deservedly very popular with those interested in outdoor sports, be it on the water, in the mountains or in the air. At the same time, its peaceful location makes it an ideal choice for those seeking a relaxing break. At the top of the site there are also a number of well equipped chalets and a shady area, mainly for tents and glamping.

Three attractive and well maintained log-built toilet blocks, two recently renovated. Facilities for disabled visitors. Laundry facilities. Motorcaravan services. Shop (March-Nov). Café/Bar serves light meals, snacks and drinks (flexible closing hours). TV. Multi-purpose hall. Play area. Volleyball. Table tennis. Boules. Gym. Fishing. Bicycle hire. Canoe hire. Climbing walls. Adventure park. Communal barbecue. Sauna. Grocery shop with eco products and electric vehicle charging station. WiFi.

Key Features

 Open All Year

 Pets Accepted

 Disabled Facilities

 Play Area

 Bar/Restaurant

 Skiing

 Bike Hire

 Fishing

Scan me for more information.

Alan Rogers Code: SV4455
80 accommodations
80 pitches
GPS: 46.55167, 16.45842
Post Code: SLO-9220

Lendava, Slovenia

Camping Terme Lendava

www.alanrogers.com/sv4455
info@terme-lendava.si
Tel: 025 774 400
www.terme-lendava.si

Open (Touring Pitches):
All year.

Camping Terme Lendava forms part of an important thermal resort holiday complex, located at the meeting point of Slovenia, Hungary and Croatia. This is an all-year site with 80 grassy pitches, most with electricity connections, and eight hardstandings. Lendava is an open site with views over the vineyards, although some pitches around the edge have shade from mature trees. Campers have access to a large swimming pool complex as well as the resort's various thermal facilities, including bathing in water with paraffin content, considered to be an effective treatment for rheumatic disorders. There are several good restaurants within the complex. Special facilities are also available for naturist bathers.

Two toilet blocks, one older and one a modern prefabricated unit, have open washbasins, controllable showers and communal changing. Laundry available in hotel. Shop, bar and restaurant in hotel. Swimming pool. Thermal complex with indoor and outdoor pools. Paddling pool. Play area. Entertainment programme. WiFi (charged).

Key Features

 Open All Year

 Pets Accepted

 Swimming Pool

 Play Area

 Bar/Restaurant

Scan me for
more information.

Alan Rogers Code: SV4200
8 accommodations
280 pitches
GPS: 46.36155, 14.08075
Post Code: SLO-4260

Bled, Slovenia

www.alanrogers.com/sv4200
info@camping-bled.com
Tel: 045 752 000
www.camping-bled.com

Open (Touring Pitches):
25 March - 15 October, 20 December
- 6 January.

Camping Bled

Camping Bled is situated on the western tip of Lake Bled. The waterfront here has a small public beach, immediately behind which runs a gently sloping narrow wooded valley. There are wonderful views across the lake towards its famous island. Pitches at the front, used mainly for overnighters, are now marked, separated by trees and enlarged, bringing the total number to 280. All are on gravel/grass with 16A electricity. A railway line passes close by but it is only a local line with few trains and they do not disturb the peacefulness of the site.

Toilet facilities in five blocks are of a high standard (with free hot showers). Three blocks are heated. Private bathrooms for rent. Solar energy used. Washing machines and dryers. Motorcaravan services. Gas supplies. Fridge hire. Supermarket. Restaurant. Play area and children's zoo. Games area. Trampolines. Organised activities in July/Aug including children's club, excursions and sporting activities. Mountain bike tours. Live entertainment. Fishing. Bicycle hire. Free WiFi over site.

Key Features

 Pets Accepted

 Disabled Facilities

 Play Area

 Bar/Restaurant

 Bike Hire

 Fishing

Scan me for more information.

Alan Rogers Code: SV4405
25 accommodations
200 pitches
GPS: 46.31168, 14.90913
Post Code: SLO-3332

Recica ob Savinji, Slovenia

www.alanrogers.com/sv4405
info@campingmenina.com
Tel: 035 835 027
www.campingmenina.com

Open (Touring Pitches):
All year.

Camping Menina

Camping Menina is in the heart of the 35 km. long Upper Savinja Valley, surrounded by 2,500 m. high mountains and unspoilt nature. It is being improved every year by the young, enthusiastic owner, Jurij Kolenc, and has 200 pitches, all for touring units, on grassy fields under mature trees and with access from gravel roads. All have 10A electricity. The Savinja river runs along one side of the site, but if the water is too cold, the site also has a lake which can be used for swimming. This site is a perfect base for walking or mountain biking in the mountains.

Four sanitary blocks have modern fittings with toilets, open plan washbasins and controllable hot showers. Washing machine. Motorcaravan services. Bar/restaurant with open-air terrace (1/5-31/10) and open-air kitchen. Sauna. Playing field. Play area. Tree-top zip wire. Fishing. Russian bowling. Excursions (52). Live music and gatherings around the camp fire. Hostel. Skiing in winter. Climbing wall. Rafting. Kayaking. Mountain bike hire. Mobile homes to rent. WiFi (free).

Key Features

 Open All Year

 Pets Accepted

 Bar/Restaurant

 Skiing

 Bike Hire

 Fishing

 Sailing

 Scan me for more information.

Alan Rogers Code: SV4340
12 accommodations
177 pitches
GPS: 46.09752, 14.51870
Post Code: SLO-1000

Ljubljana, Slovenia

www.alanrogers.com/sv4340
resort@gpl.si
Tel: 00386 1 589 01 41
www.ljubljanaresort.si

Open (Touring Pitches):
All Year

Camping Ljubljana Resort

Located only five kilometres north of central Ljubljana, on the relatively quiet bank of the River Sava, Ljubljana Resort is an ideal city campsite. This relaxed site is attached to, but effectively separated from, the sparklingly modern Laguna swimming pool complex. This is open between mid June and the beginning of September and a small, discounted charge is made in order for campers to gain access. The site has 177 pitches, largely situated between mature trees and all with 16A electricity connections. The main building and the pool complex provide several bars, restaurants and takeaways to cater for the campsite guests and day visitors.

The modern toilet block includes facilities for disabled, a baby room and children's toilet and shower. Motorcaravan services. Laundry room. Restaurant and bar with terrace. Outdoor swimming pool (17/6-31/8). Play area. Entertainment for children in July/Aug. TV lounge. Barbecue area. Fitness centre. Beach volleyball. Bicycle hire. Airport transfer service. WiFi throughout (free in reception, restaurant, pool).

Key Features

 Open All Year

 Pets Accepted

 Disabled Facilities

 Swimming Pool

 Play Area

 Bar/Restaurant

 Skiing

 Bike Hire

Scan me for more information.

Capital Madrid
Currency Euro (€)
Language Spanish and regional variants
Telephone country code 00 34
Time Zone CET (GMT/UTC+1)
Tourist Office tourspain.co.uk

Climate The north is temperate with most of the rainfall; dry and very hot in the centre; sub-tropical along the Mediterranean.

Spain

One of the largest countries in Europe with glorious beaches, a fantastic sunshine record, vibrant towns and laid back sleepy villages, plus a diversity of landscape, culture and artistic traditions, Spain has all the ingredients for a great holiday.

Spain's vast and diverse coastline is a magnet for visitors; glitzy, hedonistic resorts packed with bars and clubs are a foil to secluded coves backed by wooded cliffs. Yet Spain has much more to offer – the verdant north with its ancient pilgrimage routes where the Picos de Europa sweep down to the Atlantic gems of Santander and Bilbao. Vibrant Madrid in the heart of the country boasts the Prado with works by Velázquez and Goya, the beautiful cobbled Plaza Major, plus all the attractions of a capital city. Passionate Andalucía in the south dazzles with the symbolic arts of bullfighting and flamenco beneath a scorching sun. It offers the cosmopolitan cities of Córdoba, Cádiz and Málaga, alongside magnificent examples of the past such as the Alhambra at Granada. On the Mediterranean east coast, Valencia has a wealth of monuments and cultural sites, including the magnificent City of Arts and Science.

Shops 10am to 2pm and 4.30 to 7.30pm or 5am to 8pm weekdays. Big supermarkets and department stores generally open 10am to 10pm Monday to Saturday.

Banks 8.30am to 2pm weekdays, some also open 4pm to 7pm Thursday and 9am to 1pm Saturday.

Travelling with Children Spain is very family-friendly and has a good range of attractions for all ages. Its transport network is excellent, many restaurants cater well for kids and its beaches are safe. During the summer months, daytime temperatures in central Spain can reach 40+ degrees Celcius. The weather remains warm well into October.

Public Holidays New Year's Day, Epiphany, Good Friday, Labour Day, Assumption, Hispanic Day 12 Oct, All Saints' 1 Nov, Constitution Day 6 Dec, Immaculate Conception Day 8 Dec, Christmas Day.

Motoring The surface of the main roads is on the whole good, although secondary roads in some rural areas can be rough and winding. Tolls are payable on certain roads and for the Cadi Tunnel, Vallvidrera Tunnel and the Tunnel de Garraf on the A16.

See campsite map pages 478, 484, 485.

Camping Nautic Almata

Alan Rogers Code: ES80300
32 accommodations
1100 pitches
GPS: 42.20608, 3.10389
Post Code: E-17486

Girona, Cataluña-Catalunya

www.alanrogers.com/es80300
info@almata.com
Tel: 0034 972 454 477
www.almata.com

Open (Touring Pitches):
17 May - 15 September

In the Bay of Roses, south of Empuriabrava and beside the Parc Natural dels Aiguamolls de l'Empordà, this is a high quality site of particular interest to nature lovers (especially birdwatchers) and families. A large site, there are 1,110 well kept, large, numbered pitches, all with electricity and on flat, sandy ground. Beautifully laid out, it is arranged around the river and waterways, so will suit those who like to be close to water or who enjoy watersports and boating. It is also a superb beachside site.

Sanitary blocks of a very high standard include some en-suite showers with washbasins. Good facilities for disabled visitors. Washing machines. Gas supplies. Excellent supermarket. Restaurants, pizzeria and bar. Two separate bars and snack bar by beach where discos are held in main season. Sailing, diving and windsurfing schools. 300 sq.m. swimming pool. Tennis courts. Badminton. Paddle tennis. Minigolf. Games room. Children's play park and miniclub. Fishing (licence required). Car, motorcycle and bicycle hire. Hairdresser. Internet access and WiFi over site (charged). ATM. Torches are useful near beach.

Key Features

 Pets Accepted

 Disabled Facilities

 Beach Access

 Swimming Pool

 Play Area

 Bar/Restaurant

 Bike Hire

 Fishing

Scan me for more information.

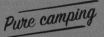

Girona cityscape

Alan Rogers Code: ES80400
100 accommodations
1500 pitches
GPS: 42.16098, 3.10777
Post Code: E-17470

Girona, Cataluña-Catalunya

www.alanrogers.com/es80400
info@campinglasdunas.com
Tel: 972 521 717
www.campinglasdunas.com

Open (Touring Pitches):
20 May - 15 September.

Camping Las Dunas

Las Dunas is an extremely large, impressive and well organised resort-style site with many on-site activities and an ongoing programme of improvements. It has direct access to a superb sandy beach that stretches along the site for nearly a kilometre with a windsurfing school and beach bar. There is also a much used, huge swimming pool, plus a large double pool for children which opened in 2015. Las Dunas has 1,700 individual hedged pitches (1,500 for touring units) of around 100 sq.m. laid out on flat ground in long, regular parallel rows. All have electricity (6/10A) and 400 have water and drainage.

Five excellent large toilet blocks with electronic sliding glass doors. Toilets without seats, controllable hot showers and washbasins in cabins. Excellent facilities for children, babies and disabled campers. Laundry facilities. Motorcaravan services. Supermarket, boutique and other shops. Large bar with terrace. Large restaurant & takeaway. Ice cream parlour. Beach bar (seasonal). Disco club. Swimming pools. Adventure crazy golf. Playgrounds. Tennis. Minigolf. Sailing/windsurfing school and other watersports. Programme of sports, games, excursions and entertainment, partly in English. Exchange facilities. ATM. Safety deposit. Internet café. WiFi over site (charged). Dogs taken in one section. Torches required in some areas.

Key Features

 Pets Accepted

 Disabled Facilities

 Beach Access

 Swimming Pool

 Play Area

 Bar/Restaurant

 Bike Hire

 Fishing

Scan me for
more information.

Alan Rogers Code: ES80500
7 accommodations
445 pitches
GPS: 42.17728, 3.10793
Post Code: E-17470

Girona, Cataluña-Catalunya

Camping Aquarius

www.alanrogers.com/es80500
booking@campingaquarius.com
Tel: 972 520 101
www.campingaquarius.com/en

Open (Touring Pitches):
15 March - 31 October

This is a welcoming and organised family site approached by an attractive road flanked by orchards. Aquarius has direct access to a quiet, sandy beach that slopes gently and provides good bathing. Watersports are popular, particularly windsurfing (a school is provided). One third of the site has good shade with a park-like atmosphere. There are 445 touring pitches, all with electricity (6/16A and 6 caravans for hire). Markus Rupp and his wife are keen to make every visitor's experience a happy one. The site is ideal for those who really like sun and sea, with a quiet situation.

Attractively tiled, fully equipped, toilet blocks provide some cabins for each sex. Excellent facilities for disabled visitors, plus baths for children. One block has underfloor heating and family cabins with showers and washbasins. Laundry facilities. Gas supplies. Motorcaravan services. Full size refrigerators. Supermarket. Pleasant restaurant and bar with 'chill-out' terrace. Takeaway. Purpose built play centre (with qualified attendant). Playground. TV room. Surf Centre. Yoga and fitness classes. Water playground for children with water slides. Fishing and sailing. Minigolf. Bicycle hire. Guided excursions (e-bikes, bikes and trekking). Live music (twice weekly in high season, once a week low season). ATM. Internet. WiFi over site (charged). Charging station for e-vehicles. Dogs are accepted in one section.

Key Features

 Pets Accepted

 Disabled Facilities

 Beach Access

 Play Area

 Bar/Restaurant

 Bike Hire

 Fishing

 Sailing

Scan me for more information.

Alan Rogers Code: ES80350
138 accommodations
692 pitches
GPS: 42.18147, 3.10405
Post Code: E-17470

Girona, Cataluña-Catalunya

www.alanrogers.com/es80350
info@campingamfora.com
Tel: 972 520 540
www.campingamfora.com

Open (Touring Pitches):
23 April 2018 - 28 September 2018

Camping l'Amfora

This spacious, friendly site is run by Michelle, Josep and their daughter. It is spotlessly clean and well maintained and the owners operate the site in an environmentally friendly way. There are 830 level, grass pitches (692 for touring units) laid out in a grid system, all with 10A electricity. Attractive trees and shrubs have been planted around each pitch. There is good shade in the more mature areas, which include 64 large pitches (180 sq.m), each with an individual sanitary unit (toilet, shower and washbasin). The newer area is more open with less shade and you can choose which you would prefer.

Three excellent sanitary blocks, one heated, provide washbasins in cabins and roomy free showers. Baby rooms. Laundry facilities and service. Motorcaravan services. Supermarket. Terraced bar, self-service and waiter-service restaurants. Pizzeria/takeaway. Restaurant and bar on the beach with limited menu (high season). Disco bar. Swimming pools with 2 new long waterslides for the 2017 season (1/5-27/9) as also SPA area. Pétanque. Tennis. Minigolf. Play area. Miniclub. Entertainment and activities. Windsurfing. Kite surfing (low season).Sailing, kayak, fishing. Games rooms. Bicycle hire. Internet room and WiFi over site (charged). Car wash. Torches required in most areas.

Key Features

 Pets Accepted

 Disabled Facilities

 Beach Access

 Swimming Pool

 Play Area

 Bar/Restaurant

 Bike Hire

 Fishing

Scan me for more information.

Alan Rogers Code: ES80720
12 accommodations
170 pitches
GPS: 42.04800, 3.18810
Post Code: E-17258

Girona, Cataluña-Catalunya

www.alanrogers.com/es80720
info@campinglesmedes.com
Tel: 972 751 805
www.campinglesmedes.com

Open (Touring Pitches):
All year.

Camping les Medes

Les Medes is different from some of the 'all singing, all dancing' sites so popular along this coast. The friendly family of Pla-Coll are rightly proud of their innovative and award-winning site, which they have owned for almost 30 years. With just 170 pitches, the site is small enough for the owners and their staff to know their visitors, some of whom have been coming for many years. The top class facilities, along with the personal attention and activities available, make this a year-round home in the sun. The level, grassy pitches range in size from 70-80 sq.m. and are shaded. All have electricity (5/10A) and 155 also have water and drainage.

Two modern spacious sanitary blocks can be heated and are extremely well maintained. Washbasins in cabins, top class facilities for disabled visitors. Baby baths. Washing machines and dryer. Dog bathing room. Motorcaravan services. Shop. Bar with snacks and pizza (all year). Good value restaurant (1/4-31/10). Swimming and paddling pools (1/5-15/9). Indoor pool with sauna, solarium and massage (15/9-15/6). Play area. TV room. Entertainment, activities and excursions (July/Aug). Diving activities. Multisports area. Boules. Bicycle hire and self-repair shop. Internet access and WiFi. Torches are useful. Dogs are not accepted in July/Aug.

Key Features

 Open All Year

 Pets Accepted

 Disabled Facilities

 Swimming Pool

 Play Area

 Bar/Restaurant

 Skiing

 Bike Hire

Scan me for more information.

Alan Rogers Code: ES81010
105 accommodations
650 pitches
GPS: 42.00113, 3.19380
Post Code: E-17256

Girona, Cataluña-Catalunya

www.alanrogers.com/es81010
info@playabrava.com
Tel: 972 636 894
www.playabrava.com

Open (Touring Pitches):
18 May - 7 September

Camping Playa Brava

This is an attractive and efficiently run site with an open feel, having direct access to an excellent soft sand beach and a freshwater lagoon. The ground is level and grassy with shade provided for many of the 650 spacious touring pitches by a mixture of conifer and broadleaf trees. All the pitches have 10A electricity and 238 have water and drainage. The large swimming pool has an extensive grass sunbathing area and is overlooked by the terrace of the restaurant and bar. This is a clean, secure and pleasant family site, suitable for sightseeing and for those who enjoy beach and water activities.

Five modern, fully equipped toilet blocks include facilities for disabled visitors. Washing machines and dryers. Motorcaravan services. Supermarket. Bar/restaurant. Takeaway. Swimming pool. Pétanque. Tennis. Minigolf. Beach volleyball. Play area. Bicycle hire. Watersports on beach. Stage show. Internet. WiFi over site (charged). Satellite TV. Gas supplies. Dogs are not accepted.

Key Features

 Disabled Facilities

 Beach Access

 Swimming Pool

 Play Area

 Bar/Restaurant

 Bike Hire

Golf

Scan me for more information.

Alan Rogers Code: ES81400
165 accommodations
371 pitches
GPS: 41.83631, 3.08711
Post Code: E-17250

Girona, Cataluña-Catalunya

www.alanrogers.com/es81400
info@campingtreumal.com
Tel: 972 651 095
www.campingtreumal.com/en

Open (Touring Pitches):
23 March - 30 September

Camping Treumal

This very attractive terraced site has been developed on a hillside around the beautiful gardens of a large, spectacular estate house which is close to the sea. The house is the focus of the site's excellent facilities, including a superb restaurant with terraces overlooking two tranquil beaches, protected in pretty coves. The site has 542 pitches on well shaded terraces. Of these, 371 are accessible to touring units and there are some 50 pitches on flat ground alongside the sea – the views are stunning and you wake to the sound of the waves. Electricity (6/10/16A) is available in all parts. Cars must be left on car parks or the site roads.

Four well maintained sanitary blocks have free hot water in the washbasins (with some private cabins) and controllable showers, and a tap to draw from for the sinks. No facilities for disabled visitors. New beach block. Washing machines. Motorcaravan services. Gas supplies. Supermarket, bar and takeaway (all season). Restaurant (15/6-15/9). Beach bar. Fishing. Play area. Sports area. Games room. Bicycle hire. Satellite TV. Internet access and WiFi (charged). ATM. Safes. Dogs are not accepted.

Key Features

 Beach Access

 Swimming Pool

 Play Area

 Bar/Restaurant

 Bike Hire

 Fishing

Sailing

Scan me for
more information.

Alan Rogers Code: ES81300
103 accommodations
466 pitches
GPS: 41.83333, 3.08417
Post Code: E-17251

Girona, Cataluña-Catalunya

www.alanrogers.com/es81300
info@intercalonge.com
Tel: 972 651 233
www.intercalonge.com

Open (Touring Pitches):
All year.

Camping de Calonge

This spacious, well laid out site has access to a fine beach via a footbridge over the coast road. Calonge is a family site with two attractive pools on different levels, a paddling pool and large sunbathing areas. A restaurant, bar and snack bar with great views are by the pool. The 466 touring pitches are on terraces and all have electricity (5A), with 84 being fully serviced. There is good shade from the tall pine trees, and there are some spectacular coastal views. Some access roads and steps are steep, but a road train operates in high season. There are wonderful views from the upper levels where there are some larger comfort pitches. The pools are overlooked by the restaurant terraces which have great views over the mountains.

Generous sanitary provision. One block is heated in winter. Laundry facilities. Motorcaravan services. Gas supplies. Shop (25/3-30/10). Restaurant (1/2-31/12). Bar, patio bar with pizzas and takeaway (25/3-30/9, weekends for the rest of the year). Swimming pools (25/3-12/10). Playground. Electronic games. Disco two nights a week (but not late) in high season. Bicycle hire. Tennis. Hairdresser. ATM. WiFi (free in hotspots). Torches necessary in some areas. Road train from the bottom of the site to the top in high season.

Key Features

 Open All Year

 Pets Accepted

 Disabled Facilities

 Swimming Pool

 Play Area

 Bar/Restaurant

 Bike Hire

Scan me for more information.

Alan Rogers Code: ES81750
90 accommodations
327 pitches
GPS: 41.81117, 3.01822
Post Code: E-17246

Girona, Cataluña-Catalunya

www.alanrogers.com/es81750
info@campingmassantjosep.com
Tel: 972 835 108
www.campingmassantjosep.com

Open (Touring Pitches):
18 May - 16 September

Yelloh! Village Mas Sant Josep

This is a very large, well appointed, open site in two parts. There are 1,023 level pitches (100 sq.m) with 327 for touring units in a separate area which has shade from established trees. All have 10A electricity connections. There are wide access roads and long avenues between the zones. The main side of the site is centred around charming historic buildings, including a beautiful, but mysterious, locked and long unused chapel. Nearby is a huge, irregular lagoon-style pool with a bridge to a palm decorated island (lifeguards) and an excellent, safe paddling pool. A large complex including a bar, restaurant, takeaway and entertainment areas overlooks the pool.

Two adequate toilet blocks for touring units (ignore the block for permanent pitches). Very good facilities for disabled visitors and pleasant baby rooms. Washing machines. Dryers. Large supermarket, bars, restaurant, snack bar and takeaway, swimming pools (all open as site). Safe playgrounds. Huge, well equipped games room. Tennis. Squash. Minigolf. 5-a-side football. Spa room and gym. Entertainment programme. Hairdresser. Internet. WiFi over part of site (charged). ATM. Bicycle hire. Torches useful. Dogs only in designated areas.

Key Features

 Pets Accepted

 Disabled Facilities

 Swimming Pool

 Play Area

 Bar/Restaurant

 Bike Hire

Scan me for more information.

Alan Rogers Code: ES84800
417 accommodations
976 pitches
GPS: 41.07546, 1.11651
Post Code: E-43840

Tarragona, Cataluña-Catalunya

www.alanrogers.com/es84800
mail@sangulisalou.com
Tel: 977 381 641
www.sangulisalou.com

Open (Touring Pitches):
23 March - 4 November

Camping Resort Sangulí Salou

Camping Resort Sangulí Salou is a superb site boasting excellent pools and entertainment. Owned, developed and managed by a local Spanish family, it has something for all the family with everything open when the site is open. There are 976 pitches of varying sizes (75-120 sq.m) all with electricity (7.5-10A). Mobile homes occupy 58 pitches and there are fully equipped bungalows on 147. A wonderful selection of trees, palms and shrubs provide natural shade and an ideal space for children to play. The good sandy beach is little more than 50 metres across the coast road and a small railway crossing. Although large, Sangulí has a pleasant, open feel and maintains a quality family atmosphere due to the efforts of the very keen and efficient staff.

The six sanitary blocks are constantly cleaned and are always exceptional, including many individual cabins with en-suite facilities. Improvements are made each year. Some blocks have excellent facilities for babies. Launderette with service. Motorcaravan services. Car wash (charged). Gas supplies. Snack bars. Indoor and outdoor restaurants with takeaway. Swimming pools. Fitness centre. Sports complex. Bicycle hire. Fitness room (charged). Playgrounds including adventure play area. Miniclub. Minigolf. Free WiFi throughout. Security bracelets. Medical centre.

Key Features

 Pets Accepted

 Disabled Facilities

 Beach Access

 Swimming Pool

 Play Area

 Bar/Restaurant

 Skiing

 Bike Hire

Scan me for more information.

Alan Rogers Code: ES84845
19 accommodations
200 pitches
GPS: 41.15008, 1.42096
Post Code: E-43830

Tarragona, Cataluña-Catalunya

www.alanrogers.com/es84845
info@camping-lanoria.com
Tel: 977 64 0453
www.camping-lanoria.com

Open (Touring Pitches):
1 April - 1 October.

Camping La Noria

La Noria is just over five acres in size with over 200 level touring pitches all having access to electricity (6A). Most of the touring pitches have good shade and the motorcaravan areas have hardstanding. A central cafeteria-style restaurant and small supermarket cater for most needs. Entertainment is available for young children with the multisport pitch and pétanque for those a bit older. The Mediterranean coast, with its clean sandy beaches, is a short, traffic free, walk away via a dedicated tunnel under the coastal railway line. La Noria is about 70 km. south west of Barcelona making it ideally situated for day trips whilst having access to sandy beaches and tranquil Catalonia countryside.

Two modern toilet blocks include open style washbasins and showers. Facilities for disabled visitors. Laundry room. Motorcaravan services. Family restaurant. Bar. Multisports court. Play areas. Accommodation for rent. Direct beach access. Free WiFi throughout (with code).

Key Features

 Pets Accepted

 Disabled Facilities

 Beach Access

 Play Area

 Bar/Restaurant

Scan me for more information.

Alan Rogers Code: ES85370
132 accommodations
300 pitches
GPS: 40.97723, 0.90093
Post Code: E-43890

Tarragona, Cataluña-Catalunya

www.alanrogers.com/es85370
info@eltemplodelsol.com
Tel: 977 823 434
www.eltemplodelsol.com

Open (Touring Pitches):
15 March - 31 October

Naturista El Templo del Sol

El Templo del Sol is a large, luxurious, terraced naturist site with a distinctly Arabesque feel and superb buildings in Moorish style. The owner has designed the magnificent main turreted building at the entrance with fountains and elaborate Moorish arches. The site has over 387 pitches of two different sizes, some with car parking alongside and 118 with full services. There is shade and the pitches are on terraces giving rewarding views over the sea. Attractive steps give ready access to the sandy beach. There is some daytime rail noise especially in the lower areas of the site where the larger pitches are located.

The sanitary blocks are amongst the best providing everything you could require. Extensive facilities for disabled campers. Washing machines. Well stocked supermarket. Health shop. Souvenir shop. Bars. Restaurant, snack bar, swimming pools (all open all season). Jacuzzi. Cinema. Games area. Boules. Separate children's pool and play area. Miniclub. Library. Entertainment. Hairdresser. Bicycle hire. ATM. Dogs are not accepted. No jet skis. WiFi over site (charged).

Key Features

 Naturist Site

 Disabled Facilities

 Beach Access

 Swimming Pool

 Play Area

 Bar/Restaurant

 Bike Hire

Fishing

Scan me for more information.

Tarragona aqueduct

Alan Rogers Code: ES85300
263 accommodations
990 pitches
GPS: 41.03345, 0.96921
Post Code: E-43300

Tarragona, Cataluña-Catalunya

Playa Montroig Camping Resort

www.alanrogers.com/es85300
info@playamontroig.com
Tel: 977 810 637
www.playamontroig.com

Open (Touring Pitches):
29 March - 3 November

What a superb site! Playa Montroig is about 30 kilometres beyond Tarragona, set in its own tropical gardens with direct access to a very long, narrow, soft sand beach. The main part of the site lies between the sea, road and railway (as at other sites on this coast, occasional train noise on some pitches) with a huge underpass. The site is divided into spacious, marked pitches with excellent shade provided by a variety of lush vegetation including very impressive palms set in wide avenues. There are 990 pitches, all with electricity (10A) and 661 with water and drainage. Some 47 pitches are directly alongside the beach. A member of Leading Campings group.

Very good quality sanitary buildings with washbasins in private cabins and separate WCs. Facilities for babies and disabled campers. Several launderettes. Motorcaravan services. Gas. Good shopping centre. Restaurants and bars. Fitness suite. Hairdresser. TV lounges. Beach bar. Playground. Jogging track. Sports area. Tennis. Minigolf. Organised activities including pottery. Pedalo hire. Boat mooring. Bicycle hire. WiFi over site. Dogs are not accepted.

Key Features

 Disabled Facilities

 Beach Access

 Swimming Pool

 Play Area

 Bar/Restaurant

 Bike Hire

 Fishing

Scan me for
more information.

PLAYA MONTROIG
CAMPING RESORT
★★★★★

"Camping in Style"

Tel. +34 977 810 637 · www.playamontroig.com · info@playamontroig.com

Alan Rogers Code: ES85400
230 accommodations
700 pitches
GPS: 41.03707, 0.97478
Post Code: E-43300

Tarragona, Cataluña-Catalunya

Camping La Torre del Sol

www.alanrogers.com/es85400
info@latorredelsol.com
Tel: 977 810 486
www.latorredelsol.com

Open (Touring Pitches):
15 March - 31 October

A pleasant tree-lined approach road gives way to avenues of palms as you arrive at Torre del Sol. This large, well designed site occupies a good position in southern Catalunya with direct access to a 800m. long soft sand beach. The site is exceptionally well maintained. There is good shade on a high proportion of the 1,500 individual, numbered pitches, all of which have electricity (700 for touring.) The site boasts three attractive pools with two jacuzzis in the bar and restaurant area. A seawater jacuzzi and Turkish sauna opened in 2012. Occasional train noise on some pitches.

Key Features

 Disabled Facilities

 Beach Access

 Swimming Pool

 Play Area

 Bar/Restaurant

 Bike Hire

 Fishing

Five very well maintained, fully equipped, toilet blocks include units for disabled visitors, babies & children. Washing machines. Gas supplies. Large supermarket, bakery and souvenir shops at the entrance. Full restaurant. Takeaway. Bar with large terrace with entertainment. Beach bar, coffee bar and ice-cream bar. Pizzeria. Open-roof cinema with permanent seating for 520. 3 TV lounges. Soundproofed disco. Swimming pools (two heated). Solarium. Sauna. Two large jacuzzis. Sports areas. Tennis. Squash. Language school (Spanish). Minigolf. Sub-aqua diving. Bicycle hire. Fishing. Windsurfing school. Sailboards and pedaloes for hire. Playground and crèche. Fridge hire. Library. Hairdresser. Business centre. WiFi. Car repair and car wash. No animals permitted. No jet skis accepted.

Scan me for more information.

CATALUNYA

SEA, WELLNESS AND ANIMATION

ANIMATION NON-STOP
15.03/05.11

TROPICAL OPEN AIR JACUZZI
JACUZZIS WITH WARM SEA WATER

✉ E-43892 MIAMI PLATJA (TARRAGONA)
Tel.: +34 977 810 486 · Fax: +34 977 811 306
www.latorredelsol.com · info@latorredelsol.com

CAMPING RESORTS
soleil VILLAGE

Alan Rogers Code: ES82340
67 accommodations
96 pitches
GPS: 41.64726, 2.76378
Post Code: E-08380

Barcelona, Cataluña-Catalunya

www.alanrogers.com/es82340
info@campingdelmar.com
Tel: 937 653 767
www.campingdelmar.com

Open (Touring Pitches):
27 March - 12 October.

Camping del Mar

Camping del Mar is situated on a quieter part of this coast, some three kilometres from the much larger resort of Blanes. Across the quiet road from the site is a long sandy beach with a lifeguard in high season. Carefully manicured lawns and a well designed site help to create a relaxed atmosphere. All the facilities are kept clean, and the 96 flat, grassy pitches all have electricity (6A) and easy access to a water point. The site is surrounded by a high hedge providing privacy and some shade to those pitches alongside, whilst most of the site has young trees and shrubs providing shade.

Two clean sanitary blocks have showers in large cubicles, open style washbasins and controllable hot water with provisions for disabled visitors and families. Laundry room with washing machines. Small shop and bakery. Bar with TV. Restaurant with varied menu. Games room. Swimming pool with safe separate children's pool. Multisports area. Tennis. Large play area. Minigolf. Children's club and entertainment (July/Aug). Fishing. ATM. Communal barbecue. Bicycle hire. Internet. WiFi over site (charged). Car wash.

Key Features

 Pets Accepted

 Disabled Facilities

 Beach Access

 Swimming Pool

 Play Area

 Bar/Restaurant

 Bike Hire

 Fishing

Scan me for
more information.

Vilanova Park

Alan Rogers Code: ES83900
431 accommodations
343 pitches
GPS: 41.23237, 1.69092
Post Code: E-08800

Barcelona, Cataluña-Catalunya

www.alanrogers.com/es83900
info@vilanovapark.com
Tel: 938 933 402
www.vilanovapark.com

Open (Touring Pitches):
All year.

Sitting on the terrace in front of the restaurant – a beautifully converted Catalan farmhouse dating from 1908 – it is difficult to believe that in 1982 this was still a farm with few trees and known as Mas Roque (Rock Farm). Since then, imaginative planting has led to there being literally thousands of trees and gloriously colourful shrubs making this large campsite most attractive. It has an impressive range of high quality amenities and facilities open all year. There are 343 marked pitches for touring units in separate areas, all with 6/10A electricity, 168 larger pitches also have water and, in some cases, drainage. They are on hard surfaces, on gently sloping ground and with plenty of shade. A further 1,000 or so pitches are mostly occupied by chalets to rent, and by tour operators.

Excellent toilet blocks can be heated and have controllable showers and many washbasins in cabins. Baby rooms. Units for disabled visitors. Serviced and self-service laundry. Motorcaravan services. Supermarket. Souvenir shop. Restaurants. Bar with simple meals and tapas. Outdoor pools (1/4-15/10), indoor pool (all year, charged). Wellness centre including sauna, jacuzzi and gym. Play areas. Sports field. Games room. Excursions. Activity and entertainment programme for all ages. Bicycle hire. Tennis. ATM and exchange facilities. WiFi throughout (charged). Caravan storage.

Key Features

 Open All Year

 Pets Accepted

 Disabled Facilities

 Swimming Pool

 Play Area

 Bar/Restaurant

 Bike Hire

Scan me for more information.

Alan Rogers Code: ES85700
85 accommodations
512 pitches
GPS: 40.12781, 0.15894
Post Code: E-12595

Castelló, Comunidad Valenciana

www.alanrogers.com/es85700
camping@torrelasal2.com
Tel: 964 319 744
www.torrelasal2.com

Open (Touring Pitches):
All year.

Camping Torre la Sal 2

Torre la Sal 2 is a very large site divided into two by a quiet road, with a reception on each side with friendly, helpful staff. There are three pool complexes (one can be covered in cooler weather and is heated) all of which are on the west side, whilst the beach (of shingle and sand) is on the east. Both sides have a restaurant – the one on the beach side has two air-conditioned wooden buildings and a terrace. The 512 flat pitches vary in size, some have their own sinks, and most have shade. All have 10A electricity and a few have a partial view of the sea. There are 85 bungalows around the two areas. This is a high-quality site offering a great choice to campers.

Toilet facilities are of a good standard in both sections, with British style WCs, hot water to some sinks, and facilities for disabled campers. Baby rooms. Washing machines (laundry service if required for a small charge). Motorcaravan services. Shop, bars, restaurants and takeaway. New swimming pool complex complete with flumes (one pool has a bar in the centre). Jacuzzi and sauna (winter). Play park. Large disco. Sports centre. Tennis. Squash. Two football pitches. Pétanque. Outdoor gym. Games room. Bullring. Hairdresser. Varied programme of activities and entertainment. WiFi (charged). Torches are useful.

Key Features

 Open All Year

 Pets Accepted

 Disabled Facilities

 Beach Access

 Swimming Pool

 Play Area

 Bar/Restaurant

 Fishing

Scan me for more information.

Camping Ribamar

Alan Rogers Code: ES85610
41 accommodations
66 pitches
GPS: 40.27028, 0.30673
Post Code: E-12579

Castelló, Comunidad Valenciana

www.alanrogers.com/es85610
info@campingribamar.com
Tel: 964 761 601
www.campingribamar.com

Open (Touring Pitches):
All Year

Camping Ribamar is tucked away within the National Park of the Sierra de Irta, to the north of Alcossebre, and with direct access to a rugged beach. There are two grades of pitches on offer here. A number of standard pitches (30 sq.m) are available for small tents, and all have electrical connections (10A). The majority of pitches are larger (90-100 sq.m) and are classed as premium, with electricity and a water supply. A number of chalets (with air conditioning) are available to rent. Leisure facilities here include a large swimming pool plus delightful children's pool and a paddling pool. A main amenities building is adjacent and houses the site's basic bar/restaurant and shop.

One spotlessly clean toilet block with facilities for babies and campers with disabilities. Laundry facilities. Bar. Restaurant. Shop. Swimming pool. Paddling pool. Multisports terrain. Tennis. Five-a-side football. Boules. Paddle court. Bicycle hire. Play area. Library/social room. Chalets to rent. Direct access to rocky beach. Fishing. WiFi (charged). Charcoal barbecues are not allowed.

Key Features

 Open All Year

 Pets Accepted

 Disabled Facilities

 Beach Access

 Swimming Pool

 Play Area

 Bar/Restaurant

 Bike Hire

Scan me for more information.

Alan Rogers Code: ES86240
23 accommodations
87 pitches
GPS: 39.32296, -0.30957
Post Code: E-46012

Valencia, Comunidad Valenciana

www.alanrogers.com/es86240
contacto@devesagardens.com
Tel: 961 611 136
www.devesagardens.com

Open (Touring Pitches):
All year.

Devesa Gardens

This campsite has recently been acquired by the La Marina Group, and the huge investment made is now starting to show as the comprehensive renovation programme gets underway. It is situated between the Albufera lake and the sea, with rice fields on both sides. The 87 level touring pitches are on sand and gravel, all with 16A electricity hook-ups (2-pin sockets). There are no water connections on pitches at the moment. They are separated by fir hedges and young trees, but there is shade from more mature trees. A modern amenities complex is at the heart of the site and includes a swimming pool, extensive play facilities for children and a large auditorium. Bungalows for rent are located in a separate area from the touring pitches.

Three heated sanitary blocks, one modern, two old and requiring updating. Facilities for disabled visitors and families. Washing machine and dryer. Bar. Restaurant and takeaway. Outdoor swimming pool (lifeguard in Apr-Oct, open to public). Riding school. Bullring. Tennis courts. Play area with bouncy castle. Children's club and entertainment. Mini farm. Boat trips. Bicycle hire. WiFi throughout (free).

Key Features

 Open All Year

 Pets Accepted

 Disabled Facilities

 Swimming Pool

 Play Area

 Bar/Restaurant

 Skiing

 Bike Hire

Scan me for more information.

Alan Rogers Code: ES86150
180 pitches
GPS: 38.93160, -0.09680
Post Code: E-46780

Valencia, Comunidad Valenciana

Kiko Park Oliva

www.alanrogers.com/es86150
kikopark@kikopark.com
Tel: 962 850 905
www.kikopark.com

Open (Touring Pitches):
All Year

Kiko Park is a smart site nestling behind protective sand dunes alongside a Blue Flag beach. There are sets of attractively tiled steps over the dunes or a long boardwalk near the beach bar (good for prams and wheelchairs) to take you to the fine white sandy beach and the sea. From the central reception point (where good English is spoken), flat, fine gravel pitches and access roads are divided to the left and right. Backing onto one another, the 180 large pitches all have electricity and the aim is to progressively upgrade all these with full services. There are plenty of flowers, hedging and trees adding shade, privacy and colour.

Key Features

 Open All Year

 Pets Accepted

 Disabled Facilities

 Beach Access

 Swimming Pool

 Play Area

 Bar/Restaurant

 Bike Hire

Four mature, heated sanitary blocks (one currently closed for renovation) include facilities for babies and for disabled visitors (who will find this site flat and convenient). Laundry facilities. Motorcaravan services. Gas supplies. Supermarket (all year, closed Sun). Restaurant. Bar with TV (high season). Beach-side bar and restaurant (lunchtimes only in low season). Swimming pools. Spa with treatments and beauty programmes (charged). Playground. Watersports facilities. Diving school in high season (from mid June). Entertainment for children (from mid June). Pétanque. WiFi (charged). Bicycle hire.

Scan me for more information.

Alan Rogers Code: ES86120
24 accommodations
298 pitches
GPS: 38.90500, -0.06600
Post Code: E-46780

Valencia, Comunidad Valenciana

www.alanrogers.com/es86120
info@eurocamping-es.com
Tel: 962 854 098
www.eurocamping-es.com

Open (Touring Pitches):
All Year

Eurocamping Oliva Beach

Approached through a new urbanisation and situated by Oliva beach with its fine golden sand, Euro Camping is a well maintained, British owned site. Spacious and flat, it is set amidst many high trees, mainly eucalyptus, so ensuring shade in summer, but plenty of sunny spaces in winter. From reception, with its helpful English-speaking staff and interesting aviary opposite, wide tarmac or paved roads lead to 298 gravel-based pitches (70-120 sq.m) which are either marked or hedged (most are for touring units). The main site road leads down to a beachside restaurant with superb views and a supermarket.

One newly built and two mature sanitary blocks are well maintained. British type WCs, preset hot water in the showers. Toilet facilities for disabled campers. Facilities for babies. Washing machines and dryer. Motorcaravan services. Well stocked supermarket and roast chicken takeaway. Restaurant/bar. Fridge hire. Entertainment in high season. Gas. Playground. Bicycle hire. Communal barbecue. WiFi over site (charged).

Key Features

 Open All Year

 Pets Accepted

 Disabled Facilities

 Beach Access

 Play Area

 Bar/Restaurant

 Bike Hire

 Fishing

Scan me for more information.

Alan Rogers Code: ES87420
36 accommodations
465 pitches
GPS: 38.12965, -0.64958
Post Code: E-03194

Alacant, Comunidad Valenciana

www.alanrogers.com/es87420
info@campinglamarina.com
Tel: 965 419 200
www.lamarinaresort.com

Open (Touring Pitches):
All year.

Camping La Marina

Very efficiently run by a friendly Belgian family, Camping Internacional La Marina has 465 touring pitches of three different types and sizes ranging from 50 sq.m. to 150 sq.m. with electricity (10/16A), TV, water and drainage. Artificial shade is provided and the pitches are well maintained on level, well drained ground with a special area allocated for tents in a small orchard. The lagoon swimming pool complex is fabulous and has something for everyone (with lifeguards). William Le Metayer, the owner, is passionate about La Marina and it shows in his search for perfection. A magnificent new, modern building which uses the latest architectural technology, houses many superb extra amenities. A member of Leading Campings group.

The sanitary blocks offer modern facilities and are regularly cleaned. Heated in winter, they include private cabins and facilities for disabled visitors & babies. Laundry facilities. Motorcaravan services. Gas. Supermarket. Bars. Restaurant and café. Ice cream kiosk. Swimming pools (seasonal). Indoor pool. Fitness centre. Sauna. Solarium. Jacuzzi. Play rooms. Extensive activity and entertainment programme including barbecues and swimming nights. Sports area. Tennis. Huge playgrounds. Hairdresser. Bicycle hire. Road train to beach. Exclusive area for dogs. Internet café (charged) and free WiFi.

Key Features

 Open All Year

 Pets Accepted

 Disabled Facilities

 Swimming Pool

 Play Area

 Bar/Restaurant

 Skiing

 Bike Hire

Scan me for more information.

Alan Rogers Code: ES87425
10 accommodations
50 pitches
GPS: 38.24020, -0.81244
Post Code: E-3330

Alicante, Comunidad Valenciana

www.alanrogers.com/es87425
laspalmeras@laspalmeras-sl.com
Tel: 965 400 188
www.laspalmerasresort.com

Open (Touring Pitches):
1 July - 31 August, 24 December - 31
December

Camping Las Palmeras

Camping Internacional Las Palmeras is set between palm trees in the south-east of Spain, located 10 minutes from Elche and 20 minutes from some of the cleanest beaches in Europe. Their outdoor pool area is perfect for small children as they have their own special little one, and for adults, there is also a lovely Jacuzzi to relax in. There is a dedicated place for barbecues and you will find a supermarket just 50 metres away where you can buy all of your provisions. If you are not interested in cooking, you can also try their fantastic restaurant. Here you will find specialities from various regions of Spain including paellas (rabbit, shellfish, lobster etc) and also an abundance of shellfish, fresh from the coast. In July and August, they offer a varied entertainment programme that is provided for children and adults and all activities are supervised by qualified staff. Camping Internacional Las Palmeras is the perfect place for creating good memories with your family in summer and for peace seekers who want to have a break in winter.

One sanitary block equipped with showers, private washing and facilities for babies and handicapped people. Bar, restaurant and takeaway. 2 Swimming pools (including a children's pool) with changing rooms. Jacuzzi. Entertainment programmes during July and August. Barbecue area. Internet access and free WiFi.

Key Features

 Pets Accepted

 Swimming Pool

 Play Area

 Bar/Restaurant

Scan me for
more information.

Alan Rogers Code: ES87435
56 accommodations
1200 pitches
GPS: 38.17790, -0.80950
Post Code: E-03330

Alacant, Comunidad Valenciana

Marjal Resorts Costa Blanca

www.alanrogers.com/es87435
reservas@marjalresorts.com
Tel: 965 484 945
www.marjalresorts.com

Open (Touring Pitches):
All Year

Marjal Costa Blanca is a fully equipped site situated 15 km. inland on the southern Alicante coast, close to the towns of Crevillente and Catral, and the Parque Natural de El Hondo. The 1,200 hardstanding pitches range in size from 90-95 sq.m, and all have electricity (16A), water, drainage, TV and high speed internet connections (charged). On-site amenities include a tropical themed swimming pool complex and a state-of-the-art wellness centre. There is full disabled access, including at the swimming pool and staffed gym. There is accommodation to rent, including 46 Balinese-style bungalows adapted for disabled visitors. The site is ideal for both family holidays in summer and for winter sun-seekers.

Six modern, spotlessly clean toilet blocks have washbasins and free showers in cabins. Facilities for children, babies & disabled visitors. Well equipped shop. Bar, restaurant and takeaway (all year). Swimming pool complex with outdoor pool (Mar-Sept), heated indoor pool (all year), sauna and Hammam. Fully equipped gym. Wellness centre. Hairdresser. Play areas. Games rooms. Library. Multisports courts. Minigolf. Tennis. Football. Entertainment and activity programme (incl Spanish lessons). Kids club. Business centre. Bicycle hire. Car hire service. Doctor and vet. Free WiFi areas, high speed internet on pitches (charged). Mobile homes and chalets to rent.

Key Features

  Open All Year

 Pets Accepted

 Disabled Facilities

 Swimming Pool

 Play Area

 Bar/Restaurant

Bike Hire

Scan me for more information.

Alan Rogers Code: ES86810
26 accommodations
303 pitches
GPS: 38.53800, -0.11900
Post Code: E-03503

Alacant, Comunidad Valenciana

www.alanrogers.com/es86810
info@camping-villasol.com
Tel: 965 850 422
www.camping-villasol.com

Open (Touring Pitches):
All Year

Camping Villasol

Benidorm is increasingly popular for winter stays and Villasol is a genuinely good, purpose built modern site. Many of the 303 well separated pitches are arranged on wide terraces which afford views of the mountains surrounding Benidorm. All pitches (80-85 sq.m) have electricity and satellite TV connections, with 160 with full services for seasonal use. Shade is mainly artificial. Reservations are only accepted for winter stays of over three months (from 1 October). There is a small indoor pool, heated for winter use, and a very attractive, large outdoor pool complex (summer only) overlooked by the bar/restaurant and attractive, elevated restaurant terrace.

Modern toilet blocks provide free, controllable hot water to showers and washbasins and British WCs. Good facilities for disabled visitors. Laundry facilities. Good value restaurant. Bar. Shop. Swimming pools, outdoor and indoor. Satellite TV. Playground. Evening entertainment programme. Safes. Dogs are not accepted. No charcoal barbecues.

Key Features

 Open All Year

 Disabled Facilities

 Swimming Pool

 Play Area

 Bar/Restaurant

 Skiing

Scan me for more information.

Alan Rogers Code: ES87430
59 accommodations
158 pitches
GPS: 38.10933, -0.65467
Post Code: E-03140

Alacant, Comunidad Valenciana

www.alanrogers.com/es87430
camping@marjal.com
Tel: 966 727 070
www.campingmarjal.com

Open (Touring Pitches):
All year.

Marjal Guardamar

Marjal is located beside the estuary of the Segura river, alongside the pine and eucalyptus forests of the Dunas de Guardamar Natural Park. A fine sandy beach can be reached through the forest (800 m). This is a very smart site with a huge tropical lake-style pool with bar and a superb sports complex. There are 212 pitches on this award-winning site, 158 for touring with water, electricity (16A), drainage, high-speed internet and satellite TV points. The ground is covered with crushed marble, making the pitches clean and pleasant.

Three excellent heated toilet blocks have free hot water, elegant separators between sinks, spacious showers and some cabins. Each block has high quality facilities for babies and disabled campers, modern laundry and dishwashing rooms. Motorcaravan services. Car wash. Well stocked supermarket. Restaurants. Bar. Large outdoor pool complex (1/4-30/9). Heated indoor pool (all year). Jacuzzi. Sauna. Beauty salon. Superb well equipped gym. Aerobics. Physiotherapy. All activities discounted for campers. Play room. Minigolf. Floodlit tennis and soccer pitch. Bicycle hire. Car rental. Games room. TV room. Full entertainment programme. Hairdresser. ATM. Business centre. High speed internet access at pitches (charged) and free WiFi areas. Caravan storage. Fishing.

Key Features

 Open All Year

 Pets Accepted

 Disabled Facilities

 Swimming Pool

 Play Area

 Bar/Restaurant

 Bike Hire

Scan me for more information.

Alan Rogers Code: ES87530
50 accommodations
800 pitches
GPS: 37.62445, -0.74442
Post Code: E-30386

La Manga del Mar Menor, Murcia

www.alanrogers.com/es87530
lamanga@caravaning.es
Tel: 968 563 014
www.caravaning.es

Open (Touring Pitches):
All year.

Caravaning La Manga

This is a very large, well equipped, holiday-style site with its own beach and both indoor and outdoor pools. With a good number of typical Spanish long stay units, the length of the site is impressive (1 km) and a bicycle is very helpful for getting about. The 800 regularly laid out, gravel touring pitches (84 or 110 sq.m) are generally separated by hedges which provide some privacy but very little shade. Each has a 10A electricity supply, water and the possibility of satellite TV reception. This site's excellent facilities are ideally suited for holidays in the winter when the weather is very pleasantly warm. Daytime temperatures in November usually exceed 20 degrees.

Nine clean toilet blocks of standard design, well spaced around the site, include washbasins (all with hot water). Laundry. Gas supplies. Large well stocked supermarket. Restaurant. Bar. Snack bar. Swimming pool complex (April-Sept). Indoor pool, gymnasium (Oct-Apr), sauna, jacuzzi and massage service. Outdoor fitness course for adults. Open-air family cinema (July/Aug). Tennis. Pétanque. Minigolf. Play area. Watersports school. Internet café (also WiFi). Winter activities including Spanish classes. Pet washing area.

Key Features

 Open All Year

 Pets Accepted

 Disabled Facilities

 Beach Access

 Swimming Pool

 Play Area

 Bar/Restaurant

 Fishing

Scan me for more information.

Alan Rogers Code: ES87620
63 accommodations
171 pitches
GPS: 36.80288, -2.07756
Post Code: E-04118

Almería, Andalucia

www.alanrogers.com/es87620
info@losescullossanjose.com
Tel: 950 389 811
www.losescullossanjose.com

Open (Touring Pitches):
All year.

Camping Los Escullos

This efficient, well maintained, medium sized site has 171 pitches (60-80 sq.m). They are divided by hedges and trees, 100 have 10A electricity and some have artificial shading. Specific taps about the grounds provide drinking water. The pool has an overlooking bar and restaurant which is kept busy serving excellent typical Spanish 'menu del dia' food at reasonable prices. It is a popular site with British tourists seeking the sun. The salinas on the approach to Cabo de Gata are famous for birdlife (including flocks of pink flamingo).

The main sanitary block is large and rather old, but clean and fully equipped with hot showers and facilities for disabled campers. A second newer block is close to reception. Fridge hire. Well stocked small supermarket. Bar/restaurant. Takeaway. Large outdoor pool (all year) and jacuzzi (1/7-1/10). Hairdresser. Massage. Well equipped gym. Internet access. Multisports court. Scuba diving. TV room. Bicycle hire. No charcoal barbecues. Entertainment programme in high season. WiFi (free).

Key Features

 Open All Year

 Pets Accepted

 Disabled Facilities

 Swimming Pool

 Play Area

 Bar/Restaurant

 Bike Hire

Scan me for more information.

Alan Rogers Code: ES90840
5 accommodations
35 pitches
GPS: 37.62300, -4.85870
Post Code: E-14547

Córdoba, Andalucia

www.alanrogers.com/es90840
info@campinglacampina.es
Tel: 957 315 303
www.campinglacampina.es

Open (Touring Pitches):
All year.

Camping la Campiña

A charming site amongst the olive trees and set high on a hill to catch cool summer breezes. Matilde, the daughter of the Martin-Rodriguez family, and her husband run this site with enthusiasm and hard work, making a visit here a delightful experience. Everything is immaculately kept with excellent amenities and standards. The 35 pitches are level with a gravel surface and most have shade. There is a large pool in a garden setting and the restaurant, with its traditional rustic charm, has a delightful menu of homemade food. Breakfast is included in pitch prices. Fresh bread and croissants are cooked to order, or you can have an inclusive breakfast on the terrace with the piquant smell of olive trees drifting from the fields. The area is famous for its natural beauty, wine and olives (excursions can be arranged to see olive oil made and to a local 'bodega' for the winemaking). Reservation is essential for high season and November-February.

Two small traditional sanitary blocks (heated in winter) have clean services including separate facilities for disabled campers (key at reception). Washing machines. Restaurant. Snack bar. Shop. Outdoor swimming pool (Apr-Oct). Bicycle hire. Play area. TV room. Yoga lessons. Torches useful. Walks and excursions arranged. WiFi throughout.

Key Features

 Open All Year

 Pets Accepted

 Disabled Facilities

 Swimming Pool

 Play Area

 Bar/Restaurant

 Bike Hire

Scan me for more information.

Alan Rogers Code: ES87810
192 accommodations
290 pitches
GPS: 36.73925, -3.94971
Post Code: E-29793

Málaga, Andalucia

www.alanrogers.com/es87810
info@campingelpino.com
Tel: 952 530 006
www.campingelpino.com

Open (Touring Pitches):
All year.

Camping El Pino

El Pino is in the Axarquia region of the Costa del Sol, east of Malaga and is surrounded by avocado groves. The old but well-maintained site enjoys some fine views of the surrounding countryside. There are now 290 pitches here, mostly well shaded, and a further 57 mobile homes and chalets to rent. Most pitches have electrical connections and vary in size from 60-100 sq.m. The site is open all year and has some good facilities including a swimming pool, supermarket and bar/restaurant. The nearest beach is 800 m. distant – a bus service runs there from the site.

Four toilet blocks with hot showers and individual cabins. Facilities for disabled visitors. Laundry facilities. Bar, restaurant and shop (all year). Takeaway. Swimming pool with new children's pool (1/6-15/9). Play area. Games room. Pétanque. Children's club. WiFi throughout (free). Mobile homes and chalets to rent. Communal barbecue - only gas or electric barbecues permitted on pitches.

Key Features

 Open All Year

 Pets Accepted

 Disabled Facilities

 Swimming Pool

 Play Area

Bar/Restaurant

Scan me for more information.

Alan Rogers Code: ES88020
65 accommodations
250 pitches
GPS: 36.49350, -4.74383
Post Code: E-29604

Málaga, Andalucia

www.alanrogers.com/es88020
info@campingcabopino.com
Tel: 952 834 373
www.campingcabopino.com

Open (Touring Pitches):
All year.

Camping Cabopino

This large, mature site is alongside the main N340/A7 Costa del Sol coast road, 12 km. east of Marbella and 15 km. from Fuengirola. The Costa del Sol is also known as the Costa del Golf and fittingly there is a major golf course alongside the site. The site is set amongst tall pine trees which provide shade for the pitches (there are some huge areas for large units). The 250 touring pitches, a mix of level and sloping (chocks advisable), all have electricity (10A), but long leads may be required for some. There is a separate area on the western side for groups of younger guests.

Five mature sanitary blocks provide hot water throughout (may be under pressure at peak times). Facilities for disabled visitors in one block. Washing machines. Bar/restaurant and takeaway (all year). Shop. Outdoor pool (1/5-15/9) and indoor pool (all year). Play area. Adult exercise equipment. Some evening entertainment. Excursions can be booked. ATM. Bicycle hire. Torches necessary in the more remote parts of the site. Only gas or electric barbecues are permitted. WiFi (charged).

Key Features

 Open All Year

 Pets Accepted

 Disabled Facilities

 Swimming Pool

 Play Area

 Bar/Restaurant

Bike Hire

Scan me for more information.

Alan Rogers Code: ES90620
33 accommodations
204 pitches
GPS: 42.43018, 0.07882
Post Code: E-22340

Huesca, Aragon

www.alanrogers.com/es90620
info@campingboltana.com
Tel: 974 502 347
www.campingboltana.com

Open (Touring Pitches):
All year.

Camping Boltaña

Under the innovative and charming ownership of Raquel Rodrigeuz, Camping Boltaña nestles in the Rio Ara valley, surrounded by the Pyrenees mountains. It is very pretty and thoughtfully planned to provide tranquillity and privacy. The generously sized, 204 grassy pitches (all with 10A electricity) have good shade from a variety of carefully planted trees and shrubs. A stone building houses the site's reception, a social room with computer and excellent WiFi connection and shop. Adjacent is a good restaurant, bar and takeaway with a large terrace that has views over the site to the mountains. Activities and excursions in the surrounding area can be organised at the helpful, English speaking reception office.

Two modern sanitary blocks include facilities for disabled visitors and children. Laundry facilities. Fridge hire. Shop, bar, restaurant and takeaway (1/4-30/11). Swimming pools (1/5-25/10). Playground. Entertainment for children (high season). Pétanque. Guided tours and information about hiking, canyoning, rafting, climbing, mountain biking and caving. Bicycle hire. Library. Communal barbecue area. Under-cover meeting area. WiFi in some areas (free).

Key Features

 Open All Year

 Pets Accepted

 Disabled Facilities

 Swimming Pool

 Play Area

 Bar/Restaurant

 Skiing

 Bike Hire

Scan me for more information.

Alan Rogers Code: ES90600
130 accommodations
330 pitches
GPS: 42.43520, 0.13618
Post Code: E-22360

Huesca, Aragon

www.alanrogers.com/es90600
info@penamontanesa.com
Tel: 974 500 032
www.penamontanesa.com

Open (Touring Pitches):
All year.

Camping Peña Montañesa

A large site situated in the Pyrenees near the Ordesa National Park, Peña Montañesa is easily accessible from Ainsa or from France via the Bielsa Tunnel (steep sections on the French side). The site is essentially divided into three sections opening progressively throughout the season and all have shade. The 330 pitches on fairly level grass are of about 75 sq.m. and 6/10A electricity is available on virtually all (no charge is made for upgrade). Grouped near the entrance are the facilities that make the site so attractive, including an outdoor pool and a heated (out of season), glass covered indoor pool with jacuzzi and sauna. Here too is an attractive bar/restaurant with an open fire and a terrace; a supermarket and takeaway are opposite.

A newer toilet block, heated when necessary, has free hot showers but cold water to open plan washbasins. Facilities for disabled visitors. Small baby room. An older block in the original area has similar provision. Washing machine and dryer. Bar, restaurant, takeaway and supermarket (all 1/1-31/12). Outdoor swimming pool (1/4-31/10). Indoor pool, sauna and jacuzzi (all year). Outdoor social area with large TV screen and stage. Multisports court. Tennis. Playground. Boules. Only gas barbecues are permitted. WiFi in bar area (free).

Key Features

 Open All Year

 Pets Accepted

 Disabled Facilities

 Swimming Pool

 Play Area

 Bar/Restaurant

 Skiing

 Fishing

Scan me for more information.

Alan Rogers Code: ES90980
9 accommodations
80 pitches
GPS: 38.48917, -2.34639
Post Code: E-02449

Albacete, Castilla-La-Mancha

www.alanrogers.com/es90980
riomundo@campingriomundo.es
Tel: 967 433 230
www.campingriomundo.es

Open (Touring Pitches):
16 March - 11 October.

Camping Rio Mundo

This uncomplicated and typically Spanish site is situated in the Sierra de Alcaraz (south of Albacete), just off the scenic route 412 between Elche de la Sierra and Valdepenas. The drive to this site is most enjoyable through beautiful scenery and from the west the main road is winding in some places. Shade is provided by mature trees for the 80 pitches and electricity (5/10A, 2-pin plug) is supplied to 70 (long leads are useful). It is in a beautiful setting with majestic mountains and wonderful countryside which begs to be explored. This is a brilliant place to relax and enjoy the beauty of nature and is ideal for those wanting to experience true rural Spain.

One sanitary block has hot showers and facilities for disabled visitors. Washing machine. Small shop for basics. Mountain-style bar/restaurant serving pre-ordered meals and snacks, with covered outdoor seating area. Takeaway (all 15/3-12/10). Swimming pool (June-Sept). Playground. Pétanque. Free WiFi. Only gas and electric barbecues permitted.

Key Features

 Pets Accepted

 Disabled Facilities

 Swimming Pool

 Play Area

 Bar/Restaurant

 Bike Hire

 Fishing

Scan me for more information.

Alan Rogers Code: ES90900
4 accommodations
150 pitches
GPS: 39.86500, -4.04700
Post Code: E-45004

Toledo, Castilla-La-Mancha

www.alanrogers.com/es90900
info@campingelgreco.es
Tel: 925 220 090
www.campingelgreco.es

Open (Touring Pitches):
All year.

Camping El Greco

Toledo was the home of the Grecian painter, El Greco, and the site that bears his name boasts a beautiful view of the ancient city from the restaurant, bar and attractive pool and terrace area. The friendly, family owners make you welcome and are proud of their site, which is the only one in Toledo (it can get crowded). The 150 pitches are of 80 sq.m. with 10A electricity connections and shade from strategically planted trees. Most have separating hedges that give privacy, with others in herringbone layouts (long leads required in this area). The River Tajo stretches alongside the site, which has an attractive, tree-lined approach.

Two sanitary blocks, both modernised, one with facilities for disabled campers. Laundry. Motorcaravan services. Swimming pool (15/6-15/9, charged). Small, well stocked shop in reception (all year). Restaurant/bar (1/4-30/9) with good menu and fair prices. Playgrounds. Ice machine. Communal barbecues. WiFi in bar/restaurant areas (free).

Key Features

 Open All Year

 Pets Accepted

 Disabled Facilities

 Swimming Pool

 Play Area

 Bar/Restaurant

Scan me for more information.

Alan Rogers Code: ES90910
23 accommodations
162 pitches
GPS: 40.04218, -3.59947
Post Code: E-28300

Aranjuez, Madrid

www.alanrogers.com/es90910
info@campingaranjuez.com
Tel: 918 911 395
www.campingaranjuez.com

Open (Touring Pitches):
All year.

Camping Aranjuez

Aranjuez, supposedly Spain's version of Versailles, is worthy of a visit with its beautiful palaces, leafy squares, avenues and gardens. This useful, popular and unusually well equipped site is therefore excellent for enjoying the unusual attractions or for an en route stop. It is 47 km. south of Madrid and 46 km. from Toledo. The site is alongside the River Tajo in a park-like situation with mature trees. There are 162 touring pitches, all with electricity (16A), set on flat grass amid tall trees. The site is owned by the owners of la Marina (ES87420) who have worked hard to improve the pitches and the site in general.

Two of the three modern sanitary blocks are heated and all are well equipped with some washbasins in cabins. Laundry facilities. Gas supplies. Shop, bar and restaurant (all year) with attractive riverside patio (also open to the public). Takeaway. TV in bar. Swimming and paddling pools, (1/5-15/10). Tennis courts. Central play area. Pétanque. Bicycle hire. Canoe hire. Activities for children (high season). WiFi over site (charged).

Key Features

 Open All Year

 Pets Accepted

 Disabled Facilities

 Swimming Pool

 Play Area

 Bar/Restaurant

 Bike Hire

 Fishing

Scan me for more information.

Alan Rogers Code: ES92120
10 accommodations
125 pitches
GPS: 40.94992, -3.72927
Post Code: E-28739

Gargantilla del Lozoya, Madrid

www.alanrogers.com/es92120
monteholiday@monteholiday.com
Tel: 918 695 278
www.monteholiday.com

Open (Touring Pitches):
All year.

Camping Monte Holiday

This picturesque and conservation-minded site is situated in an open, sunny lower valley in the Madrid area's only beech forest in the Parque Natural Sierre de Guadarrama. The area is ideal for walkers and nature lovers and offers many opportunities for outdoor sports enthusiasts. The site is mainly terraced and has 450 pitches, with 125 for touring units. These include a new area of 30 larger comfort pitches. All the pitches are mainly flat with grass or gravel surfaces and shade from mature trees. The upper area is taken by permanent units. An extensive new activity area includes a zip wire accessed via climbing walls.

The modern, heated and well equipped toilet block is well maintained. Facilities for disabled visitors and babies. Laundry facilities. Motorcaravan services. Shop (basic provisions in low season). Bar and restaurant (15/6-15/9, B.Hs and weekends). TV in bar. Library. Swimming pool with lifeguard (mid June-mid Sept). Multisports court. Tennis. Beach volleyball. Play area. Gas supplies. Barbecues are not permitted 15/5-31/10. Bicycle hire. Excursions and activities (high season). WiFi in bar (free).

Key Features

 Open All Year

 Pets Accepted

 Disabled Facilities

 Swimming Pool

 Play Area

 Bar/Restaurant

 Skiing

 Bike Hire

Scan me for more information.

Alan Rogers Code: ES90520
94 accommodations
60 pitches
GPS: 42.85139, -2.17218
Post Code: E-31800

Alsasua, Navarra

www.alanrogers.com/es90520
info@campingurbasa.com
Tel: 948 395 223
www.campingurbasa.com

Open (Touring Pitches):
1 March - 1 December.

Camping Urbasa Bioitza

Camping Urbasa is a well maintained smart site situated within the Urbasa National Park, Europe's largest beech forest, west of Pamplona. There are two large areas for tents, plus 60 pitches for caravans and motorhomes with electrical connections, of a good size, grassy and are surrounded by beech trees. Around 100 attractive natural timber chalets are available to rent. There is also a hostel with good accommodation for walkers or cyclists. The site boasts a good restaurant, specializing in Basque–Navarra cuisine. Leisure facilities here include horse riding, and accompanied excursions on horseback are organised. This is a good location for an active holiday and there are numerous opportunities for walking and mountain biking trips.

Heated sanitary facilities. Motorhome service point. Shop, bar, restaurant and takeaway (all season). Children's playground. Riding. Bicycle hire. Chalets to rent. Accompanied walks and riding excursions. WiFi throughout (free).

Key Features

 Pets Accepted

 Disabled Facilities

 Play Area

 Bar/Restaurant

 Skiing

 Bike Hire

 Horse Riding

Scan me for more information.

Alan Rogers Code: ES92270
4 accommodations
40 pitches
GPS: 42.41614, -2.55172
Post Code: E-26370

Navarrete, La Rioja

www.alanrogers.com/es92270
campingnavarrete@fer.es
Tel: 941 440 169
www.campingnavarrete.com

Open (Touring Pitches):
8 January - 9 December.

Camping Navarrete

Camping Navarrete is a clean site in which the family owners take great pride. Suitable as a base for exploring the surrounding countryside and sampling wonderful wines as it is located in the heart of La Rioja, or for stopping en route to or from Santander or Bilbao. Many of the 180 pitches are taken up by static caravans but a designated grassy area has been set aside for 40 unmarked, spacious touring pitches with 5A electricity. Some have shade and there are good views of the Rioja valley. The good facilities include a restaurant and bar which are open all year (not Mondays in low season). Noise is possible from the road.

One modern central sanitary block with heating is clean and provides open style washbasins and separate shower cubicles. Facilities for disabled visitors. Laundry facilities. Motorcaravan services. Bar with mini-market, restaurant and takeaway (closed Mon. in low season). Outdoor swimming pool and soft ball pool for young children (15/6-15/9). Games machines. Multisports court. Unfenced play area. Barbecues are allowed in special area of the campsite. WiFi in bar area (free).

Key Features

 Pets Accepted

 Disabled Facilities

 Swimming Pool

 Play Area

 Bar/Restaurant

 Skiing

Scan me for more information.

Alan Rogers Code: ES90290
37 accommodations
133 pitches
GPS: 41.49531, -5.00522
Post Code: E-47100

Valladolid, Castilla Y Leon

www.alanrogers.com/es90290
info@campingelastral.es
Tel: 983 770 953
www.campingelastral.es

Open (Touring Pitches):
All year.

Campingred El Astral

The site is in a prime position alongside the wide River Duero (safely fenced). It is homely and run by a charming man, Eduardo Gutierrez, who speaks excellent English and is ably assisted by brother Gustavo and sister Lola. The site is generally flat with pitches separated by thin hedges. The 133 touring pitches with electricity (6/10A), six with 10A electricity, water and wastewater, vary in size from 60-200 sq.m. with mature trees providing shade. The toilet block has been designed with environmental sustainability in mind, including solar heated water. This is a friendly site, ideal for exploring the area and historic Tordesillas.

One attractive sanitary block with fully equipped, modern facilities designed to include energy-saving measures and to be easily cleaned. Showers for children and baby room. Facilities for disabled visitors. Washing machines. Motorcaravan services. Supermarket. Bar and restaurant, frequented by locals, plus a takeaway service all 1/4-30/9. Swimming pool with new disability lift, plus paddling pools (1/6-15/9). Playground. Tennis (high season). Minigolf. No charcoal barbecues (July-Sept). WiFi throughout (charged).

Key Features

 Open All Year

 Pets Accepted

 Disabled Facilities

 Swimming Pool

 Play Area

 Bar/Restaurant

Scan me for more information.

Alan Rogers Code: ES90230
5 accommodations
50 pitches
GPS: 42.29130, -4.14480
Post Code: E-09110

Burgos, Castilla Y Leon

www.alanrogers.com/es90230
info@campingcamino.com
Tel: 947 377 255
www.campingcamino.com

Open (Touring Pitches):
15 March - 15 November.

Camino de Santiago

This site is located on the famous Camino de Compostela which is still walked by today's pilgrims. The path passes by the site entrance and there is an ancient pilgrims' refuge just outside the gate. It lies to the west of Burgos on the outskirts of Castrojeriz, in a superb location, almost in the shadow of the ruined castle high on the hillside. Apart from just four units to rent, the site takes only touring units. The 50 marked pitches are level, grassy and divided by hedges, with 10A electricity and mature trees providing shade. This site is also a birdwatchers' paradise – large raptors abound. Since Roman times the Camino de Santiago de Compostela, which starts from Pyrenean France, has been one of the most significant pilgrims' trails. Today it is almost as popular as ever and the campsite has a wide range of European visitors attracted by its proximity to this famous route, along with the opportunity to try some of it for themselves.

Older style sanitary block with hot showers, washbasin with cold water. No special facilities for disabled visitors or children. Washing machine and drying room. Small shop. Gas. Safe rental. Bar/restaurant and takeaway with basic cuisine. Library. Games room. Small play area. Barbecue area. Ad hoc guided birdwatching. WiFi throughout (free).

Key Features

 Pets Accepted

 Play Area

 Bar/Restaurant

Scan me for more information.

Alan Rogers Code: ES89620
11 accommodations
106 pitches
GPS: 43.14999, -4.69997
Post Code: E-39570

Potes, Cantabria

www.alanrogers.com/es89620
campinglaislapicosdeeuropa@gmail.
com
Tel: 942 730 896
campinglaislapicosdeeuropa.com

Open (Touring Pitches):
1 April - 15 October.

Camping la Isla Picos de Europa

La Isla is beside the road from Potes to Fuente Dé, with many mature trees giving good shade and glimpses of the mountains above. Established for over 25 years, a warm welcome awaits you from the owners (who speak good English) and a most relaxed and peaceful atmosphere exists here. All the campers we spoke to were delighted with the family feeling of the site. The 106 unmarked pitches are arranged around an oval gravel track under a variety of fruit and ornamental trees. Electricity (6A) is available to all pitches, although some need long leads. A brilliant small bar and restaurant are located under dense trees where you can enjoy the relaxing sound of the river which runs through the site.

Single, clean and smart sanitary block retains the style of the site. Washbasins with cold water. Washing machine. Gas supplies. Freezer service. Small shop and restaurant/bar (1/4-30/9). Small swimming pool (caps compulsory; 1/5-30/9). Play area. Barbecue area. Fishing. Bicycle hire. Riding. Free WiFi throughout.

Key Features

 Pets Accepted

 Swimming Pool

 Play Area

 Bar/Restaurant

 Bike Hire

 Fishing

 Horse Riding

Scan me for
more information.

Alan Rogers Code: ES89610
100 accommodations
140 pitches
GPS: 43.38288, -4.24800
Post Code: E-39527

Ruiloba, Cantabria

Camping El Helguero

www.alanrogers.com/es89610
reservas@campingelhelguero.com
Tel: 942 722 124
www.campingelhelguero.com

Open (Touring Pitches):
1 April - 30 September.

This site, in a peaceful location surrounded by tall trees and impressive towering rock formations, caters for 240 units (of which 100 are seasonal) on slightly sloping ground. There are many marked pitches on different levels, all with access to electricity (6A), but with varying amounts of shade. There are also attractive tent and small camper sections set close in to the rocks and 22 site owned chalets. The site gets very crowded in high season, so it is best to arrive early if you have not booked. The reasonably sized swimming pool and children's pool have access lifts for disabled campers.

Three well placed toilet blocks, although old, are clean and all include controllable showers and hot and cold water to all washbasins. Facilities for children and disabled visitors. Washing machines and dryers. Motorcaravan services. Small supermarket. Bar/snack bar plus separate more formal restaurant. Swimming pool (caps compulsory). Playground. Activities and entertainment (high season). ATM. Torches useful in some places. No electric barbecues. WiFi over site (charged by card).

Key Features

 Pets Accepted

 Disabled Facilities

 Swimming Pool

 Play Area

 Bar/Restaurant

Scan me for more information.

445

Alan Rogers Code: ES89480
152 accommodations
40 pitches
GPS: 43.55439, -6.14458
Post Code: E-33150

Cudillero, Asturias

www.alanrogers.com/es89480
camping@lamuravela.com
Tel: 985 590 995
www.lamuravela.com

Open (Touring Pitches):
June - September.

Camping l'Amuravela

This very well maintained, family run site, is close to the quaint old town of Cudillero and it is an ideal stopover when visiting 'green Spain'. Nearby is some of the most attractive mountain scenery in the region and if you stay here for one night it can easily extend to a much longer visit. There are 192 pitches, mostly used for seasonal units but with 40 good sized touring pitches on level or gently sloping grass with easy access. Some pitches can accommodate large units. Mature trees give some shade and all pitches have 6A electricity. The excellent swimming pool provides an area for relaxation. This is a relatively quiet site but can be busy and noisy at weekends when the seasonal units tend to be occupied. The spectacular Costa Verde has many places to explore and the towns of Gigon and Oviedo are places that have to be visited.

One modern and very well maintained toilet block is close to all pitches and includes washbasins and shower cubicles. Facilities for disabled visitors. Washing machines and dryers. Well stocked shop. Café/bar area. Swimming pool (June-Sept). Play area. Very little English is spoken. Gas and charcoal barbecues permitted. Free WiFi in bar area. 19 bungalows for hire.

Key Features

 Pets Accepted

 Swimming Pool

 Play Area

 Bar/Restaurant

Scan me for more information.

Alan Rogers Code: ES90240
12 accommodations
113 pitches
GPS: 42.88939, -8.52418
Post Code: E-15704

A Coruña, Galicia

www.alanrogers.com/es90240
info@campingascancelas.com
Tel: 981 580 476
www.campingascancelas.com

Open (Touring Pitches):
All year.

Camping As Cancelas

The beautiful city of Santiago has been the destination for European Christian pilgrims for centuries and they now follow ancient routes to this unique city, the whole of which is a national monument. The As Cancelas campsite is excellent for sharing the experiences of these pilgrims in the city and around the magnificent cathedral. It has 113 marked pitches (60-90 sq.m), arranged in terraces and divided by trees and shrubs. On a hillside overlooking the city, the views are very pleasant. The site has a steep approach road.

Two modern toilet blocks are fully equipped, with ramped access for disabled visitors. The quality and cleanliness of the fittings and tiling is good. Laundry with service wash for a small fee. Small shop. Restaurant. Bar with TV. Well kept, unsupervised swimming pool and children's pool. Small playground. Internet access. WiFi throughout.

Key Features

 Open All Year

 Pets Accepted

 Disabled Facilities

 Swimming Pool

 Play Area

 Bar/Restaurant

 Bike Hire

Scan me for more information.

Capital Stockholm
Currency Swedish Krona (SEK)
Language Swedish
Telephone country code 00 46
Time Zone CET (GMT/UTC+1)
Tourist Office visitsweden.com

Climate Temperate climate but very varied. Extremely cold above the Arctic Circle, mild across much of the rest of the country. Cold, short winters and summers similar to those in Britain.

Sweden

With giant lakes and waterways, rich forests, majestic mountains and glaciers, and vast, wide open countryside, Sweden is almost twice the size of the UK but with a fraction of the population.

Southern Sweden's unspoiled islands with their beautiful sandy beaches offer endless opportunities for boating and island hopping. The coastal cities of Gothenburg and Malmö, once centres of industry, now have an abundance of restaurants, cultural venues and attractions.

With the Oresund Bridge, Malmö is just a short ride from Copenhagen. Stockholm, the capital, is a delightful place built on fourteen small islands on the eastern coast. It is an attractive, vibrant city with magnificent architecture, fine museums and historic squares. Sparsely populated northern Sweden is a land of forests, rivers and wilderness inhabited by moose and reindeer.

Östersund, located at the shores of a lake in the heart of the country, is well known for winter sports, while Frösö Zoo is a popular attraction. Today Sweden is one of the world's most developed societies and enjoys an enviable standard of living.

Shops Opening hours vary throughout the year. In high-season 9am to 6pm weekdays, to 1pm Saturday.

Banks 9.30am to 3pm weekdays, some larger branches may be open until 6pm.

Travelling with Children Sweden is a fun country for children of all ages with good transport links and accommodating locals. Most museums are kid-friendly and will allow children under 18 in free. Menus often include a children's section.

Public Holidays New Year's Day, Epiphany, Good Friday, Easter Monday, May Day, Ascension, National Day 6 Jun, Midsummer 22 Jul, All Saints' 2 Nov, Christmas Day, Boxing Day.

Motoring Roads are generally much quieter than in the UK. Dipped headlights are obligatory. Away from large towns, petrol stations rarely open 24 hours but most have self-serve pumps (with credit card payment). Buy diesel during working hours, it may not always be available at self-service pumps.

See campsite map page 486.

Alan Rogers Code: SW2870
58 accommodations
170 pitches
GPS: 66.59497, 19.89270
Post Code: S-962 22

Norrbottens Län, North

Jokkmokks Camping Center

www.alanrogers.com/sw2870
campingcenter@jokkmokk.com
Tel: 097 112 370
www.arcticcampjokkmokk.se

Open (Touring Pitches):
15 May - 15 September.

This attractive site is just 8 km. from the Arctic Circle. Large and well organised, it is bordered on one side by the river and by woodland on the other, and is just 3 km. from the town centre. It has 170 level, grassy touring pitches, with an area for tents, plus 58 cabins to rent. Electricity (10A) is available to 159 pitches. The site has a heated, open-air pool complex open in summer (no lifeguard). There are opportunities for snowmobiling, cross-country skiing in spring and ice fishing in winter. Try visiting for the famous Jokkmokk Winter Market (first Thursday to Saturday in February) or the less chilly Autumn Market (end of August).

Heated sanitary buildings provide mostly open washbasins and controllable showers – some are curtained with a communal changing area, a few are in cubicles with divider and seat. A unit by reception has a baby bathroom, a fully equipped suite for disabled visitors, games room, plus a very well appointed kitchen and launderette. A further unit with WCs, washbasins, showers plus a steam sauna, is by the pool. Shop, restaurant and bar (in summer). Takeaway (10/6-10/8). Swimming pools (25x10 m. main pool with water slide, two smaller pools and paddling pool, 20/6-8/8). Sauna. Bicycle hire. Playground and adventure playground. Minigolf. Football field. Games machines. Free fishing.

Key Features

 Pets Accepted

 Disabled Facilities

 Swimming Pool

 Play Area

 Bar/Restaurant

 Bike Hire

 Fishing

Scan me for more information.

Alan Rogers Code: SW2860
122 accommodations
450 pitches
GPS: 63.84333, 20.34056
Post Code: S-906 54

Västerbotens Län, North

www.alanrogers.com/sw2860
umea@firstcamp.se
Tel: 090 702 600
www.firstcamp.se/umea

Open (Touring Pitches):
All year (full services 25/5-21/8).

First Camp Umeå

An ideal stopover for those travelling the E4 coastal route, and a good base from which to explore the area, this campsite is 6 km. from the centre of this university city. It is almost adjacent to the Nydalsjön lake, which is ideal for fishing, windsurfing and bathing. There are 450 grassy pitches arranged in bays of 10-20 units, 320 with electricity (10/16A), and some are fully serviced. Outside the site, adjacent to the lake, are football pitches, an open-air swimming pool, minigolf, mini-car driving school, beach volleyball and a mini-farm. There are cycle and footpaths around the area. Umeå is also a port for ferries to Vasa in Finland (4 hrs).

The large, heated, central sanitary unit includes controllable hot showers with communal changing areas. Facilities may be stretched in high season. Laundry facilities. Kitchen. Large dining room. Motorcaravan services. TV. Shop (27/5-31/8). Fully licensed restaurant, bar and takeaway (14/6-19/8). Giant chess. Playgrounds. Bicycle hire. Rowing boat hire. Fishing in the lake. Canoes and pedal cars for hire. Adventure golf. WiFi throughout (charged).

Key Features

 Open All Year

 Pets Accepted

 Disabled Facilities

 Play Area

 Bar/Restaurant

 Bike Hire

 Fishing

 Sailing

Scan me for more information.

Alan Rogers Code: SW2850
191 accommodations
254 pitches
GPS: 63.15942, 14.67355
Post Code: S-831 46

Jämtlands Län, North

Östersunds Camping

www.alanrogers.com/sw2850
ostersundscamping@ostersund.se
Tel: 063 144 615
www.ostersundscamping.se

Open (Touring Pitches):
All year.

Östersund lies on Lake Storsjön, which is Sweden's Loch Ness, with 200 sightings of the monster dating back to 1635, and more recently captured on video in 1996. Also worthy of a visit is the island of Frösön where settlements can be traced back to prehistoric times. This large site has 254 pitches off tarmac roads; electricity (10A) and TV socket are available on 131, while 28 are fully serviced with WiFi at extra cost. There are also 41 tarmac hardstandings available, and over 190 cottages, cabins and rooms to rent. Adjacent to the site is the municipal swimming pool complex with cafeteria (indoor and outdoor pools), a Scandic hotel with restaurant, minigolf, and a Statoil filling station. A large supermarket and bank are just 500 m. from the site, and Östersund town centre is 3 km.

Key Features

 Open All Year

 Pets Accepted

 Disabled Facilities

 Swimming Pool

 Play Area

 Fishing

Toilet facilities are in three units, two with controllable hot showers (on payment) with communal changing areas, suites for disabled visitors and baby changing. The third has four family bathrooms each with WC, basin and shower. Two kitchens have full cookers, hobs, fridge/freezers and double sinks (all free), and excellent dining rooms. Washing machines, dryers and free drying cabinet. Motorcaravan services. Playground. WiFi (charged).

Scan me for more information.

Alan Rogers Code: SW2853
36 accommodations
60 pitches
GPS: 62.79896, 17.86965
Post Code: S-870 16

Västernorrlands Län, North

www.alanrogers.com/sw2853
info@snibbenscamping.com
Tel: 061 240 505
www.snibbenscamping.se

Open (Touring Pitches):
7 May - 30 August.

Snibbens Camping

Probably, you will stop here for one night as you travel the E4 coast road and stay a week. It is a stunning location in the area of 'The High Coast' listed as a World Heritage Site. During high season, Snibbens is a busy, popular site but remains quiet and peaceful. Besides 36 bungalows to rent, there are 60 touring places, each with 16A electricity, set amongst delightful scenery on the shores of Lake Mörtsjön. The welcoming owners take you to your adequately sized grass pitch set amongst spacious trees. All the site facilities are to the highest of standards, spotlessly clean, with entry to the toilets and showers (stretched in high season) by use of a pass card presented to you on arrival. You are also provided with the security code for the site entrance barrier. To one end of the campsite, there is a beach where the waters are suitable for swimming with a zoned area for young children. Here you will also find a second play area, minigolf and additional toilets. A little further on, is the site's restaurant where your choice of food can range from a burger to 'à la carte' whilst on the terrace overlooking the lake as the sun sets.

Excellent, spotlessly clean facilities include controllable showers and partitioned washbasins. Baby changing facilities. Two kitchens with hot plates, microwaves and a mini oven. Laundry room. Small shop (20/6-15/8). Café and restaurant with breakfast service (22/6-31/8). Rowing boats and pedaloes for hire. Minigolf. Free fishing for site guests. Youth hostel. WiFi (free).

Key Features

 Pets Accepted

 Disabled Facilities

 Play Area

 Bar/Restaurant

 Bike Hire

 Fishing

 Sailing

Scan me for more information.

453

Alan Rogers Code: SW2705
90 accommodations
164 pitches
GPS: 57.70488, 12.02983
Post Code: S-416 55

Västra Götalands Län, South

www.alanrogers.com/sw2705
lisebergsbyn@liseberg.se
Tel: 031 840 200
www.liseberg.se

Open (Touring Pitches):
All year (full services 6/5-18/8).

Lisebergsbyn Karralund

Well positioned for visiting the city and theme park using the excellent tram system, this busy, well maintained site has 164 marked pitches. All have electricity (10A) and cable TV and there are several areas for tents. Pitches vary in size, 42 are hardstandings, some are fairly compact with no dividing hedges, and consequently units can be rather close together. Additionally there are cabins to rent, bed and breakfast facilities and a youth hostel. It can be a very busy site in the main season, which in this case means June, July and August. An advance telephone call to check for space is advisable.

One heated sanitary building is well maintained and cleaned, and has all the usual facilities, with controllable hot showers, a good suite for small children, kitchens with cooking facilities, and a complete unit for disabled visitors. Laundry facilities near reception. Private cabins available. Motorcaravan services. Kiosk. Breakfast buffet available and fresh bread on sale. Small playground. TV room. Free WiFi over site.

Key Features

 Open All Year

 Pets Accepted

 Disabled Facilities

 Play Area

Scan me for more information.

Alan Rogers Code: SW2842
16 accommodations
380 pitches
GPS: 59.29560, 17.92315
Post Code: S-127 31

Stockholms Län, South

www.alanrogers.com/sw2842
bredangcamping@telia.com
Tel: 089 770 71
www.bredangcamping.se

Open (Touring Pitches):
18 April - 9 October

Bredäng Stockholm

Bredäng is a busy city site, with easy access to Stockholm city centre. Large and fairly level, with very little shade, there are 380 pitches of which 204 have electricity (10A) and 115 have hardstanding. A separate area has been provided for tents. Reception is open from 08.00-22.00 in the main season (12/6-20/8), reduced hours in low season, and English is spoken. A three-day public transport card is available from the Tube station. The nearest Tube station is five minutes' walk; trains run about every ten minutes between 05.00 and 02.00, and the journey takes about twenty minutes. The local shopping centre is seven minutes away and a two-minute walk through the woods brings you to a very attractive lake and beach.

Four heated sanitary units of a high standard provide British style WCs, controllable hot showers and some washbasins in cubicles. One has a baby room, a unit for disabled visitors and a first aid room. Cooking facilities are in three units around the site. Laundry facilities. Motorcaravan services and car wash. Well stocked shop, bar, takeaway and fully licensed restaurant (Open 1 May - 15 Sept). Hostel. Cabins. Sauna. Playground. Minigolf. Frisbee Golf. Outdoor Gym. WiFi throughout (free).

Key Features

 Pets Accepted

 Disabled Facilities

 Play Area

 Bar/Restaurant

Scan me for more information.

Alan Rogers Code: SW2785
16 accommodations
75 pitches
GPS: 58.79846, 14.53849
Post Code: S-69597

Örebro Län, South

www.alanrogers.com/sw2785
info@campingtiveden.se
Tel: 058 447 4083
www.campingtiveden.se

Open (Touring Pitches):
1 April - 30 September.

Camping Tiveden

On the shore of Lake Unden, near Tiveden National Park, this friendly, Dutch-owned, family run campsite is in central Sweden and lies halfway between Gothenburg and Helsinki; the major lakes of Vanern and Vättern and numerous smaller lakes are within easy reach. There are three fields with 75 grass pitches, most with 10A electrical connections and offering a choice of full, partial or no shade. There are also nine gravel pitches for motorhomes and two tent pitches by the lakeside, but shielded from the wind by trees with the lake clearly visible between the trunks. There are various walking and cycling trails from the campsite.

Heated sanitary block with family showers (charged) and a fully equipped campers' kitchen. Motorcaravan services. Bar. Kiosk selling basic supplies and freshly-baked rolls to order. Restaurant (mid June-late Aug). Playground. Playing field. Fishing. Barbecue areas. Sauna Barrel for hire at lakeside. Bicycle, canoe, kayak, sail board and rowing boat hire. Pony rides. Fairy tale woodland walks for accompanied children. WiFi throughout (free).

Key Features

 Pets Accepted

 Disabled Facilities

 Play Area

 Bar/Restaurant

 Bike Hire

 Fishing

 Sailing

Scan me for more information.

Alan Rogers Code: SW2725
60 accommodations
220 pitches
GPS: 58.31478, 11.72344
Post Code: S-451 96

Västra Götalands Län, South

www.alanrogers.com/sw2725
info@hafsten.se
Tel: 052 264 4117
www.hafsten.se

Open (Touring Pitches):
All Year

Hafsten Resort

This privately owned site on the west coast is situated on a peninsula overlooking the magnificent coastline of Bohuslän. Open all year, it is a lovely, peaceful, terraced site with a beautiful, shallow and child-friendly sandy beach and many nature trails in the vicinity. There are 220 touring pitches, all with electricity (10A), 115 of them with water and drainage. In all, there are 370 pitches including a tent area and 60 cabins of a high standard. There are plenty of activities available ranging from horse riding at the stables on the campsite's own farm to an 86 m. long water chute.

Key Features

 Open All Year

 Pets Accepted

 Disabled Facilities

 Beach Access

 Swimming Pool

 Play Area

 Bar/Restaurant

 Fishing

Two heated sanitary buildings provide the usual facilities with showers on payment. Kitchen with good cooking facilities and sinks. Dining room. Laundry facilities. Units for disabled visitors. Motorcaravan services. Shop. Restaurant, takeaway and pub. Live music evenings. TV room. Outdoor swimming pool. Relaxation centre with sauna and jacuzzi (charged). Well equipped gym. Water slide (charged). WiFi (charged). Riding. Minigolf. Tennis. Boules. Playground. Clay pigeon shooting. Boat hire (canoe, rowing, motor, pedalo). Outside gym/fitness area. WiFi over site (charged).

Scan me for more information.

Capital Bern
Currency Swiss Franc (CHf)
Language German in central and eastern areas, French in the west, Italian in the south, Raeto-Romansch in the southeast. English spoken by many.
Telephone country code 00 41
Time Zone CET (GMT/UTC+1)
Tourist Office myswitzerland.com

Climate Mild and refreshing in the north. South of the Alps it is warmer, influenced by the Mediterranean. The Valais is noted for its dryness.

Switzerland

A small, wealthy country best known for its outstanding mountainous scenery, fine cheeses, delicious chocolates, Swiss bank accounts and enviable lifestyles. Centrally situated in Europe, it shares its borders with four countries: France, Austria, Germany and Italy, each one having its own cultural influence on Switzerland. Switzerland boasts a picture postcard landscape of mountains, valleys, waterfalls and glaciers.

The Bernese Oberland with its snowy peaks and rolling hills is the most popular area, Gstaad is a favourite haunt of wealthy skiers, while the mild climate and breezy conditions around Lake Thun are perfect for watersports and other outdoor activities. German-speaking Zurich is a multicultural metropolis with over 50 museums, sophisticated shops and colourful festivals set against a breathtaking backdrop of lakes and mountains. The south-east of Switzerland has densely forested mountain slopes and the wealthy and glamorous resort of Saint Moritz.

Geneva, Montreux and Lausanne on the northern shores of Lake Geneva make up the bulk of French Switzerland, with vineyards that border the lakes and medieval towns. The southernmost canton, Ticino, is home to the Italian-speaking Swiss, with the Mediterranean style lakeside resorts of Lugano and Locarno.

Shops Opening hours vary throughout the year and in each canton. In high-season shops are generally open 10am to 6pm weekdays, to 4pm Saturday.

Banks 8.30am to 4.30pm weekdays.

Travelling with Children Switzerland is a great destination for families as its clean and not overly commercialised. Most restaurants will provide children's menus. Public transport is good value espcially the train network where children aged 6 or under travel free and those aged under 16 get free unlimited rail travel when an annual Junior Railcard is purchased. Bern has plenty of attractions and the mountainscape train and boat journeys are perfect for all ages.

Public Holidays New Year's Day, Good Friday, Easter Monday, Ascension, Whit Monday, Corpus Christi, National Day 1 Aug, All Saints' 1 Nov, Christmas Day, Boxing Day. Saint Berchtold's Day 2 Jan, Republic Day 1 Mar, Labour Day, Independence of Jura 23 Jun, Assumption and Immaculate Conception are all regional public holidays and are observed in individual Cantons.

Motoring The road network is comprehensive and well planned. An annual road tax is levied on all cars using Swiss motorways and the 'Vignette' windscreen sticker must be purchased at the border (credit cards not accepted), or in advance from the Swiss National Tourist Office, plus a separate one for a towed caravan or trailer.

See campsite map page 487.

Alan Rogers Code: CH9015
6 accommodations
15 pitches
GPS: 47.33419, 7.14028
Post Code: CH-2883

Jura, West

www.alanrogers.com/ch9015
info@tariche.ch
Tel: 032 433 4619
www.tariche.ch

Open (Touring Pitches):
28 March - 15 November.

Camping Tariche

This lovely site is some 6 km. off the main road along a steep wooded valley, through which flows the Doub on its brief excursion through Switzerland from France. If you're looking for peace and tranquillity then this is a distinct possibility for a short or long stay. A very small friendly site (not suitable for very large units), owned and managed by Christine Lodens, there are just 15 touring pitches. It is ideal for walking, fishing or for the more active, the possibility of kayaking along the Doub. Medieval Saint Ursanne, said to be the most beautiful village in the canton, is some 7 km. In the village you will find 16th-century town gates and bridge and a 12th-century church surrounded by ancient houses. Not too far is Delemont, the Jura's capital. A local artist, Michel Marchand, runs introductory lessons in watercolour painting.

The modern, heated toilet block is of a high standard with free showers. Washing machine and dryer. Motorcaravan services. Good kitchen facilities include oven, hob and refrigerator. Restaurant with shaded terrace overlooking the play area so that adults can enjoy a drink and keep watch whilst enjoying the river views. Fishing. WiFi. Chalets and hotel rooms to rent.

Key Features

 Pets Accepted

 Play Area

 Bar/Restaurant

 Bike Hire

 Fishing

Scan me for more information.

Alan Rogers Code: CH9430
12 accommodations
90 pitches
GPS: 46.68605, 7.83063
Post Code: CH-3800

Bern, Central

www.alanrogers.com/ch9430
info@lazyrancho.ch
Tel: 033 822 8716
www.lazyrancho.ch

Open (Touring Pitches):
18 April - 13 October

Camping Lazy Rancho

This popular site is in a quiet location with fantastic views of the dramatic mountains of Eiger, Monch and Jungfrau. Neat, orderly and well maintained, the site is situated in a wide valley just 1 km. from Lake Thun and 1.5 km. from the centre of Interlaken. The English speaking owners, Stephane and Alina Blatter, lovingly care for the site and will endeavour to make you feel very welcome. Connected by gravel roads, the 155 pitches, of which 90 are for touring units, are on well tended level grass (seven with hardstanding, all with 10A electricity). There are also 30 pitches with water and waste water drainage.

Two good sanitary blocks are both heated with free hot showers, good facilities for disabled campers and a baby room. Laundry. Campers' kitchen with microwave, cooker, fridge and utensils. Motorcaravan services. Well stocked shop. TV and games room. Play area. Small swimming pool, sauna and hot tub (all season). Wooden igloo pods, XL-igloos, Love-igloo and bungalows for rent. Internet/laptop room. WiFi throughout (free).

Key Features

 Pets Accepted

 Disabled Facilities

 Swimming Pool

 Play Area

Scan me for more information.

Alan Rogers Code: CH9420
230 accommodations
300 pitches
GPS: 46.68129, 7.81524
Post Code: CH-3800

Bern, Central

www.alanrogers.com/ch9420
info@manorfarm.ch
Tel: 033 822 2264
www.manorfarm.ch

Open (Touring Pitches):
All year.

Camping Manor Farm 1

Manor Farm continues to be popular with British and Dutch visitors, being located in one of the traditional touring areas of Switzerland. The flat terrain is divided into 300 individual, numbered pitches, which vary considerably, both in size (40-100 sq.m) and price. There is shade in some places. There are 144 pitches with 4/13A electricity, water and drainage, and 55 also have cable TV connections. Reservations can be made, although you should find space, except perhaps in late July/early August when the best places may be taken. Around 40 per cent of the pitches are taken by permanent or letting units and four tour operators.

Seven separate toilet blocks are practical, heated and fully equipped. They include free hot water for baths and showers. Twenty private toilet units are to rent. Laundry facilities. Motorcaravan services. Gas supplies. Excellent shop (1/4-15/10). Site-owned restaurant adjacent (1/3-30/10). Snack bar with takeaway (1/7-20/8). TV room. Playground and paddling pool. Minigolf. Bicycle hire. Sailing school. Lake swimming. Boat hire (slipway for campers' own boats). Fishing. Daily activity and entertainment programme in high season. Excursions. Max. 1 dog. WiFi in some parts (charged).

Key Features

 Open All Year

 Pets Accepted

 Disabled Facilities

 Play Area

 Bar/Restaurant

 Skiing

 Bike Hire

 Fishing

Scan me for more information.

Alan Rogers Code: CH94205
3 accommodations
28 pitches
GPS: 46.69083, 7.78427
Post Code: 3803

Bern,

www.alanrogers.com/ch94205
camping-wang@gmx.ch
Tel: 0041 338412105
camping-wang.naturpur.ch

Open (Touring Pitches):
16 April - 31 October.

Camping Wang

Perched halfway up a mountain, 15km from Interlaken, Camping Wang will provide breathtaking views along with peace and quiet and a restful stay. This family-friendly site with spectacular mountain views and so many stars in the sky at night offers 28 spacious, grassy pitches on undulating ground for tents, campers and motorhomes. There is the possibility to rent a caravan or space in the barn on site. You are firmly immersed in Swiss nature at this lofty campsite, there is plenty of opportunity for walking and hiking and there is a gondola which operates all year between Beatenberg and Niederhorn, further up the mountain, just over a kilometre away. The centre of the village of Beatenberg, known as the Sun Terrace of the Berner Oberland, is only 2km away. Here you'll find restaurants, shops, an indoor swimming pool and tennis courts. Touring the Berner Oberland you'll find an enormous and varied amount of sight-seeing possibilities. From mountains and lakes to valleys and caves; historical castles, picturesque villages and vibrant cities. Then retreat to your peaceful idyll in the mountains to build a fire and see how many constellations you can spot in the night sky that seems to go on forever.

Key Features

 Pets Accepted

 Play Area

Smart shower and toilet block. Communal fridge and freezer. Fire pit. Communal covered area. WiFi. Children's play area. Village 2km with shops, restaurants, indoor pool and tennis courts.

Scan me for more information.

Alan Rogers Code: CH9490
6 accommodations
100 pitches
GPS: 46.63331, 8.05000
Post Code: CH-3818

Bern, Central

www.alanrogers.com/ch9490
camp@eigernordwand.ch
Tel: 033 853 1242
www.eigernordwand.ch

Open (Touring Pitches):
All year.

Camping Eiger-nordwand

Grindelwald is a very popular summer and winter resort and Eigernordwand, at 950 m. above sea level, is dramatically situated very close to the north face of the famous mountain, in a delightful situation. The slightly sloping pitches have tarmac access roads but are not marked out. There are some trees around but little shade, although there are splendid views of surrounding mountain peaks. Being so high it can become cool when the sun goes down. Some static caravans remain during the winter with about 100 places for touring units in summer, and 20 in winter. Electricity connections (10A) are available. There is a good quality restaurant and hotel at the entrance. Excursions to the Jungfrau and climbing or walking tours are organised.

A new sanitary block, heated in cool weather, is of excellent quality and includes a drying room and facilities for disabled visitors. Washing machines. Motorcaravan services. Restaurant. Hotel. Kiosk for basic supplies (1/5-20/10). Playground. Barbecue hut. Fishing. Skiing in winter. Dogs are not accepted. WiFi (charged).

Key Features

 Open All Year

 Disabled Facilities

 Play Area

 Bar/Restaurant

 Skiing

 Fishing

Scan me for more information.

Alan Rogers Code: CH9540
14 accommodations
94 pitches
GPS: 46.88390, 8.24413
Post Code: CH-6060

Unterwalden, Central

Camping Seefeld Sarnen

www.alanrogers.com/ch9540
welcome@seefeldpark.ch
Tel: 041 666 5788
www.seefeldpark.ch

Open (Touring Pitches):
All year.

One of the finest sites we have seen, Camping Seefeld Sarnen was completely rebuilt with all the features demanded by discerning campers and reopened in 2011. The location alongside Lake Sarnen is breathtaking, with views across the water to lush meadows, wooded hills and mountains topped with snow for most of the year. The seasonal pitches are immaculately maintained on their own area. There are 94 touring pitches arranged on almost level grass, each with 13A electricity and its own water tap. There is some shade from young trees which will increase as time goes on. The site not only offers active family holidays on land and on the water, but is ideally placed for exploring this beautiful part of Switzerland.

Heated sanitary facilities are in the main building supplemented by unheated facilities in the central block. Baby room and cubicles for children. Facilities for disabled visitors. Washing machines and dryers. Shop, bar and restaurant with large terrace (Easter-Oct). Campers' lounge with kitchen, TV/DVD, tables and chairs. Two swimming pools with lifeguards (20/4-15/9). Two playgrounds. Watersports. Tennis. Bicycle hire. Dog bath; dogs not accepted in high season. WiFi throughout (free).

Key Features

 Open All Year

 Pets Accepted

 Disabled Facilities

 Swimming Pool

 Play Area

 Bar/Restaurant

 Fishing

 Sailing

Scan me for more information.

Alan Rogers Code: CH9110
200 accommodations
200 pitches
GPS: 47.12548, 8.18995
Post Code: CH-6204

Lucerne, Central

www.alanrogers.com/ch9110
camping.sempach@tcs.ch
Tel: 041 460 1466
www.tcs-camping.ch/sempach

Open (Touring Pitches):
29 March - 14 October.

TCS Camping Sempach

Lucerne is a very popular city in central Switzerland and nearby Camping Sempach is an ideal base from which to visit the city and explore the surrounding countryside or, being a short way from the main A2 Basel - Chiasso motorway, is a convenient night stop if passing through. This neat, tidy site next to Lake Sempach has 200 pitches for touring units (most on grass), all with 6/13A electricity. Water connections are also available to 77 of the grass pitches. Much of the site is occupied by seasonal units, but these are well tended and not obtrusive. There are 17 chalets, with 2 fitted out for disabled guests. Two large grass areas have been provided for tents.

Three good quality sanitary blocks have the usual facilities including 14 private washing cubicles, baby rooms and excellent facilities for disabled visitors. Washing machines and dryers. Hot plates, fridges and freezers. Two motorcaravan service points. Excellent self-service bar/restaurant/takeaway with terrace overlooking the play area, lake and surrounding hills. Well stocked shop. Children's paddling pool and playground. Lakeside beach. Pedalo rental. Electric barbecues are not permitted (communal area provided). Chalets for hire. Free WiFi throughout.

Key Features

 Pets Accepted

 Disabled Facilities

 Play Area

 Bar/Restaurant

 Fishing

Scan me for more information.

Alan Rogers Code: CH9520
13 accommodations
125 pitches
GPS: 46.20583, 7.27867
Post Code: CH-1963

Valais, South

www.alanrogers.com/ch9520
info@botza.ch
Tel: 027 346 1940
www.botza.ch

Open (Touring Pitches):
All year.

Camping du Botza

Situated in the Rhône Valley just off the autoroute, this is a pleasant site with views of the surrounding mountains. It is set in a peaceful wooded location, although there is occasional aircraft noise. There are 125 individual touring pitches, ranging in size from 60 to 155 sq.m. all with 4A electricity, many with some shade and 25 with water and drainage. Pitches are priced according to size and facilities. The reception, office, lounge, shop and restaurant have all been completely rebuilt. The conservatory-style restaurant overlooks the pool and the entertainment area. Both are open to the public but free to campers. A warm welcome is assured from the enthusiastic English-speaking owner. A new barrier has been installed.

New sanitary block and another completely renovated. Some private cabins in the heated sanitary block. Washing machines and dryers. Shop. Brand new restaurant (closed Jan) and terrace. Bar. Bakery. Ice cream kiosk. Takeaway. Heated swimming pool with slides and diving board (15/5-31/8). Playground. Table football and electronic games. Tennis. Basketball. TV room with Internet corner. Entertainment stage. Multi-lingual library, board games and tourist information. WiFi on part of site (free).

Key Features

 Open All Year

 Pets Accepted

 Disabled Facilities

 Swimming Pool

 Play Area

 Bar/Restaurant

 Skiing

Scan me for
more information.

Alan Rogers Code: CH9890
86 accommodations
610 pitches
GPS: 46.16895, 8.85592
Post Code: CH-6598

Ticino, South

www.alanrogers.com/ch9890
camping@campofelice.ch
Tel: 091 745 1417
www.campofelice.ch

Open (Touring Pitches):
27 March - 31 October.

Camping Campofelice

Considered by many to be the best family campsite in Switzerland, Campofelice is bordered on the front by Lake Maggiore and on one side by the Verzasca estuary, where the site has its own marina. It is divided into rows, with 610 generously sized touring pitches on flat grass on either side of hard access roads. Mostly well shaded, all pitches have electricity connections (10-13A, 360 Europlug) and 410 also have water, drainage and TV connections. Pitches near the lake cost more (these are not available for motorcaravans until September) and a special area is reserved for small tents. A little more expensive than other sites in the area, but excellent value for the range and quality of the facilities.

The six toilet blocks (three heated) are of exemplary quality. Washing machines and dryers. Motorcaravan services. Gas supplies. Supermarket, restaurant, bar and takeaway (all season). Snack kiosk at beach. Lifeguards on duty. Tennis. Minigolf. Bicycle hire. Canoe and pedalo hire. Boat launching. Playgrounds. Doctor calls. Dogs are not accepted. New chalet for disabled visitors. Camping accessories shop. Car hire. Car wash. WiFi (charged).

Key Features

 Disabled Facilities

 Play Area

 Bar/Restaurant

 Bike Hire

Sailing

Scan me for more information.

Alan Rogers Code: CH9670
6 accommodations
95 pitches
GPS: 46.09003, 7.50722
Post Code: CH-1984

Valais, South

www.alanrogers.com/ch9670
info@molignon.ch
Tel: 027 283 1240
www.molignon.ch

Open (Touring Pitches):
All year.

Camping de Molignon

Camping de Molignon, surrounded by mountains, is a peaceful haven 1,450 m. above sea level. The rushing stream at the bottom of the site and the sound of cow bells and birdsong are likely to be the only disturbing factors in summer. The 95 pitches for touring units (all with 10A electricity) are on well tended terraces leading down to the river. Six chalets are available to rent. Excellent English is spoken by the owner's son who is now running the site. He is always pleased to give information on all that is available from the campsite. The easy uphill drive from Sion in the Rhône Valley is enhanced by ancient villages and the Pyramids of Euseigne.

Two fully equipped sanitary blocks, heated in cool weather, with free hot showers. Baby room. Washing machines and dryers. Kitchen for hikers. Motorcaravan services. Gas supplies. Shop for basic supplies (15/6-15/9). Restaurant. Heated swimming pool with cover for cool weather (6x12 m). Outdoor paddling pool. Playground. Sitting room for games and reading. Guided walks, climbing, geological museum, winter skiing. Fishing. Internet corner. WiFi in parts of site (free).

Key Features

 Open All Year

 Pets Accepted

 Swimming Pool

 Play Area

 Bar/Restaurant

 Skiing

 Fishing

Scan me for more information.

Alan Rogers Code: CH9850
40 pitches
GPS: 46.96900, 9.58933
Post Code: CH-7302

Graubünden, East

Waldcamping Landquart

www.alanrogers.com/ch9850
info@waldcamping.ch
Tel: 081 322 3955
www.waldcamping.ch

Open (Touring Pitches):
All Year

Situated close to the Klosters-Davos road and the nearby town of Landquart, this deep valley campsite provides a comfortable night stop near the A13 motorway, as well as a quiet spot for a few days rest. The 40 touring pitches are not marked or separated but are all on level grass off a central gravel road through the long, narrow, wooded site. All pitches have 6/10A electricity. The static caravans (about 100) are mostly hidden from view in small alcoves. A modern, timber-clad building at the entrance houses all the necessary facilities – reception, community room and sanitary facilities. If on arrival reception is closed (11.00-16.00), select a pitch and check-in later.

Key Features

 Pets Accepted

 Disabled Facilities

 Play Area

 Bar/Restaurant

 Skiing

The toilet block is extremely well appointed and can be heated. Facilities for disabled visitors. Baby room. Washing machine and dryer. Drying room. Motorcaravan services. Community room with TV. Playground. Free WiFi throughout.

Scan me for more information.

Alan Rogers Code: CH9835
150 pitches
GPS: 46.69686, 10.08678
Post Code: CH-7530

Graubünden, East

www.alanrogers.com/ch9835
campingzernez@gmail.com
Tel: 081 856 1462
www.camping-cul.com

Open (Touring Pitches):
15 May - 25 October.

Camping Cul

Camping Cul is a friendly and relaxed site in a good location on the banks of the River Inn, east of Davos. The site was established in 1952 and has remained in the same family ever since. Pitches are grassy and lightly shaded. Many have electrical connections and virtually all have fine views of the magnificent mountain scenery all around. On-site amenities include a bar, small shop and snack bar. There is a fully equipped communal kitchen. This is excellent walking and cycling country, with a number of routes possible direct from the site. The Rhätische Bahn is a superb mountain railway passing close to the site and discounted tickets are available for purchase at reception. A number of world class resorts are within easy reach, notably Davos, Klosters and Saint Moritz. The latter is one of the Alpine region's glitziest resorts, maybe best known for its designer shops, grand hotels and, of course, for the terrifying Cresta Run, the original adrenaline ride!

Key Features

 Pets Accepted

 Play Area

 Bar/Restaurant

 Fishing

Three toilet blocks provide the usual facilities (one only open in high season). Laundry facilities. Communal kitchen. Motorcaravan services. Small shop and restaurant (both Jun-Sept). Bar (May-Oct). TV and games in the bar. Play area. Activities and entertainment programme. WiFi (charged).

Scan me for more information.

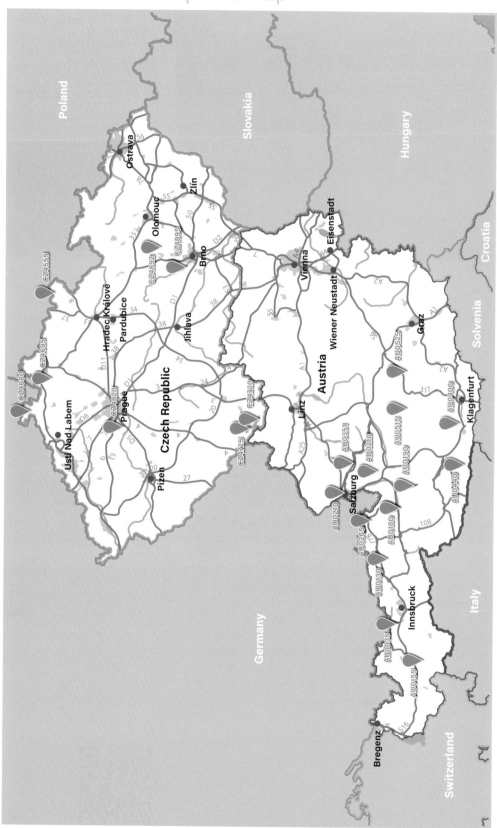

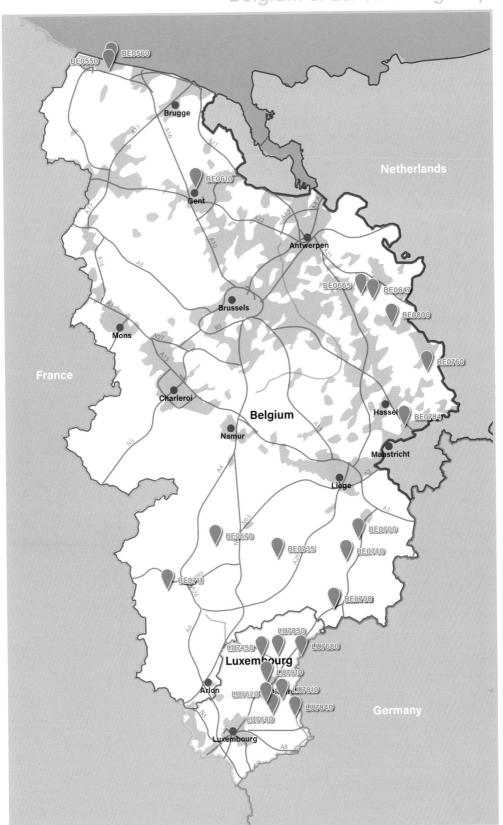

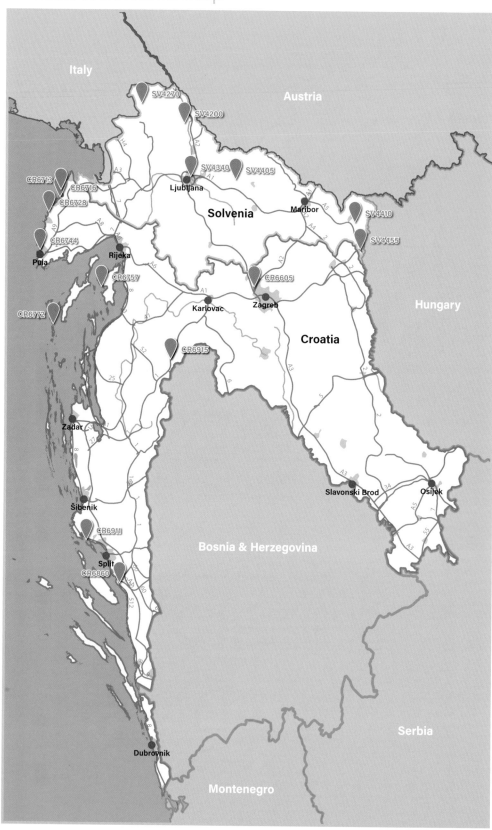

Italy

Austria

SV4270

SV4200

SV4340 SV4405

CR6713

CR6716

SV4410

CR6728

Ljubljana

Solvenia

Maribor

SV4455

CR6744

Pula

Rijeka

CR6757

CR6605

Zagreb

Hungary

CR6772

Karlovac

Croatia

CR6915

Zadar

Slavonski Brod

Osijek

Šibenik

Bosnia & Herzegovina

CR6911

Split

CR6860

Serbia

Dubrovnik

Montenegro

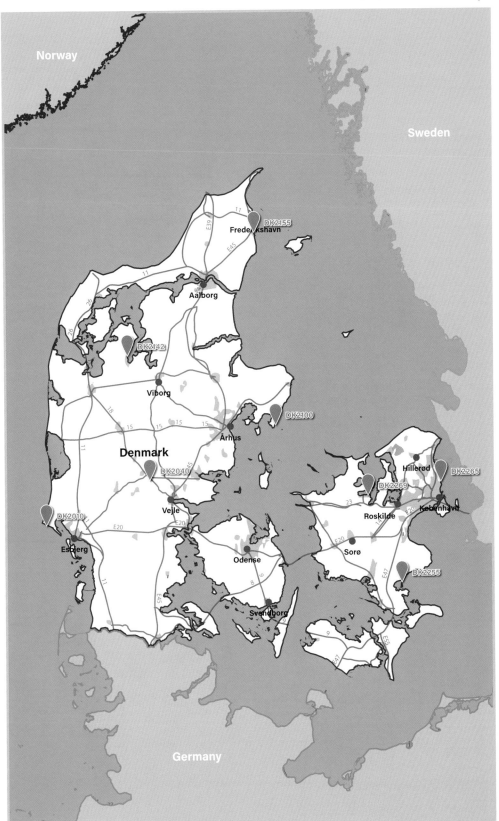

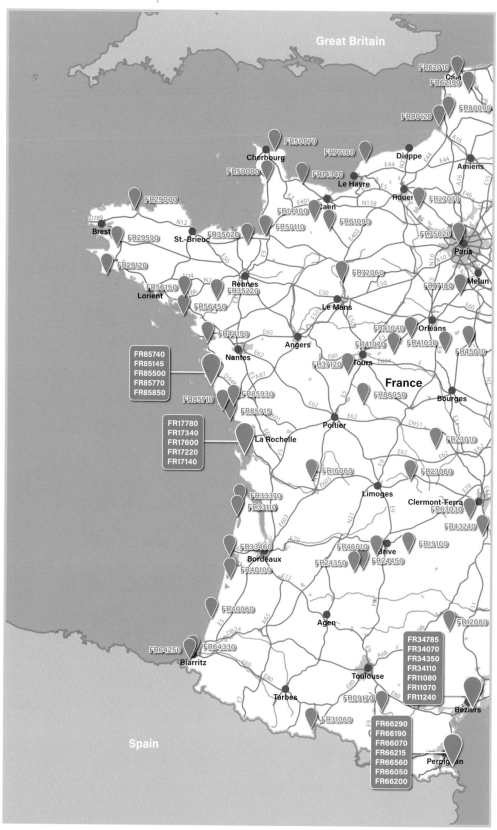

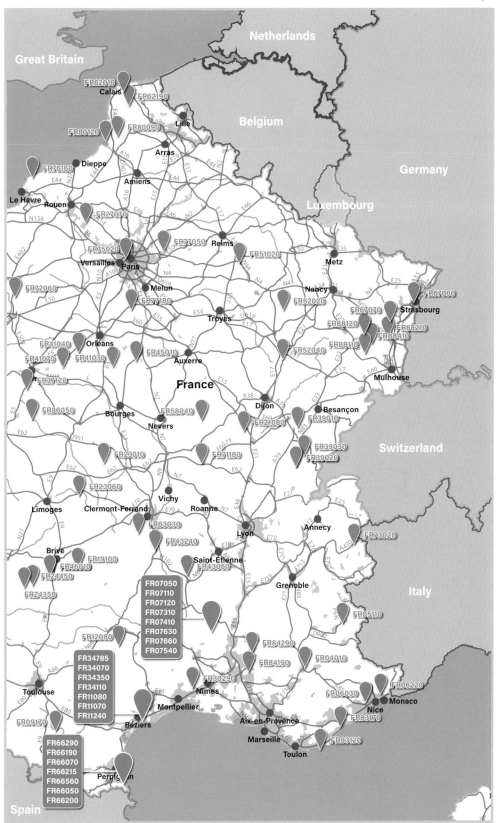

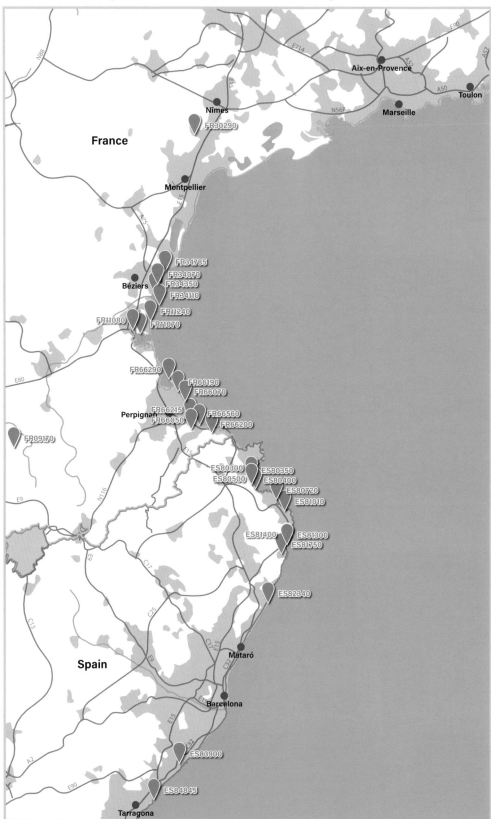

France

Nîmes
FR30290

Montpellier

Aix-en-Provence

Toulon

Marseille

Béziers
FR34785
FR34070
FR34350
FR34110
FR11240
FR11080
FR11070

FR66290
FR66190
FR66070
FR66215
FR66050
FR66560
FR66200

Perpignan

FR09170

ES80300
ES80500
ES80350
ES80400
ES80720
ES81010

ES81400
ES81300
ES81750

ES82340

Mataró

Spain

Barcelona

ES83900

ES84845

Tarragona

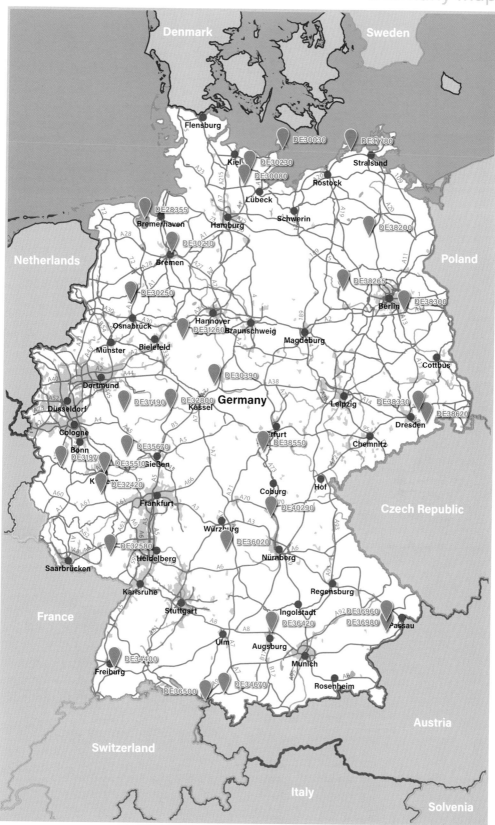

Lerwick

Kirkwall

Wick

UK7710

UK7740

UK7535

Inverness

Fort William

Aberdeen

UK7325

Dundee

Perth

Greenock

Glasgow Edinburgh

Ayr **Great Britain**

Londonderry

Donegal

UK8330 Dumfries UK6945

Omagh

Sligo

Lisburn Belfast

Carlisle Newcastle

IR8780

Muineachan

Sunderland

UK5520 UK5650 Middlesbrough

Ros Comain

Dundalk

UK4715

Ros Comain

Drogheda

Douglas

Scarborough

IR9465

Galway **Ireland**

IR9100

Blackpool

UK5360 Leeds York

IR9040

Dublin

UK6689 Liverpool Manchester Kingston UK3640

Shannon

IR9150

UK6670 Sheffield

IR9400

Chester Sheffield

Limer.

Stoke

Tra

IR9620

Kilkenny

Nottingham

UK3400

IR9570

ney

UK9510

IR9340

Waterford

UK6015 Leicester

Cork

Birmingham Peterborough

UK5995

Coventry Norwich

Swansea

Cambridge

UK0681

Cardiff

Luton UK3210 swich

Bristol

UK0745 B th UK1690 Reading London UK3055

Oxford

UK0320

Exeter

Southampton

Bournemouth Portsmouth Brighton Dover

Penzance Plymouth

France

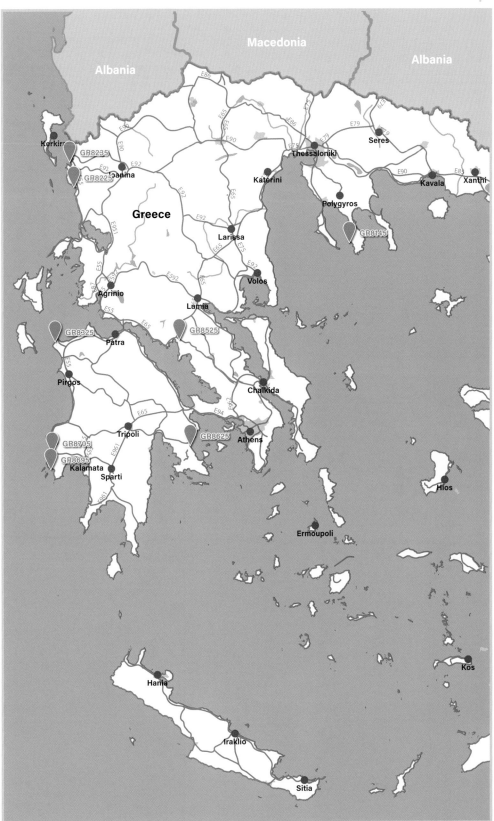

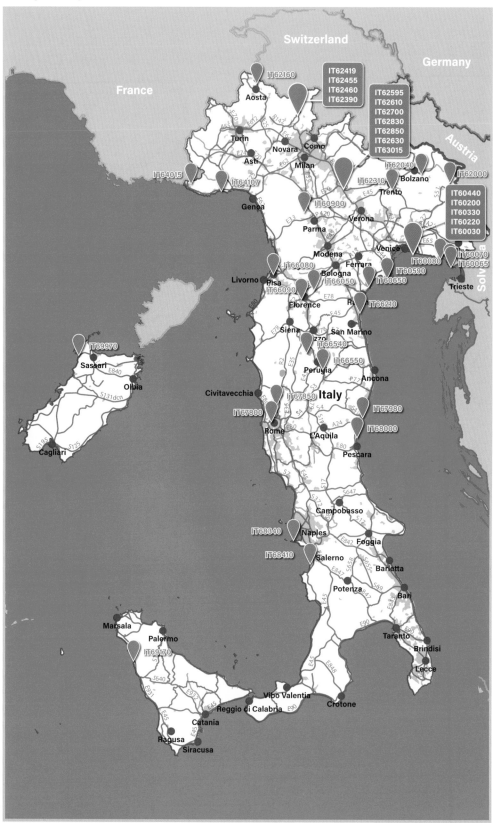

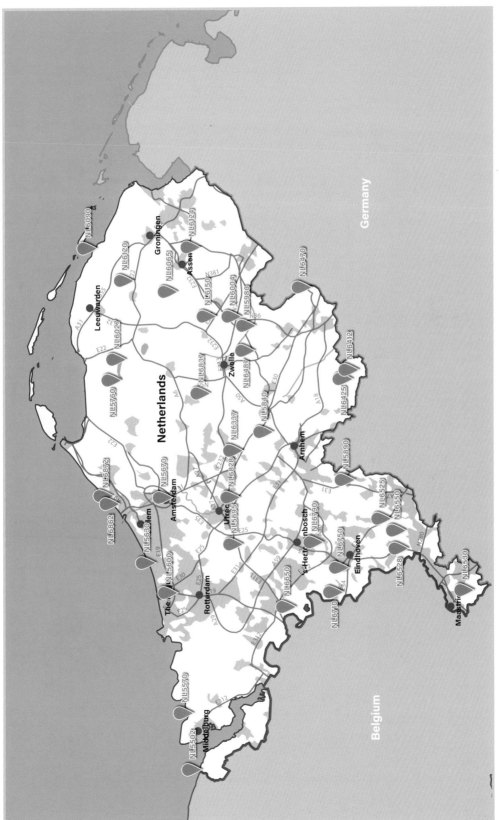

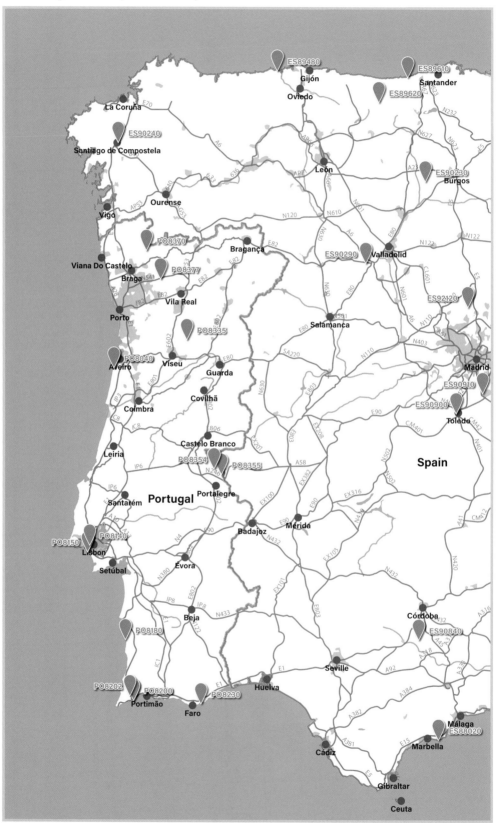

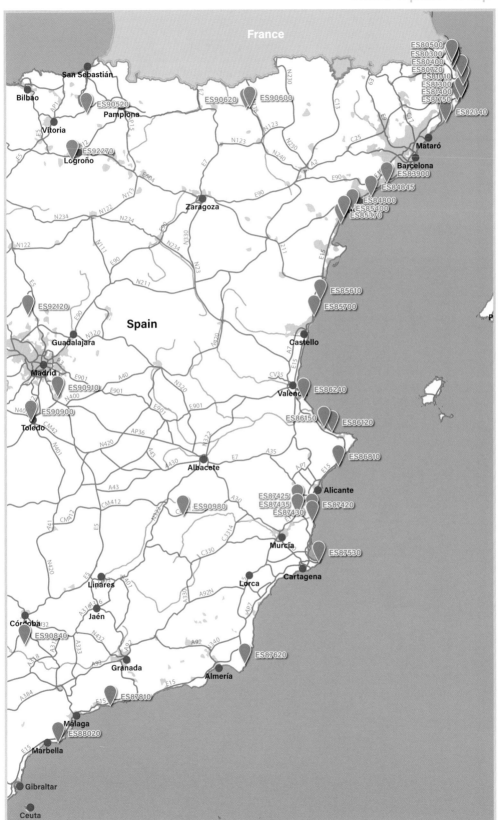

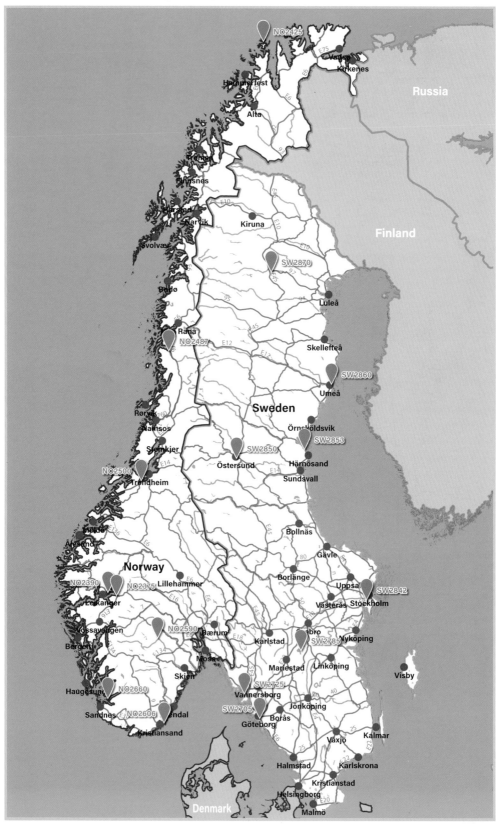